Rebel and Statesman

The Life and Times of
VLADIMIR JABOTINSKY

REBEL AND STATESMAN

The Early Years

JOSEPH B. SCHECHTMAN

Foreword by Menachem Begin

Eshel
Books

Washington • Baltimore

Eshel Books

An Imprint of Bartleby Press
PO Box 858
Savage, MD 20763
800-953-9929

Library of Congress Cataloging-in-Publication Data
Schechtman, Joseph B., 1891-1970
The life and times of Vladimir Jabotinsky.
Originally published as: The Vladimir Jabotinsky story.
New York: T. Yoseloff, cl956-61
Includes index.
ISBN 978-0-935437-48-5
Contents: v. 1. Rebel and Statesman-v. 2
Fighter and prophet.
1. Jabotinsky, Vladimir, 1880-1940. 2. Revisionist
Zionists-Biography. I. Title
DS151.Z5S23 1986
956.94'001'0924 (B)   86-13549

Printed in the United States of America

CONTENTS

FOREWORD

A versatile brain, applying itself to various fields of creation and excelling in all of them, is but a rare phenomenon in human history. Aristotle, Maimonides, Da Vinci—and, above all, the greatest of leaders and lawgivers—Moses: these are the names of the very few who prove the existence of this phenomenon and its extreme rarity. Ze'ev Jabotinsky was such a versatile brain. He was a poet, philologist, statesman, sociologist, author, orator and soldier. What has our generation learned from Ze'ev Jabotinsky, and what will future generations learn from him?

We can say about the reciprocal relationship between poetry and the era the same as has been said about the relationship between personality and the era. Materialists claim that the era creates the man, while idealists believe that man creates the era. The wisdom of life and its experience, teach us that there is a reciprocal influence between man and his time.

Here is one of the most striking examples in history: but for the French Revolution and the uprisings, the invasion, the defeats and the reawakening, the strange-sounding Italian name of an artillery officer would have been known only to his closest fellow-officers. On the other hand, however, but for the personal vision of Napoleon Bonaparte, the events of the end of the 18th century and the beginning of the 19th century (between Madrid and Moscow) would not have occurred.

There exists a similar reciprocal influence between poetry and literature in general, and the era. Sometimes, the era produces the poet. Sometimes one creates the other. But the poetry and the literary works of Ze'ev Jabotinsky preceeded an era—he created it. He wrote of Jewish strength before it came into being; of revolt before it took place; of a Jewish Army while its weapons were still a dream; of a Jewish State when many of our contemporaries still derided its very mention and of "Hadar" (honour, respect) while the manners—or lack of manners—of the Ghetto still prevailed in our people.

He used to say: "I absorb a language out of the air." And he would also say: "I must work hard in order to learn a language." Is there any contradiction between the two? Yes and no. Ze'ev Jabotinsky was capable of absorbing a new language as out of the air. But while learning its syllables, he worked hard and intensively in the search for its roots in order to master it completely; in order to open up for himself and for his pupils the new world which every new language opens up before those who learn it. In the latter half of his life, however, he devoted his unparallelled philological talents mainly to one task: the improvement and beautification of the Hebrew tongue in expression and pronunciation. We, his disciples, who were granted the privilege of drinking at his source can testify that Ze'ev Jabotinsky stood in awe before this unique phenomenon, the Hebrew tongue.

He was prepared, at any time, to bow his head in admiration and emotion before the brevity and the depth, the conciseness and the onomatopoeia contained in Hebrew—the language of the Prophets and of the vision, of the Holy Scriptures, the Psalms and the Song of Songs, the language of life and of renascence, the tongue of the Bible.

True, only the people of Israel could have resuscitated the Hebrew tongue. But it was only the Hebrew language that could have been brought back to life. And a language, so Ze'ev Jabotinsky believed, is like a garden. Just as one tends one's garden, waters it and weeds it, so one has to tend the tongue of one's people—especially eternal, reborn Hebrew. Therefore, Ze'ev Jabotinsky not only entreated us to use Hebrew as our tongue and that of our children, but also exhorted us always to remember that it is no ordinary language we are speaking, but the beautiful tongue of the Prophets.

In our Homeland, we all speak Hebrew. The language is reborn and rejuvenated. At times we are wont to smile apologetically when hearing our children mingling foreign expressions with the Hebrew mother tongue. But in such cases it is no longer the living language of the past which the proud Hebrew wishes to hear. If in days gone by—in foreign lands or on the soil of our forefathers—the command was: learn thy language and speak thy tongue, then in our day, under Israel's free sky, the command is: Honour Thy Tongue. Remember that you are using this wonderful language, the tongue of the Bible.

The Statesman

Is there a statesman? Or is the domain of politics just an open field where anyone can pitch his tent and declare: I am a statesman!

It is, at times, strange to see the lack of understanding of this conception or rather—let us not hesitate to say so—this particular wisdom which is called statesmanship.

Why do we recognize the outstanding talents of a man who takes a small instrument into his hands and draws from it sounds so heavenly that they carry us into the lofty realms of beauty whither—according to ancient thinkers—the soul, which has become detached returns on hearing or seeing splendour reincarnated? The Violinist Can Do It. You, with the same fingers, with the same instrument, cannot do it.

Why do we recognize the rare gifts of the man who takes a brush into his hands and produces a picture before the beauty of which we bow our heads in admiration: we and the generations that follow us?

Or for what reason do we recognize the particular creative talents of the man who takes a stone, a hammer and a chisel and creates beauty and splendour?

Let us recognize that just as there is the great musician, the painter, and the sculptor, so there is the statesman by virtue of specific talents which are not bestowed upon many.

But by what do we recognize the statesman? How can he be recognized? In order to answer this question let us ask another one: how does one recognize a virtuoso? One does not realize immediately that one is in the presence of talent. Years go by, talent ripens, proof is here, the melody is heard, hearts are conquered, and one day we say, now we know. Here is the maestro!

So it is also in politics. The statesman is not immediately recognized. But if, one fateful and tragic day, one man gets up and declares: "Britain will open a front in the Middle East" at the very time when most British leaders and foremost among them Kitchener, the soldier, say the contrary; and after a short time such a front is actually opened in the Middle East—then you agree the statesman was right, he foresaw events correctly.

If during World War I many believed in and demanded "Neutrality," but one man alone declared: "accursed and forbidden be neutrality. We must act; we must rise against Turkey for, if her rule over Eretz Israel is not eliminated, then there is no justification for our hopes!" Days go by, years elapse, and all admit, subsequently, that neutrality was vanity, while the alliance was justified. Then all knew, the statesman hath spoken.

If under the rule of a British High Commissioner of Jewish origin, while everyone says that he is the "Ezra of our times," an unannointed prince and bearer of all the hopes of our people—one man gets up and says: "Herbert Samuel's rule is the first attempt to liquidate Zionism"—and after but a few years all see that it is thus and not otherwise—again it is recognized that the statesman hath spoken. And if, in the days when leaders abuse the idea of a Jewish State, oppose it, ban it, repudiate it, fight it, one man stands up and declares: "A Jewish State is the command of supreme justice, it will arise, in our generation it will come true"—and but a few years elapse, and all ask themselves: "How could we ever have lived without a Jewish State?" then it also becomes clear to all: the magic fiddle of the statesman has brought forth the melody of faith in national resurrection.

If, in the days when we had no weapons, no army and no strength, and on the forehead of the eternal wanderer was written the terrible word "Hefker" (outcast)—one man stood up and demanded: "Jews learn to shoot" and added: "The Jewish army will come into being. In it there is hope. Without it there is no future and there will be no survival." And years later all the "pacifists" and all the "anti-militarists"ask themselves in naive wonderment: "How could we have done it without a Jewish army?"then it is clear that it was the wise statesman who had spoken, who foresaw events.

Such was Ze'ev Jabotinsky, the Statesman. And let us remember: the captain proves himself in a storm, the maestro in his music, and the statesman in his analysis, in his prescience.

As a sociologist, Ze'ev Jabotinsky bequeathed us the laws of true justice. He believed in the equality of man. In one of his letters he stressed that the principle of equality was an obsession with him. But his belief in equality had nothing in common with the vulgarization of "equality" which contains neither justice nor progress but is, on the contrary, injustice and regression. He believed in equality through elevation and uplifting. This is justice. This is progress.

And he also believed, with all the strength of his heart that justice and equality, without freedom, are nothing but empty phrases on the lips of those who shun the light. This was the social creed of Ze'ev Jabotinsky. And he drew it from the rising, eternal springs of the Law of Israel, of the Laws of the Prophets.

And who was proved right? All the "isms"of our time now lie prostrate before our eyes like broken idols, while the Laws of Justice of Israel's Prophets radiate their eternal teachings.

The Orator

Cicero, one of the greatest orators, wrote a small booklet on the art of speech. He explains, perhaps somewhat subjectively, that there is no art like the art of speech. According to him, there are many masters in the arts of sculpture, architecture, literature and poetry. But very few are the real orators of all times.

The truth is that the art of speech cannot be acquired by learning. Every other art, singing, music, painting or sculpture, depends in the first place on inborn talent. But in these arts, much can be acquired through learning. Without study the talent may be of no avail. Not so the art of speech. It is a fact that all the schools of rhetoric, from the dawn of history have not produced a single orator worthy of the name. The few whose names are engraved in the annals of mankind taught themselves the art of speech.

And who is an orator? Is it he who has a strong voice, who is quick-spoken, smooth-tongued, producing figures out of his sleeve while from his mouth issue flames which extinguish as they emerge? No.

The orator is he who knows how to combine logic and sentiment, heart and intelligence. It is the speaker from whose heart and brain is spun a thread reaching to the hearts and brains of his audience. And at certain moments, his listeners become one entity, and that orator becomes a part of it. Such an orator was Jabotinsky. Thus we did see him, thus we did hear him. We sat below, he stood over us, and all of a sudden we would feel— each of us individually and all of us together—that we were carried aloft, elevated towards another world which is all faith, brotherhood, love, devotion, hope, a world which is all beauty and goodness. There never was an orator like him, it is doubtful whether there will ever be another.

Descartes said: "I think,thereforeIam."Buttherearetimeswhenaman can say: "I suffer, therefore I am." And there are other times when a man has to say: "I fight, therefore I am." Ze'ev Jabotinsky proved his existence threefold: he thought, he suffered, he fought.

He was a fighter. He expressed the essence of his fighting spirit by his constant readiness to start anew. In one of his wonderful letters, he recalled what happened to the great inventor, Newton. After long years of penetrating and creative thought, Newton put his meditations in writing. The composition was almost finished when the great sage left his room, a lighted candle standing on the table next to his papers. A cat jumped on to the table, upset the candle, and the fruits of a lifetime of labour became a heap of ashes. And then, stressed Jabotinsky, Newton, standing in front of his world gone up in flames, spoke only one sentence: "I shall start anew."

And he started, continued—and completed.

A similar story, taken from life, is told of the outstanding thinker and historian, Thomas Carlyle. He wrote his famous work, one of the finest, on history and the philosophy of history—The French Revolution. A fire broke out and consumed the manuscript. The work of years was completely destroyed. And what did Thomas Carlyle say? Just as Newton did: "I shall start anew." Subsequently, Carlyle himself declared that his second composition on the French Revolution even surpassed the first one, the one that had been burned.

Thus also did Ze'ev Jabotinsky behave. He never admitted failure, but said: "This is an opening for victory. "He never despaired at a withdrawal, this was the beginning of the advance. His spirit never fell at a decline, but he said: "This is a sign of ascent." Such is the soul of a Fighter.

The greatness of Jabotinsky, the fighter, never needed any proof in our eyes. But I think that the greatness of this fighter rose to even greater heights when he fought for his ideal—abstract but real, deep and supreme, eternal and unconquered—Justice. There are times when the striving for justice by mankind in its entirety concentrates on one person alone—be it Dreyfus, Beilis or Stavsky.

Above all, Ze'ev Jabotinsky was the bearer of the vision of the State in our generation. After Herzl, there was none but him to carry on high the vision of redemption, even in the face of renegades. This is the truth. There is no need to elaborate.

Therefore we can say: here is the miracle of the standard-bearer, here— of national rebirth, here is the miracle of the Jewish Army, and here the Return to Zion.

And in all these miracles, revealed or hidden, there is a drop of Jabotinsky's lifeblood. Without him, without his vision, without his thinking and his suffering, without his fighting and without his disciples, the State of Israel would not have come into being.

Therefore, our generation, and all the generations to come, owe a debt of gratitude to him who led us and them from slavery to freedom. Is not gratitude a simple and befitting human characteristic? If a man has done his neighbor a favor, does not the latter owe him gratitude? Man cannot always return a favor. But to acknowledge a good deed—is that not a moral duty? And if such is the rule in the relations between man and man, why should it be different between one man and a community—a people? Let us be more explicit. Does not man—every individual, and mankind in its entirety—owe a debt of gratitude to men like Pasteur, Koch or Salk. They have benefited mankind. Mankind owes them gratitude.

And if a fighter appears, and gives his entire life to his people, the wealth of his thought, the warmth of his heart, all his talents, his pen of iron and the steel of his character; and toils for them, risks his life, sacrifices himself, helps his people, saves it, and sets it on the path of freedom—do not his compatriots owe him a debt of gratitude?

Gratitude, not reward. A true fighter never asks for a reward. And a reward is never offered. But simple human gratitude, coming from the heart, out of the depth of the soul—why should it be withheld from the man who fought for his people and his country?

But there also exists ingratitude. It has various forms—the most terrible of which is hatred towards the benefactor. The great student of the human soul, Dostoyevsky describes a strange psychological case. One of his heros declares: "I hate him." His friends ask: "Why? has he done you wrong?" and receives the following answer: "No, it was I who did him wrong!"

Such ingratitude was the lot of Rosh Betar, Ze'ev Jabotinsky.

But what matters this ingratitude compared with the love of tens of hundreds of thousands of our people for him, who paved for them the road to life and freedom!

What love! And what a full life did the Teacher live, who departed from us forty-six years ago.

Love. A full life. Now it is clear—only he who loves is loved; only the faithful earns faithfulness; only the devoted—devotion, even after his death, which is eternal life.

Dr. Joseph Schechtman, the author of this biography, was one of the close collaborators of Ze'ev Jabotinsky. Schechtman knew Jabotinsky intimately. They were together in times of crisis and achievement, in the hours of joy and

worry. They exchanged views in private, they appeared together on public
platforms, published their articles in the same newspapers. Indeed, not many
were privileged to know Jabotinsky as Schechtman did. Therefore, anyone
who wants to study the history of Jabotinsky's struggle for the redemption
of the Jewish People, for the renewal of its strength, for the liberation of its
Land, for the re-creation of its independent State, should read this unique
biography of Ze'ev Jabotinsky.

Menachem Begin

17 January 1986

ACKNOWLEDGMENTS

It is almost impossible for an author, in these days when space is at such a premium, to give thanks by name to every person and institution that has given him a helping hand. Many of those to whom he is deeply indebted must accept this blanket acknowledgment. Some persons, however, have played such an outstanding role in initiating, encouraging, and making this book possible that they must be mentioned.

This biography was undertaken in 1953 on behalf of the Board of Directors of the Jabotinsky Institute in Tel Aviv and is based largely on the rich material collected by this Institute. To its creator and Director, Dr. J. Paamoni, and to his collaborators the author is most sincerely grateful. For valuable material and gracious cooperation the author is also indebted to Dr. G. Herlitz, Director of the Central Zionist Archives in Jerusalem, to Mrs. Sylvia Landress, Director of the Zionist Archives and Library in New York, and to Mr. Jacob I. Dienstag, Librarian of the Yeshiva University in New York, as well as to the staff of these institutions.

Hundreds of people have contributed personal reminiscences, letters, pictures, and other materials for this biography. Many are mentioned either in the text or in the bibliographical notes at the end of the book. Special gratitude is due to Jabotinsky's sister, Mrs. T. E. Jabotinsky-Kopp, to his son, Eri Jabotinsky, to his nephews Johnny Kopp and Serge Galperin, as well as to his school friend Alexander Poliakov. It would be unfair not to single out Jabotinsky's old colleagues: Messrs. S. K. Gepstein, I. A. Trivus, and M. Grossman whose help was both generous and beneficial. Mr. Aisik Remba kindly put at the author's disposal the manuscript of his unpublished study "Jabotinsky the Defender and Prisoner"; Mr. Adolf Gourevitch rendered great service by translating excerpts from Jabotinsky's poetry from Russian and Italian. The author is also glad to be able to state that he had a large measure of cooperation from Jabotinsky's political opponents: Messrs. D. Ben Gurion, M. Sharett, J. Sprinzak, B. Locker, I. Grinbaum, and many others who shared with him their personal memories; Mrs. Vera Weizmann put at his disposal copies of Jabotinsky's letters to her late husband.

As a tribute to Jabotinsky's stature and national significance, a galaxy of outstanding leaders, representing various trends in Jewish life, formed a Committee sponsoring the Jabotinsky Biography Project. The publication of this volume is largely due to their moral encouragement.

The extensive preparatory work for this English edition has been made possible by the grants of the World Executive of the Herut Revisionist organization and of the Jewish Agency for Palestine, as well as by contributions of the following persons: H. Becker, I. B. Brodie, M. Boukstein, M. Dogilevski, M. Franco, S. Frimmerman, M. Gasner, E. Gelber, A. Goodman, F. Gordon, A. Hanin, S. Jaglom, A. Kaghan, Dr. S. Klinger, Mrs. A. Levi, B. Margolin, Dr. J. Markowitz, L. Naiditch, E. Norman, L. Oesterreich, C. Pickel, B. Pregel, Dr. O. Rabinowicz, F. Rubinstein, Dr. H. C. Schnur, O. Shainhaus, S. Shainhouse, Rebecca Sieff, N. Silver, R. Sonnenborn, J. Spector, M. Sperber, A. Streltzin, R. Szold, J. Torczyner, M. Torczyner, A. Tulin, M. Urdang, M. Weinberg, A. Weissbrod, J. Wollard, M. Yardney, as well as Revisionist groups of Los Angeles and San Francisco.

Leo Wolfson, Chairman of the Board of Directors of the Jabotinsky Biography Committee, took constant and active interest in all questions connected with the work.

Special acknowledgment is due to Dr. Harry C. Schnur who, as editor, contributed unstintingly to the preparation of this volume in its present shape.

Last, but certainly not least, justice must be rendered to the author's wife. Her help and her patience have actually amounted to collaboration. She has typed and read and re-read and criticized and made suggestions and corrected and revised the manuscript. Without her wholehearted encouragement and cooperation this book would never have been written.

J.B.S

INTRODUCTION

We live in an age that, some people tell us, should be the age of the *common man*. This is the story of the life of an *uncommon* man—uncommon by any standards.

Vladimir (Ze'ev) Jabotinsky died before he was sixty. He had been a Jew and a Jewish patriot in the same way that Lincoln and Churchill, Clemenceau and Gandhi, however different their individual backgrounds, are the type of patriots who appeal to millions, irrespective of their national backgrounds, by reason of their stature and the human value of their personality.

While Jabotinsky lived, no man in Jewry or any other Western nation surpassed him in the range and intensity of his activities, in the fertility of his thinking and the multiplicity of his interests. Here is a man of vision and action, who pursued truth where he saw it, a fighter who never admitted defeat; here is a political leader and a poet, an orator and a soldier, a publicist, diplomat, and linguist. Starting out as a noted Russian journalist, he became a man of letters who wrote in seven languages, and whose writings were published in at least twice as many tongues. Here is a man who was repeatedly arrested by the Tsarist police; a man who translated Dante into Hebrew, and the great Hebrew poet Bialik into Russian; the man who created the first Jewish Legion in World War I, and who was sentenced to fifteen years of hard labor by a British military court in Palestine for defending the Jews of Jerusalem against Arab attack. Here is a man who with his Battalion helped to liberate Palestine from the Turks, who was the first to cross the Jordan and was rewarded with the Medal of the British Empire—and twelve years later was permanently barred by the British from re-entering

Palestine. This man, reared in the best traditions of nineteenth-century liberalism, was later decried as a Fascist and militarist. For two years he was a
member of the Zionist Executive, the ruling body of the World Zionist Organization, and then quit, staying in opposition for over a decade until he
finally left the organization in order to create the New Zionist Organization.
When he died in 1940, he was in the midst of his struggle for the creation
of a Jewish Army to fight alongside the armies of the Western democracies
against nazism and fascism. No other political leader in modern Jewry has
been so passionately revered and so fiercely hated, followed so enthusiastically, and attacked so bitterly. To many, he was a prophet, to others, an irresponsible adventurer. His life was tense, stormy, controversial—the life of
a man who may be described as a political poet in action, always far ahead
of his contemporaries.

Time has a way of vindicating this kind of man. Today, fifteen years after
his death, Jabotinsky's stature is greater than ever. Appreciation of his unique
personality continues to grow, and the enduring and creative freshness of his
ideas has been justified by history. He influenced Jewish life as few men before him have done, and his name is imperishably linked with his people's
dramatic and victorious struggle for national redemption. To his followers
as well as to many of his former opponents, he is now a historic figure of
undisputed greatness. The rock that so long had been rejected by the official
builders of the Temple has now become a cornerstone of Jewish statehood.

The Bible, with sculptural simplicity, has drawn and kept alive for
all ages the portraits of the great Patriarchs, Judges, Kings, and Prophets.
Carved in the collective memory of a nation and, indeed, of the world, these
giant figures remain living and potent symbols of a great spiritual past.

Yet, post-biblical Jewry neglected to record the life stories of its outstanding men. The great figures of modern Jewry all too often are receding
into the past without their memory being preserved for future generations.
Jewish biographical literature, on the whole, is scanty and—with a few comforting exceptions—poor in quality. While thousands of biographies—bad,
good, and excellent—have been written of George Washington, Abraham
Lincoln, Thomas Jefferson, and even some minor heroes of American history, and continue to fill the shelves each year, there are very few full-size
biographies of Herzl, and we look in vain for well-documented life stories
of Moses Montefiore, Moses Hess, Leo Pinsker, Achad Ha'am, Max Nordau,
Ber Borokhov, M. Ussish-kin, Rabbi Meir Berlin, and others. Some are still

awaiting their biographer, while the biographies of others are manifestly inadequate. The dominant school in Jewish historiography is concentrating on sociological issues, on "community relations"—on faceless processes—and is neglecting the role of the uncommon personality in this our age of the common man. Whatever one thinks of the scientific value of the prevailing method, it deprives Jewish consciousness of a powerful inspirational stimulus.

A biography of Jabotinsky has long been overdue. The life story of a great man could, of course, be written a century after his passing, on the basis of the source material then available; yet, as eye-witnesses die, as libraries are destroyed and records lost, such source material diminishes in both quality and quantity, so that only a "fractional" biography can be produced—one that incorporates but a small proportion of what could and should have been recorded. Only a contemporary biographer, fully and intimately familiar with the man, his time, and environment, can produce at least the *first* reliable compilation of facts and documents, thereby providing the necessary foundation for further, more intensive studies of particular phases.

If the present writer called this biography the first, he is, of course, aware of the fact that he had predecessors: Y. Yaary, S. K. Gepstein, and Shalom Schwarz in Hebrew, Aisik Remba in Hebrew and Yiddish, Nachum Sommer in Yiddish. At least three of these publications—those written by Mr. Schwarz, Mr. Gepstein, and Mr. Remba—are extremely valuable, and the writer gratefully acknowledges having made extensive use of the material they contain. Yet none of these predecessors claims to have presented a full and comprehensive biography of Jabotinsky. Mr. Gepstein's excellent essay is very brief, Mr. Schwarz's book deals with a few isolated chapters and aspects of Jabotinsky's life and activities, while Mr. Remba's work is a collection of personal reminiscences over the period of 1936-39, when he was Jabotinsky's private secretary. Then there is, of course, Jabotinsky's own *Sippur Yamay,* one of the most interesting autobiographies ever written. Yet an autobiography can never replace a biography—at best, it is a valuable primary source for one. Moreover, *Sippur Yamay* only goes up to 1914; *The Story of the Jewish Legion,* which continues to 1919, deals with this subject exclusively. Both are in many respects strangely impersonal. They were written by Jabotinsky himself, but the "self" of the man who tells the story is often faint and elusive—deliberately so. In a letter to his sister (May 23, 1935), Jabotinsky says: "In such a condensed autobiography, everything that concerns persons must be dealt with superficially. I completely passed by the tremendous role that mother, you, Ania, Eri or Sasha* have played in my life. . . . References to oneself must surely be somewhat whimsical—otherwise it would degenerate into pomposity and lack of taste." On numerous occasions Jabotinsky obviously preferred giving an incomplete and deprecatory impression of his own feelings and deeds rather than to disclose something of his personal life and motivations. What he did reveal was scant and more carefully selected and censored than is generally supposed. The contemporary evidence often gives a different picture.

The present writer will therefore be obliged on more than one occasion to question the accuracy of some of Jabotinsky's autobiographical statements. He is well aware of the danger of presumption this implies, and is reminded of the story of the professor of German literature who, on reading in Goethe's autobiography the words "Lotte I loved above all others," appended a footnote: *Hier irrt Goethe* (here Goethe is mistaken). However, the writer may find his justification in Jabotinsky's letter to his sister, in which he acknowledges that he cared very little for factual exactitude and precision: "Exactness of dates is of no interest to me; I do not remember them and I have no time to dig for them."

Jabotinsky's memory, like anyone else's, could at times betray him, and contemporary data that are now available enable the researcher to render more accurate, or even correct, some of the accounts of events that Jabotinsky described from memory, many decades after they had taken place.

It is the aim of this biography to record the main events of Jabotinsky's life while they are still accessible and relatively fresh in the memory of his contemporaries. It will attempt to present as truthful an account of Jabotinsky's life story as is in this writer's power. He will endeavor also to relate Jabotinsky's personality and experiences to the development of his ideas.

This is, as the writer increasingly realized, a tremendous task. He had to assemble, read, and digest an immense amount of material before the work of interpretation and presentation could even begin. This material was so extensive that only a selection could be used in this book. The intention was to make this selection as representative and objective as possible, while at the same time not to crowd the story with unnecessary and irrelevant de-

---

* Ania—Jabotinsky's wife; Eri—his son; Sasha—Alexander Poliakov, schoolmate and intimate friend of Jabotinsky.

tail; to pay scrupulous respect to the facts collected, and at the same time to select those most suitable for presenting the living image which the author himself had formed. Extensive use has been made of Jabotinsky's letters, so as to enable the reader to hear him speak of his life, his work, his convictions, hopes, and disappointments. Wherever possible, preference has been given to Jabotinsky's own words over the statements of contemporaries, and to his personal letters over his other writings.

Another major difficulty is, of course, the special relationship between the present writer and the man whose biography he is writing. He has known Jabotinsky intimately for over thirty years; he has profoundly admired and—not to shy away from the word—loved the man. Yet as a biographer he must be objective, whatever his personal feelings. On the other hand, the honest biographer, in the final analysis, cannot help being partial, for he can present his subject only as he himself sees him. What he must scrupulously avoid is not so much partiality as infatuation with his subject. This is a risk inherent in every biography of a great and good man: fulsome praise is easily overdone, particularly where the man's character and achievements present the almost irresistible temptation to show him as a *chevalier sans peur etsans reproche.*

Yet this biography is not an act of hero worship, however great the writer's respect and admiration for Jabotinsky's person and achievements. The writer, if he may mention himself briefly, was apparently born without what phrenologists call the "bump of veneration." Indeed, he has paid dearly for this deficiency throughout his literary and political career. In the second place, hardly any man in the world could have matched Jabotinsky's aversion for any form of Byzantinism in human relations and in public life. No greater profanation of everything Jabotinsky stood for could be imagined than an attempt to present him as a paragon of all the virtues, a saintly and infallible figure, superhuman—and, therefore, inhuman—in its composite perfection.

Then, the semantic difficulty rears its head. You can say the same thing in two ways, conveying an exactly opposite impression. Your subject may be called obstinate or tenacious, narrow-minded or single-minded, fanatical or tirelessly zealous. This biographer will avoid wholesale use of emotive adjectives, be they friendly or derogatory. He will apply them, when necessary, with discrimination, though he is frank enough to advise the reader that he tends toward affirmative judgments. He promises, however, to keep the balance. Jabotinsky once used, in a different connotation, the formula "faithful and free." The biographer will try to follow this precept: to be faithful to the memory and to the great spiritual heritage of Jabotinsky, yet free in his approach to the single phases of Jabotinsky's life and work, and in his appraisal of them. This biography will endeavor to show a Jabotinsky who has stature without being a statue.

The original intention was to write a one-volume biography. In the process of research and writing, it became clear that this would have meant omitting or dealing too cursorily with essential and important chapters in Jabotinsky's life story. The writer was therefore compelled to divide his work into two volumes.

The present volume ends with Jabotinsky's resignation from the Zionist Executive in January, 1923. Up to that time Jabotinsky had been one of those non-party Zionists—Zionists *tout court;* he had never tried to set up a party of his own. The second volume will deal with the last seventeen years of Jabotinsky's life, which were devoted largely to building an organized movement as an instrument, first for the implementation of a clearly defined political program within the World Zionist Organization, and later for independent political action outside the framework of that organization.

YOUNG JABOTINSKY

ONE

CHILDHOOD AND YOUTH

Family Background

On Sunday, October 5th (18th), 1880, there was rejoicing in the comfortable apartment of Yona and Khava Jabotinsky, in the house of Kharlamp on Odessa's densely populated Bazarnaya Street: the third child, a son, had been born. There was his elder brother, then five years old, named Miron-Meir (Mitia), and his four-year-old sister Tamar-Therese (Tania). The boy was named Vladimir.

The Jabotinskys were a typical middle-class Jewish family. Without being wealthy, they were well off and had no major worries. Their family life ran smoothly and without complications; the couple was well-content and faced the future with calm and confidence.

This carefree existence seems to have derived to a large extent from the character and position of Yona Jabotinsky. Vladimir had almost no recollections of his father, but he heard many stories and legends about him. Yona Jabotinsky was born at Nikopol on the Dniepr and was noted all his life for his kindness and good nature. He had a good word for everybody; once, when told that an employee was stealing from him, he replied: "He who steals from me is poorer than I, and maybe he has a right to what he takes." In relating this character trait in his autobiographical *Sippur Yamay* (Story of My Life), Jabotinsky remarks that he had inherited this "philosophy" from his father.[1]

The russified form of Yona Jabotinsky's first name was Yevgenni (Eugene). Though a self-educated man, he had an important position with the semi-governmental "Russian Company of Navigation and Commerce," being in charge of wheat purchase and delivery along the entire length of the Dniepr, from Kherson to Alexandrovsk. His energy, honesty, and resourcefulness were highly appreciated by his superiors. Once, the head of the Company, Admiral Nikolai M. Tchikhatchev, said to him jokingly: "Your name is Yevgenni, but to us you are a genni (genius)." Yevgenni Jabotinsky was also widely popular with the wheat traders with whom he was dealing.

Of his mother Khava (Eva), Vladimir Jabotinsky always spoke and wrote with adoration. She was the youngest of the twelve children of Meir Sack, a well-to-do Jewish merchant from Berditchev, the most Jewish town of the Ukraine, where even the Gentile porters spoke Yiddish and those who did not spoke Russian with a Yiddish accent. While her father was strictly orthodox, she received a European education, being sent to a modern school where she was taught the German language and literature as well as European manners. German, therefore, in addition to her native Yiddish, was the language of her culture, and Schiller was her favorite poet. She learned to speak Russian only when, after her marriage, she moved to Odessa and had to talk Russian to the servants; yet she victimized that language all her life. She also understood some Hebrew, language of the Bible and of the prayers, and was deeply attached to religious tradition. When Vladimir once asked her whether his family were Hassidim, she replied, almost angrily: "And what do you think we are—Misnagdim?"* Since then, Jabotinsky used to remark half-jokingly that he always considered himself a born Hassid.

This happy family life did not last long after Vladimir's birth. In January, 1882, his elder brother Mitia, a gifted boy, died at the age of seven of scarlet fever. Some time later, Yevgenni Jabotinsky suffered a painful moral shock. Compelled to absent himself for a few weeks, he had put his younger brother in charge of his work for the Company. That brother was a charming and gifted but utterly irresponsible character, a congenital liar who abused the trust put in him and quickly bit into the Company's funds.

---

*Hassidim (literally "the pious") were members of a religious movement among Ukrainian and Polish Jews in the eighteenth century, assigning the first place in religion not to religious dogmas and ritual, but to sentiment and the emotion of faith. Misnagdim (literally "opponents") was the title applied by the Hassidim to all those who opposed them.

He was caught red-handed, and badly jeopardized his brother's good name and position with the Company. The worst, however, was that in 1884, two years after his son Mitia's death, Yevgenni Jabotinsky was stricken with two terrible diseases—tuberculosis and cancer.

For two years, the entire life of the family was dominated by a desperate but hopeless struggle against the illness. Yevgenni went to Berlin to consult the greatest German specialists who made it clear that his state of health was alarming. He wired his wife asking her to join him. She arrived in November, 1884, together with the children: the boy was placed in a kindergarten, the girl in a school. When it became evident that the illness was going to be a protracted and costly one, she left her husband and children with the family of a relative in Berlin and went back to Odessa where she sold or pawned everything the family possessed; then she returned to Germany. The winter months they used to spend in Berlin and the summer at Bad Ems. When all the money was gone, the German specialists came to the conclusion that in Russia, too, good doctors could be found. The family went to Kiev and then to Kharkov. However, the Russian specialists proved as helpless as had the German doctors, and the Jabotinskys began the painful return journey to the familiar surroundings on the Dniepr. Yevgenni Jabotinsky died at Alexandrovsk on December 14 (27), 1886, and was buried there.

The family was now ruined, the children orphaned. They returned to Odessa. The young widow, left without any means, had to support and bring up two small children, a task in which she displayed great courage and determination. A family council was held at the house of her elder brother, Abraham Sack, a well-to-do merchant, in order to discuss the children's future. The host's youngest son Miron (Meir), himself a successful lawyer, insisted that the girl should become a seamstress and the boy should be apprenticed to a carpenter. "We have enough educated people in the family already." Recalling this episode, Jabotinsky would good-naturedly say that this advice was perhaps good. His mother, however, would not hear of it. Her blunt reply was: "Miron, why don't you set an example and begin by applying this principle to your own children, while I will bring up my children as I see it fit?"

At that time, no self-respecting Jewish middle-class parents would ever think of raising their children as artisans. This would have been tantamount to social degradation of the family, for not to send one's children to school and from there to higher education was an admission of failure. Only such youngsters as proved hopelessly incapable of following a normal school curriculum were shamefacedly made apprentices. Khava Jabotinsky, proudly confident of her children's talents, was not ready to do so. She worked hard, depriving herself of elementary comforts, in order to send her children to school.

Khava tried to make a living by opening a small stationery shop at the corner of Richelieu and Yevreyskaya streets, just across from the synagogue; the family lived in a small apartment behind the shop. Business was not good, and Abraham Sack had to help out from time to time. In the fall of 1888, the family moved to an even humbler attic apartment, consisting of two rooms and a kitchen, in the house on the corner of Yevreyskaya and Kanatnaya streets. The family budget was very limited and their living standard extremely modest. However, the children somehow did not feel that theirs was an underprivileged life. There is nothing to indicate that the lean years following the father's death left the imprint of frustration on their characters. Their mother saw to it that they should be provided with some "luxuries": when Vladimir first went to school she gave him an apple for his daily school lunch; after some time, however, he told her that an apple a day meant twenty-five apples a month, that this was really too much, too expensive, and that she should not spend so much money on him. His mother was both touched by and proud of this fine gesture but did not, of course, cut out the apples.

There was a marked difference of character between the two children. Tamar was of rather austere nature, inclined to view life with a stern countenance. While still in school, she started to help the family out by giving lessons; later, with the help of her brother, she became the founder and headmistress of the first Jewish gymnasium for girls in Odessa. A woman of exceptional intellectual and moral integrity, she would always take life seriously—sometimes even too much so.

Vladimir, on the other hand, was gay and carefree; genial and of a devil-may-care disposition, he enjoyed life in all its manifestations. He was full of exuberance and often of mischief, highly strung and self-willed, often to the point of obstinacy. When he was asked on one occasion: "Whose boy are you?" he answered: "I am myself." His pride caused him to react violently to any insult, regardless of the age, strength, or position of the offender. One day, one of his former playmates told this writer, they were playing a noisy game in the courtyard of the house. Their screams annoyed a Russian officer in a nearby apartment, who upbraided them and slapped Vladimir. The boy, then hardly twelve years old, saw red and threw himself at his assailant, trying to strike back. His friends restrained him only with great difficulty.[2] One has to be aware of the universal fear and awe inspired by the uniform of a Tsarist officer to realize the reckless daring of such a reaction.

The boy was headstrong and would rarely yield to a stern rebuke. However, he was responsive to kindness. His mother, who knew how to handle this difficult youngster, would say to his sister that "with kindness and tact one can get absolutely anything from Volodia." And so it was. His mother treated him with limitless patience and tenderness, and he obeyed her eagerly and loved her dearly. Later on, he would also listen to his sister, who had early recognized his exceptional talents. They became great friends, despite the difference in their make-up.

Throughout his life, Jabotinsky remained an exemplary son and brother, affectionate, devoted, and considerate.

He adored his mother and was extremely proud of her. He would write to her regularly and often, and since reading Russian was difficult for her, he made a special effort and wrote to her in Yiddish. His mother's wish was law to Jabotinsky, and until her passing in December, 1926, at the age of eighty-six, he was always full of concern for her well-being and tried to please her in many ways. He himself was neither religious nor observant and preserved hardly any memory of his father; but since his mother wished it, he meticulously kept his promise to say *Kaddish** for his father, wherever he happened to be on the day of his passing. His mother's birthday to him and his family was always a festive occasion. On October 10, 1923, he wrote to his sister from Berlin: "Yesterday we went on a spree in honor of mama's birthday: we even drank Russian vodka." He never forgot to send her birthday greetings, and after each Day of Atonement he would inquire by telegram how his mother had sustained the fast, since he knew that she would often faint at the end of the day. In 1920, shortly before Odessa was reoccupied by the Bolshevik troops, he succeeded by superhuman efforts to bring his mother and sister safely to Palestine; his nephew Johnny preceded them by a few months. His visits to Palestine in October, 1922, and October, 1926, were motivated largely by his strong desire to see his mother. He was on a lecture tour in Germany when he was notified that

---

Kaddish—a prayer of intercession for the dead.

she had died on December 2, 1926. In Hamburg, he "went to a synagogue, ordered candles to be lit and said *Kaddish*," as he wrote to his sister. His first reaction was to cancel his remaining lectures— "my mind was not on that"—but he continued since he did not want to cause financial loss to the Revisionist groups which had arranged his tour; "so I am traveling and mechanically talking about something."[3]

In the same letter he movingly expressed his fond regard for his sister. "Taniusha, mother was always afraid that without her the two of us would drift apart and would forget each other. But this shall never happen. The arguments we had were trifles; what is essential, however, is that we always have been helping each other, that you carried me through high school, that all our lives we have been working for the same cause and valued each other's work, as well as many other things about which it is difficult to write. I am proud of you and of Johnny, just as I was proud of mother. Never will we drift apart."

Jabotinsky, that self-styled "vagabond and bohemian," had a strong family sense. He generously applied it not only to his small immediate family—his mother, sister, and nephew—but, when he married, also to the numerous family of his wife, close and distant relatives alike. This lifelong attitude of his doubtlessly derived from the warmth and affection which had permeated the atmosphere of the humble Jabotinsky apartment in that overcrowded house on Yevreyskaya Street.

Outside of the house, life was exciting, turbulent. To Vladimir, sun-drenched Odessa with its park, its acacia alleys, its harbor and seashore, was an inexhaustible source of experience and adventure. He would catch crabs in the Black Sea, he would run through the alleys of Alexander Park; in the port, which he knew intimately, he would watch the arrival of foreign ships; he would play and fight with the multilingual crowd of children that filled the streets of Odessa. In the municipal garden he enthusiastically played "Cossacks and Robbers," and would return home badly scratched, with many a shiner, but happily excited by the adventure of life.

School

Jabotinsky's schooling began early. For a year or so, while his family lived in Germany during his father's illness, he went to a kindergarten. The result of this brief experience was his strong aversion to the German language, and the memory of a fleeting encounter, in the gardens of Bad Ems, with old Kaiser Wilhelm I, with whom he exchanged salutes. It was also in Ems that he first gave signs of his inborn sense of music. A concert was given every afternoon at the City Casino. The child never missed a performance. With a little stick in his hand, he would place himself behind the conductor, gesticulating as if conducting the orchestra by himself. The conductor soon noticed a striking rhythmical correctness in the boy's movements, and his intuitive perception of the pieces that were played. The conductor was intrigued by this phenomenon, and in order to test whether or not a child was simply aping his own gestures, he several times intentionally made misleading hand movements: he was delighted to see that the boy did not follow him but continued to "conduct" in the proper way. One day Vladimir caught a bad cold and did not come to the Casino for several concerts. The conductor inquired where the Jabotinskys were staying, visited them, and told them the story. He tried to impress upon them the need for developing the boy's musical gifts. After their return to Odessa, when Vladimir began going to school, he was given violin lessons. Apparently, however, his general dislike of the entire school curriculum extended to school music as well. "I have managed to make the music teacher expel me from class," he proudly reported in his "Memoirs of My Contemporary" (music was not a mandatory subject).[4]

Vladimir acquired his first notions of the Russian alphabet from his sister Tamar at the time when the family was temporarily staying in Kharkov. At the age of seven, he entered a private preparatory school for "boys and girls of either sex," as a local wit put it. This Odessa school, owned and directed by the sisters Sussman-Lev, was of a rather unorthodox kind, and Jabotinsky later wistfully described it in a semi-autobiographical short story, "Squirrel":[5]

> It was generally considered a crazy establishment, though much later I realized that it must have been founded with quite progressive views, the two girls having apparently read books. We children were told to call the teachers by their pet names, not Anna Petrovna and Maria Sergheyevna, but Ania and Maroossia. There were two classes, with Maroossia catering for all knowledge in the lower form and Ania in the upper. There were no examinations of any kind, but sometimes Ania would rush into the lower class room just like that, in the middle of a term, in the middle of a lesson, and interrupt the proceedings by proclamation of a decree promoting Vania, Liuda, Nadia and Misha to upper class dignity; upon which the members whose names were thus mentioned would collect their books and luncheon bags

and, with great howling because Ania was reputed wicked and Maroossia good, would pass in the literal sense of the word from class to class.

In this preparatory school, Vladimir met a girl from the "upper class" whose nickname was Squirrel: she was known for her resolute character and her Amazonian methods of dealing with schoolmates "of either sex." Vladimir fell in love with her and tells the story of this stormy first romance with an ironical seriousness that is exquisitely touching.

The idyll did not last long. A year later, he was, for the first time in his life, confronted with official anti-Jewish policy. The Russian authorities were bent on barring the Jewish youth from education in government schools. A rigid *numerus clausus* provided that only one Jewish child per ten pupils be admitted, and only outstanding performance at the entrance examinations or exceptionally powerful "pull," or else a very substantial bribe, would secure admission. The Jabotinsky family had no money and no influential connections. The boy had to rely exclusively on his showing at the examinations. He tried his luck in various types of schools. Finally, he was admitted at the age of nine to the preparatory class of the second grammar school, one year later than would have been in accordance with his age. At the age of fifteen, he was automatically transferred from there to the fifth grade of the first classical high school, the Richelieu Gymnasium.

Many famous men have been infant prodigies. Pitt was a classical scholar at the age of ten; Macaulay had compiled a universal compendium of history when he was twelve; Tennyson, at the same age, had written an epic poem of six thousand lines; John Stuart Mill began his study of Greek and arithmetic at the age of three, at six he wrote a history of Rome, and by the time he was twelve he had mastered algebra and geometry and had read the works of Cicero, Ovid, Livy, Virgil, Horace, Lucretius, and Juvenal.

No such scholastic achievements could be credited to young Jabotinsky. In no sense was he a child prodigy. A highly gifted boy, with excellent memory and a wide scope of spiritual interests, he could easily have made a very good student. But he loathed the stuffy atmosphere, the limited, obsolete curriculum, and the strict discipline of the official Russian educational institutions. He turned out to be a poor student and more than once was sent home in disgrace—not, as he confessed later, because of anti-Semitism (which at that time was not yet a potent factor in Odessa), but because of his conduct. He simply would not submit to school discipline, and if he ever studied, he studied only what he himself chose. He was deliberately lazy and cut classes as often as he could. In the morning he often pretended to go to school, but on leaving the house he deposited his books at the neighboring store and, together with some other absentees, went fishing or catching crabs in the Port. He later gratefully acknowledged that parents in easygoing Odessa as a rule "would interfere very little with our activities and the way we spent our days. If we did not feel like going to class we would simply go for a walk along the sea shore: our mothers would know what was going on, but when the school would send a truant officer to inquire why her boy did not come to school today, she would state that he had gone to the dentist—a terrible toothache, he could not sleep all night. . . ." With such well-trained parents—their cooperation is probably somewhat overstated—school life cannot have been too difficult or boring. As far as teachers were concerned, there also existed "well-established and diversed ways of deceiving them." Jabotinsky claimed that "the teachers knew it very well and did not even attempt to fight this convenient system." In fact, he insisted, he and his comrades did not learn anything in school: "a *Mathmid* [diligent student] in our midst was a rare phenomenon."[6]

This picture, as he drew it in his "Memoirs," is probably somewhat exaggerated. It seems true, however, that Jabotinsky loathed school perhaps more than most of his friends and did his best to spend as little time there as possible, reducing to the barest minimum the amount of knowledge the school was supposed to impart to him. Most of the mandatory subjects failed to interest him. "Latin and Greek," he wrote in 1920, "which we studied at school, did not interest me and I do not know these languages even to this day."[7] His attitude toward mathematics was less than lukewarm: "This branch of knowledge I always despised," he wrote half-jokingly to his sister.[8] He was, on the other hand, interested in the humanities, in history and geography, and most of all in literature. Of the Russian poets he loved Pushkin and Lermontov best. Much of their poetry he knew by heart. Among prose writers, for some reason, he gave preference to Gontcharov for his novel *The Ravine*. For the rest of the curriculum he did not care at all. When he was in the third grade of grammar school, he founded, together with a group of friends, an imaginary "Republic of Lukania," named probably after Luka, a disreputable character in a satire by Prince Antiokh Kantemir, a Russian poet of the eighteenth century. The territory of this Republic, which had a most unusual constitution—a president and a king simultaneously—was a tiny valley on the seacoast of Langeron, a suburb of Odessa. Jabotinsky and his friends also published a disrespectful paper, *Shmarovoz,* in which, among other similar material, there appeared a mock degree of the Tsarist Ministry of Public Education, prescribing a radical reform in the teaching of classical languages: "to replace Greek by Latin, and Latin by Greek. . . ."[9] The principal of the grammar school, Jungmeister, fully recognized the boy's ability but often complained angrily of his utter intractability. At the final examinations in the grammar school, he was caught passing a "gyp-sheet" to a schoolmate in difficulties and stood in danger of being refused a diploma; in the end, however, Jungmeister was mollified and agreed not to ruin the further "academic career" of this troublesome pupil.

But in the gymnasium, too, Vladimir was more than once in trouble. Just as in grammar school, he would always cut classes, this time mostly in favor of youthful sea pleasures: fishing, catching crabs, trips in hired or "borrowed" boats, with boys and girls, singing and indulging in horseplay. He was a normal youth who loved company, adventure, a good laugh, a practical joke, and flirting with the girls. He was far from handsome, and he knew it: short, stocky, and with a negroid profile and lips. But a high fore-head, keen eyes, and an animated expression lent a kind of attractiveness and charm to his plain face. According,to local Odessa tradition, he was by no means unsuccessful in his early romantic ventures.

The time he could not help spending in school he used to ask the teachers embarrassing questions; to write bitingly satirical verse about the pedagogic and administrative personnel who, of course, resented this bitterly; to draw caricatures, and in many other ingenious ways to annoy his teachers. There was a widespread rumor in town that one of the teachers, whom Jabotinsky for some reason disliked particularly and systematically derided, committed suicide because he could not bear the flood of the boy's epigrams, parodies, and caricatures.[10] This was probably a rumor based on Odessa's vivid southern imagination rather than fact; but it was characteristic of the reputation young Jabotinsky established for himself inside and outside the school.

At the age of sixteen, Vladimir with a group of friends edited a clandestine mimeographed schoolpaper called *Truth.* It was clandestine, not because it covered, God forbid, political matters: the editors had no interest in politics whatsoever. But the very fact that such a paper did appear was in itself a challenge to the political regime and to school regulations in particular: both definitely prohibited any kind of school publication. This defiance of state and school authority made Jabotinsky and his friends "revolutionaries," whether they wanted it or not. In one of his early Russian poems, "Schafloch," written in 1900, Jabotinsky thus described himself to a girl he was courting:[11]

> In my early youth, dear Fräulein,
> I annoyed every grown-up;
> For I was a mighty Liberal, Never ready to give up.
> *(Translated by A.G.) 35*

On the authority of "those who knew him well," Itamar Ben Avi described young Jabotinsky as "so cocksure of his natural abilities that he always spoke in superlatives: 'I will do that great thing, I shall come out on top. I am absolutely sure of winning a victory'—those were the words which continually recurred in his conversations with pals, teachers, relatives and even parents."[12] This intense self-confidence may be traced back to his mother's great pride and love for him. Freud insists that "a man who has been the indisputable favorite of his mother keeps for life the feeling of a conqueror, that confidence of success which often induces real success." Quoting this statement, Ernest Jones, Freud's latest and most penetrating biographer, stresses that the self-confidence of the founder of psychoanalysis, which was one of his salient characteristics, was only rarely impaired, and that Freud was undoubtedly right in tracing *it* back to the security of his mother's love: "His mother's favorite, he [Freud] possessed the self-confidence that told him he would achieve something worth while in life, and the confidence to do so, though for long the direction this would take remained uncertain."[13]

Spiritual Background

As stressed before, school played an insignificant role in Jabotinsky's spiritual life. The center of his interests and preoccupations lay outside. He read widely and indiscriminately, using the well-stocked library of the "Jewish Salesmen's Society" on Remeslenaya Street, which played an outstanding role in the spiritual formation of almost three generations of the Russian-Jewish intelligentsia. Yet, the specifically Jewish background of Jabotinsky's youth was very scant.

Odessa was a cosmopolitan city, a metropolis, founded and built up by
at least half a dozen various nationalities. Its first settlers in the eighteenth
century were not Russians but Greeks, Italians, and Albanians; then came
Ukrainians, Russians, Jews, Armenians, Poles. On the whole, it was a city
of newcomers: according to the census of 1892, 58 per cent of the city's
population had settled there recently, as against only 42 per cent "native"
Odessans.

It also housed all kinds of Jews: orthodox and free-thinkers, Hassidim
and Misnagdim, Litvaks, Polish Jews, and Galicians.

The late Professor Ch. Tchernowitz aptly described Odessa as "the
Alexandria of its day."[14] The Jewish community was of recent origin, without deeply rooted traditions. It was attracting thousands of orthodox provincial youths longing for "modern enlightenment" and was considered as
a dangerous and demoralizing center of free-thinking and heresy by orthodox Jewish circles. A current proverb said that "Hell is burning seven miles
around Odessa."

The community leaders were for the most part liberal in their views,
but even the average Jew, while not consciously assimilated, had a very poor
Jewish background. Jewish learning was scarce and the tenor of everyday
life was devoid of any traditional color. Occasional attempts at observance
were spiritless, superficial, sterile. Passover was not a real Passover, Hanukkah not a genuine Hanukkah. For a boy reared in this atmosphere, there
was little to remember, to treasure, and to cherish in later life. Jewishness
was largely personified by an old grandfather or grandmother, guardians of
the vestiges of a long outlived past.

There was no "Jewish quarter" in Odessa, at least not in the usual sense
of this term. The Jews were, though unevenly, scattered throughout the entire city, and not even the most exclusive residential sections were without
their stately Jewish houses. Neither were the poverty-stricken suburbs of
Moldavanka and Peressip *Judenrein*. Odessa Jews, therefore, felt very much
at home in the city, not isolated or segregated; at that time, they were as
yet not constantly on the defensive, nor were they acutely aware of being
a minority. They did not consider themselves as strangers, because almost
everybody in this young and dynamic Black Sea port was a newcomer, belonging to some minority group.

The absence of anti-Jewish pressure, combined with the weakness of
Jewish religious and cultural tradition, produced a very lax and detached

attitude to Jewishness on the part of a typical Odessa Jew. The Jabotinsky family was no exception from this pattern.

The language of the family was Russian. While Jabotinsky's mother talked to her sister in Yiddish, she would speak only Russian with the children, though she "murdered Russian grammar." The children did understand Yiddish, but it never occurred to them to speak it, be it at home or in the street. It was only at the age of thirty-four that Jabotinsky first attempted to speak Yiddish in public. During the first year after his father's death, Vladimir said *Kaddish* three times daily in the little Jewelers' synagogue nearby, but, he recalls, he did not acclimatize in its atmosphere and, except for saying *Kaddish*, never participated in the prayers. His mother, who still had strong ties with Jewish tradition, strictly observed *kashrut*, lighted candles on Sabbath eve, and taught the children a few prayers (*Modeh Ani* and *Kriath Shma*). But, says Jabotinsky, all these traditional practices in no way affected him either spiritually or emotionally.

There exists a widespread notion that Jabotinsky acquired his first ideas of Hebrew when he was already a grown man. Jabotinsky himself, however, indignantly denied this legend. When, at a banquet in a Latvian town in 1923, one of the speakers mentioned this current version, Jabotinsky proudly retorted that this was simply untrue. "My mother," he said,[15] "made me learn the *aleph-bet* when I was six years old."* A neighbor, the noted Hebrew writer and scholar Yoshua Ravnitzky, volunteered to teach her children Hebrew; they translated from the Bible into Russian and learned a little grammar. Vladimir continued his study of Hebrew at long intervals until the age of thirteen when, according to Ravnitzky's son, he declared defiantly: "What is the use of studying a dead language?"[16] Another teacher, whose name Jabotinsky forgot, prepared the boy for his Bar Mitzvah and read with him Hebrew poems by Yehuda Leib Gordon.

Despite these stray ingredients of Jewish education, Jabotinsky frankly admitted that in his youth he "had no inner contact with Judaism." In the

---

*The Hebrew alphabet nevertheless remained forever alien to Jabotinsky. Even at a time when he was an accomplished Hebrew stylist, writing articles and poetry in that language, he still complained that it was very difficult for him to read any text written or printed in Hebrew characters, be it in Hebrew or in Yiddish. Whenever possible, he wrote Hebrew in Latin characters. In 1934, in a letter to S. D. Salzman about the *Autobiography* he was then preparing, he said: "I will write it in Hebrew, but in Latin characters, for otherwise it would be difficult for me to proofread" (Letter from Paris, March 22, 1934).

library which he frequented assiduously, he rarely read books of Jewish content. When he tried to do so, he did not find in them "any action, merely mournfulness and sadness," and his devastating youthful verdict was— "uninteresting." So it came about that young Jabotinsky, born and bred in a city with a Jewish community of 140,000, a city where every third person was a Jew, where the leaders of the Jewish intelligentsia-men of the stature of Achad Haam, Bialik, Dubnov, Ben Ami, Lilienblum, Levinsky, Ravnitzky, Chaim Tchernowitz—were or had been active, that living close to a *Yeshiva,* frequenting Jewish families only and making friends almost exclusively with Jewish schoolmates—despite all these things, young Jabotinsky had no interest whatsoever in anything Jewish. Not that he was ashamed of being a Jew or trying consciously to avoid being involved in Jewish problems; he was not an assimilationist, but simply unconcerned and spiritually aloof. He admits that in his youth he never "breathed the atmosphere of Jewish cultural tradition, did not even suspect that such an atmosphere exists on God's earth."

There was nothing in his school life to awaken his dormant Jewishness. There were thirty students in his class: they belonged to eleven different nationalities, among them ten Jews. "One would in vain be looking among those Jews for at least a spark of what is now being called 'national consciousness,'" Jabotinsky recalled. "I do not remember that one of us was interested, for example, in the *Khibat Zion* [Lovers of Zion] movement, or even in anti-Jewish discrimination, though we all had personally suffered from it. It was very difficult for every one of us to be admitted to the school, and every one knew that it was going to be even more difficult to enter the University. That we, of course, knew; but we somehow did not 'realize' it; it did not play any role in our consciousness, in our thinking and dreaming. At home, some of us had perhaps studied *Loshen Kodesh* [the Holy Language], because the father so ordered, but I never knew who among my comrades did or did not do so—to such an extent was this matter unimportant in our eyes; something like taking or not taking private piano lessons. When we were once offered in school to register for lessons in Jewish *Zakon Bozhiy* [God's Law, i.e., prayers and some Jewish history], one hour a week, only three out of ten responded, and even they did so only because their parents wanted it. Among the books we used to read together, I don't remember one single book of Jewish contents. The entire field of Jewishness simply did not exist for us."[17]

Jabotinsky stressed that the same attitude did on the whole character-ize other ethnic minority groups in his class, for instance the Greeks and Armenians; only the Poles made an exception.

Yet, despite this apparently complete lack of national consciousness, there was among his schoolmates a clear and sharp segregation into na-tional groups, in particular as far as the Jews and the Poles were concerned. Without any propaganda, without any "idea" behind this spontaneous occurrence, the ten Jews and the five Poles would sit on separate rows of benches in class, each nationality with its own. When the Jewish pupils formed a "circle" to read books on philosophy together, it just did not occur to them to invite any non-Jews; in the evenings, their non-Jewish comrades would very rarely be found as guests in their homes. It was with Jewish boys only that they would go for walks and only with Jewish high-school girls was it customary to flirt in the park.

Why was it so? "I don't know," answered Jabotinsky. In the nineties of the nineteenth century, a dead and empty period in Russian political his-tory, even anti-Semitism was sleeping in Russian society. "We were friends with our Christian comrades; with some of them we were even intimate; but we still lived separately and regarded this state of affairs as quite a natural one, as something that just could not be different—or we did not regard it at all."[18] Jabotinsky himself did not know what to make of this contradictory situation: was it indicative of assimilation or of an instinctive nationalism? Perhaps of both, he thought. But "instinctive nationalism" was dormant while cultural assimilation was very much alive. Young Jabotinsky avidly absorbed the fascinating spiritual values of Russian and Western European culture, discussing literary and social problems with his friends.

This Jewish boy thought and felt Russian. In his receptive mind the romantic epic of Russian literature found an echo: Pushkin, Lermontov, Tiutchev—but also Tolstoi, Chekhov, Gorki. He devoured the writings of leading Russian thinkers, literary critics, and sociologists—Pissarev and Bielinsky, Herzen and Lavrov, Mikhailovsky and Kropotkin. They took firm possession of his soul and mind, they shaped his first literary taste and incli-nations, molded his language and awakened the poet and the writer.

Many years later, Jabotinsky felt it necessary to insist that the Russian culture in which he was reared had remained "half alien" to him: Shake-speare and Walter Scott, Dante and D'Annunzio, Victor Hugo and Maupas-sant, even Mickiewicz or the Swedish poet Tegner, he asserted, were "closer to his heart than, for example, Tolstoi or Turgeniev."[19] This statement is less than convincing to anyone who knew Jabotinsky well. There is no doubt that he thoroughly enjoyed and cherished the works of those great writers of world literature; but it is more than improbable that the Russian writers—not necessarily Tolstoi or Turgeniev—were less close to his heart. No other language, not even Italian, was as intimately interwoven with his innermost spiritual fabric as was Russian. A powerful writer and speaker in several tongues, he was nevertheless at his very best in a speech or an article in Russian as compared with any other language. With the partial exception of Hebrew, it was in Russian only that he wrote poetry. He was deeply imbued with the spirit and tradition of Russian literature. He knew and at every occasion would fondly quote thousands of lines from Russian poets, old and new. It is true that, as he himself pointed out in *The Five*, he was "indifferent to Russia" even when he was young.[20] But that was his attitude to Russia as a country: he never was a "Russian patriot." Yet this indifference did not extend to Russian literature. While Russia was not Jabotinsky's spiritual motherland, Russian literature was—his own denial notwithstanding.

His love of Russian literature did not prevent him, even in his early years in Odessa, from hungrily and indiscriminately absorbing everything that Europe sent over to Russia, whether it was in the field of literature, theater, music, and art, or political and social ideas as they flowed into the broad stream of Russian liberal thinking.

Some of the foreign books he was able to read in their original language. His first linguistic experiences he described in 1920: "I learned German when I was between two and four years old; I went to a kindergarten in Berlin. I spoke it then as well as a German, but soon afterwards I forgot the language. At the age of nine I began to learn Spanish through the medium of a text book which I happened to find. At that stage I also began to learn French with the help of my cousin who lived with us. . . . I attempted to write in Esperanto which interested me when I was between twelve and fourteen years of age and I wrote some very bad poems in that medium."[21] To this must be added that his sister shared with him the scant knowledge of English she was acquiring at her gymnasium; in his last letter to his sister, written in English in New York on July 28, 1940, just a few days before his death (the letter arrived in Palestine after his burial), Jabotinsky wrote: "Taniusha dear, when you taught me my first English lesson forty-five years ago, we never imagined that a day might come when we both should have to correspond in that language" (because of military censorship both in the United States and in Palestine). Finally, thanks to his Polish schoolmates, he was able to read Mickiewicz's *Pan Tadeusz* in the original.

These extracurricular interests, too, had some connection with his shortcomings as a student. He neglected his school work in order to give himself to reading—and writing.

Literary Beginnings

Jabotinsky began his literary work quite early. At the tender age of ten, he tried his hand at some juvenile poetry. His poems were "published" in a handwritten paper edited by two of his friends who were pupils at another school. Between his thirteenth and sixteenth birthdays, he concentrated on translations into Russian, starting, characteristically, with part of the "Song of Songs" and of the poem "Sea Depths" by Yehuda Leib Gordon. While still in high school, he wrote an outstanding translation of Edgar Allan Poe's "The Raven," even though his knowledge of English at that time was rather scanty and he had to make extensive use of the dictionary. He sent the poem to the journal *Severny Kurier* (Northern Courier), but the paper rejected it unceremoniously; other publications to which he kept trying to sell his literary efforts did the same. These first literary misadventures were not surprising. Most of Jabotinsky's earliest writings were far from mature in form and style, and hardly fit for publication; one notable exception was his translation of Poe's "The Raven," which later became a classic and was published in a popular anthology known as *Chtetz-Deklamator* (The Reader-Reciter). Young Jabotinsky was, however, by no means discouraged by these early failures. To him they were a challenge, an inducement to do better. He continued working on himself, enriching and polishing his vocabulary, absorbing new values from world literature. The famous Russian writer Vladimir Korolenko, the editor of the leading progressive monthly *Russkoye Bogatstvo* (Russian Treasure), to whom Jabotinsky sent his first full-length novel, refused to publish it, but volunteered the encouraging advice: "Continue writing."

In 1897, Jabotinsky, then only sixteen, made his first attempt to "conquer" the daily press of Odessa. He turned first to the influential liberal paper *Odesskiya Novosti*, founded in 1895. Its editor-in-chief, I. M. Heifetz, recalls how one day a "youth with an original, somewhat aggressive face" brought him an article against the use of marks in school and, "without the shyness usual in such cases," asked whether it would be acceptable to the editor.[22] It was not; later, however, the article appeared in another Odessa newspaper, *Yuzhnoye Obozreniye,* under the pen name of Vladimir Illiritch—the first literary production of Jabotinsky's ever to appear in print.

Heifetz says that he was "amazed by the simplicity and brightness of the style and by the serious approach to such an elementary and seemingly insignificant question." He therefore asked: "Have you by any chance sinned in the field of belletristics?" A few days later, Jabotinsky brought him a lighter piece—"some kind of a legend or a fairy-tale"—which was gladly accepted. Since then, Heifetz recalls, *Odesskiya Novosti* started to publish periodically short belletristic feuilletons "signed with unknown initials, but attracting general attention by their colorful form and daring topics."

Encouraged by these first literary successes, Jabotinsky, early in 1898, made an adventurous decision. He came to Heifetz and asked him for a quarter of an hour for a "serious conversation."

"I am leaving for Italy," he said, "and I want to ask you whether you can use the services of a correspondent there."

"But you are a high-school student," argued Heifetz, "and, I understand, you are already in your last year. What is the sense of leaving Russia just now, one year before graduation?"

"Pardon me, Mr. Editor," said Jabotinsky, "I did not come to you for advice; I am simply asking for the position of a correspondent."

Heifetz liked this rejoinder, but would not assume the responsibility for entrusting an inexperienced youth with representing his paper in a foreign country. Jabotinsky turned to a rival newspaper, *Odessky Listok,* which was older (established in 1880) and somewhat more conservative. To its editor, V. V. Navrotzky, he was warmly recommended by the noted Russian poet A. M. Fiodorov, who had read Jabotinsky's translation of "The Raven" and liked it very much. Asked whether he would accept Jabotinsky's articles from abroad, Navrotzky answered: "I might, but on two conditions only: if you will write from a European capital where we have no other correspondent, and if you will write no stupidities. . . ."[23]

Many years later Jabotinsky himself admitted that from the average, common-sense viewpoint this youthful venture of his was sheer madness: "The young reader of our day will find it hard to understand what a gymnasium education meant for a Jew forty years ago. It meant a diploma, the right to enter a [Russian] university, the right to live outside the 'Pale'—in short a human instead of a dog's life. And here I am already in the seventh grade and in another year and a half will be entitled to don the blue cap and black uniform of a university student. What madness is this to throw it all away and ruin all my prospects, and why?"

The answer given to this "Why?" in his *Autobiography* is a valiant attempt to justify *post factum* an irrational decision by brilliantly developing an enticing, though hardly convincing, and even somewhat mystical theory of an all-embracing and all-explaining "just because." There is every reason to believe that the real motive for Jabotinsky's daring step was his abhorrence of the official Russian school system, his irate teachers having become increasingly hostile, and his impatient longing to see the wide world, to have a chance to develop fully the creative forces he felt seething in him. He craved for a Europe he vaguely knew or guessed about from literature—for this free, shining, magnificent Europe; and he badly wanted to get out of the Russian police state.

His mother and sister begged him to reconsider his decision and to "stick it out" until he would obtain his high-school diploma; but he remained adamant. The only concession he made was a definite promise to return in time for his final examinations, for which he would present himself as an "extern," so that he might get a diploma together with his classmates.

TWO

BERNE AND ROME

The Berne Interlude

In April, 1898, Jabotinsky left Russia for the first time in his life. When choosing the university where he intended to study, he was to be guided by "professional" considerations: it had to be in some capital where *Odessky Listok* did not have a correspondent. There were two such capitals: Berne and Rome. His mother asked him to choose Berne, because two older sisters of his friend A. Poliakov were studying medicine at Berne University and could be counted on as chaperons of the inexperienced youngster. Jabotinsky agreed. At that relatively idyllic time most of the European universities were as yet not very formalistic with regard to admittance of foreign students, and Jabotinsky—even without a high-school diploma—had no difficulty in enrolling in the Law School of the University of Berne.

On his way to Switzerland, he had to pass through the thickly populated Jewish communities of Galicia and Hungary. The journey was a long one, with several stopovers. There, for the first time in his life, Jabotinsky witnessed the full degradation of ghetto poverty and misery; he got an inkling of what the existence of the Jewish masses was like, and it impressed him painfully and repellingly. In his Russified Odessa he had never seen anything like it, and he thought with horror and bitterness: This is my people!

However, these impressions seem to have been of a superficial and passing nature. In Berne, they were quickly overshadowed by the novelty of student life.

In the beginning, Jabotinsky tried to play the role of a lone wolf, of an "original." He unexpectedly embraced the vegetarian "faith." Following the strictest precepts of vegetarianism, he courageously prepared and cooked various vegetables on his primitive alcohol stove. However, after some two weeks of this experimenting, tired of eating tasteless food and of being constantly hungry, he went to the same restaurants as did the other students. Together with his vegetarianism, his aloofness came to an end, and he made contact with the "Russian Colony."

"Russian colonies" abroad were a peculiar phenomenon. They consisted of political emigrés who fled persecution by the Tsarist police, and of Jews who, under the existing *numerus clausus*, could not enter Russian universities. Though not revolutionaries in the accepted sense of the word, and sometimes offspring of wealthy or well-to-do families, most of these students held Leftist opinions and were strongly influenced by Marxist theories. It was most unpopular to stress any specific nationalist aspirations and demands, which were branded as obsolete and reactionary. Political Zionism as well as the anti-Zionist Jewish Socialist Bund were at that time only one year old and still quite insignificant in the Russian colony of Berne—about three hundred strong and 80 per cent Jewish.

According to the noted Yiddish publicist Sh. Stupnitzky, who at that time was studying in Berne, Jabotinsky did not actively participate in the life of the colony. "He used, of course, to come to the meetings and to listen to the discussions between the Zionists and the Socialists, but he would sit there with a clever smile on his thick lips and keep silent. He would not utter a single word and nobody knew what he was." The two Poliakov sisters, with whom he used to spend much time and who, "of course," were Socialists, said that he "had some sympathy for Zionism, but a Zionist, God forbid, he was not."[1]

Only once did Jabotinsky break his silence. A few months after his arrival in Berne, Dr. Nachman Sirkin, the first theoretician of Socialist Zionism, came to that city. His lecture was followed by a lively and acrimonious discussion between Socialists and Zionists. Everybody was surprised when Jabotinsky asked for the floor. This first public speech, which he reported in his *Autobiography* in his usual self-deprecating manner, was something of a sensation to the audience. The gist of the speech was that he was little acquainted with the teachings of socialism and therefore could not say whether he was a Socialist or not. But he was undoubtedly a Zionist, he said. In the Diaspora, the Jews were facing a St. Bartholomew's Night. The enemies of Jewry were not completely wrong, since in dispersion the Jews are a painful abscess in the organisms of other nations. Only a wholesale emigration to Palestine could save the Jewish people.

In the perspective of the tragic experience of the last decades, this speech of a seventeen-year-old student sounds almost prophetic. But at that time it provoked great indignation, in particular as the chairman of the meeting "translated" Jabotinsky's words into German (from Russian) in a grotesquely distorted and vulgarized way: "The speaker is not a Socialist, because he does not know what socialism is; he is, however, an anti-Semite and he advises us to hide out in Palestine in order that all of us should not be massacred. . . ." Since Jabotinsky spoke an exceptionally pure and accent-free Russian and neither his looks nor his name indicated his Jewishness, many may have taken him for a Russian and an anti-Semite. After the meeting, one of the Socialist participants, Charles (Chaim) Rappoport* bluntly told him: "I never suspected that among Russian youth there existed such a type of zoological anti-Semite. . . ." Jabotinsky laughingly assured the audience that he was a Jew, but his statement did not convince his opponents.

It is probable that Jabotinsky himself did not attribute much importance to his first "Zionist" speech. For years to come it was to remain just a fleeting utterance on his part, to which he did not give further thought. In his *Autobiography* he recalled that at the age of seven he once asked his mother: "Will we Jews, too, some day have a state of our own?" And his mother answered curtly and sharply: "Of course, we will, you little fool." "Since then," said Jabotinsky, "I did not ask any more: this was enough for me." This delightful little reminiscence may partly account for his impromptu "Zionist" debut in Berne. However, for at least four to five years to come, this speech remained but an episode and was not followed by any advance in his political thinking.

Jabotinsky's sojourn in Berne was brief. According to Stupnitzky, he was not very assiduous in his university studies. He enrolled in the Law School, but later confessed that, with the exception of Professor Reichesberg, who was the first to introduce him to the teachings of Karl Marx, he could not remember a single name from among the professors who were supposed to have been his teachers. His scant knowledge of and dislike for

---

*He later became one of the leaders of the Communist Party in France.

the German language was likewise hardly conducive to diligent study. Neither did he enjoy the specific atmosphere of the "colony," which had little contact with the life of the country and was completely absorbed in futile interparty discussions. Miss Liubov Axelrod, who already then, at the age of thirty, was considered the most important political personality in the "colony,"* once indignantly said to Jabotinsky about another Russian emigré who came to Lausanne to give a lecture: "He is now, in 1898, saying things which are directly opposite to what he had written in 1892." "There was," Jabotinsky mockingly recalled thirty-five years later, "such horror in her voice that I understood: wherever you go and wherever you move, you must always carry with you all the archives containing all your previous writings and lectures; and you must reread all this stuff before you sit down to write a new article or before you mount the platform to make a speech."[2] This mock-horror describes very accurately Jabotinsky's organic aversion to any stiff and pompous orthodoxy. The spiritual climate of the Berne "colony" even then was too stuffy for his mind.

Jabotinsky's literary contributions to the *Odessky Listok* were few and not outstanding. The only significant product of the Berne period was the poem "Gorod Mira" (City of Peace) which appeared in the summer of 1898 in the St. Petersburg Jewish monthly *Voskhod* (Sunrise) under the pen name of Egal. In this juvenile and rather feeble, though melodious, legend, an old Arab sheik says that God had in olden times promised Zion to the Jews who for centuries had been living "without motherland or honor."

After several rather empty months spent in Berne, Jabotinsky, in the fall of 1898, obtained the consent of *Odessky Listok* to transfer to Rome, though the paper already had a correspondent there —a Russian with the Italian name of Corradini.

The Imprint of Rome: City and Teachers

It is difficult to overestimate the decisive role Italy played in Jabotinsky's spiritual formation. While Berne left almost no imprint on his personality, Rome exercised a tremendous and all-embracing influence. "If I ever had a spiritual fatherland," said Jabotinsky, "it was Italy more than Russia." He began to study Italian about six months before his departure for Rome, and after six months there he spoke the language very well.

---

*She later became, under the pen name "Orthodox," an outstanding Marxian philosopher.

In Rome he did not find a Russian colony. Italy at that time had not yet attracted political emigrés and Jewish students in any considerable numbers; they preferred the more familiar grounds of Switzerland, Germany, and France, partly because established Russian colonies already existed there, and partly because they were more conversant with German and French than with Italian. In the Eternal City, Jabotinsky had almost no Russian-speaking friends. "There were no Muscovite students in Rome at that time; for months on end I hardly ever got the taste of a Russian word on my tongue" ("Diana"). Nor was there any organized Russian milieu that would have constituted a barrier between him and Italian life. He was completely on his own. Rome and Italy were his—to see, to hear, to study, to absorb, and to love. And the eighteen-year-old youth made full use of this opportunity.

The Italian period in Jabotinsky's life was most important for the shaping of his intellectual world. In his semi-autobiographical short stories ("Diana," "Via Montebello 48," "Bichetta," "Trattoria of the Students"), he spoke very lightly of his studies at Rome University as if endeavoring to create the impression that he was just an idler, that he avoided any mental effort and rarely read a serious book. All this is deliberate self-deprecation. He did not obtain a diploma from the University of Rome and he hardly followed a regular university curriculum. He came from Russia, imbued with an intense hatred and contempt for stiff regimented education. It was largely in order to escape this bureaucratic type of learning that he had left Odessa. He deeply enjoyed the freedom—and even laxity—offered by the very liberal university rules. He did not study for the practical purpose of receiving a degree conferring some privilege, honor, or power; and in fact, when three years later he left Italy for good, he did so without having graduated; likewise, no record could be found in the archives of the University as to whether he ever passed any examinations in single subjects. But it was in Rome that he first quenched his intellectual thirst with a large variety of subjects which were of particular interest to him: sociology, history, law, philology. He himself worked out a university curriculum of his own, selected his professors, established his timetable. All this was, of course, most unwise from the practical viewpoint; and he most likely made some grave mistakes in his youthful predilection for certain subjects and teachers. But, within the self-chosen field, he worked hard, read voluminously, and made meticulous observations on everything that fell within the range of his insatiable spiritual curiosity.

He made a thorough study of ancient Rome, its institutions, and legal system. According to official university records,[3] "Giabotinsky Vladimiro di Eugenio et di Eva Marcovna, nato a Odessa il 9 ottobre 1880," enrolled as a student in 1898, and in the first school year, 1898–99, registered for the number of prescribed courses in Roman Law, Procedure, and Political Economy, while in the second school year, 1899–1900, he took a number of courses in Roman Law, Political Economy, and Statistics.* This list, however, apparently includes only mandatory courses, for which Jabotinsky registered officially and obtained "attestazioni di frequenza" (certificates of attendance). There were undoubtedly several other professors whose lectures he attended more or less regularly. At the turn of the century, the University of Rome was rightly proud of the high level of its law faculty, and Jabotinsky always gratefully remembered some of the lecturers from whom he learned much.

Of all his university professors, the most outstanding and influential at that time was Antonio Labriola. A distinguished philosopher and sociologist who had numerous scholarly studies to his credit, he had, like Socrates, a passion for oral teaching and conversation, through which he spread a large number of ideas of which only a fraction ever appeared in his essays, formal addresses, letters, and books. Jabotinsky was one of Labriola's most assiduous and attentive listeners: he always admitted to having learned a lot from this first exponent of historical materialism at a European university. Labriola impressed Jabotinsky largely because, while being a Marxist, he nevertheless always rebelled against confining himself within any one system of ideas. To him, historical materialism implied a monistic outlook, because he regarded it as a unified entity of theory and practice, rising above the theoretical abstractions of all-explaining historical factors. To Labriola, there was no predetermination in human life; progress is not fated. Men themselves must produce the future, and in progress there are always regressions, deviations, and errors.[4]

---

*Here are the exact names of the courses and of the professors for which Jabotinsky registered: First year: Institutions of Roman Law (Professor Gaetano Semeraro); History of the Roman Law (Professor Gaetano Semeraro); Political Economy (Assistant Professor Eteocle Lorini); Penal Law and Procedure (Avv. Enrico Ferri); Philosophy and History (Professor Antonio Labriola); Filosofia Morale (Professor Antonio Labriola). Second year: Political Economy (Professor Angelo Messedaglia); Statistics (Professor Angelo Messedaglia); Roman Law (Professor Vittorio Scialoga); History of the Roman Law (Professor Gaetano Semeraro).

Some of the teachings of Labriola, whom Sorel regarded as a landmark in the history of socialism, left a lasting imprint on Jabotinsky's thinking. His Zionist monism—the very basis of his Zionist philosophy—is clearly reminiscent of Labriola's monistic approach, though in a different field. His belief in the role of individuals in history and his fierce opposition to any attempt to substitute alleged "iron laws of history" for free determination of men and nations is also deeply rooted in Labriola's ideas. And it must not be forgotten that Jabotinsky returned from Rome to Russia a firm believer in the economic doctrine of socialism (though, as we will see, he strongly opposed Marxian mechanistic philosophy and its disregard for the rights and interests of individuals). As late as October, 1906, when he already was a leading and militant Zionist, he volunteered a most orthodox Socialist credo: "I belong to those who believe that there is an irreconcilable and steadily growing contradiction between the interests of the employer and the worker; that the only possible and inevitable solution of this contradiction is the socialization of the means of production; that the natural instrument of this upheaval is the industrial proletariat; and that the way to this upheaval is class struggle and seizure of political power. Together with the overwhelming majority of those of my age, I am so imbued with this concept of the social problem that I am organically incapable of thinking about this problem differently."[5]

Jabotinsky was never a Marxist, but he recognized that Marx had long become a "classic," profoundly influencing a whole generation. He frequently dealt with Marxism and historical materialism, often criticizing it severely, but always seriously. He would not hesitate to label his own view "psycho-Marxism," or "psycho-historical materialism." Especially interesting are those essays in which Jabotinsky dealt with so-called "laws" established by Marx, such as the labor theory, the class structure of society, and the one-sided materialism (see for instance his essays: *Socialism or Jubilee?*—1931; *Robot and Workman*—1932; *Crisis of the Proletariat*—1936; *The Big Five, A Dialogue*—1934; *The Social Philosophy of the Bible*—1936).

Jabotinsky admitted that an even more potent influence than that of Labriola was exercised by Enrico Ferri, professor of Penal Law, outstanding exponent of the positive school in criminology and the founder of the science of criminal sociology. In addition to Ferri's immediate topic—Penal Law—he introduced his listeners to an almost encyclopedic variety of fascinating subjects—problems of sociology and psychology, heredity, literature, art, music. He was a powerful orator, whom many compared with Jaurès. Ferri's personality—possibly even more than his teachings—deeply implanted itself in Jabotinsky's mind, and he used to recall its various aspects many years later.[6]

He vividly remembered how in 1903, when Tsar Nicholas II intended to visit Italy, Ferri—then a Socialist deputy—overcoming the pandemonium of the aroused Parliament with his formidable voice, triumphantly uttered the Leftist slogan: "And we will hiss (whistle) him off." The Tsar's visit was subsequently canceled. On another occasion, trying to define the subtle charm of Maroossia (the main character of his novel *The Five*), Jabotinsky could not help suddenly recalling an expression of Enrico Ferri's during one of his lectures in Rome: *ché bella pianta umana*—"what a beautiful human shoot."[7]

There were at least two more outstanding Italian scholars at whose feet Jabotinsky sat during his Rome *Lehrjahre:* one was Maffeo Pantaleoni, the other Benedetto Croce.

In his essay *Crisis of the Proletariat,* which was devoted to criticism of the Marxian theories, Jabotinsky wittily but affectionately mentioned his teacher Pantaleoni, who "spent so much time on disputes with Marxism that what remained in his students' memory was Marx rather than the theory of marginal utility, which to him was an article of faith." In the *Encyclopaedia of the Social Sciences,* Umberto Rucci describes Pantaleoni as "a man of broad culture and immense erudition, a fascinating teacher who wrote brilliantly on many topics on the borderline between economics and sociology." His chief work *Principi di economia pura* (Florence, 1889) "marked a turning point in the history of economics, at least in Italy."[8]

In another essay, *The Revolt of the Old Men,* Jabotinsky admitted that "Benedetto Croce was perhaps the first who taught me to discern the vibrations of the aesthetic nervous system which underlies the clockwork that drives the wheels of history." This Italian thinker, a moderate and liberal neo-Hegelian, vigorously asserted the identity of concrete philosophy with history.

It was the inspiring effort of Italy's struggle for national unification and freedom that helped to form Jabotinsky's own concept of normal and dignified national existence. In Mazzini, Garibaldi, and Cavour he saw the living symbols and trailblazers of liberation. Garibaldi especially remained forever his most beloved hero. In the controversy which for decades occupied historians, as to who was the decisive force in Italy's resurrection, Giuseppe Garibaldi or Count Cavour, he always took sides for the former. Many years later, when he heard his son Eri, then a student at a Paris *lycée*, reading aloud the chapter of his history text book dealing with Italy's liberation, Jabotinsky was greatly annoyed at the official school version, which ascribed all the merit to Cavour while deprecating Garibaldi's role. For more than an hour he heatedly explained to Eri his own concept of this eventful and dramatic period of Italian history, picturing Garibaldi as *the* liberator of his country. To Jabotinsky, the most endearing feature of Garibaldi's personality was the synthesis of ardent, fanatic nationalism with the broad-mindedness of a citizen of the world. In an article published in 1912, he had the statue of Garibaldi on the hill of Janiculum remind those who reproached him with being a "narrow-minded nationalist" that in 1870, when the German armies invaded France, he gathered around him his old comrades and rushed with them to Dijon, to defend the liberty of the French people; that he fought in the ranks of the liberation armies of Brazil, Argentina, and Peru. He gave his life to Italy, yet the great humanitarian Herzen called him "the knight of humanity."[9] Garibaldi once told Herzen that there was a tragic paradox in his career: it so turned out that he was almost at all times a military man, fighting on some front, while he always hated war and was a convinced pacifist. When S. K. Gepstein quoted these words of Garibaldi, Jabotinsky thoughtfully said: "I, too, have been labeled a 'militarist and a war monger'; yet, God is my witness, that I loathe war and army; to me, they are but cruel and revolting necessities."[10]

During the three years of his stay in Italy, Jabotinsky not only studied—he lived. And his was a happy and full life.

He fell in love with the Eternal City. He knew the City's "every nook and cranny, got acquainted with the most heterogeneous classes of population, became familiar with all the city gossip, nicknames, jokes, and ambiguities."[11] Rome heightened Jabotinsky's esthetic perception, giving him an acute and exacting longing for harmony and beauty.

In Rome, Jabotinsky did not limit himself to university studies, or to frequenting museums, art galleries, and libraries. He was passionately interested in all aspects of Italian life—politics and the theater, the labor movement and art—but first and foremost, in *people*. He had numerous friends among his Italian colleagues at the university, as well as in literary and artistic circles, but also among simple people, young and old—shopkeepers, workers, even beggars. At that happy age—he was eighteen—he had a great facility for striking up acquaintances and making friends. It is significant that Jabotinsky, who all his life was almost physically allergic to rubbing shoulders with human multitudes, never felt this way about an Italian crowd: "There always is about them some nobility, some inborn dignity both in color and tumult, and they never degenerate into what one meets in the East—the permanent noise of a yelling rabble dressed up in gawdy, savage rags."[12]

Not only Rome, but the whole of Italy deeply penetrated Jabotinsky's spiritual world—a blessed, sunny country, simultaneously inspiring and easygoing, simple, bent on playing and dancing. Italy was to him a divine revelation, wonderful, almost unbearably beautiful. He wandered through its picturesque provinces, sometimes by train or carriage, often on foot, admiring and deeply inhaling the charm and flavor of its landscape and people, churches and skies, taverns and museums—a unique human and cultural entity, without which Europe and the world would have been hardly half of what it had been since the Middle Ages. Roman classicism and the Italian way of life decisively influenced his own pattern of thinking and expression. During his entire life, iron-clad Latin clarity, logic, and studied simplicity never deserted Jabotinsky's reasoning; his style, both in writing and speaking, became easy, elegant, and bright. The Italian language itself— that unique Roman eloquence, decorous yet resounding, simple and ingratiating, yet also martial and manly—was a source of inspiration to him, and under its influence his Russian not only became more sonorous, rhythmic, and musical, but also lighter.

In July, 1922, when Jabotinsky had occasion to revisit Italy on a Zionist political mission, he took with him his twelve-year-old son Eri and found time to show the boy this wonderful country.[13] Young as he was then, Eri was deeply impressed by what was revealed to him of the greatness and beauty of his father's beloved places, mostly in Rome, but also in Milan, Turin, and Florence.

Jabotinsky was far from being a saint during the Italian period of his life. There was no lack of flirtations and more serious romantic adventures. One of them is related, with delicate thought-fulness, in his short story "Diana"; some more were candidly described in several feuilletons entitled "From a Frivolous Copybook," which he later published in *Odesskiya Novosti*. In *The Five* he recalled how, on a moonlit night in Rome, a crazy painter admitted him to his studio on Babuino where Lola, *il più bel torso a piazza di Spagna*, serving as a model, was clad to the waist in moonlight only.[14]

His then "philosophy of life" was crudely formulated in his poem "Schafloch":[15]

> In this business of living
> There is little sense, 'tis right;
> But the Alps of Bern in moonlight
> Shine like silver through the night.
> And in kissing lips of coral
> Under cover of the night,
> One may find perhaps a meaning
> In life's business, all right.
>
> (*Translated from Russian by A.G.*)

Beauty of nature and the cult of love were the main ingredients of Jabotinsky's *Weltanschauung* at that happy and carefree period of his life.

The Arch of Titus

We have seen that Jabotinsky came to Rome with a very scanty knowledge of Jewish affairs. Italy could do nothing to enrich and enliven his Jewish background. There were some eight to ten thousand Jews in Rome; but, said Jabotinsky, during the three years he spent there, he, who knew intimately all the aspects of Roman life, had no occasion ever to identify an Italian Jew.

There was, to begin with, no Jewish problem in Italy to speak of. In a pamphlet *The Strangers. Sketches of a Happy Ghetto*, published in 1903 when he already was a convinced Zionist, Jabotinsky admitted that "there is no other country where the Jews have attained everything about which those of our race, who see the ideal of our happiness not in the creation of an independent state but in full equality on foreign soil, could even dream. The Italian Jews enjoyed the fullest, the most ideal equality."[16] Jews were well represented among judges, university professors, senators, and deputies. The parliamentary leader of the Italian "Irredentist" movement, striving for the unification with the motherland of the Austrian-held Trento and Trieste, was the Jew Barzilai.

The second reason was the deliberate self-effacement of the Italian Jews themselves. "Deeply assimilated—to an extent that even a discussion about assimilation was out of place among families with such names as Della Seta, Piperno, Volaterra—they concealed and avoided pronouncing aloud the name of their nationality. . . . During those three years [which he spent in Italy] I literally not even once came across the word *ebreo*—either in the press or in conversations. . . . As far as I am concerned, Roman Jews have fully attained what apparently constituted their ideal: I did not notice their existence."

There were, of course, no Zionist leanings whatsoever in Italian Jewry at the turn of the century. Jabotinsky quoted the journalist Primo Levi who wrote under the pen name of "L'Italico" and treated Zionism in a most detached way: "Every one is free to bother about the resurrection of Israel, but I personally am glad to be of Jewish origin only because our [Jewish] race is especially inclined to patriotic feelings, so that, as a Jew, I feel particularly strongly my being an Italian." The sole Zionist in Rome was at that time a certain Izzaco G. (Jabotinsky did not even dare to reveal his full name).

Jabotinsky left Rome in 1901. In 1903, after the Sixth Zionist Congress in Basel, he revisited the Eternal City, this time as an ardent Zionist who "saw Rome with different eyes." In his *Autobiography* he wrote: "I was looking for and I found Jews among my friends I had parted with two years ago. I visited several times the historical ghetto—not for the sake of the Cenci Palace, but in order to have a closer look at the poor Jewish people who, despite civic equality and absence of anti-Semitism, did not abandon the Jewish quarter mentioned in Cicero's speeches and in Juvenal's Satires." Now, with his new acute Zionist perception, he realized that, though the Jewish intelligentsia in Italy were "classical specimens of a full and absolute assimilation, such as the Jews have not attained even in Germany, France and England," all of them— students, merchants, journalists—"in the very first conversation used the term 'goy'; in their hearts I found seeds of fear, uneasiness, some *feeling* of possible danger."

"All this," Jabotinsky averred, "I have not seen before." His poor Jewish background was, therefore, in no way enriched during the Roman period of his life. He saw, of course, in the Forum, the Arch of Titus, with the sacred seven-armed candelabra, stolen and profaned by the Roman conqueror. He may have been told that to this day no self-respecting Jew will pass under this monument of national defeat and humiliation. But he was not ready to grasp and to appraise the spiritual meaning and implication of this symbol.

The Emergence of Altalena

Jabotinsky came to Rome in the fall of 1898 as correspondent for the *Odessky Listok*. He wrote for this paper under the pen name of "V. Egal," "Vl. Egal," "Egal," "V.E." Contrary to the prevalent notion, the little-known *Listok* period lasted for more than a year. "Egal's" correspondence can be traced as late as the December 17, 1899, issue of the *Odessky Listok*. According to J. M. Heifetz, these reportages, "lively, witty, made him regret his skepticism" which had caused him to reject Jabotinsky's services for the *Odesskiya Novosti* in 1898. He recalls that later he received a letter from Jabotinsky saying that he longed for the *Novosti*, did not demand a fixed salary, and was ready to collaborate on the basis of the usual "per line" honorarium. "Is there a need to say," wrote Heifetz, "that I immediately wired my consent? In less than a month's time I myself was glad to give him a salary, since his correspondences were becoming increasingly more meaningful, more interesting and fascinating."[17] Simultaneously, though less often, Jabotinsky used to write from Italy for the liberal *Severny Kurier* in St. Petersburg.

Having switched from the *Listok* to the *Novosti*, Jabotinsky also changed his pen name. He chose the pseudonym of "Altalena," doing so, as he himself confessed, by mistake. He believed that this Italian word meant "elevator," while its real meaning is "swing." In a letter to Heifetz he explained that he felt as yet "by no means stable or constant," but rather rocking and balancing, so that the pen name "Swing" fitted him all right (some of his articles were signed "Vladimir Altalena").[18]

Nothing in Egal's or Altalena's reportage from Rome can be taken as indicative of Jabotinsky's future as a Zionist leader and thinker. His writing was light, witty, brilliant, somewhat Heinesque—mostly about everything and nothing, yet giving a widely varied and vivid picture of various aspects of Italian life. He wrote about Pope Leo XIII and the operetta *Maestro Calcagni* (a parody on Pietro Mascagni's opera *Iris*); about early Italian aspirations to colonial power, and the popular Italian novelist Edmondo De Amicis; he wrote about the worker's league against the popular Italian custom of settling arguments by knifing (*Lege Operata con il contello*), and about the actor Ermette Novelli; about the star Sarah Bernhardt, and banditry in Sicily and Sardinia; he chatted about a new opera by Mascagni *Le maschere*, and the street life of Rome; he wrote about the striking contrast between the ignorance of the Italian masses and their innate culture and intelligence. From time to time he would forsake his reportage for an elegant short story, a fairy tale, or a bit of poetry, as light and pleasant as his prose. The general impression conveyed to the reader of these pieces is that the writer possessed two great qualities: an unmistakable literary talent and the delightful intoxication of carefree youth.

True to the promise made to his mother, he came to Odessa in the spring of 1899 to pass his final examinations for a "certificate of maturity" at the same Richelieu Gymnasium which he had left in 1898. The teachers, however, had apparently not forgotten all the troubles they had had with this unruly young man, and were not disposed to treat him too gently at the examinations. He failed in Latin and Greek, and for a long time abandoned any attempt to obtain a high-school diploma (it was not before 1909 that he did so in St. Petersburg). According to available evidence, he was not particularly disheartened by this setback, and returned to Rome in high spirits. In 1900 he once more spent his vacation in Odessa and then returned to Italy.[19]

The Italian period was probably the happiest in Jabotinsky's life. Young, carefree, easily earning his livelihood by journalistic work, without a worry in the world, not burdened with any political creed or obligation, he enjoyed life in all its aspects. He almost completely forgot that he was a Jew or, for that matter, that he was Russian. He became Italianized to an amazing degree; he frequented Italian circles only and learned to speak Italian without a trace of an accent; however, he later admitted that the people of the South regarded him as a Northerner and vice versa, and that he never met anyone who took him for an Italian from his own province. He achieved perfect mastery not only of the generally accepted literary language, but he also learned to distinguish between all the "twelve accents of the Italian tongue," as he puts it in his delightful short story "Diana": "Venetians sang in a naive and caressing lilt and called their city 'Venessia.' Neapolitans moaned their vowels with a sort of eager and passionate longing; Sicilians pouted and talked in the tone of a peevish child." Jabotinsky was free from the customary prejudice against slangs: "Jargons are always more intimate, more alive than the official idiom of books and lawyers; they suck life's atmosphere from the very source."[20] In an article on the Ukrainian national poet Shevchenko, he invoked the memory of the great Roman poet Belli who lived in the forties of the nineteenth century: his sonnets in the Romanesco dialect were magnificent, while his elegies in classical Italian were watery, rhetorical, and insignificant.[21]

Jabotinsky retained his mastery of several Italian dialects until the end of his life. The present writer vividly remembers a dinner he had

together with Jabotinsky in a large Italian restaurant in Soho Square in
London in 1932, where Jabotinsky addressed each of the five waiters
in their respective provincial dialects, creating a happy uproar among
them. They abandoned all other guests and gathered around our table,
admiringly gaping at this marvelous polyglot stranger who was doing
something that none among the native Italians could imitate. And Jabotinsky himself was as happy as a child who was given the opportunity of
playing again with his most beloved toy.*

According to his own account, Jabotinsky also tried to write poetry in
Italian.[22] In 1900, after some bitter disappointment in a love affair with a
charming but not very consistent Italian girl, he spent a sleepless night—
"the horridest night in my life!"—and toward dawn sat at his table and
wrote a sonnet:

> É lungi omai quel giorno. Di zaffiro
> pareva il mar che voi chiamate Nero.
> La zingara dagli occhi di vampiro
> chiese: "Dammi la man—ti svelo il vero."
>
> Disse: "Tua madre é morta.—In un ritiro
> di calma e pace svolgerai intero
> il filo della vita.—Hai nome Piero.—
> Darai a donna indegna il tuo sospiro."
>
> Disse e fuggi. Molti anni poi fuggiro:
> mamma é sorretta ancor dal sangue fiero
> della Tribú; il mio nome é Vladimiro;
>
> fra tempeste serpeggia il mio sentiero . . .
> Pur ella non menti: folle, deliro,
> per una indegna donna io mi dispero.

---

*Thirty-five years after Jabotinsky's Italian sojourn, in 1938, following a reception
arranged by the Rotary Club in Johannesburg, an Italian Count approached Jabotinsky
and in broken English complimented him on his speech. Jabotinsky replied in perfect
Italian. "I had no idea that Mr. Jabotinsky was of Italian origin," said the Count and,
when told that Jabotinsky was a Russian Jew, refused to believe it (Interview with
Nahum Levin, Tel Aviv).

è lungi omai quel giorno di zaffiro
pareva il mar che voi chiamate Nero
la zingara dagli occhi di vampiro
chiese: „Dammi la man — ti svelo il vero"

Disse: „Tua madre è morta. In un ritiro
di calma e pace svolgerai intero
il filo della vita. - Hai nome Piero. -
Darai a donna indegna il tuo sospiro"

Disse e fuggì. Molti anni poi fuggiro:
mamma è sorretta ancor dal sangue fiero
della Tribù, il mio nome è Vladimiro,

fra tempeste serpeggia il mio sentiero..
Pur ella non mentì: folle, deliro,
per una indegna donna io mi dispero.

V. Jabotinsky —
aber 1900.

Facsimile of sonnet on facing page in Jabotinsky's own hand.

The day was long ago. Like pure sapphire
shone the great sea which you misname Black Sea.
The gypsy-girl, with flaming eyes of fire,
whispered: "The truth in thy own palm I see."

"Thy mother is dead.—In peace shalt thou retire
to spend a lifetime in sweet agony.—
Thy very name I know: Pierre they call thee.—
Unworthy woman shall claim thy desire."

She spoke, and fled. Many a year went by:
mother is still sustained by the fierce blood
of our clan; not Pierre, Vladimir am I;
fate drives my ship through storm and gale and flood . . .
And yet, alas, the gypsy did not lie:
a worthless girl I worship next to God.

(*Translated by A.G.*)

Jabotinsky revealed that afterward he sent the sonnet to several editors who never printed it; this, however, did not dampen his "own admiration for the little masterpiece." An unbiased reader would probably be inclined to agree with the editors rather than with the youthful author in regard to the poetical value of the sonnet, which is rather immature both in content and form. Yet, it offers testimony of Jabotinsky's easy mastery of the language.

In 1901 there appeared in the leading Italian publication *Nuova Antologia* (Vol. 96) an eleven-page article signed Vladimiro Giabotinski and titled "Anton Cekhof E Massimo Gorki" devoted to "impressionism in the Russian literature"; for this article he received the then considerable honorarium of one hundred French francs (about eighteen dollars). Another Italian periodical, the weekly *Roma Litteraria* accepted his article on the Russian epic legends—but without an honorarium.[23] He translated into Italian a few short stories of Chekhov and, together with a friend, Gorki's "Old Iserguyl." Several articles of his on the role of the college students in the Russian liberation movement appeared in the Socialist paper *Avanti*; they were a passionate defense of the progressive student youth, whose protests against the Russian regime had been described in the rightist Italian paper *Tribuna* as vile excesses by rowdies and hooligans. Shortly before leaving Italy for Odessa, he wrote to his mother and sister: "In the meantime, toward the end of my stay here, I am working feverishly and probably just because of that I feel so contented and pleased as I was not for a long time."[24]

Jabotinsky returned to Russia by boat, via Venice-Constantinople, late in July, 1901. The immediate reason for this journey was that at the age of twenty-one he was liable for military service and had to appear before the conscription board.

This departure marked the end of the Italian chapter, one of the most meaningful in Jabotinsky's spiritual development. He occasionally returned there for brief visits, but those were fleeting episodes in his busy life. Possibly it was just because of this brusque interruption that Jabotinsky always retained in his heart an unreserved fondness and admiration for Italy. His "romance" with Rome was like any other romance in human life: if it had been allowed to continue, inner conflicts, misunderstandings, and disappointments would have been bound to arise and might have marred the enchantment. Yet he was early torn away from the object of his affection and at the distance it remained in his memory as beautiful, as pure and magnificent as he had seen it in his youthful enthusiasm. There was no time and no opportunity to lose this enthusiasm or to water it down. To him, Italy forever remained a living symbol of everything great and wonderful in his own life and that of humanity—a "spiritual fatherland if I ever had one." Italy retained a deep and lasting influence on Jabotinsky's spiritual development.

THREE

BACK IN ODESSA

Journalistic Career

Jabotinsky returned to Odessa in 1901. At that time, Odessa was Russia's most Europeanized and cosmopolitan city. Its harbor was full of ships, coming and going to the far world. Its grain exchange was in permanent and active communication with those of Hamburg, Liverpool, Berlin, Vienna, Chicago, and Winnipeg. Odessa was the outlet of the young oil industry of the Baku and Batum regions, the center of the flourishing Ukrainian sugar industry, and had a dominant position in Russia's import and export trade with the Mediterranean countries and the Far East. It was the most eloquent incarnation of the Western spirit of enterprise which had begun to permeate the wide steppes of the Ukraine, spelling a new era for the entire South Russian region. Bursting with initiative, expanding and growing exuberantly, the Odessa of those happy times was a busy, lively, multicolored, and joyous city.

To this city Jabotinsky returned with a vague idea of completing his studies and becoming a lawyer. But his reputation as a journalist was already well established, and Heifetz, the editor of *Odesskiya Novosti*, suggested that Jabotinsky become a daily contributor to his paper and offered him the then princely monthly salary of 120 rubles (sixty dollars) a month. This temptation was too great: Jabotinsky accepted.

His feuilletons, said Heifetz, had "no strict consistency in their philosophy"; they contained "ideas and paradoxes, which were free from party blinkers, from canons fixed once and for all." The chief editor actually had some trouble with several old members of his editorial staff who deemed themselves entitled to uphold the purity of these canons. "But," said Heifetz, "this dissatisfaction of my colleagues did not affect me at all. . . . I knew well that one feuilleton of Altalena's was worth ten articles by other contributors."[1]

The feuilleton is a form of journalism that has never taken root in the American press. It is not exactly an essay, neither is it precisely a short story, not necessarily a topical article, nor timely criticism—yet it partakes of all of them. The feuilleton, indeed, was an art form highly developed in European journalism and particularly by Jewish writers, beginning with Heine and Börne down to Herzl and Jabotinsky, not forgetting the many Jewish journalists of Prague who wrote in German. As most of these ephemeral productions are lost, so, alas, is the bulk of those little feuilletons by Altalena. They are buried almost irretrievably in the ancient files of *Odesskiya Novosti* which are no longer accessible.

Those feuilletons were almost completely non-political. Most of them dealt with subjects of minor, often local and passing, significance. Altalena would write on the deficiencies of the city's communications system run by a Belgian company, or of limitations of the rights of university students; of citizens' demands that the city fathers improve streets and parks, or of current performances in the municipal theater. He would discuss the new public library, but also topics of more essential and lasting interest: problems of youth, of ethics, art, literature. All of them, irrespective of their content, were remarkable specimens of brilliant writing, done with a light and provocative touch; more often than not they were controversial, frequently ironic, occasionally caustic, but always bubbling with the exuberance of youth, with the irrepressible urge to proclaim truth, beauty, and justice, whenever the writer felt those values to be involved. The very language of those little masterpieces was an object of admiration and envy to Odessa's intelligentsia. Odessa was a city which could not boast of a very pure, correct Russian. Subjected to the influences of half a dozen languages, it developed a dialect of its own, with many notable deviations from classical Russian both in vocabulary and pronunciation. Jabotinsky, on the contrary, wrote and spoke an impeccable, rich, and expressive Russian, which was both polished and colloquial, vibrant in rhythm, felicitous in phrasing, high-spirited, and pithy. It was a language written deftly and full of wit, of unexpected and charming sallies, overflowing with genial sympathy and hearty laughter. For each of these nuances Altalena instinctively found the proper selection and order of words—good, simple Russian words, old and new, which in his presentation always sounded mint-fresh and young, as if created for that moment. For thousands of readers, almost every causerie of Altalena's was a stylistic marvel, an esthetic treat.

As mentioned above, politics played very little, if any, part in Jabotinsky's writings of that period. He was much more attracted by problems of literature, theater, and art.

In the fall of 1901, a dramatic three-acter in verse, *Krov* (Blood), by Jabotinsky was staged in the Odessa Municipal Theater. The play was much commended in Odessa's society. It was inspired by the recent Anglo-Boer War and was devoted to the spirited apotheosis of pacifism. The audience applauded it fervently. Unfortunately, no text and not even a detailed description of the plot of Jabotinsky's first theatrical venture is available. Yet, his second try was likewise a play in verse, *Ladno* (All right), which the Municipal Theater presented in 1902, and which seems to have been less successful. From the little we know about this abortive attempt (S. K. Gepstein, who read the galley proofs of *Ladno* in 1903, remembers the plot), it was a passionate defense of the right of the individual to dispose of himself and to follow his own inclinations in love, even against the conventional morals of society. Many years later, in a letter to his sister dated March 23, 1935, Jabotinsky from memory reconstructed a few lines from *Ladno*, which give eloquent expression to his philosophy:

> There is no duty. Thou art free. Then light thy candle
> Before Desire.—Desire shall be thy law.
> Wherever it might lead, to altar high or low,
> To sweet home or dark tavern, or black night
> Of suicide, or service to the nation:
> No lesson is my deed, no task of Errant Knight,
> Nor God's command—but only my own fashion,
> My own desire, my Sovereign Desire.
> *(Translated from Russian by A.G.)*

Commenting on this quotation, Jabotinsky stressed: "Individualism has remained my credo up till now. If I were writing a philosophic treatise, I would fully reconcile it with my service to the nation: I am serving not because I have to—nobody 'has to' do anything for anybody—but because I so please."

In 1902, Jabotinsky wrote a poem, *Poor Charlotte*, which was published in St. Petersburg in 1904 as a separate pamphlet. It gives a new, original interpretation of the famous terrorist act of Charlotte Corday, the exalted French girl who stabbed to death the Jacobin leader Marat: in a letter to a friend written on the eve of her execution, Charlotte recounts her empty, uneventful, and insignificant life, without any meaning, beauty, and glory; even in the illegal group of Girondist conspirators she was assigned to some subordinate, prosaic duties. Her pride revolts. She longs for a heroic deed, for a bold strike of her own—and she is ready to die striking, like a bee who dies stinging.

Galley proofs of the poem were sent for a preview to Maxim Gorki, who at that time stood at the peak of his popularity and headed the leading Russian publishing house "Znaniye." Gorki was strongly impressed with *Poor Charlotte* and ordered "Znaniye" to buy the entire edition for distribution. S. Gepstein, who was in charge of the poem's publication, was delighted by this opportunity, but warned Gorki that the censor might confiscate the brochure. It was agreed that most of the copies would be delivered to "Znaniye" *before* the poem would be submitted to censorship. When officials of the "Chief Administration on Printing Matters" appeared at the printer's with an order to confiscate the entire edition, they were shown and were able to carry away eight hundred copies only, while in fact three thousand had been printed.[2] The poem (considerably edited) was republished in 1930 in Paris in a collection of Jabotinsky's poetry.[3]

Odessa Patriotism

Jabotinsky always insisted that Italy was to him more of a spiritual fatherland than Russia. This claim can be accepted only under the assumption that the Black Sea harbor of Odessa never constituted a part of the Russian Empire. For Odessa signified to Jabotinsky much more than a native town commonly means to a man. He was an "Odessite" not simply by accident of birth and registry, but first and foremost by deep and passionate conviction. He often argued that anyone can be born in Odessa and there is no merit in being just recognized by the city's registrar. Those are just incidental facts of life, which in themselves do not mean anything and oblige to nothing. Many thousands of people have borne the title of Odessite without any emotion, completely deprived of "Odessa consciousness." To them, being an Odessite meant as much or as little as being a native of Yekaterinoslav, Moscow, or Irkutsk. There was in those characters not the slightest trace of love for and pride in their own city. There even were among them some snobs who—good-naturedly or maliciously—were publicly making fun of "Odessa patriotism."

Jabotinsky wholeheartedly despised those ungrateful "Odessites by chance." To him, Odessa was not an indifferent accident, but a precious gift of fate. All his life he was deeply appreciative and immensely proud of being an Odessite. In his scale of values, the rank of an Odessite was the highest and the most honorific in the entire world. He was more than a patriot of Odessa; he was an Odessa chauvinist.

Though deeply permeated by Russian culture, Jabotinsky had no love and attachment for Russia. In *The Five* he stated with the utmost frankness: "I have been indifferent to Russia even in my youth; I remember that I was always happily tense when leaving for abroad, and was reluctant to return." Broadening the statement, he said: "I am indifferent not to Russia only. I am not really 'attached' to any country at all; there was a time when I was in love with Rome, and not just for a little while; but even this is over." The only glorious exception from this wholesale detachment was Odessa. "I love Odessa . . . when the train would approach Razdielnaya [a railway station near Odessa], I was already feeling exultantly excited. Even now, if I were approaching Odessa, my hands would probably be trembling." Love for Odessa "is not over and will never be over."[4]

In 1933, Jabotinsky started publishing, in installments, in the Paris *Rasswyet*, a novel, *The Five*—a broad and delightful picture of Odessa at the beginning of the twentieth century (early in 1936 it appeared in book form in Paris; later it was translated into Hebrew and partly into Yiddish; in 1947, the Jabotinsky Foundation published an American edition of the original Russian text). Jabotinsky loved this novel dearly. When he received the first copy of *The Five* in London, he wrote to his brother-in-law, I. Galperin: "I was so happy that the whole day I was going from one movie to another."[5] And to S. D. Salzman he wrote: "I am leaving to the Odessites a memory of their youth. . . . I think that they will read this novel with a sweet and melancholic feeling. . . . Maybe even not all Odessites will understand me. . . . Odessa was a Metropolis not only for the Jews, but for the entire world."[6]

This metropolis aspect of Odessa was to Jabotinsky an inexhaustible source of pride. He called himself "a native of Babylon" and described his "own brand of Babylon" as "a tornado of a place where every corner of local life used somehow to get entangled with affairs and questions of a world-wide range. Brokers on the Corn Exchange were compelled to discuss the chances of a war between Uruguay and Paraguay, or a probable outcome of a revolt in Persia; for on all that, in some crooked way, the stability of our grain market was eminently dependent. Card-players at their baize-tables, while pondering over their next lead, chatted about Lee Hung Chang and Jaurès. The whole life was like the Italian soup minestrone—overspiced and too thick."[7] And Jabotinsky loved minestrone. This "overspiced" life was stimulating, challenging, broadening a man's horizons. Odessa was not just one of the big provincial towns of Russia: it was the "heart of the Universe."

With Jabotinsky this was an article of faith. Once, in a hospitable Russian home in Paris, a discussion arose about the size and value of the various capitals of Europe. Jabotinsky listened attentively and then quietly and casually said: "Sure, sure. . . . But still, the biggest and most beautiful city in the world is—Odessa." No amount of argument was able to sway him from this statement—he just ignored it. But then somebody said: "Well, as far as the most beautiful is concerned, it is a matter of personal taste, which is *non disputandum*. But what about the biggest? You will, I hope, not deny that London has a population of eight million?" "Oh, I certainly will not deny that," Jabotinsky answered calmly. "Let it be eight million. But then, Odessa has a population of nine million. . . ." The question was thus settled, so far as he was concerned.

This glorification of Odessa remained with him throughout life: Odessa, *Odessa über alles, über alles in der Welt*. When Jabotinsky was living in Paris—*la ville lumière*—he wrote two feuilletons, "My Capital City" and "My Village." And, of course, in this juxtaposition, the "Capital City" was Odessa, and Paris was the "Village." When still in Russia, he published in *Odesskiya Novosti* a brilliant feuilleton in defense of some peculiarities of the "Odessa language," which was notorious for its numerous deviations from classical Russian. Jabotinsky boldly justified these usually much ridiculed and scorned specific oddities. He eloquently argued that, in fact, these derided "Odessisms" represented, not an illiterate and clumsy distortion of the commonly accepted Russian language, but wonderful neologisms, which had vastly enriched and enlivened the existing Russian vocabulary. Odessa, young and creative, and not burdened by shackles of obsolete grammatical tradition, found the courage and the imagination to go its own way in the struggle for a more adequate and picturesque expression of the thoughts and feelings of its multinational population.

The Rebellious Individualist

The individualistic trend that strongly prevailed in Jabotinsky's plays and feuilletons very soon made him the talk of the town, in particular after he started venting his unorthodox ideas also as a lecturer.

The center of Odessa's intellectual life was the "Literary-Artistic Circle," whose weekly Thursday meetings attracted the cream of the city's multinational intelligentsia.[8] The topics were "innocent" ones—literature, philosophy, art, sometimes economics. But the thinly veiled underlying *leitmotif* of the lectures and the subsequent discussions was invariably in some subtle way connected with politics, with the all-pervading struggle against Tsarist absolutism and for a constitution. The dominant trend among the intellectually active society was socialism in its various shades, mostly of the orthodox Marxian blend, with its strong emphasis on the collective as opposed to the individual. The majority of those who frequented the Circle had, of course, never read Marx or Engels and had a very vague idea about the meaning of the "collectivist" (a current pseudonym for Socialist-Marxian) philosophy and program. But every self-respecting intellectual or semi-intellectual somehow felt that this philosophy was synonymous with progress and that each deviation from the "collectivist" canon smacked of obscurantism and reaction.

Jabotinsky brought with him from Italy a different concept of socialism. Reared in the unorthodox Socialist teachings of Labriola and Ferri, he was an inveterate enemy of any stiff and narrow dogma, an iconoclast by nature and conviction. He had no respect for "sacrosanct" formulas. In his poem "Schafloch" he answered a direct question of a pretty girl as to whether he was a Marxist by a bold confession that neither the Goddess of Freedom nor the Queen of Morals were holy to him:

> Only cowards, fools or paupers
> Worship idols wrapped in rags.
> High above the rest of mankind
> Soar the people with no tags.
> *These* are men! The broad horizons
> Stretch before their eagle's eyes;

All the marvels of Creation,
God's own world, become their prize.
                    (*Translated from Russian by A.G.*)

Least of all was he prepared to condone the prevalent contempt for the rights of the sovereign human personality; he was ready and eager to challenge this attitude vigorously and at all times.

It is against this background that we have to appreciate the effect of the first public appearance at the Circle of the popular feuilletonist. I. A. Trivus, who was present at that memorable evening, vividly recalls the discussion that followed Jabotinsky's speech.[9]

Jabotinsky's basic contention was that the only eternal reality in human life is the individual. The only ideal that is worth working and fighting for is to secure the happiness of the individual, the fullest freedom of development of his personality. It is wrong to put the stress, as it was then being done, on the collective, on the "masses," on uniformity. Progress consists in freeing the individual from the chains of the collective: for individuals, and individuals alone, are the real creators and promoters of progress. They are the trailblazers for the masses, for humanity. Collectivism, bent on mechanical equalization, on subordination of human personality to uniform rules and way of life, is nothing but a new form of slavery—reactionary and despicable. Neither an anthill nor a beehive, highly and efficiently organized as they are, can serve as an ideal for the human society.

The audience, which precariously held its temper for over an hour, could stand such heresies no longer. From all sides arose booing, hissing, trampling, shouting, cursing: Enough! Reactionary! Anarchist! Bourgeois! Spy! Shame on you! One opponent after another bitterly and abusively attacked Jabotinsky.

In his rejoinder, Jabotinsky, hurt and excited by defaming personal attacks, delivered an impassioned and powerful oration:

"I shall not answer personal insults. But I was accused of anarchistic leanings. It is true that I value highly Proudhon, Bakunin, Kropotkin, Reclus, none of whom you have, of course, ever read; but I am not an Anarchist, since I recognize the necessity of state power. The difference between you and me is that in my concept the state is merely the supreme judge that acts only when individual freedom is in danger and does not interfere with the normal process of economic, social and personal life, while to you it is a stick which has to govern everything."

This challenging rejoinder only increased the indignation of most of his hearers. The shouting and hissing became threatening, and only the appearance of the police prevented further trouble.

The next day and for many weeks to come, "all Odessa"—those who had been present at the meeting and those who had not—was seething with excited discussions on these "unheard of" utterances by "that Altalena." Yet Jabotinsky was not in the least disturbed by this pious indignation. He was sure of his ground, having thoroughly studied the abundant literature dealing with the problems of individual freedom vs. collectivism. I. Trivus, who visited him at that time, saw in his library works by Stirner, Bakunin, Marx, Proudhon, Spencer, Kropotkin, Lavrov, Mikhailovsky—though possession of some of these books was then illegal and could lead to administrative banishment to Siberia. Jabotinsky reiterated his opposition to full-fledged anarchism: he believed in the necessity of state-organized human life, but, as he put it, he was half-way inclined toward the anarchist philosophy, which attracted him by its emphasis on individual freedom and its hatred of leveling tendencies.

His flirtation with anarchism was of short duration. It was hardly ever serious; its most probable source was Jabotinsky's highly developed *ésprit de contradiction* and his mischievous enjoyment of the uproar he provoked. No traces of any weakness toward any form of anarchist philosophy are discernible in his subsequent spiritual development. What remained was the strong, almost religious belief in the inalienable rights of the individual as the supreme criterion for determining what is progress and what is not.

Enter Zionism

In the spring of 1902, police and gendarmes paid a visit to Jabotinsky, made a search, and confiscated two "incriminating" items: an illegal edition of the memorandum on "County Self-Government and Autocracy" submitted to the Tsar by the Russian Minister of Finance, Count Sergey J. Witte, and four issues of the Italian Socialist paper *Avanti* in Milan with Jabotinsky's reportages.

The more suspect of the two impounded items were the articles. A police officer with the Russo-Hungarian name of Samoilenko-Mandjaro told Jabotinsky in all seriousness that, being written "in unintelligible language," they had to be handed over to an official translator "to establish whether they do or do not contain offenses against His Majesty." This investigation took a full seven weeks. It was found that nothing was said against His Majesty's honor in the *Avanti* articles, and Jabotinsky was released from prison.* For the offense of possessing Count Witte's memorandum he had to remain under police observation.

Many years later, Jabotinsky described the seven weeks spent in Odessa prison as one of the most delightful episodes of his life. There he met for the first time the peculiar and fascinating world of the revolutionary underground. These revolutionary jailbirds deeply impressed him with the "moral purity of their conversations, thoughts and, apparently, of their way of life outside of the prison." Three-quarters of the inmates were Jews. Even their conspiratorial nicknames were often purely Jewish: *Zeide* (Grandfather), *Riboino-shel-Oilom* (Master of the World); Jabotinsky's nickname was "Lavrov." Though supposed to be strictly separated in solitary confinement, they managed to live a very active social life, organizing lectures, concerts, and recitals. Jabotinsky jokingly recalled that, after having listened to three lectures by *Zeide* on the history of the Jewish Socialist Bund, he irrevocably became a Zionist.[10]

This last remark is correct only so far as it describes his Zionist leanings. In 1902, as in 1898, Jabotinsky had understanding and sincere sympathy for the Zionist solution of the Jewish problem. But he was not as yet a Zionist, for he simply was not sufficiently concerned with the Jewish problem as such. Theoretically, he realized the justice and greatness of the Zionist cause. But there was in him no powerful innermost impulse to draw actual personal consequences from this mental realization. He was still much more involved in general problems of literature, art, ethics, politics. His "Jewish soul" was pleasantly dormant. It needed some potent incentive to be awakened.

Jabotinsky stated in his *Autobiography* that the beginnings of his Zionist activities were connected with the Italian opera, and with the organization of the Odessa self-defense.

---

*Jabotinsky jokingly wrote to his mother from prison that she should not worry, since politically he was "as clean as a cleanly wiped glass." According to Mrs. Jabotinsky-Kopp, he owed the attention of the Tzarist gendarmery to the fact that the two sisters of his close friend, at whose house he was a frequent guest, were known as Socialists.

The opera episode was insignificant in itself: somewhat hesitatingly Jabotinsky yielded to the request of an Odessa Zionist, S. D. Salzman, whom he met first at a performance of the Italian opera and later at a reception by the famous Italian diva Amanda della Abati, and induced the management of the Municipal Theater to include in the repertoire *La Juive* by Halevi and *Queen of Sheba* by Carl Goldmark, as well as plays by Herzl and Nordau.[11] He also convinced the famous Italian actor Ermette Novelli to abstain from beginning his guest appearances in Odessa with the performance of Shakespeare's *Merchant of Venice*, in which Novelli was to play the role of Shylock. In the specific Russian atmosphere, such a beginning could easily have been interpreted as an anti-Semitic gesture.

It seems that it was Salzman who first provided Jabotinsky with the classics of Zionist literature, of which at that time there were not many. He gave him Pinsker's *Autoemancipation*, as well as the writings of Herzl and Lilienblum and reports from the first five Zionist Congresses. The impression Salzman gained was that Altalena was beginning to take a lively interest in Zionism, and he passed this good news to his Zionist friends; he stressed that though the popular feuilletonist was as yet not a regular Zionist in the (then) accepted sense of the word, he had a "Zionist conception of his own, a romantic and activist one, different from our Zionism. . . . Just as Herzl wrote his *Judenstaat* without knowing the world in which Pinsker lived, so has Jabotinsky created his own Zionism." Zionist circles were rather dubious about the prospect of Altalena's joining their ranks—and they decided not to try to "push" him in this direction and to let him find his way to active Zionism unhurriedly and freely.[12]

It is certainly not accidental that the immediate lane through which Jabotinsky did find his way was through the idea of self-defense.

In the early spring of 1903, about six weeks before Passover, anti-Jewish excesses took place in the small town of Dubossary, not far from Odessa. There were no killings, but this outbreak was ominous, and there were rumors of a possible pogrom in Odessa itself. In Jewish circles the vague idea of self-defense was growing: and it awakened powerful dormant forces in Jabotinsky.

It is not correct to credit Jabotinsky, as it is sometimes done, with having been "the founder of the first Jewish self-defense corps." He himself never claimed this distinction, and we shall see from the available evidence that he neither "invented" nor was the first to begin implementing the self-defense idea. When he got involved in self-defense activities, it was with an already existing, though small and hardly influential, student Zionist body. But he came to the self-defense idea independently, through spiritual channels of his own.

We read in Exodus II, 11-12: "And it came to pass in those days, when Moses was grown, that he went out unto his brethren, and looked on their burdens; and he saw an Egyptian smiting a Hebrew, one of his brethren. And he looked this way and that way, and when he saw that there was no man, he slew the Egyptian, and hid him in the sand." There were thousands of Jews in the ghetto of Goshen who saw hundreds of times "an Egyptian smiting a Hebrew." But in none of them did this familiar sight provoke the urge to react by "slaying the Egyptian." They had been reared in the slavish mentality of the Goshen ghetto, in fear and submissiveness. Moses grew up at the court of the Pharaoh, among warriors and priests, with a proud and even haughty master mentality, with a highly developed sense of personal honor and dignity. Jabotinsky's mind and soul were likewise formed outside the spiritual ghetto, in which the overwhelming majority of Russian Jewry still lived. He was deeply influenced by the proud philosophy of the Italian national Risorgimento: *Italia fará da se*—Italy will be liberated by herself.

When, in 1903, the terrifying and humiliating menace of a pogrom appeared on the horizon, Jabotinsky, like Moses, may have "looked this way and that way" in a vague expectation of comfort and help from the outside world; but "he saw that there was no man" to help. No protection would come either from the corrupted Tsarist administration which openly encouraged the anti-Semitic forces, nor from the Russian so-called "progressive elements" which were both helpless and passive. Jabotinsky's reaction was to rely on and to call for Jewish self-defense. Irrespective of the practical value of this defense, it was to him a powerful means of awakening Jewish self-esteem, of the same magnificent self-assertion which inspired the victorious slogan *Italia fará da se*. A congenial echo of this longing he found in Zionism. More than two decades later he wrote: "I learned my Zionism not from Achad Haam, and not even from Herzl and Nordau; I learned it from non-Jews in Italy."[13]

The actual sequence of events, so far as can be gathered from the available evidence, seems to have been as follows:

Stirred by the pogrom rumors, Jabotinsky sent out letters to a dozen influential Jewish leaders, "sedate city fathers," most of whom he did not even know personally, urging the organization of a self-defense corps in Odessa. The addressees, horrified by such a radical suggestion, did not even answer. But one of them passed the letter to a Zionist self-defense group which at that time was already in existence in the city. The group naturally was pleased to have the support of the popular feuilletonist and got in touch with him.

This group was a special self-defense committee appointed by the Zionist student circle "Yerusholayim." One night, when the committee was working on the mimeographing of an illegal leaflet to be distributed in ten thousand copies (recalls I. Trivus), Jabotinsky suddenly appeared with two friends (A. Poliakov and M. Ginsburg) and said: "I see that you are already dog-tired; get some rest and let us continue the job." When invited to make some corrections in the text of the leaflet, he sharply retorted: "We came here, not to correct anybody or anything, but to work as simple soldiers, and that is all. Besides, I believe that it does not matter whether you use one word or another. What matters is the new spirit expressed in this appeal, the spirit of national honor and dignity, and of open struggle against aggressions. 'Yerusholayim' has performed a historical service to the Jewish people by calling to arms, and my friends and myself have come to help you; you can use us for any purpose."

The leaflets were ready at dawn and were distributed all over the city. The next morning, on behalf of the committee, Jabotinsky and I. Trivus visited the popular and influential Zionist leader M. J. Disengoff (later the founder and first mayor of Tel Aviv) and enlisted his cooperation. Together with Disengoff, Jabotinsky started collecting funds. A respectable business-man and a popular feuilletonist proved to be a highly successful team. The same evening they supplied the committee with the first 5,000 rubles (2,500 dollars)—at that time a very considerable amount. Jabotinsky and Disen-goff joined the general staff of the self-defense. During these weeks, recalls Trivus, Jabotinsky worked with unparalleled energy. He was busy day and night, running around like one possessed, from the houses of the rich to the tenements of the poor. He won over to the cause of self-defense intellectual circles who, before he embraced this cause, had looked upon it warily and even with antagonism.[14]

There was no pogrom in Odessa on Passover of 1903. Organized self-defense had no occasion to go into action. But a bloody pogrom did take place on April 6–8 in Kishinev; it left behind fifty corpses, several hundred wounded, and many raped women. These three days of massacre in the Bessarabian capital in many ways marked the birth of a new Jewish mentality. For the first time in modern Jewish history the main feeling provoked in the community was not one of horror and grief but of shame, humiliation of a people who allowed themselves to be beaten and killed like cattle. Bialik found a dramatic and powerful expression for this new feeling in his poem "Massa Nemirov": "Great is the sorrow, and great is the shame—and which of the two is greater—answer thou, oh son of Man."

The poem, comparable only to the twenty-eighth chapter of Deuteronomy in the bitterness of its invective against Jewish meekness and cowardice, caused a deep and lasting spiritual upheaval in wide Jewish circles. But it was available only to those who understood Hebrew. In 1904, Jabotinsky translated the poem into Russian. He put into this translation all the deep feeling of his own soul, all the fire of his indignation, and all the intensity of his pride. So imbued was this Russian version of Bialik's poem with the spirit and personality of its translator that it came to be regarded as an original poem of Jabotinsky's rather than the translation it was supposed to be.

Since the censorship at that time would not permit the printing of this rebellious piece in Russian, it had to be mimeographed. L. Sherman, who lived at the time in Odessa, recalls that "the national Jewish youth and the members of the self-defense corps would come together and read aloud the Russian translation of that stirring poem. The one who obtained a mimeographed copy was fortunate, but even luckier was he who had the privilege to hear Jabotinsky declaim the poem at one of our secret, illegal meetings."[15] The present writer remembers that many of the younger generation learned Jabotinsky's translation by heart and would recite excerpts from it in their private conversations and group discussions. Later, in 1905, when the censorship's grip relaxed considerably, it was published by S. D. Salzman in the form of a separate pamphlet under the title *Skazaniye o Pogromye* (The Tale of the Pogrom).

Most impressive was Jabotinsky's poetic introduction to the poem. In it he reminds Bialik—his "older brother in spirit, magician and master of that musical tongue which was called his own by my remote ancestor and which my grandson shall call his own" —that, besides him, "another Poet has written a formidable tale about this pogrom. . . . Yours is full of passion, vivid and vigorous; but *the other* is more powerful":

Once, in *that* town, under a heap of garbage
I noticed a piece of parchment—
A fragment of the Torah.
I picked it up and carefully removed the dirt.
Two words stood out: *Be'erets Nokhriya,* "In Alien Land."
This scrap of parchment
I nailed above the door to my own home.
For in these two words out of the Book of Genesis
Is told the entire story of the Pogrom.*

(*Translated from Russian by A.G.*)

After the Kishinev pogrom, Jewish self-defense units were created throughout the Jewish communities of Russia. In several cases (the most spectacular was that of Gomel on September 1, 1903) they went into action and contributed much to the strengthening of Jewish self-esteem and national consciousness.

Nevertheless, Jabotinsky was far from the illusion that self-defense as such was an answer to the pogrom plague. As early as 1906, he bluntly put the question: "What can be done against the pogroms?"—and pitilessly answered: "Self-defense—one hardly can speak about it in earnest. In the final analysis, it did not do us any good; in the beginning, the fear of it actually prevented a few pogroms, but now, when *they* have seen it in action and have compared the number of Jews and pogromists killed—who takes it seriously? When they wish, they start a pogrom and kill as many Jews as they want, and self-defense is just of no use. Of course, there is [moral] consolation in self-defense. But its practical balance amounts to zero and will remain zero, and it is time quietly to recognize it aloud, so that people should not hope in vain."[16]

Notwithstanding this realistic appraisal of the actual usefulness of self-defense, Jabotinsky never ceased his energetic participation in

---

*This was not just a poetic license. Jabotinsky actually picked up a fragment of a torn Torah scroll and kept it for many years. In Alexandria, when (on February 23, 1915) hundreds of volunteers signed up for the first Jewish military unit, he showed them this piece of parchment, on which the two words *be'erets Nokhriya* were still distinguishable, told them its story and said: "Here is your reply to it—the document you have just signed." (D. Yudelovitz. "The Legion and the Torn Torah-Scroll." *Hamashkif,* September 9, 1940.)

its organization. As usual, Jabotinsky himself deliberately minimized his personal role in this work. "As to the self-defense," he wrote in his *Autobiography*, "I was not very active in this field. I participated in some conference, if I am not mistaken, in Odessa." He only reluctantly admitted that his "proclamations and pamphlets which were being distributed illegally, have helped this movement, in particular Bialik's *Tale of the Pogrom* published in my translation and with my introduction."

There is, however, authoritative evidence that the role he actually played was much more important. Bernard Kahn, Honorary Chairman of the European Executive Council of the American Jewish Joint Distribution Committee, wrote on February 9, 1943, to the Jabotinsky Publication Committee in New York: Jabotinsky "was very helpful to me in my work in 1905–1906 after the revolution and the terrible pogroms. We tried all possible ways, both legal and illegal from the Russian point of view, to provide means of self-defense to the Russian Jews in towns. We relied on our Russian friends who cooperated with us, and among them Vladimir Jabotinsky was one of the most outstanding."

LIFE AND STRUGGLE IN RUSSIAN ZIONISM

FOUR

IN THE ZIONIST STREAM

The First Congresses

It would be wrong to connect the beginning of Jabotinsky's Zionist activities with the shock produced by the Kishinev pogrom (April 6–8, 1903). S. D. Salzman claims that he had sold his first shekel to Jabotinsky early in 1903, and S. M. Dubnov mentions in his autobiography Jabotinsky's Zionist speech in the Odessa club "Bessyeda" (Assembly) on April 7, 1903, i.e., before the news of the Kishinev slaughter had reached Odessa.[1] Jabotinsky had always insisted that no pogrom ever "taught" him anything.

Kishinev, however, played a considerable role in Jabotinsky's Zionist life in another sense: it brought him together with a galaxy of Russian Zionist leaders. Soon after the pogrom, Jabotinsky went to Kishinev on behalf of *Odesskiya Novosti* to deliver funds and clothing collected by the paper. There he met for the first time such Zionist stalwarts as M. M. Ussishkin (from Yekaterinoslav), V. Y. Tiomkin (from Yelisavetgrad), Dr. J. B. Sapir (from Odessa), and J. M. Kogan-Bernstein (from Kishinev); he also made the acquaintance of the poet Ch. N. Bialik, whose very name was then unknown to him.

Soon after his return from Kishinev, the Zionist circle *Eretz Israel* offered to send Jabotinsky as a delegate to the Sixth Zionist Congress in Basel. After some hesitation due to his uncertainty as to the adequacy of his Zionist knowledge, he accepted the nomination. Invited to a meeting of the circle, he found its membership consisting of middle-aged and elderly middle-class people— not a single young man participated—who asked him, as was customary in such cases, "to present his program." Jabotinsky spoke very deprecatingly of "all the silly things" he then probably told this august electoral college and ascribed the fact that they did not "take him by the scruff of his neck and throw him out" to the kindhearted clemency of the *Eretz Israel* leaders. This is, of course, a misinterpretation. For the Odessa Zionists the chance to have the already famous Altalena as their representative at the Congress was a godsend. Instead of "throwing him out," they most earnestly put to him several quite pertinent questions concerning some problems which the Congress was likely to face. One of them was: "What would be the prospective delegate's attitude toward the pending project of Jewish colonization of the El Arish area, on the Sinai Peninsula, on the frontier between Egypt and Palestine?"* Jabotinsky, who had learned of this project only a few days earlier, remembered answering the question in a noncommittal way: his vote would depend on the conditions prevailing at the Congress; if there was no danger of a split, he would vote in the affirmative; should he, however, feel that such a resolution was going to split the movement, he would consider this as proof that Zionism was in favor of Palestine only, and he would vote against the proposal. This answer, apparently, satisfied the patriotic feelings of the *Eretz Israel* leaders, and they confirmed Jabotinsky as their delegate. At that time he was only twenty-two and a half years old, while the prescribed age for a Congress delegate was twenty-four. But "good false witnesses gave evidence" that he was twenty-four years old, and he therefore qualified to receive his delegate's card.

To Jabotinsky, the experience of his first Congress was anything but a happy one. With the exception of a few colleagues from Odessa, nobody knew him. He felt lost and wandered around forlorn among the delegates who hardly took notice of the strange-looking young man. He knew little of the routine of the Zionist organization and of the problems before the Congress. "I was introduced," he recalled, "to a tall and slim young man with a black goatee and a shiny bald head. His name was Dr. Weizmann, and I had been told that he was the head of the 'opposition.'** Immediately I felt that

---

*The project was mooted by Davis Trietsch, and Herzl started unsuccessful negotiations on El Arish in 1902.

**At the Fifth Zionist Congress at Basel (1901) there appeared for the first time an official oppositionist group, the "Democratic-Zionist Fraction." Its leading spirits were Leo Motzkin, Chaim Weizmann, Victor Jacobson, and Martin Buber. It aimed at the promotion of more evolutionary, more deeply rooted nationalism, a greater degree of democracy in the leadership of the movement, a stronger influence of youth and its ideas, and a program of *Gegenwartsarbeit*—immediate day-to-day activity—of a cultural nature throughout the Diaspora.

my place, too, was in the 'opposition,' though I did not know what or whom to oppose. . . . Later, when I saw the same young man in a cafe, surrounded by friends and engaged in a spirited discussion, I came over and asked: 'Would I disturb you?' and Weizmann answered: 'You *are* disturbing me,' and I went away."

Jabotinsky's first speech at the Congress proved to be the innocent cause of much annoyance and trouble. Dr. Herzl's recent trip to Russia (August, 1903), where he conducted negotiations with von Plehve, the reactionary and anti-Semitic Minister of the Interior, provoked much criticism among Russian Zionists; all parties had, however, agreed not to mention the matter, in order to spare Herzl public embarrassment. Jabotinsky was aware of this understanding. He believed, however, that it did not apply to himself: he was confident that as a Russian journalist who thoroughly learned the difficult art of dealing with the most explosive matters without arousing the ire of the censorship, he would also be able to tackle safely this delicate issue. But he underestimated the sensitivity of a Zionist audience. When he started arguing that it was necessary to avoid confusing ethics and tactics and thus—though by implication only—defended Herzl's hotly disputed political move, the opposition immediately "smelled a rat" and started shouting: "Enough! No more!" German Zionists then played a leading role in the Zionist movement, and the official stenographic minutes of the Congresses were kept in German, which was the only language understood by the great majority of the delegates. Since Jabotinsky spoke Russian, the official *Protokoll*, while listing him as speaker, does not record his speech, simply mentioning: *Delegierter Schabotinsky spricht Russisch.*[2] When N. Sokolov was later called upon to translate the speech into German, he said that he could not do so because of the many interruptions and the unrest with which Jabotinsky's speech was received. He only mentioned that Jabotinsky spoke against fractions within the Zionist movement and demanded a united organization.[3] At the height of the commotion provoked by Jabotinsky's speech, Herzl, who at that time was closeted with a few friends in a nearby room, rushed on the platform and asked the people at the presidium what the young man was saying. Dr. Weizmann supplied the answer by stating: *Quatsch* (nonsense). Relying on this information, Dr. Herzl said the only words which he ever spoke directly to Jabotinsky: *Ihre Zeit ist um* (Your time is up). These were "the first and the last words I had the privilege to hear from him," recalled Jabotinsky. Dr. Adolf Friedemann, one of Herzl's closest lieutenants, made the meaning of these words clear in his inimitable Prussian style: "Get off the platform, and if you don't, you will be carried off forcibly."

Many years later, in a light vein, Jabotinsky good-naturedly told a group of friends a joke which reminded him of this only encounter with Herzl: a Jew boasted in a synagogue of a conversation he had with the Governor of the town they lived in.

"How come that the Governor spoke to you? And what was the conversation about?"

"Oh, it was very simple. I came to see the Governor during his reception hours. As soon as I uttered the first few words, he shouted: 'Get out!' "

Jabotinsky did not speak again at the Sixth Congress. He did not participate in the debate on the British promise "to consider favorably proposals for the creation of a Jewish colony or settlement" in the Uganda area of the British Protectorate of East Africa, "under such conditions as will seem to the members to guarantee the retention of their national custom." The East Africa scheme, which became known as the "Uganda Project," aroused a passionate opposition, particularly among the Russian delegates. They saw in it an attempt to substitute Uganda for Palestine and combated the proposal to appoint a commission which should make a thorough investigation of the East African offer. When Herzl's motion favoring the dispatch of such a commission had been accepted, one hundred seventy-seven delegates who opposed it left the Congress hall. Jabotinsky voted with the minority and left together with them.

Dr. Weizmann asserted in his autobiographical *Trial and Error* that Jabotinsky's position at the Sixth Congress was not "very distinct": "one did not know, for instance, whether he was for Uganda or against, whether he condoned Herzl's visit to von Plehve . . . or condemned it."[4] This is, of course, absolutely incorrect. We have seen that, contrary to the position taken by many Russian Zionists, Jabotinsky defended Herzl's visit to Plehve; and that, together with the majority of the Russian delegation, he voted against the sending of a commission to East Africa, leaving the Congress with the opposition after the vote.

The same evening, Herzl came to the closed meeting of the secessionist minority and in a powerful speech reassured them of his fidelity to the Zionist program, which "remains integral and unaffected." The next day, the opposition reappeared in the Congress. In his closing speech, Herzl solemnly declared: *Im Eshkahech Yerushalayim tishkah yemini* (If I forget thee, oh Jerusalem, may my right hand forget its cunning).

At the Sixth Congress, Jabotinsky saw and heard Herzl for the first and last time. But this brief and fleeting contact was sufficient to convey to him the full greatness of Herzl's personality and the everlasting profundity of his teachings. In his *Autobiography* Jabotinsky described Herzl's impact as follows:

> Herzl made a colossal impression on me—the word is no empty phrase. There is no other description that will fit—but colossal—and I am not easily impressed by personalities. Of all my acquaintances I remember no person who made such an impression on me, not anyone before Herzl nor anyone after him. Here I felt that I really stood before a man chosen by fate, before a prophet and a leader—that even to err and blunder in following him was justified. And to this day it seems that we still hear the resounding voice as he swore before us: "If I forget thee, Jerusalem. . . ." I believed his pledge. Everyone believed.

Throughout the whole of his life, Jabotinsky remained imbued with the spirit of Herzl's Zionism.

During and after the Congress, a serious conflict developed between Herzl and representatives of Russian Zionism, who accused Herzl of autocratic leanings and methods. This controversy gave Jabotinsky the opportunity to formulate his concept of the role of a leader in a national movement. He did it in a feuilleton on "Current Problems," which appeared in the first (January, 1904) issue of the St. Petersburg Zionist monthly *Yevreyskaya Zhisn*:

"There is no doubt," he wrote, "that a strong personality cannot work in narrow limits, and the more outstanding the personality is and the more energetic, the more difficult it is for him to remain within the limits of his own square on the general chess board. A man of great caliber is bound to sin against the collegiate principle. In the best case, it might be a concealed, masked, ennobled lack of collegiality, but the energy of an outstanding personality is in its very essence directly opposed to the collegiate principle. . . . Those who appreciate outstanding working forces have to recognize their right to sin against the collegiate principle. But—only to a certain extent, and here is the crux of the problem. . . . Other men are also not sheep, or at least should not be sheep: they must know what is being done in their name or with their means; they must be able to protest when they consider unnecessary what is being done and to restrain the swing of an autocratic, though loving hand, if the scope of this swing seems to them to be excessive or wrongly directed. . . . This friction is the regulator—the only possible *modus in rebus*—in the relationship between a strong personality and a collective body. It is this friction that at any given moment indicates to the leader how far his autocratic energy can go, and which limit cannot be transgressed; the tact of an outstanding leader consists in his ability to feel instinctively and faultlessly at any moment, to what extent he can act independently and where he is risking to meet excessive resistance. . . . The best constitution is not one which once and for all strictly limits authority's freedom of action, but one which, on the contrary, allows the possibility of friction and resistance. . . ." A man of truly great stature, Jabotinsky insisted, "is not afraid to surround himself even with hard and unyielding personalities. He must remember *qu'on ne s'appuie que sur ce que résiste*. Herzl quoted this sentence when closing the Sixth Congress."[5]

Jabotinsky voted at the Congress against any attempt even to investigate the British proposal of a Jewish colonization of East Africa. Many years later, trying to analyze his vote, Jabotinsky was still puzzled by its innermost motivation: "At.that time, I had no romantic love for Palestine—and I am not sure whether I have it even now; and I could not know whether there was a danger of a split in the movement—I did not know that [Jewish] people, and its delegates I saw there for the first time and had no opportunity to come closer to any one of them." Many among those who came from Russia together with Jabotinsky raised their hands in favor of the Uganda Project. Nobody influenced his vote. He had full confidence in Herzl's solemn promise "not to forget Jerusalem" and was deeply impressed by Herzl's greatness. Still he voted against him: "And I don't know why—simply because. This is one of those 'simple' things which counterbalance thousands of arguments."

During the two-year period between the Sixth and Seventh Congresses, Jabotinsky took an active part in the struggle for Palestine as the only goal of Zionism. Many years later, Jabotinsky told his son Eri that the only time when he temporarily doubted the soundness of his vote and of the subsequent campaign against the Uganda Project, was during the early years of his desperate struggle for the Jewish Legion. In 1915–16, he was sometimes tempted to think: If by that time there were in existence a Jewish Commonwealth in Uganda, it would automatically provide a ready-made nucleus for a full-fledged Jewish Army.[6] And to this writer he said in 1938, after his return from South Africa, that when his airplane was flying over the flourishing and well-cultivated Uganda territory, he thought of the tragic plight of the masses of East European Jewry who were in desperate need of speedy evacuation and had nowhere to go, the doors of Palestine being almost hermetically sealed by a nearsighted and callous British government; and he caught himself doubting whether it really was just and wise to have rejected, thirty-five years before, the chance of salvation offered by a generous British government. "I know," he added, "that it is an unforgivable heresy to allow even a shadow of such a doubt to penetrate one's mind when all our efforts must be concentrated on the struggle for Palestine; but I just couldn't help wondering. . . ."

In 1905, the Odessa Zionists once more delegated Jabotinsky to the Seventh Zionist Congress, where he again spoke Russian. The official *Protokoll*, therefore, only briefly mentioned that, "greeted with approval and applause," delegate Schabotinsky "defined the essence of politics. Politics is power. This power we do not possess. Zionism must endeavor to become a power."[7] A report in the *Khronika Yevreyskoy Zhisni* (July 29, 1905) supplemented this brief account by saying that Jabotinsky "stressed the difference between *Hoveve Zion** and political Zionism and outlined the way Zionism has to follow: wTe must become a *force*, to unite, indefatigably to labor for our goal."

Jabotinsky's speeches at the Sixth and Seventh Congresses, though summarily and badly reported, are in many respects characteristic of his later Zionist concept and program.

At the Sixth Congress he stressed the basic difference between "ethics and tactics" and defended Herzl's negotiations with von Plehve as a Zionist political necessity. After Herzl's death, he again contemptuously deprecated "this aesthetically fastidious criticism of [diplomatic] visits and handshakes, these all-comprehensive investigations of the question whether or not it is permissible and necessary to send greeting telegrams to the Sultan or to come to Petersburg. . . . Aesthetical appraisals are in order with regard to works of art, but they are completely out of place with regard to facts of actual life, which must be measured solely by the criterion of their usefulness to humanity. . . . The moral appraisal of the means and methods used by a fighter must

---

Hoveve Zion (literally "Lovers of Zion")—groups of supporters, in the latter part of the nineteenth century, of small-scale Jewish settlement in Palestine on a philanthropic basis, without a clearly defined political goal.

be governed exclusively by the measure of the real public good or public harm they result in."[8]

In later years, Jabotinsky remained faithful to this early concept of national policy when, in 1921, he himself entered into an agreement with Petliura's Minister, Maxim A. Slavinsky, for the purpose of organizing Jewish self-defense units against pogrom bands and pursued the "policy of alliances" with the so-called "anti-Semitic regimes" of Poland and Rumania (1936–39).

At the Seventh Congress he defined the essence of politics as power, and insisted that Zionism as a national political movement of the Jewish people must become a force. This remained his Zionist *leitmotif* for the rest of his life.

At the same Congress, he identified his ideological antipode: the *Hoveve Zion*. The struggle against philanthropic Zionism and for Herzl's political concept filled all his Zionist activities.

To St. Petersburg

By the end of 1903, Jabotinsky apparently still had no definite plans as to his future career. As he put it in his usual playful manner, he might have dreamed of the laurels of a Russian writer or have strived to become the captain of a Zionist ship; but "fate in the person of a huge and fat police officer named Panassiuk decided everything for me."

As theater critic of the *Odesskiya Novosti*, Jabotinsky had a permanent seat in the fifth row of the Municipal Theater, among the notables of the city. In appearance, however, he was anything but impressive: he was short, looked boyish, and dressed like a bohemian. At one of the performances, Panassiuk, who attended the show, could not imagine that the place for such a character was not in the balcony, and shouted at Jabotinsky, accusing him of sneaking in where he had no right to be. Greatly offended, Jabotinsky gave Panassiuk a piece of his mind and did the same for the General of the gendarmery, Bezsonov, who tried to intervene. A scandal broke loose. Two days later Jabotinsky was summoned to appear before the Governor of Odessa, Count Neidgard, who was known for his extravagant and wild temper. He could easily guess what was in store for him. Therefore, he later related to a group of friends in St. Petersburg, he put on the dinner jacket which he had ordered the year before for the premiere of his play *Krov*, packed his meager belongings, mobilized all his cash (thirty rubles), and told his faithful friend Ginsburg: "If in two hours I am not back, bring my suitcase to the railroad station, just in time for the noon express to St. Petersburg." Count Neidgard received Jabotinsky in the presence of Panassiuk and said: "He [Panassiuk] is always shouting at everybody, including myself—such is his manner; as to your punishment, you will hear from me in a few hours. Good-bye." Jabotinsky decided not to wait for Neidgard's decision, took a cab to the railroad station, and bought a ticket to St. Petersburg.[9]

Except for a cousin (a student at a dental school), Jabotinsky knew in St. Petersburg only one person, and that by correspondence: a young Jewish lawyer, Nikolas V. Sorin, who had written to him about a certain literary anthology to which Jabotinsky contributed poetry (*Petersburgsky Sbornik*). Almost directly from the railway station, Jabotinsky went to 11 Pushkinskaya Street where Sorin lived, and was received with the utmost friendliness.[10] Since Jabotinsky had no right to live in St. Petersburg, Sorin found him a hotel whose owner had a permanent arrangement with the police: in consideration of a substantial bribe they never interfered with his Jewish guests. Later, Jabotinsky "legalized" his sojourn in St. Petersburg by registering as Sorin's "domestic servant."

Shortly before Jabotinsky's arrival, Sorin succeeded in obtaining from the Tsarist administration a license (then very difficult to get) for the publication of a new monthly, *Yevreyskaya Zhisn* (Jewish Life), which he intended to convert into a serious organ of Zionist thought. Early in 1905, a weekly, *Khronika Yevreyskoy Zhisni* (Chronicle of Jewish Life), was added to the monthly. Banned by the administration in 1906, the weekly reappeared under the name *Yevreysky Narod* (Jewish People) and, in 1907, under the name *Rasswyet* (Dawn). It existed, with interruptions, until 1934—in St. Petersburg, Moscow, Berlin, and Paris—playing a tremendous role in the evolution of Zionist thought and action; most of the time it was closely connected with Jabotinsky.

Sorin immediately introduced Jabotinsky to the staff of the new publication. From that day on, Jabotinsky became one of the mainstays of the monthly and later of the weekly as well. "What was Jabotinsky doing in *Rasswyet*? Everything that was necessary," testifies S. K. Gepstein.[11] He was a leading member of the editorial board, the initiator of and the daring skirmisher in almost all Zionist political campaigns. His articles were avidly read and commented upon by the entire Zionist family in Russia. The struggle against assimilationists and semi-assimilationists of every brand; victorious duels with the Bund; molding the ideological foundations of

Jewish national policy in Russia and of the program for practical work in Palestine—in all this great and constructive collective effort of the St. Petersburg organ, Jabotinsky's personal note merged harmoniously with the rest but was clearly discernible, strongly individualistic, with a peculiar and inimitable timbre of its own. Dr. Julius Brutzkus, himself one of the pillars of the St. Petersburg *Rasswyet*, formulated the division of work among the two mainstays of the paper— A. D. Idelson (who in 1905 became chief editor) and Jabotinsky—as follows: "Idelson devoted all his spiritual forces to the exposing of the fantastic abnormalcy of our [Jewish] life. He was clearing the field for new ideas, new realistic goals. The positive part of the work was taken over, in the main, by Jabotinsky. He acquainted the Jewish public with the struggle of other nations for their existence and with European methods of this struggle for real interests. . . . Jabotinsky's brilliant preaching of Jewish national renaissance was always preceded by profound study of this problem in other peoples' history. . . . Jabotinsky had become the indefatigable political tutor of Russian Jewry."[12]

Tsarist censorship often made life difficult for *Yevreyskaya Zhisn* and *Rasswyet*. But, testifies Sorin, the censors had a high opinion of Jabotinsky's literary talents and greatly enjoyed reading his articles. "When, as often happened, the red ink of the censorship was about to obliterate an editorial, I more than once ascribed its authorship to Jabotinsky, and the censors always yielded in order not to grieve their favorite," recalls Sorin.

The Orator

In St. Petersburg, Jabotinsky very soon established his reputation as an exceptionally daring and powerful orator. The Russian capital liked and appreciated good oratory, but was very hard to please. The best speakers of the country—F. I. Roditchev, V. A. Maklakov, A. S. Zarudny, A. F. Kerensky, N. P. Karabtchevsky, O. O. Grusenberg—either lived or were often heard there. To emulate them was not an easy task.

The St. Petersburg Jewish community at large first took notice of the orator Jabotinsky at the memorial meeting for Theodor Herzl in the Great Synagogue in 1904. There, Jabotinsky read his powerful *Hesped* poem and then delivered a speech on Herzl (both were later published in the June issue of *Yevreyskaya Zhisn*). He fascinated and conquered the audience. Since then no hall in St. Petersburg was considered too large for a lecture or speech by Jabotinsky.[13]

One of the most dramatic demonstrations of his great ascendancy over mass audiences was Jabotinsky's performance at the huge public meeting arranged by the Zionists at the large hall called *Soliany Gorodok* (Salt Town) in the winter of 1905. Thousands packed the hall to protest against the recent wave of government-sponsored pogroms. The atmosphere was stormy. Everyone in the audience was united in condemnation of the reactionary policy of the government. But the ominous silence of the Russian Liberal and Socialist circles with regard to the pogroms was considered a "taboo" topic among "progressive" Jewish society. It was M. M. Ussishkin who launched a frontal attack in this delicate field: "The followers of Marx and Lassalle will forget about the sufferings of the people which produced these leaders just as easily as the followers of Jesus Christ and the Apostle Paul have forgotten their origin." Social-Democrats and Bundists, who constituted a considerable group among the audience, raised a storm of indignant and riotous protest; Zionists were no less turbulent in their refutation of the Leftists' reproaches. The incoherent uproar of the public was deafening and steadily growing: the hall resembled a Bedlam. Everybody considered the meeting as hopelessly disrupted. At the very climax of the hysterical din, there appeared, far above the incensed crowd, the stocky figure of Jabotinsky: one foot on the shoulder of Victor Kugel, the tallest student of the entire St. Petersburg University, whose nickname was "a Jew-and-a-half," and the other on the shoulder of the six-footer Max Soloveitchik. The diapason of his first word—his beloved *Basta*—was powerful enough to overcome the uproar, and when everybody realized that it was Jabotinsky speaking, complete silence prevailed.

Jabotinsky boldly elaborated Ussishkin's challenging theme. Only two days before the meeting, the two Russian Socialist parties—the Social-Democrats and the Socialist-Revolutionaries— had published a manifesto accusing the government of all possible crimes, without even mentioning the murder of Jews in a hundred cities of slaughter. Fully dominating the subdued audience, Jabotinsky delivered a fiery indictment of the Socialist and Liberal circles for hushing up the Jewish tragedy: "People have tried to comfort us by telling us that there were no workers among those who murdered us. Perhaps. Perhaps it was not the proletariat who made pogroms on us. But the proletariat did to us something worse than that: they *forgot* us. *That* is a real pogrom."[14]

The impression produced by Jabotinsky's speech was overwhelming. N. Sorin reports that he received the stormy plaudits of the entire audience.[15]

Along similar lines, and with the same staggering impact, Jabotinsky delivered his speech at the crowded protest meeting called by the leaders of the Russian intelligentsia in the hall of the Tenishev School. The chairman was the noted Socialist writer and humanitarian, V. A. Miakotin; his colleagues in the presidium were the best representatives of Russian literature, press, and political parties; the audience was, however, 80 per cent Jewish. The most eloquent speakers of that time—Zarudny, Miakotin, Grusenberg—addressed the enthusiastically responsive public. Jabotinsky's speech provoked consternation. He started by stressing active Jewish participation in the liberation movement, hand in hand with the Russian revolutionaries. But the Russian intelligentsia never paid much attention to Jewish sufferings. Enumerating, one by one, the most terrifying chapters of the Jewish tragedy during the last four decades, Jabotinsky concluded each chapter with the refrain: "Where have you been then, you, the Russian progressive intelligentsia?"[16]

The impression produced by this powerful challenge was tremendous.

Not less impressive was Jabotinsky's oratorical performance at a meeting of Jewish lawyers called in this stormy period at the house of the noted lawyer M. E. Sheftel. The Zionists were accused of an "emigrant mentality": while living in Russia, they were permanently "sitting on their suitcases" and were thus excluding themselves from the common effort in favor of building a free Russia. Jabotinsky's fiery reply subdued—if not convinced— the opponents. The noted Russian-Jewish writer Ossip Dymov, a non-Zionist, who was present at that gathering, gives an enthusiastic report of Jabotinsky's long speech, which was avidly listened to and applauded by the entire audience. The host Sheftel—a staunch anti-Zionist—smilingly acknowledged Jabotinsky's oratorical superiority: "We lawyers have already heard plenty of good speeches; speeches impress us very little; but oratory of such kind —this is outstanding, indeed. . . ." And he said to Sorin: "A pity that he is a Zionist. . . . However, he is yet so young, almost a boy. . . . Either he will mend his ways—and then he will be ours, or, if he will stick to his Zionism, he will be heir to Herzl."[17]

Jabotinsky's colleagues on the *Rasswyet* editorial board vividly remember an intimate supper at the Northern Hotel in St. Petersburg on the night Count Paolo Trubetskoy's famous monument of Tsar Alexander III was unveiled. They gathered to watch through the hotel windows the ceremony of the monument's illumination. Everybody was in high spirits after a fine supper and a few drinks, and it somehow happened that Jabotinsky—half-earnestly, half-jokingly—made a political speech, in which he gave an impressive and masterful picture of contemporary Russia. The most striking feature of this speech was that he divided it into four sections, delivering each of them in a different language: in Russian, Italian, French, and Hebrew. Not all present understood every language; but, A. M. Soloveitchik and S. K. Gepstein recall, his elocution was so expressive, his voice so infectious, his gestures so eloquent, that they followed him easily.

In 1904 and during the first months of 1905, Jabotinsky's more or less permanent residence was St. Petersburg. He was busy on journalistic and editorial work in the monthly *Yevreyskaya Zhisn* and the weekly *Khronika Yevreyskoy Zhisni* where his was the main responsibility. But in the second half of 1905, when the editorship was largely taken over by A. D. Idelson who came for this purpose from Moscow, Jabotinsky was released by the Zionist leadership for extensive propaganda trips. He became a "traveling salesman" of Zionism, a "permanent inhabitant of railroads," as he put it in his *Autobiography*.

"When I was young, there was an entire category of people who lived more in railway carriages than at home; or, to be more exact, they had no home at all at that time, so that one should say: they lived more on the railroads than in hotels. . . . For people of this category many notions were just inexistent: what is 'far'? and what means 'to be tired'? or 'out of the way'? One of them was traveling with me from St. Petersburg [in the North] to Baku [in the Caucasus]. On the station Mineralny Vodr he received a telegram: 'After Baku, immediately to Zhitomir [Ukraine].' He glanced at it, yawned and telegraphed: 'All right.' "

These excerpts from "Fairy Vagabunda" give a vivid picture of the hectic life of a "Zionist salesman." It was the life Jabotinsky was leading in those years. In his article "Your New Year," written on January 1, 1908, he gave an exact account of how he spent the previous four New Year's Eves: January 1, 1904 he was in a railway car near the station of Luga; January 1, 1905, in the car somewhere north of Dvinsk; January 1,1906, in the car near Berditchev; January 1, 1907, in the car somewhere near Rovno.[18] There was hardly a town in the vast and densely populated Pale of Jewish settlement, in the provinces of Lithuania, Volhynia, Podolia, Kiev, where he would not have delivered a lecture, or participated in a debate with assimilationist or Socialist opponents—and not once, but several times. The owner of a Vilno hotel reminded him on one occasion that it was the fifty-fifth time that he had stayed at his place. Together with I. A. Rosov, he visited all the Jewish communities along the Volga River. A few months were spent in Odessa, where the administration had apparently forgotten the political "crime" which forced him to escape to St. Petersburg in 1903. Jabotinsky himself reminded the police of his troublesome existence at a mass meeting shortly before the 1905 revolution: he concluded his speech with his favorite expression *Basta*, addressed to the Tsarist regime—and paid for this pleasure with a relatively brief visit to the Odessa prison. A second time he was arrested at Kherson for participation in an illegal Zionist gathering.[19] Such incidents belonged to the routine of Russian political life.

In the provinces, every lecture by Jabotinsky was an event of great significance. Friend and foe alike came to hear him: many were carried away by his compelling eloquence. For some years he was under the strong influence of the Italian school in oratory: fervent, stirring, passionate; lavishly using every possible modulation of his rich and expressive voice; appealing not merely to the mind, but also very much to the soul and sentiment; bent on the striking effect of a well-turned phrase or slogan. All this was new and fascinating and made Jabotinsky the idol of Jewish audiences throughout the Pale of Jewish settlement and beyond it. Zalman Shazar (Rubashev), now a *Mapai* member of the *Knesset* and of the Jewish Agency Executive, told this writer that even now he "remembers every word" of Jabotinsky's memorial speech on Herzl, held in the synagogue of Vilno in 1907.[20] According to I. Grinbaum, Jabotinsky was at that time the "most beloved child" of the entire Zionist movement in Russia: "everybody admired him and nourished the highest expectations for his future. Everything was his for the asking."[21] Particularly enthusiastic was the youth. J. Sprinzak, now the Speaker of the *Knesset* and at that time one of the exponents of the *Zeirei Zion* movement (a precursor of both *Hapoel Hazair* and *Poalei Zion*), told this writer that in 1905, when he first met Jabotinsky in Grodno, he suggested that Jabotinsky become its leader. "Is this movement already in existence?" was Jabotinsky's first question. When Sprinzak answered that it had begun to crystallize, Jabotinsky retorted: "I am not the man to continue something that is already existing; either I will create a movement myself, or I will simply write and give lectures, just as I am doing now."[22]

Sprinzak did not like this answer at all. It was, however, indicative of the self-assurance of the young Jabotinsky. In fact, until 1925, he never tried either to "create a movement by himself" or to join any particular faction in

Zionism. He unreservedly devoted himself to an uphill struggle for "Zionism without any adjectives" as he used to say, and against "the foes of Zion."

The main target of Jabotinsky's crusades, both oral and publicistic, were the Jewish assimilationists, and even more the Jewish Socialist Bund.

Jabotinsky conceded that at that time there already was no longer a "pure" assimilationist camp in St. Petersburg. The anti-Zionist group around M. M. Vinaver and H. B. Sliosberg and their weekly *Voskhod* were already fully aware that Russia was not France or Germany, and that "Russians of the Mosaic Faith" had no place in the Russian-Jewish community. But they were not ready to draw consequences from this state of affairs and to put forward any program of Jewish national demands; they were still passionately committed to the elementary slogan of civic equality only and were bitterly opposed to any concept of national rights for the Jews. The *Rasswyet* staff used to call them "National-Assimilationists."

The program of the Bund was more articulate. It not only recognized the fact of a distinct Jewish nationality, but also contained the demand for "cultural autonomy," which was based on the teachings of both the noted Austrian Socialist theoretician Rudolf Springer (Karl Renner) and the "bourgeois" historian S. M. Dubnov. "No progressively minded bourgeois could write an article or make a speech without compliments for the mighty proletarian movement," Jabotinsky recalled. He, however, had the *chutzpah* (daring) to describe the historical function of the Bund as a kind of "bridge" to carry the Jewish workers from pure Marxism to pure Zionism. It was his contention that "as a national Jewish party, the Bund had accomplished its mission . . . and is doomed to stagnation; there is no more sense in its existence, no chance for development." At the same time, Jabotinsky did not underestimate the positive role the Bund played in the early years of its existence: "As far as political alertness and physical courage is concerned, it undoubtedly heightened the spirit of the Jewish working masses and through them of the entire nation; it has thus written into our history splendid pages of heroism and it would be foolish not to bow before them with deference and gratitude. . . . But all this has already been accomplished; the Bund has nothing more to offer; it has outlived its social usefulness."[23]

In his struggle with the Socialist Bund over its national program, Jabotinsky could not possibly avoid the more general issue of socialism as such.

As mentioned before, Jabotinsky returned from Italy imbued with the teachings of socialism. However, even before he became a Zionist, he never joined any Socialist party and never engaged in any form of Socialist propaganda. He had to give an explanation for this apparent contradiction between his creed and his actions, and tried to do so in one of his "Sketches Without a Title."

"One can be deeply conscious of his Socialism," he wrote, "and still realize that there are many grave problems besides Socialism, and not only in the field of pure culture, science, art and poetry, but just in the field of social creativeness. . . . I humbly submit that according to the spirit and the letter of the Socialist creed, the mission of Socialism is limited to the solution of one single problem—the problem of the full product of human labor; and all other reforms, beginning with the equality of women and ending with disarmament, international courts and even federation of states, can and will be achieved independently, still within the framework of capitalist economy."[24]

Simultaneously, Jabotinsky started to revise the orthodox Socialist dogma on the value and future of the various classes of society. In his polemics with the Bund, he still admitted that "objectively, the proletariat is the bearer of the future Socialist upheaval."[25] But writing about Herzl, he pointedly stressed that Herzl occupied "one of the first places in the glorious list of the great men of the *tiers état*" and continued: "From the fact that you and I foresee the arrival of a time when this class will have to yield its dominance to another, more numerous layer of society, it does not follow at all that we have the right to forget the progressive role the bourgeoisie has played in world history. . . . And it would be utterly naive to think that this role has already been played to the very end and that there is nothing more left for classical 'liberalism' to accomplish on earth. I submit, for instance, that there is as yet no country in the world where the best ideals of classical liberalism have been fully implemented; and I even dare to believe that not only in 1923 [the deadline foreseen in Herzl's *Altneuland*], but in 1950 as well, a good fifty per cent of the civilized world of that epoch will still be only dreaming of and longing for a complete fulfilment of a genuine bourgeois liberalism."[26]

Maturing

Jabotinsky's travels through the centers of Jewish mass settlement were a great spiritual experience for him. "A new world was revealed to me in Vilno. . . . It was a kind of university for a man of my background, who until then had not even breathed the atmosphere of Jewish cultural tradition, who did not even suspect that there existed such an atmosphere in God's world. . . . I saw a Jewish world, autonomous in the literal sense of this term, governed by internal laws of its own, and connected with Russia politically only, but not spiritually. . . . Yiddish—a powerful instrument of thought and culture, not merely a 'jargon' as in Odessa or St. Petersburg; Hebrew as a spoken language used by the daughters of Itzhak Goldberg [noted Zionist leader]; poems by Bialik, Tchernikhovsky, Cohen and Schneur directly influenced the growing generation." He now looked at the Jewish masses whom he was meeting during his travels with different eyes than in 1898, when passing through the densely populated Jewish communities of Galicia and Hungary on his way to Switzerland. He saw now not only misery and ugliness, but also spiritual greatness which impressed him deeply.

It was a busy and difficult life, this life of a traveling Zionist propagandist. But Jabotinsky obviously enjoyed every bit of it. In a letter from Vilno, dated April 3, 1906, he exuberantly told M. M. Ussishkin: "In a few days I may go to Zhitomir. . . . On the whole, I am traveling a lot. It is a gay time now, and if only we had our [all-Russian Zionist] convention, we could conquer the entire world!"

Then came a time when Jabotinsky somehow got tired of and even disgusted with his oratorical successes. He began to realize that his influence on his audiences was largely due to the skill of his delivery rather than to the persuasiveness of his arguments; and he bitterly resented this state of affairs. He did not want to be looked upon as a mere artful performer, a highly successful prestidigitator, admired for his mastery of words and not for the justice and greatness of the truth of which he was the bearer. He felt that the "Italian school" of oratory was "too beauteous," often substituting form for content. And he started deliberately to curb his eloquence, to speak in a more restrained, less flowery manner, to avoid impassioned appeals to his listeners, to present his case in a matter-of-fact way. He knew that thereby he was depriving himself of a great deal of popular enthusiasm. But he wanted it so. He once told Gepstein, half-jokingly, half-seriously: "Yesterday I spoke at a meeting where in the first rows there were sitting 400 adoring college girls with sumptuous hairdos. Basta! From now on I shall speak in such a manner that my lectures will be attended by not more than forty Jews, who jointly would have a total of only forty hairs."[27]

The "new look" began not only to dominate Jabotinsky's oratory but also his writings. They were growing more serious. It was not that deliberate, ponderous, make-believe earnestness which is bound to be both dull and unconvincing. The new quality of Jabotinsky's writing arose from the simple fact that the things he was now writing about really mattered to him. He was no more that Altalena who so easily and often flippantly could compose hundreds of feuilletons and articles on scores of topics, each one interesting and stimulating. In his largely autobiographical article (written in 1908) "Your New Year," Jabotinsky reminded his contemporaries in Odessa of this "nice, naive period five years ago": "You expected every day something great and joyful. Like children, you fussed a lot and got excited. Your inner flame grew hotter and brighter every day, and there was no such trifle for which you did not have enough ardor and which you would not debate with passionate eagerness. Everything seemed terribly important, everything played a part in your life." Throughout this tirade, Jabotinsky used the pronoun "you"; yet more accurate would have been the pronoun "we," because this characteristic fully applied to himself as well until the year 1903.

There was a lot in common between Jabotinsky and his readers of those happy times. They all shared an indiscriminate ardor for everything. But since everything seemed to be equally important, *nothing* was of genuine, deeply personal concern to him. Even when crusading for or against some idea, he was doing it mostly because his was a fighting and passionate nature and he was enjoying the very process of intellectual fencing. In fact, his attitude was that of mental curiosity or infatuation. The objects of this infatuation were many, diversified, and changing; therefore, none of them really mattered. They were sufficiently interesting to produce many scintillating feuilletons, but his concern for them was skin-deep. There was no backbone in the motley variety of his interests.

Zionism imperiously and tyrannically invaded this medley world of intellectual flirtation. It drastically changed Jabotinsky's entire outlook and filled him with a new spirit. Jabotinsky the Zionist had an idea and an ideal to convey, a truth to announce, a gospel to preach—something holy and beautiful, all-pervading, overriding everything else in the world. Of course, there were other problems and ideas—right and wrong ones, good and bad, magnificent and ugly. But to Jabotinsky they all became merely components of an overall picture, the center of which was Zionism. This new sense of dedication decisively influenced his entire personality and bearing in this crucial period of his life. His colleagues on *Rasswyet* did not fail to notice a marked change in his demeanor. He remained gay and easygoing, always willing and eager to participate in any escapade, responsive to a good joke; just as before, he enjoyed the company of his friends and comrades, Jews and non-Jews alike. But there was in him something—Dr. M. S. Soloveitchik* told this writer—that prevented familiarity: one could be friends with Jabotinsky, but not chummy. There was always a feeling of distance. Not that he was in any sense haughty or forbidding. But the pointed courtesy for which he was noted was indicative of a deep-seated, intense respect for other people, as well as of personal reserve. As Dr. Soloveitchik penetratingly formulated, even his closest friends could never forget that "they must every time knock at his door and obtain a special ticket to enter his world."[28] To Jabotinsky, his newly born faith was something so precious and sublime that it had to be approached with the utmost deference and care—by others, and by himself.

This attitude left a deep imprint on his writings. Beneath their usual brilliancy, they acquired the underlying mark of passionate earnestness; without losing a shred of their elegance, they were permeated by intense missionary zeal. Hardly any writer in Russia exceeded him in ease and familiarity of style, in perspicacity of expression, and in simplicity and gracefulness of language. He wrote a fine, clear, meticulous script, revealing the neat precision and beauty of a demanding and esthetic mind, fully aware that each word counted, as indeed it did. His articles were usually richly documented, but he presented his data not as dry facts, but as muscle reinforcing a point of view. Many among his writings were really sculptural essays on vital problems of Russian Jewry.

Some admirers of Jabotinsky's literary talent looked at this new quality of his style with mixed feelings. They regretted the disappearance of the sparkling lightness and carefree casualness of his pre-Zionist era; they felt that much of his specific charm was irretrievably lost with this new earnestness. Even some leading Zionists shared this view. A. D. Idelson, the chief editor of *Rasswyet*, once told Jabotinsky: "Please don't write intelligent articles, write brilliant ones." Repeating to this writer this advice of an

---

*At that time Jabotinsky's colleague on the *Rasswyet* editorial board and now Director of the Jerusalem Radio.

older colleague, Jabotinsky deeply resented it. He could not help writing brilliantly—just as a true singer can't help singing beautifully —but he hated the idea that the stylistic elegance of his articles should overshadow their content and message. Now he did not care any more for the approval of literary gourmets or for the glory of a journalistic wonder boy. The *Great Love* had come into his life.

Though deeply romantic in his innermost self, Jabotinsky was chaste and meticulously restrained in displaying his feelings. He hated sentimental outpourings and loud manifestations of love. There are, however, in some of his articles a few breakthroughs, dramatically revealing the almost religious profundity and intensity of his Zionist faith.

In his article "In the Days of Mourning," written in 1906, the first anniversary of the 1905 wave of pogroms, he wrote:[29]

I have no remedies against the pogrom—I have my faith and my craft. . . . My faith tells me that the day will come when my people will be great and free, and through the sweat of her sons Palestine will scintillate with all the rays of her rainbow nature. My craft is the craft of one of the masons building a new Temple for my supreme God, whose name is—Jewish People. When lightning cuts through the black skies of the alien land, I order my heart not to beat and my eyes not to look: I add one more brick and this is my only answer to the roar of destruction.

In the article "Your New Year," he said about himself:

For me there exists only my tomorrow, only my dawn, in which I believe with the whole palpitation of my being, and I need nothing else. . . . Once I felt strongly the beauty of a free-lance, a man above and beyond the rank and file, having no allegiance, without obligation toward anyone on earth, impartial toward his own people and to strangers alike, pursuing the way of his own will over the heads of kin and strangers. Today I also see beauty in that. But for myself, I gave it up. In my people there was a custom, cruel but profound: when a woman gave herself to her husband, she cut off her hair. As a common rite it is savage. But there does exist, though rarely, such a degree of love that one wants to surrender everything, even one's beauty. Perhaps I too could soar in glorious freedom, sing songs of beauty, bathe in the cheap favor of your applause. But I do not want it. I cut off my hair because I love my faith. I love my faith, in it I am happy, as you never were happy and never will be, and I want nothing else.

In his article "Jews in Russian Literature," he told an assimilated Socialist writer of Jewish origin who enthusiastically pledged allegiance to the
Russian people and Russian culture:[30]

If we speak of a personal frame of mind, I would like to point out to you one
more detail of it: *our* hardened, condensed, cold-mad determination to stick it out
on the post the others have deserted, and to serve the Jewish cause with whatever is
possible—with our heads and hands and teeth, with truth and untruth, with honor
and revenge, at any price. You went over to the rich neighbor—we will turn our
backs on his beauty and kindness; you worship his values and have left our little
patrimony to rot—we will clench our teeth and from the depths of our soul will cry
out to the world that every Hebrew-speaking tot is to us dearer than anything on
earth wherever your masters may live, from Aachen to Moscow. We will exaggerate
our hatred to make it help our love; we will strain our sinews to the very last limit,
because we are few and every one of us has to work for ten others, because you have
run away and others will follow you on the same way. Yet, somebody has to remain
. . . if only we do not break our backs, we shall try to do the job for you as well.

This new frame of mind changed everything in Jabotinsky's journalistic
climate.

During his St. Petersburg period, Jabotinsky continued writing for
the Russian press. His own account of this chapter of his journalistic life
is good-humoredly deprecatory. In the moderately liberal *Rus* (which paid
him the then exceptionally high salary of four hundred rubles [two hundred dollars] for eight articles a month), the chief editor, Alexey Suvorin,
often kept Jabotinsky's manuscripts in his desk drawer instead of publishing
them, because they did not conform with the "policy of the paper."[31] Jabotinsky hoped that in a more "radical" paper he would fare better and when,
in 1904, he received an invitation from Professor L. V. Khodsky, the editor
of a new St. Petersburg daily, *Nasha Zhisn* (Our Life), to join the editorial
staff, he eagerly accepted it. But this new journalistic venture proved to be
even more disappointing. *Nasha Zhisn* paid regularly and well, but most
of his articles never appeared in print. To the paper's somewhat primitive
radicalism, Jabotinsky's more subtle and sometimes ironical handling of
political matters was unacceptable. After his sojourn in the Odessa prison
(because of the *basta* incident), Jabotinsky wrote that the entire town was
laughing at the stupidity of the police; the editors refused to publish the article, arguing that in such a case one must not laugh but indignantly protest.

In reply to Jabotinsky's astonished query: "Why, then, have you invited me?" Mrs. Yekaterina Kuskova, a leading member of the editorial board, innocently explained: "Mr. Jabotinsky, yours is a beautiful literary style, and we expected your brilliant pen to expound the ideas that will be submitted to you."

To the fiercely independent Jabotinsky this was both an insult and a lesson. He rushed to Suvorin and repentantly asked: "Would you take me back? You at least don't consider me to be just a gramophone record!" Suvorin's answer was: "With pleasure." Jabotinsky gratefully commented that the editor of *Rus*, being a personality himself, duly respected the other man's personality; when Jabotinsky in his articles used the expression "We Jews," Suvorin did not feel that this was a violation of the best traditions and principles of the Russian liberal press as did more "progressive" editors.

Jabotinsky wondered "who spread the rumor that at that time I allegedly occupied a high position in the general Russian press" and asserted that this was "an exaggeration, one of the legends about me, which were in circulation." His contention was that in Odessa and in South Russia in general, he was popular indeed, predominantly in Jewish circles; but he "did not conquer St. Petersburg." This self-appraisal of his journalistic achievements in Russia's capital does honor to Jabotinsky's modesty, but is highly misleading. There was no publicist in the Russia of that troubled period who could have boasted of "conquering" or dominating the literary world of St. Petersburg. And Jabotinsky certainly did not aspire to this position. When he settled in the Russian capital, the Russian press and its interests were already a sideline in his journalistic activities. His main allegiance belonged to *Yevreyskaya Zhisn* and to Jewish and Zionist topics. *Rus* and *Nasha Zhisn* were foreign, though friendly and accessible, territory. He knew it himself, and the editors of these Russian papers probably felt it instinctively. There was no genuine congeniality between his sphere of interests and theirs. Jabotinsky was already distant and aloof in regard to Russian problems as such. There was a kind of transparent glass wall between him and the Russian press. A Suvorin could be broad-minded enough to have permitted the use of "We Jews" in some of Jabotinsky's articles, but to "conquer" St. Petersburg's press with a "We Jews" approach was, of course, sheer impossibility.

It is, therefore, all the more remarkable that, in spite of this handicap, Jabotinsky succeeded in becoming a widely published and widely read "Russian journalist."

Highly appreciated and much commented upon was a series of challenging articles by Vladimir J. published in *Rus* in 1904. The following hypothetical question was put to a group of intellectuals: Suppose that all the books in the world were to be burned save ten—which books and authors should be picked for survival?

The Old and New Testament were accepted unanimously. A lively discussion developed on the candidacy of Homer, whom some of the participants tried to discard as "obsolete" and no more in harmony with the spiritual world of a modern reader. He was, however, confirmed after a passionate plea by his proponent who stressed the eternal epic beauty of Homer's characters who "knew how to laugh and to eat"—qualities thoroughly forgotten by the present generation. Boccaccio's *Decameron* was chosen, after spirited debate, as a powerful and convincing rebuttal of the Church's philosophy of the inherent sinfulness of joy and love in human life. Unopposed was the choice of Shakespeare, his gallery of human characters being considered the most "encyclopedic" in world literature. *The Arabian Nights* was selected as the most colorful expression of the "fantasy and storytelling" element in life and literature—an element which has become so rare in the writings of modern authors. In the group's decision to select Byron, the determining factor was his protest, the outcry of a strong personality against the conventional lies of society. The candidacies of Alfred de Musset as a poet of love and of Jonathan Swift's *Gulliver's Travels* as a satire were both discarded in favor of Heinrich Heine, whose love poems were great in their tenderness and whose irony was biting in its crusading spirit. Edgar Allan Poe, even though a literary favorite of Jabotinsky's, was rejected after much discussion: it was considered improper to include in a highly selective list of ten books and authors "intended to serve best the education of the human race for a healthy and sensible life, works written to satisfy unhealthy and irrational tastes of a perverted generation." Instead, Dostoyevsky was chosen unanimously. No opposition was raised against Cervantes whose *Don Quixote* was recognized as the symbol of the human capacity for chivalry and self-sacrifice for an ideal. This was the ninth book on the list. For the tenth place were proposed Goethe, Dante, Shelley, Voltaire, Tolstoi, Schiller, and Russian epics. The competition was strong and fierce. It was finally decided to call upon the public to make their choice.

These articles were published in 1905 in St. Petersburg as a separate pamphlet entitled *Ten Books*. The thirty-six-page pamphlet makes interesting reading even now. It is lively and gives evidence of a wide range of literary interests.

Very popular were the political "fables" in verse (an imitation of Krylov's classical fables), which Jabotinsky used to publish in *Rus* over his full signature—until the censor started threatening to close down the paper; the appearance of each of those fables was the talk of the town. Salzman later printed a collection of the fables, of which unfortunately not a single copy has been preserved.

Leading Russian writers highly appreciated Jabotinsky's role in Russian literature and deeply regretted his gradual but steady withdrawal from the Russian cultural scene.

In 1910, A. I. Kuprin, then at the peak of his talent and influence, told a group of young Zionists in Odessa who discussed with him the merits of the Russian-Jewish writer, Semion Yushkevitch: "Yushkevitch you can keep for yourself. But there is another Odessan—a genuine talent who could grow to become an eagle in Russian literature—him you have just stolen from us, simply stolen. . . . And, my God, what have you done with him, with this young eagle? You dragged him into the Jewish Pale of settlement, you have cut his wings, and soon he will probably become a hen which will be cackling just like the others! A pity! A great loss to Russian literature which counts so few authors possessing his style, his acumen, his great understanding of our soul."[32] The same regret was expressed by another outstanding Russian novelist, Leonid Andreyev, who wrote to Jabotinsky from Finland in 1912 that it was a pity that "you have half-way or completely abandoned Russian literature, which is so much in need of you." Maxim Gorki wrote to O. O. Grusenberg on September 20, 1913: "Jabotinsky is a wonderfully interesting man in his [literary] works."[33] M. Ossorgin, Jabotinsky's colleague on the *Russkiya Vyedomosti* (Russian Gazette), the leading Moscow daily, and a first-class novelist in his own right, wrote in 1930, on the occasion of Jabotinsky's fiftieth birthday, that he "was sincerely mad that national Jewish affairs have snatched Jabotinsky away from Russian literature"—that he had become "for us Russians a foreigner— though a polite and well-disposed one. . . . There are in Russian literature and journalism very many Jews living—and fervently living—with Russian interests only. With all my fullest respect for them, I would still take a large percentage of them, tie them together with a string and deliver them to you, Jews, in exchange for this one coldly amiable Jabotinsky."[34]

FIVE

IN RUSSIAN POLITICS

The Struggle for Equality

Uppermost in the mind of Russian Jewry at the beginning of kJ the twentieth century was the problem of civic equality. In Tsarist Russia, the Jews were in many vital respects second-class citizens, deprived of such basic privileges as the right to live wherever they chose, to have their children freely admitted to state schools and universities, to be represented in the civil service and the officer corps. When, as a consequence of a lost war with Japan, the internal tension burst out and revolutionary strikes disorganized the country, the Tsar and his advisers saw themselves constrained to relax autocracy. In 1905, elections to a Duma (Parliament) were announced, although on a very narrow suffrage. It seemed as if the general political climate of the country was to become somewhat milder, affording some liberty of self-organization. In March, 1905, a convention of public-spirited Jewish personalities assembled at Vilno. There, a non-partisan political organization was formed under the name "League for the Attainment of Equal Rights for the Jewish People in Russia." The most influential group in the League were the old-time St. Petersburg leaders with assimilationist leanings. But as a tribute to the growing nationalistic spirit, the broadly formulated program of the organization called for "the realization to their full extent of the civil, political and national rights of the Jewish people in Russia."[1] Almost immediately after its creation, the League became the battlefield on which the divergent political forces in Russian Jewry were fighting for their specific interpretation of this program.

There is no record of Jabotinsky's participation in the first Convention of the League, but there is ample evidence of his active interest in its program and progress. At the following conventions of the League, Jabotinsky played an outstanding role in the struggle for a more outspoken nationalistic program.

The major issue facing the second Convention of the League (November 22–25, 1905) was the proposal to call a Jewish Constituent Assembly as the only authoritative body entitled to determine the contents and character of Jewish national demands and action. There was at the beginning considerable opposition to this idea. Jabotinsky was nominated as the main spokesman for the proposal. "The irrepressible Jabotinsky," says Oscar J. Janowsky in his study *The Jews and Minority Rights*, "insisted that the national problem of a people could be formulated only by a constituent assembly; the League could only act as a preparatory body; it must not arrogate to itself the right to speak in the name of the Jewish people."[2] The main stress in Jabotinsky's argumentation was put on the necessity not to get submerged in general Russian politics, not to expect salvation from outside, but to rely first and foremost on self-organization and self-help. "We must concentrate all our forces on a policy which is the only one open to us—on our Jewish internal policy. . . . Let us turn our backs on the outside political world which has long since turned its back on us; let us face internal, national policy only. We have to write a manifesto not to Russian society* but to the Jewish people itself, to call the Jews to a new life, to urge them to take their fate into their own hands."[3]

Jabotinsky carried the day. When it came to a show of hands, all but two delegates voted in favor of a democratically elected All-Russian Jewish Constituent Assembly.

The almost perennial issue before the League's conventions was the problem of the organization of Jewish parliamentary representation. Twelve Jewish deputies, among them five Zionists, were elected to the first Russian Duma (April 27-July 8, 1906). The Zionists and nationalists demanded the establishment of an independent Jewish Parliamentary Club with mandatory discipline in all matters of Jewish interest; joining other parliamentary factions was to be forbidden. The assimilationists were against this "separatism"

---

*Publication of such a manifesto was suggested by those who believed in the solution of the Jewish problem in Russia by Russian progressive forces.

and insisted that much more could be achieved by joining the existing general Russian parties. The latter prevailed at the third Convention of the League in February, 1906. Voicing defiance to this decision, Jabotinsky announced that "nationalists will endeavor to prevent from being elected to the Duma a single Jew who will not bind himself openly and clearly to raise in the Duma the banner of a Jewish party."[4]

At the fourth (and last) Convention (in St. Petersburg, May 9–12, 1906), the question was raised again. This time a majority decided in favor of a "distinct Jewish parliamentary group which works in unison in all questions affecting complete Jewish emancipation." But the assimilationist minority immediately announced their withdrawal from the League. To prevent a split, a new and meaningless resolution was accepted, favoring a parliamentary group "without a stringent discipline."

The Zionists deeply resented this outcome of the Convention. Together with leading Zionist publicists, Jabotinsky came to the conclusion that further cooperation with non-Zionists would only compromise Zionist principles and undermine Zionist influence with the Jewish masses; he was determined to launch a strong movement for the creation of an independent Zionist political party in Russia. "He left the League, and afterwards we, under his influence, decided henceforth to march under our own Zionist banner," recalls S. Gepstein.[5]

Molding the Zionist Political Program

A great, possibly a decisive, role in the political evolution of Russian Zionism was played by the three "conferences of the Zionist press" held at Vilno in 1906–07. They did the ideological spadework, prepared the ground for new ideas and concepts, formulated them in carefully worded draft resolutions. Each one of them can be considered as a spiritual laboratory of creative Zionist thought. S. Gepstein testifies that the initiative of convening the press conferences was Jabotinsky's, and J. Brutzkus confirms that Jabotinsky was "the head and the chief participant of the work" which brought about both the press conferences and later the Helsingfors Convention.[6]

The first conference took place at Landvorovo (near Vilno) on July 7–9, 1906. The three Zionist periodicals (*Yevreyskaya Zhisn*, St. Petersburg, *Dos Yiddishe Folk*, Vilno, and *Glos Zydowsky*, Warsaw) were represented by the best minds in Russian Zionism. The conference worked out a program demanding the recognition of Russian Jewry as a distinct national entity with self-government in all affairs of national life. It also advocated the active participation of the Zionist Organization in Russian politics as an independent body, in defense of the civic and national rights of Russian Jewry.

Jabotinsky actively participated in the work of this first press conference. His personal share in the collective effort which forged what was soon to become known as the "Vilno platform" is, of course, difficult to establish. But he undoubtedly became the leading and most articulate champion and spokesman of this platform in the Zionist ranks.

Aware of the gravity of the political situation in Russia and of the need for a clear-cut Zionist program, an unofficial conference of seventy active Zionist workers was convened in Odessa (July 29–August 1, 1906).[7] At this Convention, Jabotinsky's influence was overwhelming. He gave the report on the chief subject—political action—and submitted, in substance, the platform adopted at the Vilno conference. The gathering was apparently not ripe to take a clear and definite stand on most of these complicated problems. The only question on which it was ready to decide was that of an independent Zionist political party. With few exceptions, all participants favored a strictly Zionist political activity, and a resolution to this effect submitted by Jabotinsky was finally adopted without dissent.

Jabotinsky also actively participated in the second (October, 1906) and third (April, 1907) press conferences.

In June-July, 1906, Jabotinsky published a series of five articles (a total of thirty-seven columns) under the general title "Our Tasks," in which he dealt comprehensively with the problems of civil rights of Russian Jewry, national autonomous rights, national civil rights, forthcoming activities in Russia, and work inside Jewry.[8] This extensive treatise was a lucid and comprehensive presentation of a new Zionist program as conceived by the press conferences.

This program was presented for consideration and decision to the long-awaited Third All-Russian Zionist Convention in Helsingfors, the capital of Finland. This gathering took place in an atmosphere of strong unrest and great expectation among the national minorities of the multi-national Russian Empire. Either from conviction or policy—such demands for political independence would have been high treason—many national groups, for instance the Poles, the Letts, the Ukrainians, were demanding territorial autonomy within the Russian Empire. In the Jewish camp there were various trends in regard to the position the Jewish minority had to take in this struggle for national autonomy. The Bund, while expecting full solution of the Jewish problem from a victory of socialism, demanded autonomy in cultural matters only; the *Folkspartei*, led by the noted Jewish historian S. M. Dubnov, advocated a broader program of national autonomy in Russia as the final answer to all Jewish needs; Zionists, on the other hand, were eagerly debating the question as to whether advocacy of such autonomy was compatible with their then almost Messianic aim of exodus.

It is against this background that the Helsingfors Convention must be viewed.

The Convention met from November 21–27, 1906. It consisted of seventy-two delegates from fifty-six localities. The best minds of the movement attended this historic gathering. Its deliberations culminated in the formulation of a new revolutionary concept of "synthetic Zionism" which organically combined the traditional Zionist negation of the *Galut* with the struggle for Jewish survival and national organization in the countries of dispersion; simultaneously, the necessity of practical colonizing work in Palestine was recognized over and above the political activities of the world movement.

The Helsingfors program was the product of collective thinking and molding by an exceptionally gifted and brilliant group of Russian Zionist intellectuals: A. D. Idelson, Dr. Joseph Lurie, Itzhak Grinbaum, Arnold Seideman, Appolinary Hartglass, Alexander Goldstein, Solomon Gepstein, Daniel Pasmanik, Leo Motzkin, and others. It is, of course, difficult to apportion Jabotinsky's individual share in this collective effort. It can, however, be safely said that the role he played at the Helsingfors Convention was an outstanding and often a predominant one.

In the general debate on the political platform of Zionism he spoke twice. One of the major problems the Convention faced was the place of *Gegenwartsarbeit* (national and political activities in the Diaspora countries) in the Zionist *Weltanschauung*. Leo Motzkin insisted that national action in the countries of dispersion was not a "supplementary means but a primary goal." The majority, however, says Janowsky, "followed Jabotinsky and Pasmanik in admitting only the present value of a national program as an effective means; in principle the old negation of the Diaspora persisted, and national rights were demanded with the full realization that little might be expected of the new claim in the way of solving the Jewish problem."[9] One of the originators and a fervent advocate of the *Gegenwartsarbeit* program, Jabotinsky opposed every attempt to distort the proper correlation of values and factors in the Zionist concept. He also rejected I. Grinbaum's contention that Jewish national renaissance was possible in the *Galut:* "In the *Galut* we don't create any values. . . the only motivation for the necessity of *Gegenwartsarbeit* is the organization of Jewry for national self-help in the direction of exodus." With the same vigor Jabotinsky opposed M. Aleinikov's claim that Zionist work in the Diaspora and Zionist activities in Palestine were on different and fundamentally incompatible levels: "There are no such two levels; one single red thread, leading from Zion to Zion, traverses the entire history of our people, and everything that occurs in Jewish life will sooner or later discharge itself into the channel of Zionism."[10]

This integral philosophy of Zionism prevailed in Helsingfors. It was Jabotinsky who submitted to the Convention the final text of the resolutions formulated by a special committee on *Gegenwartsarbeit.*

He was also the reporter on the highly controversial question of a Zionist tactical platform. Analyzing the realities of the Russian political scene, he advocated an alliance with such ethnic groups which constituted a minority within the country's single territorial units and whose interests were therefore akin to that of the Jewish minority. He insisted that in their struggle for Jewish rights and interests the Zionists must act as an independent party. This party should, however, conduct a separate policy as distinct from other Jewish parties only when working within the Jewish community. On the general political scene, in Russian national or municipal elections, he favored a united Jewish front; joint electoral committees, coalitions, and federations should be sponsored if the candidates proposed by single groups pledged to support a nationalistic program and to champion the establishment of a Jewish parliamentary group in the Duma.[11]

Opponents of Jabotinsky's main thesis advocated the creation of a united Jewish Party with a nationalistic program, which would include non-Zionists of S. Dubnov's *Folkspartei.* They insisted that there was no substantial difference between the demands and slogans of either group. In his concluding speech Jabotinsky stressed that while the slogans might sound identical, Zionists and "just nationalists" were bound to expound them in quite a different way. The latter would present the demands as the final ideal, while the *leitmotif* of Zionist propaganda must be: "Let us struggle for our national rights in Russia, but remember that national rights as such offer no ultimate solution of your national problem, and there is before you still a long and hard way to go. . . . We will often have to quarrel and to fight with the *Folkspartei*—not with their slogans, but with their interpretation of these slogans."[12]

The gist of Jabotinsky's proposals was overwhelmingly accepted by the Convention. It was decided that Zionists must act as an independent party. For specific ends, coalition with other groups was recommended. For election purposes, the Convention favored a united Jewish election committee selected by the Jewish population or by the various parties. Candidates must pledge themselves to join the Jewish parliamentary group.

All his life Jabotinsky remained faithful to the Helsingfors program, though the clamor for its abolition or for substantial changes arose very soon. At the Fourth All-Russian Zionist Convention at The Hague in August, 1907, Dr. D. Pasmanik, Sh. Levin, V. Jacubson, J. Brutzkus, Leo Motzkin, and B. Goldberg demanded, for various reasons, far-reaching amendments to the Helsingfors decisions. Dr. J. Klausner insisted on the complete rejection of any Zionist political activities in the Diaspora. Jabotinsky, who was the reporter on the question of "Independent Zionist action in Russia," strongly defended the Helsingfors program in its totality. In Helsingfors, he said, the Zionists "decided to abandon the boycott of the *Galut* and endorsed a broad system of utilizing the *Galut*. . . . We explained to the masses that we are going to the Duma—at least for the time being—in order to realize not the *aims* but the *prerequisites* of Zionism. . . . Now the masses know that we intend to liquidate the *Galut* not through the deterioration of the *Galut* existence, but through its normalization." Later, answering the numerous objectors to the Helsingfors program, Jabotinsky said: "Listening to many arguments of the opponents of independent Zionist political action, I involuntarily thought that if the spirit of Zionism would come to this hall, it would have uttered the words of Marquis Posa [in Schiller's *Don Carlos*]: 'The times are not ripe for my ideal. I live a citizen of those which are to come.' (*Das Jahrhundert ist meinem Ideal nicht reif. Ich lebe ein Bürger derer, welche kommen werden.*) I see that we are by far not yet ripe for Zionism as a full and unadulterated philosophy (*Weltanschauung*)."

The Convention accepted Jabotinsky's motion to confirm the Helsingfors decisions in full.[13] In his last book *The War and the Jew*, published posthumously in 1942, Jabotinsky stressed that he "would be prepared to sign that program again," with the usual reservation that this program never meant to perpetuate the *Galut* as a normal and everlasting form of Jewish existence.[14]

Electoral Campaigns

In October, 1905, Jabotinsky reached the age of twenty-five, which gave him the right to vote and to be elected to the Russian Duma. Electoral franchise in Russia was then conditional upon either an educational degree (which Jabotinsky did not have as yet, since he had left high school before getting his diploma), or ownership of real estate. Intending to contest the elections in the province of Volhynia, Jabotinsky bought from an old Zionist, Benjamin Melamid, a one-story house in the township of Alexandria and thus became eligible for election to the second Duma. In accordance with the policy he advocated (and which later was officially endorsed by the All-Russian Zionist Convention in Helsingfors), he presented himself openly as a Zionist candidate. In November, 1906, a conference of Zionist clubs convened in the township of Miropol and confirmed Jabotinsky as the Zionist candidate for this province. However, this candidate looked so youthful that on one occasion, when he came to an electoral meeting at which he was supposed to speak and presented his voter's card to the official Russian doorkeeper, the man laughed good-naturedly and told him: "Listen, young fellow, you better stop pretending, go home and do your homework for school—this card is certainly your father's and not yours. . . ." Jabotinsky had to summon witnesses to prove that he was entitled to come in.

When the anti-Zionist Jewish *Folkgroup* in St. Petersburg, headed by such outstanding leaders as M. M. Vinaver and H. B. Sliosberg, learned of Jabotinsky's candidature in Volhynia, all their "pamphlets and leaflets not even for one moment lost sight of their final aim—to defeat Jabotinsky," wrote *Rasswyet* on February 22, 1907. One of their favored arguments was: "It is not permissible to campaign for the Russian Parliament under the Zionist banner; even our progressively minded Russian friends will abandon us, saying: If you are Zionists, why are you demanding civil rights in Russia?" To counter this demagogic propaganda, Jabotinsky rushed to St. Petersburg and mobilized his friends in the press, in particular S. L. Poliakov-Litovtzev, a veteran Zionist and skilled journalist. Poliakov-Litovtzev interviewed the top leaders of the Russian opposition parties—P. M. Milyukov, M. M. Kovalevsky, A. F. Annensky, P. B. Struve, I. V. Zhilkin—and every one of them categorically stated that he would defend Jewish rights irrespective of whom the Jews were going to elect as their representative in the Duma. Jabotinsky published these interviews in the widely read liberal paper Rus. At the same time he published in the St. Petersburg daily *Ryetch*, the official organ of the same "Cadet" (Constitutional Democratic) Party, of which the *Folkgroup* leaders were influential members, "An Open Letter to M. M. Vinaver." In this letter, whose arguments now, almost half a century later, sound as timely and mint-fresh as in January, 1907, Jabotinsky vigorously refuted the allegation that Zionists considered the Jews as "strangers" in the countries of dispersion:[15]

> I never hid my banner and I will never try to hide it; I am a Zionist and I do not conceive of Jewish welfare outside of Zionism. But I don't consider Jews in Russia as strangers or foreigners; our forefathers had been living in many regions of Russia hundreds of years before their present masters arrived there; we have contributed to Russia's economic development, we have created her flourishing commerce in the south-west, we have enlivened and enriched her border towns; our nation has sacrificed many—maybe too many—lives of our youth for her liberation. We are neither newcomers nor foreigners, we are deeply rooted citizens of this country; we wish to bear all the obligations, all the duties that will be imposed on all her citizens, and we demand for ourselves all the rights which will be granted them. But while doing so, we are not going to take an oath, as has been done in the proclamation of your group, that the large masses of the Jewish people "will never leave" the countries where they are dwelling now; we are not going thereby to insult the millions of our emigrants who have been going overseas not only from Russia, but, to no less an extent, also from the ghettos of Galicia where they enjoy equality. . . .
>
> We, Zionists, do not "appeal" to anybody to leave Russia: one has to be completely ignorant of the essence of modern Zionism not to realize that, first of all, we don't believe in any "appeals"—we reckon only with the force of events which is an elemental force; it is this force of events which started the inevitable process of elimination and which is bound to consummate it. And nobody has the right to swear that the Jewish masses will "never" yield to the force of events. . . . And nobody can demand from the Jews to take an oath that they shall remain where they are at any price, even in spite of the elemental force of social circumstances; and nobody is entitled to make their civic equality dependent on taking such an oath. The course of events is being created not by the Jews, and not the Jews are responsible for its implications; full civic equality is being granted not for their renouncing forever, for themselves and for their progeny, the right to ask for traveling papers: their only obligation is conscientiously to serve the country in all fields of civic duty. This is

the sole engagement that will be asked from the Jews by those political parties in Russia which are being led by the ideal of justice.

After the publication of this "Open Letter," which made a great impression in Jewish and non-Jewish circles alike, Jabotinsky returned to Volhynia.

The situation in this province was delicate. The Jews constituted only 13.24 per cent of the population and had to look for electoral alliances. The main non-Jewish groups were the peasants who belonged to an "oppressed class" and therefore enjoyed Jewish sympathy; and the landlords who represented the "dominant" class and were considered as unfit for any partnership. Endeavoring to be realistic in this complicated situation, Jabotinsky induced the first conference of Jewish electoral committees to accept the following tactical line of conduct: in principle, an agreement with the peasants was to be sought; however, should the peasants turn reactionary, an agreement with the landlords was permissible—if the latter would allocate a sufficient number of seats to the peasants.

This apparently sensible and fair decision unleashed a vicious attack in anti-Zionist circles, beginning with the Socialist Bund and ending with the assimilationists of the Jewish *Folkgroup* who, in matters of general Russian politics, followed closely the lead of the bourgeois "Cadet" Party. The Zionists and Jabotinsky personally were accused of preaching a bloc with the landlords against the peasants. Nevertheless, the second conference of the Jewish electoral committees confirmed the decision. The third conference was organized in such a way that Jabotinsky was unable to attend. In his absence, a new line was accepted: electoral agreements are permissible only with such groups which are "not to the right of the 'Cadet' Party."[16]

The campaign against Jabotinsky's candidature was conducted with unparalleled vehemence and hatred. Many years later he still remembered the poisoned atmosphere of this electoral struggle.[17] His typewriter reminded him of

an electoral meeting in Rovno, a list of candidates that included your name, and a room full of people using that name as an imprecation. The type of people? All classes from all walks of life—the pillars of society, the doctors, businessmen and lawyers, as well as the poor carpenters.

Practically all of them rage against you and refuse to work with you. What was your sin at that time? A simple one—you were a Zionist. . . . What does the crowd shout? Everyone yells that you will ruin the Jewish people, bring Zionism into the Duma, and hinder the struggle for equal rights.

Whom do the people want instead of you? A Social-Democrat or perhaps a Bundist who will at least represent the interests of the carpenters? Perish the thought! They want a bourgeois "cadet," probably one less radical than you (you, by that time, had at least been imprisoned in Russian prisons several times). Anyone but a Zionist. Even the carpenters want the bourgeois cadet rather than you at whom the shouts of "down" are hurled. And you, at that time a mere lad, greatly influenced by the surrounding atmosphere and the opinion of a group of people, feel shocked by a group hatred and ask yourself quietly:—Is it a sin to be a Zionist?

Proclamations by some specially established committee appeared in the streets of Rovno with a slogan: "Don't vote for Jabotinsky!" The Bund made common cause with this committee and also published proclamations full of attacks and insinuations against Jabotinsky and the Zionists. Agents of the anti-Jabotinsky committee visited hundreds of Jewish electors, trying to induce them to erase Jabotinsky's name from the voting bulletin and to replace it with the name of an assimilationist candidate.[18]

All these efforts proved to be of no avail. The Jews of Rovno gave Jabotinsky an overwhelming majority and sent him as one of their three representatives to the province's electoral college.[19] But there the situation turned out to be hopeless. It very soon became obvious that no agreement with the peasants was possible. All the sixty-nine peasant "secondary electors" appeared at the electoral assembly adorned with the badges of the reactionary and militantly anti-Semitic "Union of the Russian People." The anti-Zionist Jewish leaders were already prepared to make common cause with a less progressive party than the "Cadets," even with the aristocratic Count Pototzky. All this was of no avail. The peasants and the landlords formed a bloc against the Jews, and all the thirteen Duma deputies elected were extreme reactionaries and anti-Semites.[20]

The second Duma, to which Jabotinsky failed to be elected from Volhynia, was short-lived. It was dissolved on June 3, 1907, and elections to the third Duma were announced for the fall of the same year, on the basis of a new, much more restrictive, electoral law.

Jabotinsky's native city of Odessa was one of the few urban centers where the election of a Jewish deputy seemed to be reasonably sure. Odessa Zionists asked Jabotinsky to be their candidate. Unlike the overwhelming majority of electoral districts, the elections in Odessa were direct ones. The electorate was divided into two *curiae* (divisions): to the first belonged the well-to-do classes, to the second, the less privileged. In the first *curia*, the election of a converted Jewish lawyer, P. J. Pergament (who had also been elected to the second Duma), was considered certain. To the Zionists and nationalists, however, a *meshumed*, who never showed any concern and understanding for Jewish interests and problems, was certainly not a candidate to their heart. They announced Jabotinsky's candidacy in the second *curia*. His competitors were non-Jews: the reactionary and anti-Semitic Count Konovnitzin, the "Cadet" A. Nikolsky, and the Social-Democrat V. Maliantowicz. But his most bitter and vocal opponents were various Jewish groups of anti-Zionist tendencies. The Odessa correspondent of *Rasswyet* reported that "a tripartite alliance is being formed to defeat Jabotinsky; it comprises the higher bourgeoisie, the assimilationist intelligentsia, and the united extreme Leftists of all denominations."[21]

Paradoxically enough, this motley coalition found itself in an unholy alliance with the Tsarist administration of Odessa. For reasons of their own, this administration was doing its very best to silence the press favorable to Jabotinsky and to favor the paper advocating the Socialist candidature. As a result of this policy, Jabotinsky found his lips sealed, so far as press propaganda was concerned, while his Socialist opponents had all the advantages.[22]

This situation bore the expected fruits: on the first ballot, Maliantowicz received 3,898, Count Konovnitzin 3,112, Nikolsky 1,673, and Jabotinsky 1,580 (about one-third of the Jewish vote). No candidate having obtained an absolute majority, a second ballot became unavoidable. Then the administration played its card: they found a legalistic trick by which Maliantowicz was declared ineligible. The voters had to choose between the reactionary Konovnitzin and a progressive candidate. In order not to split the progressive vote, Jabotinsky, who received ninety-three fewer votes than Nikolsky, withdrew in the latter's favor. Nikolsky was thus elected in the second *curia*, while Pergament was victorious in the first.[23] There were no Zionists among the three Jewish representatives in the third Duma.

Having a stable reactionary majority, this Duma was allowed to serve a full five-year term. It was not before the summer of 1912 that the population of Tsarist Russia started preparing for the elections to the fourth Duma. Asked by the Zionists to stand again in Odessa, Jabotinsky advised them to nominate another candidate. But only his name was sufficiently popular in Jewish circles, Zionist and non-Zionist alike.

For electoral purposes, Odessa was again divided into two *curiae*: in the first the Jews constituted about 48 per cent of the electorate, in the second, about 42 per cent. The assimilationists were in favor of a Jewish candidature in the first *curia*; their nominee was the noted St. Petersburg lawyer H. B. Sliosberg. The All-Jewish Electoral Committee, however, unanimously (with one abstention) decided to nominate V. Jabotinsky in the second *curia*.[24]

The situation was awkward. It was clear that the Jews could not claim both deputies from Odessa. In the second *curia* Jabotinsky's competitors were two progressive Gentile candidates and the reactionary and anti-Semitic Bishop Anatoly. There was a danger of splitting the Jewish and progressive vote and thus securing the election of Bishop Anatoly. A strong tendency arose to withdraw the Jewish candidate from the second *curia* in the hope of thus preventing the election of Bishop Anatoly. In the Jewish Electoral Committee the vote on this proposal was divided fifty-fifty and the Committee dissolved.[25] Nor was there unanimity in the Zionist circles themselves. Jabotinsky, supported mainly by the youth, insisted on continuing his election campaign; he believed in the possibility of a success, but even if he should be defeated, Zionist election propaganda alone would have contributed to the national education of Odessa Jewry and would have been worth the effort. M. M. Ussishkin, together with many other local Zionist leaders, advocated the withdrawal of the Zionist candidature. The All-Russian Zionist Central Committee in Vilno was asked to pass judgment. This writer was with Jabotinsky when he received the telegram from Vilno instructing him to withdraw. He was at that moment writing an article for *Odesskiya Novosti*. Interrupting the work, he quickly read the telegram, handed it over to me, and quietly returned to his writing. When the article appeared the next morning in the paper, its title was "Without Nervousness." His younger partisans took this move with less equanimity. A special youth delegation called on Ussishkin, protesting against the "anti-Jabotinsky decision." Ussishkin upbraided them for this "interference" and called them "rebels"; Jabotinsky himself counseled discipline and self-restraint.

In a brief letter to the editor of *Odesskiya Novosti*, Jabotinsky announced that "submitting to the new decision of the leading bodies of

Zionism," he was withdrawing his candidature in the second *curia*.*
Motivating this move in an interview published in the same paper, M. M.
Ussishkin admitted that it was decided upon "not without some internal
struggle within the [Zionist] party itself. . . . We did not want to give
anybody the pretext for saying that the victory of the Rightist parties was
the result of Zionist tactics." Obviously trying to sweeten the pill of Jabotinsky's enforced withdrawal, Ussishkin insisted that "Jabotinsky is now
too mature, too much grown in stature, that we should permit ourselves
to let him be a candidate at random. He is one of those whose candidature
must be secure."[26]

All these calculations and sacrifices proved to be in vain. In both *curiae* the Rightist candidates were victorious. In the first, the reactionary and
anti-Semitic Professor Levashov overwhelmingly defeated H. B. Sliosberg;
in the second, Bishop Anatoly received 60 per cent of the votes.

Outwardly, Jabotinsky took the enforced withdrawal of his candidacy with equanimity; but inwardly he was boiling with indignation.
D. Bar Rav Hoi, then a youth of twenty, who was active in the technical
work during the abortive election campaign, happened to travel together with Jabotinsky on the train which left Odessa on October 13th. They
had supper in the dining car and for hours Jabotinsky bitterly criticized
the leading Zionist bodies for their attitude toward him. "Jabotinsky
was full of bitterness," Bar Rav Hoi recalls. "He spoke of the prevailing
tendency in Zionist ruling circles to give him no play, not to utilize his
capabilities. He gave a scathing characterization of the members of the
Zionist Central Committee, who were unable to appreciate the value
and the possibilities of an outstanding personality and were constantly
clipping his wings."[27]

It was with a feeling of deep and intense distaste that Jabotinsky left
Odessa, in the fall of 1912, to settle in St. Petersburg.

---

*H. B. Sliosberg says in his memoirs that "Jabotinsky did not obtain a majority," thus
implying that he stood for elections and was defeated. (*Dyela Minuvshikh Dney*. Vol. III.
Paris, 1934, p. 316.) This is, however, not correct. Jabotinsky withdrew his candidature
before elections.

SIX

HOME AND HEARTH

Courtship and Marriage

It goes without saying that not all of the time Jabotinsky spent in the cities and towns he visited was devoted to meetings and politics. Very sociable, he frequented many Jewish—as well as non-Jewish—homes and struck up numerous personal friendships with men and women alike. As a famous and popular speaker and journalist, he was considered a highly eligible bachelor. Local gossip was only too eager to label as Jabotinsky's fiancée every pretty girl from a good family with whom he spent an evening or two. Such "fiancées" used to be reported from almost every place Jabotinsky ever visited; this topic was often discussed among his *Rasswyet* colleagues, who once played a mischievous trick on him.

"I received," Jabotinsky smilingly recalled many years later, "a current issue of *Rasswyet* and found in the column 'The Zionist Week' the following piece of news:—'We are informed from Bialystok that the noted Zionist orator and writer, Vladimir Jabotinsky, is engaged to the charming daughter of the local industrialist and Zionist leader P. Similar information is reaching us from many other towns and townships. . . .'—I was dumbfounded. I already saw in my imagination everybody laughing and ridiculing me; I expected a swarm of my friends who, I knew, were getting *Rasswyet*, descending on my room with more or less appropriate jokes. I was boiling mad at my *Rasswyet* colleagues for putting me in such a predicament. However, the day passed and nobody came. I ventured to take a walk and met several *Rasswyet* subscribers: none of them so much as mentioned the story. I went to the library and asked for the latest *Rasswyet* issue, opened it and —the incriminating notice was not there: the *Rasswyet* gang printed *one single copy* including this piece of news, and sent it to me, joyfully savoring in advance the effect it would produce. And you may believe me that the first effect was devastating. Only much later was I able to appreciate this joke and to admit reluctantly that they 'had a point' in exposing the 'bride' legend."

"As a matter of principle," Jabotinsky, in fact, was rather in favor of multiplicity of romantic interests in the life of a young man. When his son Eri was seventeen and they were spending the summer in the mountain region of the French *département* of Vosges, Jabotinsky jokingly wrote to his sister: "Eri has a blonde fifteen-year-old girl friend by the name of Guena. He begins early. 'Exactly like his papa,' our old nurse Liaksandra [Alexandra] would say. Unfortunately, not exactly: what is lacking, is that variety and many-sidedness in his attachments which helped his 'papa' to choose from the available material. But maybe this, too, will come in due time."[1]

Among Jabotinsky's manifold attachments there was, however, one stable, or at least recurrent, feature: Ania-Anna (Johanna) Markovna Galperin. According to his own account, he met the girl when he was fifteen and she was just ten years old. This was his first year in the Richelieu Gymnasium; his classmate Ilya Galperin invited him to his parents' house and introduced him to his sisters. One of them was playing the piano when he crossed the room. She admitted to him afterward that behind his back she laughed heartily because of the strange impression she formed of him: "a Negro profile under a disheveled mop of hair." But that very evening, Jabotinsky recalled, "I won her favor by calling her (for the first time in her life) 'mademoiselle.' "

This first encounter initiated a lasting relationship. At the beginning, there was, of course, no real "romance" between a fifteen-year-old boy and a girl five years his junior. But a kind of *amitié amoureuse*, as the French call it, was born which, in various forms and in various degrees of intensity, withstood the test of twelve eventful years. A. Poliakov, who was a frequent guest in the house of the Galperins, told this writer that in the beginning Jabotinsky's pals often teased him because of his fondness for "this baby": at that age, a difference of five years was—or seemed to be—tremendous. But the youngster was not in the least impressed—let alone influenced—by this mockery.[2] Little by little the age difference was losing its significance. When, after almost three years of absence, Jabotinsky returned from Italy, he was twenty-one and Ania was sixteen—a pretty and lively young girl; very soon she was a young lady. The relationship grew and deepened. At certain periods the noun *amitié* prevailed, at others the adjective *amoureuse*. However, for several years there was no definite commitment on either side. As mentioned above, Jabotinsky's "attachments" were many and variegated. Some of them were widely popular and much discussed in Russian Zionist circles.

One evening, Jabotinsky himself recalled, after having received his salary from *Odesskiya Novosti* (and as usual having spent most of it immediately), he still had one gold coin left. In the presence of Ania's brother Ilya and three other students—Ilya Epstein, Alexander Poliakov, and Moshe Ginsburg—he handed it over to Ania and playfully recited before these four witnesses the slightly varied traditional marriage formula: "Behold, with this ring thou art joined to me in holy wedlock according to the law of Moses and Israel." This was, of course, meant as a jest, though Ginsburg's father, an orthodox Jew, later warned the would-be bride that she must demand a "divorce" from Jabotinsky "if she intended to find a more solid match."*

In the winter of 1903–04, Jabotinsky settled in St. Petersburg. But he often visited Odessa, and in 1905 he provided Ania with a technical job in the administration of *Rasswyet*, so that for some time they again lived in the same city. To this period belongs an amusing episode related to this writer by Jabotinsky's sister: it so happened that Ania's older sister and her brother got married without previously informing their mother, who was very much upset by this procedure and so was Jabotinsky's mother; his sister, therefore, made him promise that, should he decide to marry, he and his bride would never confront their mothers with a *fait accompli*. One day, however, a telegram arrived from St. Petersburg saying: "Volodia and Ania got married." Both sister and mother were flabbergasted: he had promised to advise them in advance! Then they looked at the date of the telegram: April 1st. It was an April fool's day prank.[3]

In July of the same year, Ania joined Jabotinsky's mother, aunt, and sister, as well as the latter's two sisters-in-law and their mutual friend, A. Poliakov, in their journey to the Seventh Zionist Congress in Basel. She was not a Zionist and was not interested in Zionist affairs; but this was a wonderful occasion to see Switzerland and to meet interesting people.

---

*According to strict orthodox usage, utterance of the complete formula establishes a valid marriage. This is why in stage weddings the word *li* (to me) is omitted.

After the Congress, a gay group of young men and girls, which included Jabotinsky, Ania, Rose Kopp, and A. Poliakov, undertook an ambitious excursion on foot over the Swiss mountains. According to Jabotinsky, they walked as far as Venice without a nickel in their pockets. Poliakov recalls that in Venice they practically starved for about a week, because the money which Jabotinsky confidently expected from Suvorin, the editor of the paper *Rus*, as his monthly honorarium, failed to arrive. Jabotinsky spent the rest of his scanty cash on telegrams to St. Petersburg, only to find out later that the money was waiting for him in some obscure Italian bank where he did not even think to look for it.[4] It was with the greatest fondness that Jabotinsky always remembered this carefree youthful adventure, in which Ania and Sasha (Poliakov) proved to be wonderful companions.

In 1906, when Jabotinsky paid a visit to Warsaw, Ania accompanied him. I. Grinbaum and his wife, who met them at the Palace of Arts and did not know anything about their relationship, very soon noticed the "possessiveness" with which she treated Jabotinsky and came to the conclusion: Here goes our Vladimir's freedom. . . .[5] However, it took more than a year before he finally gave up his "freedom." To the very last moment his own family was not sure whether and whom he was going to marry. His sister recalls that when, almost on the eve of the wedding, he came to his mother and asked her to buy two wedding rings, his mother asked: "And who is the bride?" She guessed, but she was not sure. Jabotinsky insisted that nobody but the closest relatives on either side should be present at the ceremony.[6]

The wedding took place in Odessa on October 14/27, 1907, just in the midst of the election campaign for the third Duma. Jabotinsky reported this event with his usual brevity in all personal matters: "A few days before the elections, I ordered a buggy and, accompanied by my mother and sister, set off for the synagogue. On the steps of the synagogue I met Ania—she, too, was in the company of her mother, brother, and sister. . . . In the synagogue there were already waiting the deputy of the Rabbi [Avinovitzky], a minyan of Jews and a canopy. I said 'behold thou art consecrated to me' to Ania, and in my heart I made a vow 'behold I am consecrated to thee.' From there I rushed to attend an electoral meeting."

The same afternoon, the newlyweds and the closest family had coffee at the home of Jabotinsky's mother, and in the evening numerous friends assembled in Ania's mother's house; fearing lest the Tsarist administration would arrest Jabotinsky on the eve of the elections, M. M. Ussishkin persuaded him to spend the night in Ussishkin's house.[7] After the unfavorable outcome of the elections, the newlyweds left Odessa. Jabotinsky went to Vienna and his wife to Nancy, to study agronomy. Why agronomy? Poliakov's explanation is that at that time the progressive Russian "intelligentsia" strove to acquire such knowledge as could be utilized in the service of the people, first and foremost of the Russian peasant masses: agronomy suited this purpose and, not being a Zionist, Ania followed this then fashionable trend.[8]

The rest of 1907 and the greater part of 1908, Jabotinsky lived and studied in Vienna and his wife in Nancy. But he visited her in Nancy and spent several weeks there. This visit was an unexpected and happy event in the life of the relatively small and weak Zionist group in that French university town; the Zionists had a hard time holding their ground against the attacks by the Socialist majority in the Russian student colony of about four hundred. The Socialist camp was privileged to have in its midst a certain Szyrin, a highly schooled theoretician, who knew Marx by heart and was a skillful debater. Since Marx was at that time considered the oracle in all problems concerning humanity, Szyrin's abundant quotations from Marxian writings constituted the final authority. No local Zionist was a match for this Socialist big gun. The most outstanding French Socialist leaders—Jean Jaurès, Aristide Briand, Sebastian Faure—used to speak in Nancy, and the Zionists had nobody to counterbalance their influence. Jabotinsky's arrival was a godsend for them. His Italian teachers—Labriola, Ferri, Pantaleoni—had trained him well in Marxian theory and phraseology: Szyrin was quickly and easily deflated, and Jabotinsky's fiery oratory was not inferior to the harangues of a Jaurès or a Briand. He gave new life and strength to the Zionist student group which thereupon started a successful uphill fight.[9]

The Constantinople period (1909–10) was one of the few interludes which the Jabotinskys spent together. When they returned to Odessa in the summer of 1910, they first lived at Ania's mother's rented country house, and then in Odessa itself, together with her older sister, who was married to Dr. Epstein. There, on December 13/26, 1910, was born to them their first and only child Eri-Theodore. In the latter half of 1912 they left Odessa and settled in St. Petersburg. When this writer visited them there in the fall of 1912, Mrs. Jabotinsky told him with disarming frankness that she had no illusions whatsoever as to the impression Jabotinsky's choice of a helpmeet had produced among his friends and admirers: "I knew that all of you were deeply disappointed. You expected him to marry, if not a princess, then at least some striking beauty or some outstanding intellectual luminary. And he unexpectedly married just Anitchka Galperin, a plain Odessa girl! . . . I couldn't even blame you for that, though, of course, I wasn't happy about this attitude. I decided to do my very best to remedy this situation and to make his friends accept me as I am. I hope that to a great extent I have succeeded in this."

She succeeded indeed. Jabotinsky's friends stopped regretting that he had not married a princess. They very soon recognized in Anna Markovna a personality of her own, a willingness and a capability to bear with honor and dignity the great responsibility of being Jabotinsky's life companion. As mentioned above, she was not a Zionist when she married, and for at least twenty-five years afterward she took no active interest in Zionist affairs and activities. A. Poliakov, an intimate friend of the family, testifies that at least in the beginning she was far from happy about her husband devoting all his time and energy to Zionist work, and that she resented his all too frequent journeys and changes of domicile which this kind of life implied. But on this subject Jabotinsky was unyielding, and Anna Markovna was wise enough not even to try to interfere with his Zionist activities. She never complained, never objected to his travels and prolonged absences. And they were many and long indeed. The afternoon of her fifteenth wedding anniversary, October 27, 1922, Mrs. Jabotinsky spent with this writer and his wife in Berlin, while Jabotinsky was in Palestine: according to her calculation, out of those fifteen years they had spent together a total of about two and a half years. When they celebrated their silver wedding jubilee in 1932, they did so by exchanging telegrams; some time later, when they met, they estimated that they had lived together hardly one-fifth of these twenty-five years.[10]

Mrs. Jabotinsky never complained about the financial worries caused by her husband's neglect of the practical aspects of life and by his extreme generosity.

Jabotinsky deeply appreciated her understanding and cooperative attitude. At the same time he had a strong and ever growing feeling of guilt toward his wife, for whom he was not able to provide a normal, quiet, and secure existence, to which he believed every woman was entitled. He considered himself undeservedly fortunate in having such a life companion, and never failed to stress his deep affection for her. In a letter to S. Jacobi (October 31, 1930) he wrote: "I am sending you a photo of Ania that I love very much

(I have in mind the photo; but I also like the original ever better and better)."
In 1938, congratulating the young and promising *Betar* leader, Menachem
Begin, on his wedding, he wrote to him that the best and happiest day in his
life was the day when he put on Ania's finger a thin gold ring and recited the
traditional nine-word formula.

Vienna Interlude

Jabotinsky's marriage coincided with a turning point in his spiritual
development. At the peak of his political and publicistic career, he started
feeling increasingly uneasy. Always inclined to revision, he began a critical
re-examination of his own balance sheet. For several years he had been
performing his Zionist journalistic and propaganda work without complaint, and indeed even with pleasure. But a moment came when he was
overcome by a feeling of spiritual fatigue and dissatisfaction; "not this is the
way,"* he suddenly realized, and "revolted against himself." There was no
definite line in his life, he mused dejectedly. Too easily did he "adapt" his
personality to different environments: when he was writing frivolous feuilletons—to bohemian circles; in Rome—to his Italian friends with whom
he drank Frascati and Grotta-ferrata, and to *Sartinas* (Roman equivalent
of French *midinettes*) with whom he flirted and who often found him very
simpatico; now, he had become "absorbed" by the Zionist crowd. "But who
am I myself?" he asked. He realized that, since he had left the university,
he had acquired but little knowledge. He was mentally hungry. And he told
himself: "Basta." No more spending without replenishing his intellectual
equipment. The time had come for thought and study.

Jabotinsky abruptly canceled all his journalistic and propaganda com-
mitments. He longed to be alone and to work. To his bride, who was preparing to leave for France to study agronomy at Nancy, he said: "I will go
together with you to Berlin—there we will part, and I will go to Vienna; I
want to study."

The choice of Vienna was not accidental. Jabotinsky was then profoundly interested in the problems of nationalities, minority rights, national
renaissance movements. Vienna, the capital of the multinational Austro-
Hungarian monarchy, was the logical place for studying these problems.

---

*The title of a famous article by Achad Haatn (literally "One of the People"), pen name
of Asher Ginsburg, 1856-1927, the philosopher of cultural Zionism.

Jabotinsky threw himself fully into the work. After years of hectic public life, he was deeply tired, both physically and morally, and he enjoyed his solitude in the big city, where he painstakingly avoided involvement in any public or Zionist activities. In a letter to M. M. Ussishkin, dated December 1, 1907, he wrote: "I avoid people in order not to be disturbed; besides, I am so tired that a conversation of half an hour leaves me exhausted. Apart from my journalistic duties, I am working on nationality problems. I intend to acquire a thorough knowledge of all theoretical studies in this field, and, first and foremost, to master fully the factual picture of national relations and conflicts in Austria and Hungary. For the time being I am reading books in the library; later on I will start interviewing leading personalities." Jabotinsky would spend the whole day, from morning till evening, at the university or *Reichsrat* (State Council) Libraries. In addition to German, Polish, Italian, English, Russian, and French (languages he already knew), he learned to read Czech and Croat. He carefully studied the abundant literature on the problem of nationality in its relation to the state: the standard works of Rudolf Springer (Karl Renner), Herman von Herrnritt, Ludwig Gumplowicz, Georg Jellinek, J. C. Bluntschli, Fr. I. Neumann, Ernest Renan, Pasquale S. Mancini, Aurel Popovici, R. Charmatz, and L. Bernhardt.

On December 24, 1907, and on April 4, 1908, he reported to M. M. Ussishkin: "My studies are progressing. . . . I am working regularly, and on the whole it seems that I will be satisfied with my Vienna. I intend to stay here till June." The only thing that troubled him were financial worries. "My worries are of a financial nature. What I am afraid of is that I might be forced to cut short my stay in Vienna and to go to St. Petersburg to earn money. This would be hard. This will spell doom for me. But I am struggling with all my might."

Jabotinsky managed to stay in Vienna for almost a year. It was a studious and highly creative period in his life. He thoroughly enjoyed the quiet and diligent existence to which he was so unaccustomed. The eve of the year 1908 was the first since 1904 when he "went nowhere, neither by train nor by foot," he wrote in a "letter from Vienna," published under the title "Your New Year." This was a strange and wonderful human experience for the vagabond Jabotinsky, which he masterfully described in this highly personal feuilleton:[11]

The people of Vienna wait for New Year's midnight on the square in front of St. Stephen Cathedral, enjoy themselves and make lots of noise; but I did not go anywhere. I am weary, I have heard too much noise during these four years.

My lamp was burning on the table and coals were glowing in the hearth. I had tea, a sofa, books, the curtains were drawn, and it was warm in my room. It was probably that self-same thing people call "petty bourgeois" cosiness. That is all right with me. I have earned my right to await for once New Year's midnight basking in the caress of homelike warmth and snugness. Once in a while you have to live as everybody else does. If you always wear different boots from everybody, in the end your soul will not stand for it. The best medicine for overstrung nerves is the everyday and the commonplace. And, besides, after such a life, precisely the commonplace presents all the charm of novelty. . . .

Tomorrow I shall put on my hat, raise the collar of my overcoat, and continue on my chilly windswept way—but one evening I feel entitled to spend in the warmly heated bath of my own, guileless, tranquil egoism.

So I sat and celebrated, not knowing myself what exactly.

I bathed my dust-covered soul in quiet and remembrance of people far away and of days gone by, of the year about to die, and of the whole sad alley of years, born and gone before my eyes.

The Vienna interlude did much good for Jabotinsky's mind. It was not only a period of intensive study, but also a kind of recuperative "spiritual bath." Planning to return to St. Petersburg in September of 1908, and to settle there, he was full of "truly great and earnest designs," as he wrote to M. M. Ussishkin on April 4, 1908.

Events in Turkey, however, gave a new direction to Jabotinsky's life.

Farewell to Odessa

In the spring of 1909, shortly after his return from Palestine and Turkey, one of his *Rasswyet* colleagues, Arnold Seideman, who had a university diploma in mathematics, decided to turn lawyer and to try to pass the state examination at the Faculty of Law; he induced Jabotinsky to do the same. But Jabotinsky, who in 1897 had left the Odessa gymnasium before completing his course, had first to obtain a high-school diploma. At the age of twenty-eight he started rehashing high-school subjects: Latin grammar, even Russian grammar, Russian history, geometry, etc. Most of his tests he passed with flying colors. The only subject in which his marks were rather poor, was—Russian composition: Jabotinsky, at that time already famed as a writer throughout Russia, was not good enough for the teacher of Russian literature at the Fifth St. Petersburg gymnasium. A local press reporter was eager to publish this sensational episode in his paper, but Jabotinsky took pains to dissuade him from doing so.

Further progress in Jabotinsky's delayed "academic career"— a university diploma—was prevented by his assignment to Constantinople. It was not before 1912 that he found time and opportunity to present himself for a state examination at Demidov's Lyceum in Yaroslavl. He passed the examination *summa cum laude* and obtained a university diploma,* which—for the first time since 1903—entitled him legally to establish domicile in St. Petersburg.

It was also the first time since his marriage that he possessed an independently rented and furnished apartment, and when this writer visited him in the fall of 1912, Jabotinsky was almost childishly proud of this achievement. The guest had to make a "conducted tour" of all four rooms, to admire every piece of furniture, and to learn that the beds had been bought with the proceeds of Jabotinsky's lectures on "The Language of Our Culture"; the dining room was furnished out of his earnings from his lectures on "Assimilation of Nationalities"; and the study owed its desk and bookshelves to the fees he was receiving for his articles in *Odesskiya Novosti*. Many years later, traces of this state of mind were easily recognizable in Jabotinsky's short story "Fairy Vagabunda," in which one of his former colleagues, when asked what he was doing now, gravely answered: "Oh, now I have a passport, a winter coat and a furnished room." In this answer, commented Jabotinsky, many overtones were discernible: "respect for himself, at the same time an unaccustomed feeling of being settled, and a bit of nostalgia for the vagrant period of his history."

For all practical purposes, this settling in St. Petersburg marked the end of the Odessa period in Jabotinsky's life. After 1912, he only occasionally and briefly visited his native city, though his articles regularly appeared in *Odesskiya Novosti*. Only much later did he realize that in October, 1912, he had actually said farewell to Odessa.

---

*In order to obtain his law diploma, Jabotinsky submitted a thesis on "State and Nation," dealing with legal aspects of the autonomy of national minority groups. He made extensive use of this thesis in the study "Rights of the National Minorities," which he published in the authoritative Russian monthly *Vestnik Evropy* (European Messenger).

SEVEN
ZIONIST THOUGHT AND ACTION

Not all the many contributions Jabotinsky made to Zionist thought and action can be listed and discussed in this biography, which is necessarily limited in scope. However, some "samples" must be mentioned. Even though they belong to different periods and there is no direct connection between them, they are —both separately and in their totality—indicative of the volume and value of Jabotinsky's "investment" in the spiritual treasury of Russian Zionism.*

The First Call for Halutziut**

All his life Jabotinsky was a "political Zionist" par excellence. At the same time he was also a determined partisan of immediate practical colonizing work in Palestine. He insisted that *Rasswyet* must devote more space to information on Palestine and put more emphasis on problems connected with Palestine's upbuilding. A. D. Idelson, the chief editor of this only Zionist periodical in the Russian language, did not share Jabotinsky's view, and the majority of the older members of the editorial board supported him in

---

*S. Gepstein notices the interesting fact that, formally, Jabotinsky had no official position in the Russian Zionist hierarchy, with the exception of that of a member of the editorial staff of *Rasswyet*. Though probably the most popular man in the movement, he was never a member of the Central Committee of the Zionist Organization in Russia or of any other governing body.

**Halutz* (plural *Halutzim*)—Hebrew for pioneer, term applied to young Jewish labor immigrants to Palestine who undertake physical work in both rural and urban areas. *Halutziut—the Halutz* movement.

this negative attitude. Jabotinsky was therefore instrumental in the establishment in Odessa of a second Zionist weekly in Russian, *Yevreyskaya Mysl* (The Jewish Thought), where particular stress was put on practical work in Palestine. The first issue of the new publication appeared on October 18, 1906.

However, in about six months' time, Jabotinsky came to the conclusion that the parallel existence of two Zionist organs published in Russian was inadvisable.[1] He therefore proposed to discontinue the Odessa organ; in return, *Rasswyet* agreed to devote every week about eight columns to a Palestine section, which would be edited in Odessa by representatives of the Palestine Committee, the initiator and sponsor of *Yevreyskaya Mysl*. This solution was accepted.

Jabotinsky insisted that practical work for Palestine must play the main role not only in Zionist activities, but in the entire life of the Zionist movement. "It is irrelevant that the majority of the Zionist rank and file will be unable directly to participate in these activities. What is important is that preparatory work in Palestine should be considered as the main instrument, as the only one that leads *directly* to the fulfillment of Zionism, and that all the rest—organization of Jewry, diplomatic work, culture, etc.— are sidelines, subsidiary courses only."[2] In accordance with this Zionist concept, Jabotinsky was probably the first leading Zionist to launch the idea of organized *Halutziut* in Russia. As early as 1905, advising Russian Zionists "what to do," he insisted that "the time has come to create a new *Bilu*."* To him, this was not a "betrayal" of political Zionism: "All our hope I see in political Zionism, and would there be no political Zionism, there would be no sense in and no need for new *Biluim*. But in order to enable political Zionism to conquer Palestine for the Jews, the Jews must prepare the country with the labor of their hands. ... The revival of *Bilu* is necessary not in order to colonize Palestine 'at the rate of a tablespoonful per hour,' but in order to prepare Palestine for mass settlement."[3] When, in 1906, a "Neo-*Bilu*" organization was created, Jabotinsky sent a letter to its first (clandestine) conference at Yelissavetgrad, in which he developed a program and an ideology for the prospective pioneers. The main points of the letter were these:[4]

Bilu (plural *Biluim*)—abbreviation for "*Bet Yaakov lechu venechla*" (O House of Jacob, let us go forth), the name given to the first organized group of Jewish settlers, who left Russia to live in Palestine between 1880–90.

There are two kinds of immigrants to Palestine: the so-called "natural immigrant," who is going there in order to make a living, and the pioneer. The immigrant belonging to the first category is useful only if he does make a living; the pioneer is always useful; he is in all circumstances contributing to the economic and cultural conquest of Palestine. He must, however, possess two qualifications: he must be physically and spiritually fit, and he must be organized and disciplined. Without organization, not a single pioneer should leave for Palestine. "Only to prepared jobs, only to pre-designed positions" must they go. The pioneers must be educators of Palestine Jewry. The country is not ripe for class struggle, in particular for the excesses of such a struggle. Good relations with the Arabs must be established. . . . We must have in Palestine a population which "in the future will be capable of fighting for our political independence."

"The Alien Land"

In the winter of 1907, in the midst of his scholarly research in Vienna, Jabotinsky conceived the idea of and started working on a drama in verse, *Extern Abram*, devoted to the spiritual crisis of Russian Jewry. In 1908, Jabotinsky read this play, which he renamed *Chuzhbina* (The Alien Land)— a comedy in five acts—before a select gathering of St. Petersburg writers. The opinions of those present were divided. Some praised it very highly, others questioned its literary value and saw in it but a "publicistic feuilleton in rhymes or rhythmic prose." Nevertheless, the manuscript was sent to the printers and proof sheets were submitted to the censor. The latter started making difficulties: he demanded substantial cuts and changes and threatened to confiscate the work upon its appearance. The publication of the play was therefore suspended—for fourteen years; it was not before 1922 that S. D. Salzman published it in Berlin. In Russia, extensive excerpts from *Chuzhbina* appeared in 1910 in *Rasswyet*, where S. Gepstein devoted to it an extensive review, based on a set of proof sheets salvaged from the censor's clutches.[5] Since *Chuzhbina* has not been translated into any European language, it seems advisable briefly to review its contents.

A large, half-Jewish, south-Russian harbor city (presumably Odessa) is full of pre-revolutionary tension. The leading role is being played by the Social-Democratic Party, which is in this city overwhelmingly Jewish in its composition. Intellectuals and the frightened bourgeoisie slavishly pay court to the new masters of the situation. Everybody believes that a new force has arisen— truly powerful, self-confident, majestic. A lonesome Jewish intellectual, Gonta, challenges this illusion. At a revolutionary banquet, amidst enthusiastic and boastful toasts, he pitilessly reminds his Socialist fellow Jews that, while they imagine themselves to be the moving spirit of the mighty hurricane raging all over the country, they are, in fact, merely "wood splinters on the waves of another nation's vortexes": "Unable to start or to stop, to ignite or to extinguish a world-wide conflagration, holding a harmless sword in a nerveless hand, you are useless in this struggle!" Gonta refuses to be a partner to this delusion. He preaches to his contemporaries the bitter truth of their utter and hopeless impotence in Russia's great upheaval. He has no "solution" to offer. His prescription is: "cold, inexorable, unconquerable, hard-hearted, bottomless pride of a King who has been deprived of his throne and crown."

Gonta's rebuke is received with scorn and indignation. The Jewish revolutionary leaders refuse to realize both their Jewishness—I am a Jew merely "because of my passport and my nose," says Makar, the most outstanding of them—and its impact on popular feelings. Styopa, the only genuine Russian proletarian in the entire crowd, a simple soul who is keenly sensitive to the temper of the Russian masses, warns, in his somewhat awkward, inarticulate way, that these masses are longing for a "chieftain" of their own, with a "Russian voice . . . with a flavor of the steppes and of the Volga": "He may be less clever than Makar, provided that he and myself be alike as two peas, that our spirits can talk to each other as if by phone."

Such a chieftain is not available. Clever and fervent speeches of the Jewish political propagandists are unable to reach the innermost emotions of the Russian crowd. Makar himself is puzzled. He feels that something vital is missing: "There is no access. A wall. Maybe some button hasn't been pushed, some magic word not said to the end—Sesame did not open. Mystery. Mystery."

The mystery culminates in a pogrom. Upset and discouraged, Jewish revolutionary youth assembles in a synagogue to discuss the organization of self-defense. But precious time is being wasted on vain theoretical debates. The curse of utter helplessness dominates the scene. Everybody feels lost. Gonta stubbornly repeats his refrain: "Our struggle is a mirage, we are mere shadow, there is no role for us to play, events run their course independent of our will." And he calls on the Jews "to cut off the last bridge between ourselves and the alien land, and to pronounce an anathema! Not to accept and not to bestow anything!"

But even Gonta's passionate negation is still not the climax of nihilism born out of abysmal disappointment and despair. Extern Abram, a strange youth who till now has been silent and watching, suddenly takes the floor and, brushing away all hopes of life and struggle, calls each and everyone to indulge in the last privilege that is left to those who are doomed—to debauch: "To cynicism toward all idols and to debauch in every public place. . . . Into the gutter! Into the gutter!" Swayed by the elemental force of this despair, having lost the last remnants of willpower and faith, the crowd follows this "prophet of doom," pathetically trying to drown in somber orgies of depravity their hopelessness and horror before the iron mask of "the alien land." Only a few religious old Jews remain, calm and impassive, in the abandoned synagogue. They had been interrupted in the middle of divine service by noisy and forlorn unbelievers—now they are alone again. They continue their prayers.

Most of the play is in verse; prose parts are few, and the use of prose is almost always determined by a specific purpose, in accordance with the character of the theme or of the person. A definite purpose can also be seen in the variety of the rhythmical patterns used. Certain characters speak in well-measured, sonorous verse, full of pathos, faith, love, or hatred; others, in abrupt or humorous, often deliberately awkward, sentences. The dialogue is lively and sparkling. In 1922, when *Chuzhbina* was published, it could be read with almost the same deep interest and tension as in 1908, when it was written.

Crusade Against Assimilation

The main target of Jabotinsky's journalistic crusades was Jewish assimilation in its various forms and expressions. What angered him most was the pathetic—and to him sickening—longing of the Jewish intellectuals to penetrate into the Russian spiritual world and to pretend being "at home," on a par with "genuine" Russians. There was wholesale desertion of Jewish life and culture in pursuit of this fallacy. Jewishness had begun to be considered as something obsolete that could be easily dropped for the sake of any prospective advantage, be it a literary career or a university diploma. Some were still maintaining their formal allegiance to Jewry; others did not hesitate to go through the ceremony of baptism.

It would take very many pages to describe the manifold facets of Jabotinsky's struggle against all these shades of assimilation. Only two or three will be briefly outlined here.

In February, 1909, a Russian translation of Sholem Asch's play *Yikhus* (Blue Blood) was read to a gathering of fourteen Jewish and twelve non-Jewish writers assembled in the house of the noted Russian actor of the Imperial Theaters, Khodotov. On that occasion some disparaging remarks were made about the Jewish influence in Russian literature and on the press. The well-known Russian novelist, Eugene N. Chirikov (whose philosemitic, though rather inept play, *The Jews*, was very popular with the Jewish public) said in the discussion that the Jews, who allegedly dominated the entire literature and in particular literary criticism in Russia, were showing lack of understanding of and an unfriendly attitude toward the tenor of every-day Russian life; another Russian writer, K. Arabazhin, who also used to be known for his philosemitic tendencies, cautiously seconded this view. The Jewish writers present felt offended; they heatedly disputed the accusations, stressing their attachment to Russian culture and spirit.

When *Rasswyet* published this story in its issue of March 1, 1909, Jabotinsky commented on it in a powerful article "Deserters and Masters." He discounted the soothing argument that Messrs. Chirikov and Arabazhin were both mediocrities and not typical of the Russian intelligentsia: just because they might have been nothing out of the ordinary, their utterances must be considered as indicative of the mentality of an average Russian intellectual—otherwise they would not have dared to put them forth. And the Jews who had made their way into the Russian literature, press, theater, and publishing business, would sooner or later have to face a gradual dismissal. It would be wrong to brand this coming trend as "anti-Semitism." The "genuine" Russian intelligentsia was simply beginning to feel the urge to be "among themselves, without the ever-present Jewish witness, who acclimatized himself too much, feels too much at home, is meddling with everything, and whose voice is being heard everywhere." Jabotinsky bluntly refused to sympathize with the prospective victims of this impending *Judenrein* policy, who had long ago deserted their own people and its culture and who now felt so terribly hurt because their Russian masters unceremoniously rebuked them for not being sufficiently "Russian." He wrote:

We, who have always been insisting on the concentration of [Jewish] national forces and demanding that every drop of Jewish sweat should fall on the *Jewish* cornfield, we can only from afar follow the development of this conflict between our deserters and their masters—in the best case as indifferent onlookers, in the worst—with a bitter smile. . . . For what interest can the Jewish nation have in individuals whose supreme pride consisted in the fact that they had, with very few exceptions, renounced their people?

Rasswyet's report and Jabotinsky's article produced great consternation in Jewish assimilationist and Russian progressive circles. Some Russian liberal and radical papers (*Ryetch, Nasha Zhisn*) at the beginning tried to kill the unpleasant issue by a conspiracy of silence. But this strategy failed, and very soon such pillars of *Ryetch* as P. N. Miliukov and M. M. Vinaver, together with P. B. Struve of the *Slovo,* Alexey Poroshin of the *Novaya Rus,* and many others became engaged in a revealing and stimulating discussion on the problem of those Jews who considered themselves Russians. Jabotinsky devoted four articles to this issue in *Rasswyet* and in the Russian daily *Slovo:* each was a penetrating analysis and a scathing indictment of both the pathetic bankruptcy of the Jewish assimilationists and the hypocrisy of the Russian progressive camp.[6] It is difficult to convey to the present-day reader even a pale notion of the shattering blow these articles dealt to the very roots of the assimilationist creed, and of their almost revolutionary impact on Jewish intellectual circles during these pre-World War I years.

In February, 1912, there appeared in *Odesskiya Novosti* the article "A Strange Phenomenon" by Altalena.[7] In it, Jabotinsky called attention to the fact that the various "Literary Clubs" functioning in the cities were usually frequented by Jews only: "genuine" Russians were very rare and vanishing guests. Many and various explanations of and excuses for this state of affairs were offered by both Jews and Gentiles. Jabotinsky lucidly and ruthlessly analyzed each one of them and reduced the problem to its bare essentials: the Russians, even those who were free from any anti-Semitic prejudices, preferred to be among themselves, and the Jewish urge to be *à tout prix* in Russian company was both undignified and self-defeating.[8]

Two years earlier, the same *Odesskiya Novosti* had published "Our Everyday Phenomenon"—a quietly scathing denunciation of the baptism epidemic which was then raging among Jewish academic youth.[9] Probably only those who have witnessed the atom-bomb effect it produced among the younger generation are able to appreciate the sociological significance of this article. It suddenly shattered the resigned complacency, the passive acceptance of this "everyday phenomenon" by Jewish society; it dramatized the issue, made it an object of passionate discussion in every high school and university; it brought about sharp conflicts between parents and children, between relatives and comrades; many friendships fell apart, many romances were broken. It is difficult to ascertain to what extent all this numerically stemmed the flood of conversions. There can, however, be no doubt that for the first time public attention was forcibly focused on this flood, which had been for so long a time considered as too "delicate" a matter to be openly discussed, and was thus permitted to rage unhindered.

Published in an Odessa paper, "Our Everyday Phenomenon" had an influence which far transcended the local scene. It was reprinted in full by *Rasswyet*, which had a country-wide circulation. It was later republished as a separate pamphlet and sold in tens of thousands of copies.

Creating Zionist Propaganda Literature

The beginning and expansion of printed Zionist propaganda in Russia is closely connected with Jabotinsky's prodigious effort. The most popular and effective form of party literature was at that time the "brochure"—a 16-, 24-, 32-, or 48-page pamphlet with a paper or cardboard cover. Hundreds of such brochures were being published in millions of copies by all parties. The Zionist movement was very poorly represented in this flood of pamphlet literature, both in quantity and quality. Jabotinsky played an outstanding role in overcoming this handicap.

Together with a group of friends (S. D. Salzman, Dr. M. S. Schwartzman, M. S. Aleinikov), Jabotinsky in 1904 founded in Odessa a Zionist publishing house "Kadima," to which each of them contributed one hundred rubles (fifty dollars). This capital very soon proved insufficient. Jabotinsky went to Kiev where he was given the opportunity of presenting the case for "Kadima" to a small gathering of some twenty Jewish businessmen, mostly of assimilationist leanings. His address made a strong impression. When some of the participants objected to the Hebrew name "Kadima" and ironically asked whether its founders intended to publish Pushkin in Hebrew, Jabotinsky replied: "This suggestion of yours is excellent, and I am most certainly going to avail myself of it—for your benefit! The day will come when, if not yourself, then your children will be able to enjoy Pushkin in Hebrew." The gathering netted two thousand rubles which secured "Kadima's" existence and development. In the course of the following three years it published an entire Zionist library of thirty pamphlets: twenty-three in Russian (among them six by Jabotinsky), and seven in Yiddish. Jabotinsky was taking an active part in "Kadima's" management. The administrative work was in the hands of Salzman, but Jabotinsky was in full charge of selecting and editing the material; he did not spurn even the prosaic work of proofreading.[10]

The work which "Kadima" started in Odessa was continued and amplified by the publishing house "Vostok" (Orient) in St. Petersburg. It embarked on publication of books rather than pamphlets. Its first edition was Jabotinsky's translation of Bialik's poetry; then followed Herzl's *Feuilletons* (with a preface by Jabotinsky) and a series of other major publications. "Jabotinsky was the moving spirit of this venture," Salzman testifies. "I never undertook anything without first consulting him, and during his absences I constantly remained in touch with him."[11]

Jabotinsky's major articles dealing directly with Zionist problems were usually republished in pamphlet form very soon after their appearance in the periodicals. There was, however, a large variety of articles on issues which were, so to speak, on the borderline of Zionism; they had an unquestionable bearing upon the most vital questions of national Jewish policy, without being directly Zionist or even sometimes purely Jewish in their immediate contents. A collection of thirty such articles was published in 1912 under the unpretentious title of *Feuilletons*. They had previously appeared at different times and were destined for different audiences; some were the result of long and painstaking study, others had a predominantly polemical or lyrical character. But, as Jabotinsky wrote in a brief introductory note, "there is in all this heterogeneous material one common feature: each line was born in the atmosphere of struggle, every word was a response to a fighting challenge; this explains the nervousness of the tone, the predominance of temperament."

To those who had been following Jabotinsky's journalistic skirmishes and battles over the years 1904–12—and there were many of them—this little, tastefully printed book was a real treat. They excitedly recapitulated the specific occasions that gave birth to this or that of the republished articles, the immediate reaction each of them produced among Jewish and non-Jewish readers, and their more lasting aftereffects. *Rasswyet*, from which Jabotinsky had broken away in 1911, devoted an enthusiastic review (by S. Gepstein) to the book. Stressing its contagiously militant spirit, the reviewer reminded Jabotinsky of an "old story": having listened to the speeches of the famous Roman orator Servius Tullius, the Romans used to say that there was "no better orator than our Servius"; after the speeches of Demosthenes, denouncing Philip, King of Macedon, nobody praised his oratory, but everybody was clamoring: "War on Philip."[12]

The *Feuilletons* could be found in thousands of Jewish homes. Together with Jabotinsky's translation of Bialik's poems, they became the most popular present on many festive family occasions, and one could easily discern numerous—often unconscious—quotations from them in conversations and discussions among the Jewish intelligentsia. The book (two printings) was almost completely sold out within a few years. In 1922, S. D. Salzman published a new edition in Berlin, which was widely read by the Russian-Jewish emigrés. It is now almost impossible to find a copy of this Berlin edition in any bookstore in Paris, New York, or Tel Aviv. It is perhaps worth while to note that Jabotinsky was the only Russian Zionist writer whose books (*Feuilletons, The Alien Land,* his translations from Bialik's poetry) have been republished abroad after the forcible isolation of Russian Jewry by the Communist régime.

Poles and Jews

In unpublished, handwritten autobiographical notes, Jabotinsky said that during the years 1910–13 he "began a systematic press offensive against the last fortresses of assimilationism in South Russia; all my best work as a Jewish publicist in the Russian language belongs to this period."

There is no boastful exaggeration in this self-evaluation of his writings in the last three prewar years. Jabotinsky was then at the peak of his matured journalistic talent. Clear and courageous thinking, vast knowledge, exceptional mastery of the Russian language, elegance of style, and spiritual militancy combined to make almost each of his articles a literary and political event.

It would be wrong, however, to assume that all, or even the bulk, of Jabotinsky's journalistic work of this period was Jewish in its contents. Far from it. A careful perusal of his articles published from 1910 to 1913 in *Odesskiya Novosti*—his main mouthpiece—shows that probably 70 per cent of them were devoted to general subjects: literary, political, theatrical—Russian as well as international. The range of Jabotinsky's interests was very wide and manifold. But if not in quantity, then certainly in intensity, the "Jewish sector" occupied the central position in his journalistic work; his Jewish articles were usually signed "V. Jabotinsky" or "V.J." Polish-Jewish relations held the forefront of the Jewish sector.

The Polish-Jewish issue was no new item on Jabotinsky's national political agenda. As far back as October 5, 1906, he published in *Khronika Yevreyskoy Zhisni* an article "The Autonomy of Poland," which culminated in the sentence: "Poland's freedom shall not be permitted to be used for the oppression of other national groups." He expressed similar views in the Warsaw Zionist weekly *Glos Zydowsky*.

In 1910, a violent polemic broke out between Jabotinsky and the leader of the Polish anti-Semites, Roman Dmowsky. This was a three-cornered fight—Odessa-Warsaw-St. Petersburg—which was hotly commented upon even in the Duma lobby. "I think," said Jabotinsky in his quoted autobiographical notes, "that no other campaign of mine contributed as much as this one to putting Jewish nationalism on the map in the eyes of Jews, Russians and Poles alike." This was largely so because, in the 1910 discussion, Jabotinsky broadened the issue between the Jews and the Poles; he introduced into the picture Polish persecution of the Ukrainians in Galicia, municipal autonomy in Russian Poland, anti-Semitic tendencies in democratic Finland, discrimination against the Negroes in the United States. His conclusion was: democratic principles, even democratic régimes, do not in themselves guarantee justice and equality. Polish (as well as Finnish) anti-Semitism, Jabotinsky stressed, is for the Jews "more offensive and ideologically more harmful than any other form of anti-Semitism, just because its bearer is a nation that is itself complaining of oppression." He insisted that only then would the Polish people prove itself worthy of full national freedom, when it would realize and accept the fundamental truth that "Poland is the country of Poles and Jews alike; Polish towns—hearts and depositories of the country's culture—belong to both nations equally."[13]

This claim provoked furious reaction in nearly the entire Polish press of Warsaw. *Odesskiya Novosti*, where Jabotinsky's article was published, arranged a survey among the local Polish leaders: all of them, even the most "progressive," violently attacked Jabotinsky's views. The Odessa Polish colony proclaimed a boycott of the paper as a reprisal for its hospitality to Jabotinsky's ideas.[14]

These ideas later aroused opposition even in certain Zionist ranks. In the spring of 1913, Jabotinsky published in *Rasswyet* a series of three articles under the heading "Resistance," in which he insisted that we must "remove from the idea of Poland's self-determination the halo of a dogma which is unfailing under all circumstances." With anti-Semitism dominating Polish public opinion, autonomous Poland would mean not equality but slavery for Polish Jewry. Therefore, "in the Polish question our [Jewish] interests coincide not with the line of decentralization, but with the line of state concentration."

The Hebrew organ of Polish Zionists, the daily *Hatzefirah* in Warsaw, heatedly questioned Jabotinsky's "competence" in Polish affairs and his "right" to state publicly his opinion in this matter; it also expressed astonishment that *Rasswyet* published Jabotinsky's articles without editorial reservations. The editors of *Rasswyet* explained that "until competent Zionist bodies take a definite decision," the problem of Polish-Jewish relations remained an "open question," and they were going to publish articles for and against Jabotinsky's views. Taking advantage of this statement, one of the leading Polish Zionists, A. Hartglas, wrote an article in *Rasswyet* titled "Resistance to Resistance," strongly opposing Jabotinsky's stand.[15] *Hatzef ira*, in turn, reacted to the *Rasswyet* attitude in such a violent manner that the latter's editors were obliged to qualify it as both "out of place and inadmissible."

The correctness of Jabotinsky's position in the Polish question was belatedly admitted some two years later. M. S. Aleinikov, a staunch opponent of Jabotinsky's "activism" and of the Legion idea, could not help recalling, in March, 1915, "the prognosis made several years ago by V. Jabotinsky . . . it is now already impossible to contest the justness of his fundamental contention that the Polish-Jewish problem must become the very center of Jewish national policy."[16]

EIGHT

ASSIGNMENT TO TURKEY

The Young Turk Revolution

Since Palestine was a province of the Ottoman Empire, the attitude of the Turkish government toward Zionism had always been of paramount importance. Theodor Herzl's attempts to obtain from the Sultan a Charter for an autonomous Jewish settlement in Palestine proved to be unsuccessful. In 1908, Zionism was confronted with a new situation: the autocratic régime of the Sultan Abdul Hamid II was overthrown by the revolutionary Young Turk Party, and the Ottoman Empire became a constitutional monarchy, with the Young Turks in power.

This event both impressed and encouraged the Zionist world. It was generally felt that it would be easier to conduct settlement and cultural activities in Palestine under a constitutional government, and it was widely believed that the political activities of Zionism would meet with understanding and sympathy on the part of the victorious Young Turk revolutionaries. Ambitious plans were made for a systematic political enlightenment campaign in Constantinople, and for the Zionization of Turkish Jewry which so far had remained almost completely untouched by Jewish national and Zionist tendencies. The Central Committee of the Russian Zionist Organization took the initiative for creating in Turkey a network of press organs and conducting widespread Zionist propaganda.[1] For this purpose it raised considerable funds and put them at the disposal of the Zionist Inner Actions Committee with headquarters in Cologne; this body was headed by Herzl's successor, David Wolffsohn.

115

While still in Vienna, Jabotinsky was keenly interested in the national-ity problem in Turkey. As early as April 4, 1908, he wrote to Ussishkin that he was negotiating with the editors of *Rus* about a trip to Turkey on their behalf. In the meantime the Young Turkish Revolution broke out and the paper was glad to accept his offer. Jabotinsky arrived in Constantinople in the early winter of 1908–09; from there he paid a brief visit to Palestine and returned to Turkey for a few weeks before going back to Russia. In Constantinople he found no difficulty in carrying out his journalistic du-ties. The Young Turks craved publicity and, as he put it, "countless were the ministers who received me and proclaimed unanimously that their country from now on and forever was a Paradise; that there was no longer any difference between a Turk, a Greek or an Armenian—they all were Ottomans: one nation, one language." With regard to Jewish immigration, the general attitude was: "Why not? We shall be very glad if they would scatter over all our provinces, above all in Macedonia—particularly if they undertake to speak the 'Ottoman language.' "

After his return from Turkey, Jabotinsky published a series of seven articles on "New Turkey and Our Perspectives."[2] He stressed the fact that while Young Turkish emigré leaders in Paris were rather favorable toward Zionism, those living in Turkey were not. This unfriendly attitude was motivated by three main reasons: their scant knowledge of Zionism, their fear of Jewish separatism in Palestine, and their tendency to assimilate all non-Turkish ethnic groups. Jabotinsky insisted that since the Turks con-stituted but a minority—about one-third—of the entire population, and were culturally certainly not superior to any ethnic group in the country, they could not assimilate or peacefully dominate non-Turkish nationalities. "The development of national relations in Turkey will very soon reconcile the Young Turks with the inevitable strengthening of the national charac-teristics among the country's ethnic groups and with the latters' striving for self-government and concentration." Particularly delicate were Turkish-Arab relations, which were bound to develop into "competition between two equally strong adversaries." The position of Jewry in this impend-ing conflict was likewise delicate. "Our Palestine vanguard is inclined to overestimate Arab strength," Jabotinsky pointed out; if this *terror arabicus* would lead merely to stressing our wish to live in friendship with the Arabs, this attitude would be useful; but it should not foster attempts to make us conform to Arab political aspirations or to support their anti-Turkish or particularist trends. In the near future such an attitude would certainly "do us more harm in Constantinople than it would help us in Palestine." Palestine Jewry's "foreign policy must take into account not only local pressures, but first and foremost the overall interests of Jewish colonization."

Jabotinsky rejected outright the slogan "silence and work," which at that time was popular as a precept for Zionist work in Palestine, foreshadowing the curious doctrine of "avoiding politics" and concentrating on practical colonizing activities only, which later became dominant in Zionism and which Jabotinsky so consistently combated. Jabotinsky argued "that it was too late, after twenty-five years of Zionist propaganda, to pretend that we are going to Palestine just to till the land. . . . The political method in our movement is absolutely inseparable from the practical work."

First Trip to Palestine

As mentioned above, Jabotinsky squeezed in between his two sojourns in Turkey a hurried trip to Palestine. It was his first visit to the Holy Land. He spent only a very short time there, and this first encounter does not seem to have made a strong and lasting impression on him. There are few traces of this journey in his literary and journalistic production, and he devoted one single page to it in his *Autobiography*.

In the colonies, Jabotinsky talked to small groups of Jewish workers who gave him a brotherly reception. His own version is that he addressed them "in his bad Hebrew." Sh. Schwarz, on the contrary, asserts that at workers' and colonists' meetings Jabotinsky "spoke calmly and self-assuredly and answered questions from the floor in excellent Hebrew."[3] However, Jabotinsky and his audience had different problems. Jabotinsky, who had just come from Turkey, was trying to tell them about the Turkish political scene, while they usually answered: "This is unimportant; what is important is—why isn't there immigration from Russia?"

Jabotinsky was favorably impressed by the well-armed Jewish watchmen and their quiet self-assurance. He was even more impressed by the younger generation in the colonies, the product of the new Zionist colonization and education, to whom he devoted two affectionate feuilletons.

The first—"Tom Thumb, the Little Peasant"—appeared in *Odesskiya Novosti* in January, 1911.[4] Its main personage was Itamar, "going on thirteen... well-versed in the affairs of this world, sensible and talkative, a bit-of-a-man, only of small stature." He spoke a simple and voluble, "natural"

Hebrew and knew intimately every nook and cranny of the country and
their historical backgrounds. His was "an organic perception of the homeland, in which past and present, tradition and hopes for the future, personal
and historical elements, were interwoven." Gay and carefree, as it was normal for a boy of his age to be, Itamar looked disturbed and unhappy when
acknowledging that there was not a single *dunam* in Jewish hands in the
Valley of Jezreel. When (together with Jabotinsky, whose guide he was) Itamar paid a visit to a Catholic monastery and had to face an arrogant Catholic friar, his gaze was "full of cold anger and contemptuous self-assurance;
it was the look of a builder who meets some trammel that has not yet been
put away; the look of a woodcutter measuring a tree that has to be stumped;
the look of a conqueror—and even more than that: of a master."

Avinoam,the hero of the second feuilleton—"The Jew-Boy"[5]— could
have been the twin brother of Itamar. He was also only a few weeks short of
thirteen, and had come to Palestine from the South of Russia when he was
six years old. Jabotinsky particularly appreciated the boy's "inborn breed-
ing" and determination: "he never spoke till he was spoken to . . . answered
questions unhesitatingly." His opinions about the curriculum of the colony's
school were both outspoken and radical: "We learn too much rubbish there,"
was his verdict.

This verdict was based, not on some theories or prejudices, but on a
very personal experience of Avinoam's early childhood in his native Ukrainian village of Bolshaya Lepeticha on the Dniepr River. Once, when he was
fishing for tadpoles with his elder brother Mendel,a member of the youth
group *Pirche Zion*, some Russian boys started teasing the Jewish boys. Mendel defiantly declared that he was proud to belong to the Jewish nation. But
the leader of the native boys answered: "The Jews are not a nation," and
started to prove this thesis as follows:

"If you were a nation, you could swear in your own language. I am a
Russian and so I swear in Russian (and here he pronounced an oath which
was so utterly shocking that Avinoam would not repeat it). Now say the
same thing in your language!"

But Mendel could not.

"And the second thing," said the native boy, "is this: if you were a nation,
you could hit back. Now you see, I am a Russian and I'll give you a good sock
on the jaw (which he at once proceeded to carry out). Can you give me one
like it?"

Mendel could not.

This experience, Jabotinsky reported, apparently formed the basis of Avinoam's entire scholastic program: "Arithmetic and all the rest of it are nonsense. A pupil must learn only two branches of science—to speak Hebrew and to punch hard."

The two feuilletons about Itamar and Avinoam offer an illuminating insight into Jabotinsky's vision of Jewish youth: already at that early stage of his Zionist development, the main features of this vision—the result of his first encounter with Palestine's younger generation—were Hebrew and fitness for defense. Fifteen years later, he made them the fundament of the *Betar* movement.

First Political Appointment

Jabotinsky's first visit to Turkey had produced a favorable impression. Dr. Victor Jacobson, who at that time was responsible for all Zionist activities in Turkey, wrote to David Wolffsohn on December 12, 1908: "He [Jabotinsky] has spent over three months in this country, knows conditions fairly well, and is well equipped with all qualities required in one of our collaborators here: a great oratorical talent and the capacity to inspire confidence in people and win them over. In addition he is very intelligent, possesses wide erudition, is very energetic, etc." Jacobson, therefore, warmly advocated securing Jabotinsky's services for the planned daily paper and in general for Zionist propaganda and enlightenment work in Turkey.

Wolffsohn was apparently impressed by this description of Jabotinsky's qualities and of his usefulness to the expansion of Zionist influence in Turkey. On December 29, 1908, he wrote to Jacobson: "I am familiar with the excellent capabilities of Mr. Jabotinsky, and I consider it only a great advantage to our cause that he should be conducting in Constantinople the propaganda, for which he is so eminently suitable. Please give him my best personal regards. I hope that Mr. Jabotinsky will find an ever increasing scope for his activity, and if conditions shall bring us to undertake something there, his talents will, of course, be taken into consideration."

After a few months' sojourn in Russia, Jabotinsky returned in June, 1909, to Constantinople. There he found a galaxy of leading Zionist personalities: David Wolffsohn arrived together with Nahum Sokolov from Cologne; the Russian Central Committee delegated M. M. Ussishkin and I. A. Rosov. As a result of their deliberations, a Zionist-controlled press

network was established consisting of: a) A daily paper in French, not specifically Jewish in content but advocating a policy of understanding for the
aspirations of all ethnic groups. For this purpose, the newspaper *Courier
d'Orient* was won, which later changed its name to *Jeune Turc*; its nominal
editor and publisher was Djelal Nuri Bey, a Turkish nobleman and son of
a Minister; b) A weekly in French, *L'Aurore*, edited by Lucien Sciutto; c) A
weekly in Judeo-Spanish, *El Judeo —Ha-Hehudi*, edited by David El Kanon;
d) A weekly in Hebrew, *Ha-Mevasser*.

Sokolov and Jacobson suggested that Jabotinsky be in charge of this entire press network; Ussishkin and Rosov, who represented the Russian Central Committee and its funds, readily concurred. There apparently was some
difficulty in getting Wolffsohn's approval. Emil Bernhard Cohn, Wolffsohn's
biographer, rather derisively mentions "a very self-confident young man
from St. Petersburg, named Vladimir Jabotinsky,"[6] and A. Hermoni, who at
that time lived in Constantinople, adds that "Wolffsohn had a weakness for
people holding diplomas from Western Europe."[7] Nevertheless, Jabotinsky's
candidacy was accepted. He was appointed for two years with a yearly salary of 7,200 francs ($1,450). For Jabotinsky, these conditions represented a
great financial sacrifice. As a Russian journalist he earned much more with
less work (*Rus* alone paid him $2,400 yearly for eight articles per month).
A press committee was established consisting of Jabotinsky, Jacobson, and
Hochberg.* It was stipulated that any change in the composition of the committee could take place only with the consent of the Inner Actions Committee
(D. Wolffsohn, Prof. Otto Warburg, and Jakobus Kann) of the World Zionist
Organization; of the representatives of the Russian Zionist Organization
(M. Ussishkin, B. Goldberg, and E. Chlenov); and of the press committee itself.

Building Up a Zionist Press

The bulk of the work lay on Jabotinsky's shoulders. He became the
chief editorialist of *Jeune Turc*. His editorials, recalls Hermoni, "very soon
became an event in the world of the press in Constantinople; people read
and re-read them, quoted them, looked for the possible meaning between
the lines, became enthusiastic over their pungency, simplicity and directness." Jabotinsky soon overcame the difficulties of writing in French which

---

*An old Zionist from St. Petersburg who had lived in the Near East for twenty years and
was thoroughly acquainted with local conditions.

at that time he had not mastered perfectly. Lucien Sciutto, editor of *L'Aurore*, who also supervised the style of the *Jeune Turc*, showed Hermoni various manuscripts of Jabotinsky's articles written in French: at first there were many corrections, errors of style and grammar, Russian and German turns of sentences, in general, solecisms. Three months later, there was practically nothing for Sciutto, who was an astute and excellent editor, to correct. "Now he [Jabotinsky] writes French better than I," Sciutto used to say. "Every passing day," testifies Hermoni, "confirmed Jabotinsky's position as one of the foremost journalists in the Turkish capital." Under his guidance, *Jeune Turc* became one of Constantinople's leading and most influential dailies.

Equally satisfactory were the achievements of the weekly publications. The French organ *L'Aurore*, reported Jabotinsky, "soon earned an authoritative position in all circles of the Jewish intelligentsia in Constantinople and Salonica; it is being read by everybody, even by adversaries and indifferents; its opinions on all pending Jewish questions are expected with impatience, and eagerly discussed." The Judeo-Spanish *El Judeo* had penetrated even into the remotest Jewish communities of Macedonia, and its circulation equaled that of the oldest Sefardic periodical, *El Tiempo*. The Hebrew *Ha-Mevasser* was, of course, limited in its possibilities by the small number of Hebrew-reading people, but through its high literary level, which was appreciated even in the Hebrew press abroad, it considerably strengthened the prestige of the Hebrew language in Turkish Jewry. Jabotinsky contributed several articles to *Ha-Mevasser*—on Hebrew language and literature, on Hebrew as a spoken language, on Bialik, and so on.

Jabotinsky's activities in Turkey were, however, by no means limited to the literary field. Hermoni, who was an eye-witness to Jabotinsky's hard struggle for Zionism on the virgin soil of Turkish Jewry, recalls that Jabotinsky "participated in all the discussions and stormy meetings of active Zionists" and made deep Zionist inroads into the Turkish-Jewish community. Before definitely settling in Constantinople, Jabotinsky spent several weeks in Salonica, at that time "the most Jewish city in the world," where even the post office was closed on Saturdays. During those weeks he "won the admiration and affection of the population of Salonica, particularly of the youth and intelligentsia of this 'Jerusalem of Turkey.' " The local Jewish press related that the brilliant style of this master orator and the charm of his personality wrought a powerful spiritual revolution in this dormant Jewry, "as if a legendary prince had touched it with his magic sword and roused it from its long sleep."

No less impressive were Jabotinsky's achievements in Constantinople. His first lectures on "Our National Revival," "Bialik's Poetry," and other topics "were most inspiring and brought hundreds of people into the Zionist movement, which was new in these circles. The entire Jewish *jeunesse dorée* of the capital began to flock to the meetings of the 'Maccabi'. . . . During the several months of Jabotinsky's activity in Constantinople, the small Zionist nucleus grew into several hundred Zionists, devoted, active and faithful."

The "conquest" by Jabotinsky of two influential Jewish members of the Turkish Parliament—Nissim Russo and Nissim Matzliach Effendi—must be considered a major Zionist achievement. Both were among the founders of the Young Turk movement and had been until then completely indifferent to the Jewish national idea. Sh. Schwarz relates that at the conference of Zionist leaders in Constantinople in December, 1909, Russo stated in his own and Matzliach's name that they fully agreed with the Zionist program as expounded to them by Jabotinsky and were ready to work for his ideas.[8] Another Jewish member of the Turkish Parliament as well as a member of the powerful Young Turk Central Committee, Carasso, also stated in an interview published in the Salonica paper *L'Epoca* that, after a discussion he had with Jabotinsky and Jacobson, he was "in complete agreement with them in regard to Zionism."[9]

Jabotinsky hardly exaggerated when he stated in his letter to the Zionist press committee in Constantinople (May 4, 1910) that "during the last tew months the attitude of the Constantinople Jews toward national consciousness and Zionism has changed strikingly. The fear that Zionism might be high treason is gradually disappearing. Considerable strata of the youth (whose majority was educated in the Alliance schools) feel inspired by our [Zionist] ideals. This attitude has already enabled us to register many victories in the Jewish community and has considerably shaken the moral position of our most influential adversaries."

Political Disappointments

Jabotinsky had every reason to be satisfied with the achievements of his Zionist work in the Jewish community. Much less satisfactory appear to have been the results of his political activities in Turkish governmental circles. This he frankly admitted in his *Autobiography*: "I was not successful with Nazim Bey, the Secretary General of the Young Turk party, the author and initiator of the revolution, and possibly the decisive personal factor which accelerated the downfall of the Ottoman state.... Again the same re-frain:—There are no Greeks, no Armenians, we, all of us, are Ottomans; and we would welcome Jewish immigration—to Macedonia. The same refrain I heard from everybody—Ministers, members of Parliament, journalists.... And I felt that no pressure would help: for them, wholesale assimilation is a *conditio sine qua non* for that nonsense which is their state; and there is for Zionism no other hope but the destruction of that nonsense. I hated Constantinople and my useless work." In this mood, Jabotinsky said, he went to the Ninth Zionist Congress in Hamburg in December, 1909, and returned to Constantinople "with a heart full of dissatisfaction."

Jabotinsky's *Autobiography* was written a quarter of a century after the Constantinople period of his life, and it is probably but natural that he somehow transposed the actual sequence of his political experiences and conclusions and ascribed to the end of 1909 the inferences to which he came only much later; for it seems highly improbable that he would be able to come to such far-reaching conclusions within the short time at his disposal. He arrived in Turkey in June, 1909, and the Hamburg Congress took place in December of the same year: five to six months can hardly be considered a sufficient time for forming so far-reaching and definite a judgment. Much more accurate seems to be Jabotinsky's own timing as expressed in his book *Turkey and the War*, published in London in 1917: "On the eve of the Great War [1914] the disappointment [with the Young Turkish régime] was general and forever incurable." But at the end of 1909 and the beginning of 1910 hardly anybody, including Jabotinsky, was of the opinion that Turkey "must go." There is no conclusive evidence to indicate that Jabotinsky was at that time already in a frustrated frame of mind or irretrievably disappointed as to the possibilities of Zionist political work in Constantinople.

Available testimony concerning Jabotinsky's mood at the Hamburg Congress is contradictory. In a short biography of Jabotinsky, published in Tel Aviv in 1941, S. Gepstein, his intimate lifetime friend, recalls that at the Hamburg Congress Jabotinsky bitterly complained of Young Turkish blind-ness toward Zionist aspirations, saying: "The Young Turks are the worst basis for Zionism. Nothing will be achieved until they leave Palestine." But on December 20, 1909, i.e., when the Congress was still in session, the same S. Gepstein reported in *Rasswyet* a conversation he had with Jabotinsky: "He [Jabotinsky] is as always in a hearty and cheerful mood. 'I am,' he told

me, 'as you know, an incurable optimist, and the last six months in Constantinople did not reform me.' " There is every reason to rely on Gepstein's
report of 1909 at least as much as on his recollection of 1941, thirty-two
years later. The first fully squares with Jabotinsky's appraisal of Nordau's
speech at the Congress, in which Nordau vigorously reasserted the irreduc-
ible minimum of Zionist demands on Turkey. "I am very satisfied," said
Jabotinsky, "with Nordau's speech; it will put an end to all the rumors that
the Zionists are allegedly prepared to make all possible concessions. Now
it is clear that we never forsake the formula: concentration in Palestine and
Jewish nationalism." When saying so, Jabotinsky must have believed that
this formula could, with a reasonable chance of success, be submitted to the
Turkish government and public opinion. It did not sound at all like a *lasciate
ogni speranza* with regard to Zionist chances in Turkey. It is true that even
if Jabotinsky at that time had held very pessimistic views in regard to such
chances and had believed the destruction of the Ottoman Empire to be
both inevitable and desirable, he could not have expressed such views in
public. But he certainly could have refrained from public statements to the
contrary. The fact that he did not do so permits the inference that *at that
time* his pessimistic views on the Turkish problem and theater of action
were at least not yet as strong and definite as they became later.

There can, however, be no doubt that, notwithstanding the striking
success of his journalistic and oratorical activities in Turkey, Jabotinsky was
not only far from smug self-satisfaction, but was getting increasingly unhappy in Constantinople. For this there were several reasons.

In the first place, he violently disliked the Orient in general and Constantinople in particular. We read in his short story "Edmée": "The East? It is
entirely foreign to me.... Mine is a Westerner's mentality.... I must confess
that I did not like Constantinople at all. To begin with the celebrated Bospo-
rus. I cannot stand that crude brilliance, that sun that knows no half-tones,
no shades, and daubs with coarse, screaming colors like a pavement artist....
I have nothing against tortuous, up-and-down streets.... But there must be
in addition some sort of architecture, style, tone. The little streets of Stam-
boul, in my opinion, are merely ugly.... And the mob!—a sort of permanent row of a yelling rabble dressed up in savage-painted rags."[10]

In the second place, there were considerable financial troubles. No political paper in Turkey was financially self-sufficient. Notwithstanding its
moral success, the Zionist-controlled press was no exception from this rule.

When Jabotinsky returned from the Congress (alone, because Dr. Jacobson was taken ill in Hamburg and had to stay in Europe for a cure), Hochberg, who was in charge of finances, showed him the accounts of the press committee proving that from the funds collected in Russia very little remained. Letters to Wolffsohn, Ussishkin, and Goldberg produced no tangible results. Jabotinsky, of course, continued the work unabated, but disappointing difficulties were accumulating.

The Kann Controversy

Then came the "Kann incident."

After a trip to Palestine, made in the spring of 1907, Jakobus H. Kann, one of the three members of the Inner Actions Committee of the World Zionist Organization, published in 1909 a political travelogue in German—Erez Israel. In this book he expressed with the utmost frankness his Zionist political credo and program. He demanded an autonomous Jewish government in Palestine under the sovereignty of the Sultan: "The Turkish government transfers its authority to the Jewish administration which for the duration of the agreement takes over all rights and obligations in respect to the population already settled in the country from the present Turkish administration, so that Turkish taxes will be replaced by Jewish taxes." Palestine frontiers in the author's conception were: Lebanon in the North, the Damascus-Aqaba railway to the East, Egypt to the South, the Mediterranean to the West. All the land belonging to the Ottoman state was to be leased to the Jewish people for at least one hundred years. The Jewish government was to possess sovereignty in matters of taxation and an army and police of its own.[11]

These demands, though fully conforming with the Herzlian concept of Zionism, were in striking contradiction to the policy officially proclaimed and pursued by the Zionist Organization. Jabotinsky was sent to Constantinople with a clear mandate to convince the Turkish government and public opinion, which were highly sensitive to and suspicious of any tendency to further dismemberment of the Ottoman Empire, that Zionism did not aspire to a Jewish state in Palestine and was striving merely for free Jewish immigration to Palestine and purely cultural autonomy. This was the foundation of the entire Zionist propaganda and enlightenment work among Jews and non-Jews alike. It was on this basis that Jabotinsky succeeded in enlisting the cooperation of outstanding Turkish-Jewish personalities in the

Zionist work. Any authoritative Zionist pronouncement to the contrary was tantamount to both a betrayal of their confidence and a wanton destruction of the entire painfully built Zionist position in Turkey.

Even when Kann's book was available in its German text only, it provoked considerable criticism in Zionist ranks, according to Adolf Böhm, the historian of the Zionist movement.[12] It became a real menace when, shortly after the Hamburg Congress, Kann published a French edition of his book and started sending it to leading Young Turkish statesmen and politicians, as well as to the press.[13] Jabotinsky and his colleagues on the press committee were alarmed. They felt that this action was badly jeopardizing all their modest and still very unstable political achievements. Jewish assimilationist circles eagerly jumped at this heaven-sent opportunity and attacked the Zionists with the accusation that because of their "extremist demands" the attitude of the Turkish government toward the Jews had worsened considerably; they demanded restriction of Zionist propaganda in Turkey. In the hope of somewhat alleviating the situation, Dr. V. Jacobson wrote to Wolffsohn demanding that the chapter on "Zionist aspirations" be eliminated from the French edition of Kann's book; the press committee insisted that the Inner Actions Committee should state publicly that Kann's views were not identical with the position of the Zionist organization. Wolffsohn categorically refused to heed these demands. The Central Committee of the Zionist Organization in Russia fully endorsed the position of the press committee. But Wolffsohn did not give in.

Jabotinsky repeatedly urged Wolffsohn to realize the seriousness of the situation. In a letter dated January 29, 1910, he wrote: "Our adversaries will not accept the argument that Jakobus Kann, as a private person, can write whatever he likes. The French edition was published already after the [Young Turkish] revolution* and immediately after the [Hamburg] Zionist Congress. A book by a member of the Inner Actions Committee will be considered as an authoritative interpretation of Nordau's Congress speech. A *dementi* by the President of the Organization will not be trusted. People will say:—It is improbable that one of the [three] members of the [Inner] Actions Committee would have written against the wishes of the two other members. The press committee went on record against the publication of

---

*The preface to the French edition was dated The Hague, May, 1909.

the French edition. . . . It should not be forgotten that the publishers of
L'Aurore and *El Judeo* are Ottoman subjects and that there is martial law in
the country. It will be sufficient that some paper should reprint from the
book the paragraph concerning the Jewish army and Jewish government,
to put our colleagues in a deplorable position. Political consequences are
also possible. The first result will be that all those who have been speaking about Zionism in a formulation which is different from that given by
Kann, will be considered liars. Sciutto, El Kanon and Djelal Nuri will cease
to trust us."

All these arguments were of no avail. Then, on February 7th, the press committee unanimously decided to cable Wolffsohn demanding an official
condemnation by the Inner Actions Committee of Kann's book as being
in contradiction to the Zionist program formulated by the Congress and
Kann's immediate and unconditional resignation; both demands, together
with their motivation, were to be communicated to Zionist organizations
and press in all countries. The telegram was signed on behalf of the committee by Jabotinsky and Hochberg. The very next day Wolffsohn cabled
back that by his "meddling in affairs which are not of his concern," namely
by his appeal to the Zionist organizations in various countries, Jabotinsky
had exceeded his competence: "I forbid further steps in this direction." On
February 10th, he wrote to Jabotinsky:[14] "You and the other gentlemen in
question have been appointed by the Zionist leadership for the sole and
single purpose of working on behalf of the press created there in accordance with the instructions of the leadership"; he even threatened to "draw
consequences" from Jabotinsky's stand—having apparently in mind the latter's dismissal.

In a reply dated February 15th, Jabotinsky politely but firmly explained to Wolffsohn that "everything which is in some way capable of
influencing the position of the [Zionist] press in Constantinople," is—*eo
ipso*—his and the press committee's concern. He also reminded the President that according to Art. 6 of the agreement entered into in August,
1909, any changes in the composition of the press committee required
the consent of the Russian Zionist Central Committee and of the press
committee itself. He respectfully disagreed with Wolffsohn's concept of
the rights of the President of the Inner Actions Committee: "It does not
belong to the competence of the President to permit or to forbid me anything outside of my immediate field of work."

Wolffsohn was both amazed and angered by the independent and firm stand taken by Jabotinsky. His own concept of the relationship between himself and those Zionist personalities working for the Zionist cause in Constantinople, was that of an employer to an employee, of a boss to a subordinate. He did not tolerate any objection or argument. In February, 1909, when Dr. V. Jacobson wrote to him trying to put forward and to insist on certain ideas of his own, Wolffsohn rebuked him bluntly and sternly: "You are mistaken if you think you are the representative of the Zionist Organization. You are, in fact, acting in Constantinople as *my* representative. . . . I give you my orders and you will see how to carry them out."[15] Dr. Jacobson found it possible to accept and to confirm this haughty interpretation of his rights and duties.[16] Wolffsohn was, therefore, flabbergasted when a young Russian Zionist dared so firmly to assert his independence and refused to be considered and treated as a mere functionary, or some obscure member of a press committee.

This exchange of arguments and recriminations between the President and Jabotinsky lasted for quite a long time. The situation had obviously become untenable. No action whatever was taken in regard to Kann's book. The Inner Actions Committee decided to discontinue the subsidy to the press fund, which was the very basis of the existence of the Zionist press in Constantinople, and accepted the following motion: "In view of the fact that the behavior of Mr. V. Jabotinsky towards the Inner Actions Committee is incompatible with the duties of an official of our organization, the Inner A. C. expresses to Mr. Jabotinsky its censure." Dr. Jacobson was asked to inform Jabotinsky of this resolution.[17]

Even Dr. Jacobson, who only two months earlier had accepted Wolffsohn's rebuke to himself, revolted and notified him that he would not convey to Jabotinsky the vote of censure, in which Jabotinsky was treated as a *Beamte*. Wolffsohn was unable to understand this sudden outburst of independence on the part of the usually supine Jacobson. "If the Inner A. C. sees fit to have its views conveyed by one of its representatives to one of its officials in Constantinople, it is the duty of that representative simply to carry out his orders," he wrote on May 19th to Jacobson. "That you personally do not agree with the views of the Inner A. C. is something which you could tell him if you think it necessary." The letter contained a formal injunction "to transmit to Mr. Jabotinsky the vote of the Inner Actions Committee."[18]

Resignation

However, this command came too late. In the meantime, Jabotinsky, on May 4th, submitted to the press committee his resignation as committee member. The letter of resignation contained a detailed report on the activities and achievements of the Zionist press in Turkey; it reiterated Jabotinsky's belief that "influencing Ottoman public opinion is for us [Zionists] of tremendous importance, that it is presently the most decisive and at the same time the only possible political activity, and that this work can be done only through the press." Since the Inner Actions Committee "seems not to feel this way," he "considered that there was no possibility of cooperation."

The two other members of the press committee (Jacobson and Hochberg) refused to accept Jabotinsky's resignation. They signed an official protocol (dated May 6th) in which they "request Mr. Jabotinsky to continue putting at the disposal of the Zionist Party his collaboration which is of eminent value to us and can hardly be replaced." Jacobson wrote to Wolffsohn begging him "not to accept Jabotinsky's resignation as we have done, for it would really be a great loss for the work here." Wolffsohn, however, was obviously only too glad to get rid of the non-conformist collaborator, whom he persisted in considering and treating as just a hired official. With heavy irony he wrote to Jacobson: "As far as the resignation of Mr. Jabotinsky is concerned, I must confess that the views and the behavior of this gentleman become more and more incomprehensible to me." Referring to the clause of August 2, 1909, protocol which provided for a two years' engagement as director of Zionist propaganda in Turkey, Wolffsohn said: "There can thus not be any resignation on the part of Mr. Jabotinsky. His services have been engaged for a period of two years, and at the most he could request us to release him from his obligations ahead of time. Under these circumstances I can consider Mr. Jabotinsky's step only as an illegal notice, which, by the way, I will accept without further ado. As you see, I do not at all share your view that it would be better not to accept his resignation. I do not regret at all that our relations with this gentleman, who may be a passable Zionist but who lacks even a trace of responsibility and discipline, have now been dissolved."[19]

In order to prove that Jabotinsky's resignation would in no way affect the interests of the Zionist cause in Turkey, Wolffsohn found it possible to try to depreciate the value and importance of Jabotinsky's achievements in the field of Zionist and pro-Zionist press. "I am delighted to hear that *Aurore* is good and is gaining influence among Turkish Jewry; but I do not see at all that this should be a merit of Mr. Jabotinsky's. It rather seems to be thanks to the work of Mr. Sciutto. Even before Mr. Jabotinsky joined its editorial staff, *Jeune Turc* was friendly to our cause and on every occasion stood up for Zionism."[20] To this deprecatory attempt, Jacobson replied by giving exact figures on the growth and development of *Jeune Turc* under Jabotinsky's editorship: "If *Jeune Turc* on November 1, 1909, was selling 5,000 copies per week but by the end of April, 1910, 10,000, and at the beginning of May already 11,000; if subscribers in November numbered 1,272 but in April 2,115; if advertisements in November brought Frs. 7,381— but Frs. 9,573 in April—these figures speak for themselves. I am not now talking of the content of the papers where a tremendous advance must be noted." All this, Jacobson stressed, "happened thanks to the leadership and in the first place the efforts of Mr. Jabotinsky."[21]

When Jabotinsky submitted his resignation to the press committee, he stated that he would have to go to Russia for two or three weeks "in order to arrange some personal matters, but he intends to return and remain in Constantinople." The committee decided "to request him to write regular articles for our papers during his trip."[22] When Wolffsohn so eagerly jumped at the occasion to sever all relations with Jabotinsky, the latter's intentions obviously became irrelevant. The further development of Zionist political work in Constantinople belongs to the history of Zionism and not to the biography of Jabotinsky.

The Paradox

Thus the Constantinople chapter of Jabotinsky's life came to a disharmonious end.

In the light of his entire Zionist background and of the further development of his Zionist philosophy and action, it can indeed be considered as a dramatic paradox, a bitter irony that his first conflict with the official leadership of the World Zionist Organization was caused by his fierce opposition to a book forcefully expressing ideas and demands which were Herzlian in their spirit and later became the very foundation of Revisionism. Many years later, when writing his *Autobiography*, Jabotinsky was fully aware of this striking confrontation. He always was a political Zionist, he stressed, and "there is for me no other Zionism; but logic is dearer to me." And the unsparing logic, as he saw it, was that a national movement cannot decide that its policy in Turkey was going to be "immigration and Hebrew language," and not even a single micromillimeter more—in particular not a word about autonomy, which was anathema to the Young Turks—and at the same time condone the distribution of a book by one of the three official World Zionist leaders, openly preaching a Jewish government and a Jewish army. Moreover, the lack of logic in this case was not merely theoretical—it implied very practical and nasty consequences: "deportation of all of us from Turkey and closing down of our press." Jabotinsky was not ready to accept this state of affairs. He felt particularly strongly about the predicament in which this inconsistent policy put those of his colleagues in Constantinople who were not foreigners like himself or Jacobson, but Turkish subjects. In a letter to Wolffsohn (February 15, 1910), he quoted one of the best among them, Sciutto, who at the meeting of the press committee said (in French): "Gentlemen, you can at any moment pack your bags and leave; but I have to remain in Turkey and I don't want to become compromised in the eyes of my government."

It was fortunate that Jabotinsky's apprehensions as to the impending disastrous effects of Kann's book—apprehensions which were fully shared by all his colleagues in Constantinople—proved to be unfounded. No major political complications occurred. Relating this episode a quarter of a century later, Jabotinsky himself seemed not to be very happy—and rightly so—about both the controversy as such and its outcome.

Jabotinsky left Constantinople with mixed feelings of regret and relief. He regretted the necessity of leaving behind him "unfinished business" and the Sefardic Jewish community, of which he had become very fond. "If before my birth God Almighty would have given me the right to select for myself a race and a nation, I would have said:—Israel, well—but a Sefardi," he wrote in his *Autobiography*. On the other hand, he was glad to put an end to an obviously nonsensical situation of permanent friction with World Zionist headquarters, combined with a steadily increasing dislike of and disbelief in the Young Turkish régime. This disbelief eventually developed into an essential element of Jabotinsky's geopolitical Zionist concept.

NINE

THE STRUGGLE FOR HEBREW

Jabotinsky the Hebraist

Jabotinsky was one of the few in the younger Zionist generation O in Russia who took the cultural aspect of Zionism with utter seriousness. To him, the idea of the renaissance of Hebrew as the living language of the Jewish people, both in Palestine and in the Diaspora, was not just an article of the Zionist program to be reverently quoted and paid lip service only; in his spiritual "naiveté" —or honesty—of a neophyte, he considered it as an essential element of the Zionist concept, which had to be realized. The first decade of his Zionist work, the Russian era, is largely filled with an incessant struggle for Hebrew.

With a directness which was so characteristic of his approach to all problems, Jabotinsky started this struggle by resolutely attacking his own deficiency in Hebrew. He approached Yoshua Ravnitzky, his former teacher, with the request to renew their Hebrew studies. Ravnitzky replied that even though he was extremely busy, he would always find time for such a pupil. Three times a week Jabotinsky would come to Ravnitzky, learning avidly and intensely. After a few months he said: "How could I ever have called such a language a dead one?" Recalling this episode, Ravnitzky's son, Eliahu, vividly remembered how much *naches* (enjoyment) his father derived from teaching Hebrew to Jabotinsky, who was very soon able to read in the original writings of Achad Haam and Bialik.[1] In 1904, he was already able to carry on a correspondence in Hebrew. On August 9, 1904, he wrote from St. Petersburg to his "dear teacher" Ravnitzky, in a rather awkward Hebrew, about the progress of fund-raising for the schools in Palestine. He admitted that "this time" his Hebrew style would probably be "worse than on previous occasions," since he was writing the letter in the office of the daily *Rus*, where there was no Hebrew dictionary and not "a live Jewish soul"; he was therefore not sure whether or not he really knew "the holy language" and hoped that this time his teacher "would forgive him more than usually." Later, Jabotinsky attended a number of lectures on Talmud and Hebrew literature at the Odessa *Yeshiva*. In a passing remark in his pamphlet *On Territorialism* (1905), he stressed that "having relatively recently started studying Talmud, I most respectfully admire the depth of wisdom which is treasured up in its pages."[2]

By 1904, Jabotinsky was already capable of masterfully translating from Hebrew Bialik's *Massa Nemirov*. But he was far from being satisfied by this achievement. In Vienna (1907-08), where he concentrated on nationality problems, he also found time and energy for continuing, without a teacher, his Hebrew apprenticeship: he copied entire chapters (in Latin characters) from Hebrew books, to increase his vocabulary and to improve his style. In a letter to M. M. Ussishkin (December 24, 1907) he mentioned that he was preparing himself for an article he undertook to write for a Hebrew publication "in a very original way"—by compiling for his own use a Russian-Hebrew dictionary on the basis of Klausner's Hebrew-Russian dictionary. "As soon as I will be at least half through [with this spadework], I will start writing the article." In Constantinople (1908-09) he was already a regular and brilliant contributor to the Hebrew weekly *Ha-Mevasser*.

The next stage of his Hebrew curriculum was the shift from prose to poetry. In 1910, he told Bialik of his intention to translate into Hebrew *The Raven* by Edgar Allan Poe, but expressed doubts whether his command of the Hebrew language was sufficient for the task. Bialik advised him to try, and promised to make any necessary corrections. When Jabotinsky brought the translation of the first stanza, Bialik made a few minor changes; the second stanza called for fewer corrections; the rest was translated by Jabotinsky entirely by himself—"and it was a remarkable translation," Bialik told L. Sherman.[3]

Simultaneously Jabotinsky started assiduous work on the translation into Russian of the major poems of Bialik. Several Russian publishing houses to which he submitted the manuscript were hesitant to undertake its publication, or were offering ridiculously unfavorable conditions.

S. D. Salzman, who happened to come to Odessa from St. Petersburg where he then resided, boldly took the risk. The book appeared in an elegant edition, with a biographical-critical "introduction" by Jabotinsky, and was an immediate and startling success. It became a best-seller not only on the Jewish but on the general Russian book market. Seven consecutive printings of thirty-five thousand copies were sold within two years.[4]

In 1911, Jabotinsky founded in Odessa a publishing house "Turgemon," whose aim was to make available to the Hebrew-reading youth the classics of world literature. The funds for this undertaking (twenty-five thousand rubles) were provided by the widow of the Zionist leader Moshe Zeitlin; the board of directors included M. M. Ussishkin, Chaim Nachman Bialik, and Yoshua Ravnitzky. Until the outbreak of the war, "Turgemon" published among others Giovaniole's famous novel *Spartaco* (in Jabotinsky's translation), Cervantes' *Don Quixote* (translated by Bialik), and *The Arabian Nights* (translated by Yeyvin). Jabotinsky was also interested in the publishing house "Maddo," established by a group of friends of Hebrew in order to publish text books in that language. In a letter to Dr. E. V. Chlenov (April 25, 1914), Jabotinsky expressed his concern about the intention of the publishers to limit the use of vowel signs to foreign terms and "dubious" cases only. He argued that this was insufficient. Many students of the planned Hebrew University were going to be youngsters without any Hebrew background and would be unable to read a Hebrew text lacking such signs. He therefore insisted that all text books intended for use by University students be printed with vowel signs.

The first-known public appearance of Jabotinsky with a speech in Hebrew was his address at the celebration of the seventy-fifth birthday of the "Grandfather of Yiddish literature," Mendele Mocher Sforim, which was held in the beautiful hall of Odessa's Municipal Stock Exchange on December 29, 1910. The Russian-Jewish poet S. Frug and even Ch. N. Bialik spoke in Yiddish. Jabotinsky's address, delivered in a perfect Hebrew, was the sensation of the evening. He used the Sefardic pronunciation which was at that time not yet so current in Russia. Mendele, though not a friend of modern Hebrew, and accustomed to the Ashkenazi pronunciation, listened intently, and when Jabotinsky finished, he rose and warmly shook Jabotinsky's hand.[5]

In Odessa, Jabotinsky belonged to a small group of zealots who always spoke only Hebrew among themselves. S. Ben Baruch (Sh. Schwarz), who worked in the editorial offices of *Odesskiya Novosti*, relates that even there they talked only Hebrew to each other, though none of their colleagues understood the language. This was the only field in which Jabotinsky—known for his meticulous observance of the strictest code of consideration and good manners—was ready to disregard etiquette.[6]

Reformatory Attempts

From the very inception of his Zionist career, the problem of national education was uppermost on Jabotinsky's spiritual agenda. In so far as organized modern Jewish education existed in Russia at the beginning of the twentieth century, it was largely in the hands of the "Society for the Advancement of Learning Among the Jewish Population." In Odessa, this body was controlled by die-hard assimilationists; thirteen elementary schools, four courses for adults, eight schools for boys, etc., maintained or subsidized by the Society, were very poor in Jewish content and were conducted in the spirit of outright Russification.

In 1901–02, about forty Zionist and nationalist leaders of Odessa established a special "Committee for Nationalization," headed by Achad Haam, S. M. Dubnov, M. Disengoff, J. Ravnitzky, and Ch. N. Bialik, to work for the reform of the Jewish schools. They demanded that the Society increase the number of hours devoted to Jewish subjects and improve the quality of teaching of these subjects.[7] When Jabotinsky became a Zionist, he eagerly joined this struggle, giving it a fresh and militant impulse and introducing an argumentation of his own. Almost all of the leaders of the "Committee for Nationalization" were themselves reared in the atmosphere of Hebrew culture and Jewish tradition; they fought against the Russification of the younger generation. Jabotinsky himself belonged to this Russified generation, and he combated assimilation out of his own spiritual experience. The objective of the intellectuals of the past generation, he argued, had been to arouse interest in secular culture among Jews. But now, when this revolutionary goal had already been widely achieved, those responsible for the education of youth were completely neglecting their duty of imbuing the new generation with the spirit of faithfulness to and love for their own people. This system was responsible for the evaporation of Jewish ideals from the upper and middle classes of the Jewish community and for the desertion of youth, which was reared in the spirit of unlimited adoration for Russian culture and life and knew nothing of the greatness and beauty of Jewish spiritual values; in Jewish life, they saw only the misery, ugliness, and humiliation of the ghetto existence. It was, therefore, again necessary to revolutionize the educational system: to make the study of Judaism the center of the school curriculum, to strengthen spiritual ties between the individual and the nation, to give the youth the proud feeling of belonging to a great people.

Jabotinsky developed this complex of ideas in a pamphlet *Jewish Education*, published in 1905.[8] At this early stage, his concrete program of reforms to be introduced in the existing school system was a relatively modest one. He energetically denied the allegation by the assimilationist camp that the proponents of a national Jewish school were demanding the immediate introduction of Hebrew as the language of instruction for all the subjects of the school curriculum. "What is of foremost importance," he wrote, "is not the language but the very foundation on which the entire educational structure is based." He maintained that it would be sufficient to infuse into the Jewish school a new spirit: to make national consciousness the very core of the educational system, to imbue the pupils with the proud feeling that Jewish history and culture are both great and beautiful, that being a Jew is not a curse, but a privilege.

It was in line with this concept that he had been for years actively interested in the gymnasium for girls, which his widowed sister, Mrs. T. E. Jabotinsky-Kopp, had established in Odessa in 1901. The language of instruction was Russian, but special attention was being paid to the study of Hebrew and Jewish history. Up to 1906, when the school was granted the status of a regular private secondary school, Jabotinsky covered its rather substantial deficits out of his journalistic earnings; from 1906 on it became self-supporting and existed until 1920.[9] An entire generation of Jewish girls received a fairly good Jewish education in this institution of learning.

The Odessa "Committee for Nationalization" was very active in the years 1901–04. Then, Achad Haam left for England, Dubnov and Jabotinsky went to St. Petersburg, Disengoff to Palestine, and the battle against the assimilationist policy of the "Society for the Advancement of Learning" calmed down.

In 1910, Jabotinsky returned to Odessa and again joined in the struggle. The slogan of the nationalist group was "Two-Fifths," meaning that at least 40 per cent of the curriculum of the schools controlled by the Society must be devoted to the teaching of Hebrew and Jewish history—a much more ambitious program than that of 1903–05. It was a fierce and long war. Jabotinsky was, of course, not the only one to wage it. But because he was the most dynamic orator of his group and had at his disposal the columns of *Odesskiya Novosti*, widely read by the Jewish intelligentsia, he became in the eyes of the opposing camp the incarnation of the entire nationalist crusade and the main object of all their anger and attacks. The list of candidates presented by the nationalist group to replace the then ruling Committee of the Society was headed by such names as Ussishkin, Bialik, and Druyanov, but, recalled Jabotinsky many years later, "since you shout the loudest in Russian, all the wrath is concentrated on you." The assimilationists mobilized all their forces and defeated the entire nationalist slate. Jabotinsky vividly described the atmosphere of this final contest:[10]

A select crowd was there, unquestionably the most popular and respectable gentlemen of the Odessa community. About midnight, after the theater or concert, their bedecked wives appear; none of them are interested in the discussion, but they also come to cast their ballot against the nationalists, look hatefully at you, and cheer every speaker who demonstrates that you are opposed to cultural advancement, a religious fanatic and a demagogue of hate against the Russian people and European civilization.

This was a painful defeat of an earnest concerted effort by the nationalist camp to achieve a reasonable degree of nationalization through compromising with the existing system of Jewish education and introducing some reforms into the prevailing curricula. Yet, by that time, Jabotinsky's own concept of national education went much further than the "two-fifths" program. He came to the conclusion that no useful purpose could be achieved by partial mending of the existing school pattern and by merely increasing the number of hours devoted to Jewish subjects. His own program was completely different and more ambitious.

Struggling for the Hebrew School

Jabotinsky devoted the years 1910-13 mainly to propaganda for the idea that the language of all instruction in Russia's Jewish schools, from the lowest form to the highest, must be Hebrew. This concept of national education looked both revolutionary and fantastic, not only to assimilationists or Yiddishists, but also to the leading minds in the Zionist movement. He conducted this struggle almost singlehanded.

Jabotinsky flatly rejected the contention that the *cheder*—the "old" and the "new" alike—was an adequate instrument of a truly national education, because only Jewish subjects (Bible, Talmud, Hebrew language, Jewish history) were taught there. He also rejected the then popular scheme of a Jewish school network with a full-fledged program including both Jewish and general subjects, where the first would be taught in Hebrew and the latter in Russian. This type of bilingual school, he insisted, was not an instrument of national education but, on the contrary, merely a tool for complete Russification. A normal, average child is not interested in specifically national subjects as such. What fascinates him is a complex of everyday questions: What is electricity? Where is America? Why aren't there any horses in front of a train? The basic factor forming a child's mind and soul is, therefore, the language in which the so-called general subjects are taught. The most dangerous thing would be to erect two separate sectors of knowledge in the pupils' minds: one that is purely national in content, Hebrew in its linguistic form, which has no bearing upon the realities of life; and the other, which embraces everything that is of general human interest and is being acquired through the medium of another language. Jabotinsky's scheme provided for a Hebrew school which devotes sufficient time to both Jewish and general subjects, and wherein *all* topics, both Jewish and general, are taught in Hebrew only, from the first to the last day of school.[11]

With this program Jabotinsky came before Jewish public opinion in Russia. For two years he traveled over half of the country with a lecture theme "The Language of Our Culture." He repeated it in fifty Jewish communities, each time before thousands of listeners; in some cities he spoke twice, three, even four times. On the whole, he presented his views to more than one hundred thousand listeners. "I memorized this lecture word by word," he recalled, "and though I do not think too much of the orator in me, this is the only lecture upon which I shall pride myself all my life."

"The Language of Our Culture" was indeed a perfect specimen of clear and courageous thinking, of rich documentation and of masterly delivery. To prove his point, Jabotinsky mobilized an abundant arsenal of experience gained by other nations which were striving for national renaissance. With almost cruel logic he demonstrated the futility of half-measures, of the attempts to have a national school "divided against itself"—half-Russian, half-Hebrew and/or Yiddish. Though repeated tens of times almost without any changes, the lecture was on each occasion an impassioned, oratorically powerful plea, listened to with rapture by enthusiastic audiences.

There is a widespread notion that as a rule Jabotinsky wrote his lectures and speeches, memorizing them word by word and delivering them by rote. This is not true. Neither at that time, nor at any other time, did Jabotinsky ever write his speeches. True, he prepared them most carefully and minutely, both in content and form. To him, a speech or a lecture was an important and responsible public service, which must not be performed impromptu; every thought, every argument and fact had to be carefully and earnestly weighed and checked, molded into an organic entity and presented in a polished and elegant form, embellished with wit and bland irony. He therefore labored on each of his lectures like a scientist or artist laboring on a scholarly treatise or a work of art. Very little, if anything, was left to offhand inspiration—not even an intonation or a gesture. Every possible avenue of conveying the idea and of implanting it in the audience's mind and soul was explored in advance. The result was a perfectly integrated oratorical unit, from which he rarely deviated.

What prevented his lectures from becoming stale and sounding like a worn-out record, was the stage fright from which Jabotinsky was never free, even if it was the twentieth or thirtieth time that he had to deliver the same speech. He was nervous and jittery before every public appearance, avoided speaking to anybody, needed solitude and concentration. Only after the lecture was over did he feel relieved and relaxed; and it is a fact that more than once a lecture, which was masterfully delivered and had made a tremendous impression one day, sounded flat and failed to captivate the audience the very next day.

In many places, a lively and often passionate discussion followed Jabotinsky's lecture. His main and most bitter opponents usually were the partisans of Yiddish, whose arguments Jabotinsky countered alternatively by an array of well-arranged facts and witty repartee. After a lecture in Kiev, which was a fortress of Yiddishism, several opponents made abundant use of the sentimental appeal of Yiddish to the Jewish masses. The very sound of a Yiddish word, they argued, evokes a powerful response in every Jewish heart, brings forth tears—something Hebrew could never achieve. Jabotinsky answered by an unexpected sally: Certain arias from popular operas are beloved in whatever language they are sung; they appeal to the sensitivity, to the ear and the heart of any music lover. *Nu, is wos?* (So what?), he asked in Yiddish. Will anybody ever claim that the original language of such an opera is his own national language? This *Nu, is wos?* won the day for

Hebrew. It became a household word in Kiev; the entire local Russian press amusedly quoted this repartee, together with the rest of Jabotinsky's rich factual and logical argumentation.[12]

Another town where Jabotinsky's wit and sense of humor prevailed was Bialystok. In this industrial town the Socialist Bund was firmly entrenched and appeared in strength at Jabotinsky's lecture, demanding that their spokesman be given the floor after Jabotinsky. The chairman of the meeting was, however, forced to announce that the Russian police had barred any discussion. The Bund people then started shouting that in that case they would not let Jabotinsky speak either. For about a quarter of an hour Jabotinsky remained quietly sitting on the rostrum. Finally he indicated that he wanted to say a few words. The audience, curious, fell silent. Addressing himself to the "Gentlemen my opponents," Jabotinsky advised them not to be too disappointed. Every experienced lecturer who expects opponents and hecklers and knows who they are going to be, he said, deliberately leaves a few weak spots in his speech and at the same time carefully prepares beforehand the most potent answers to their possible objections. The opponents and hecklers, however, do not know what is in store for them and that they are being trapped: they eagerly jump at the weak spots, concentrate their attacks on them, and pay little attention to the rest of the lecture. Having the last word, the speaker makes ample use of his stratagem and victoriously displays the heavy artillery of previously hidden powerful arguments. So, don't be too unhappy about the missed chance of a discussion. . . . The audience liked this subtle little revelation of a lecturer's "professional secret." Even the Bundists could not help smiling and let Jabotinsky deliver his lecture in peace.[13]

However, Jabotinsky was not fooled by the oratorical success of his propaganda tour, and least of all in the Zionist circles themselves: "In every city the Zionists listened and applauded, and after the lecture they came to me and, in a tone one uses when talking to a naughty little boy, said: 'Fantastic!' . . ." This Zionist attitude was particularly painful to Jabotinsky. In a series of articles published in *Rasswyet* in April-May, 1913, he bitterly accused the Zionist movement in Russia of a complete lack of clarity and action in the field of national culture: "Our most serious defect is that we Zionists, as a collective body, do not conduct any cultural work." Jabotinsky demanded that the Zionist Organization as such should undertake the task of full Hebraization of Jewish education in Russia.[14]

A lively discussion followed. Dr. D. Pasmanik, one of the foremost theoreticians and leading minds in the movement, published a series of five articles on "Jewish Creative Power in the Diaspora," in which he strongly defended a much more limited program.[15] It would be enough, he insisted, if Hebrew would be used in Jewish schools for teaching Jewish subjects only. A Jewish youth must learn to read and write Hebrew, and an adult, to know our national cultural values in the original. "This can be implemented, but no more, since more than that Diaspora Jewry never achieved," Pasmanik asserted. For this purpose, the existing "Society for the Advancement of Learning Among the Jews" would be sufficient. "Cultural work in the national spirit must become an all-Jewish matter, and not a purely Zionist one. . . . It is impossible to introduce into this field a sectarian spirit."

The internal dissensions in Russian Zionism came to a head at the conference of the Russian delegates to the Eleventh Zionist Congress held in Vienna in August, 1913. Jabotinsky refused to accept a mandate to the Congress, but he was a delegate to the Russian conference. He came with the sole purpose of inducing the Zionist movement in Russia to take a definite stand in the question of Hebrew education and to create the necessary machinery for starting practical work in this field.

In the debate on the report of the Central Committee, Jabotinsky accused the leadership of Russian Zionism of lack of *ratzon* —lack of the will to work and of faith in what they had been doing; in particular, in the domain of culture and school, "nothing tangible was created, and no definite program was even worked out, and no directives for activity were given." He delivered this speech in Hebrew, though, as he said, he realized that some of the delegates would not understand him and that he himself was thus weakening the influence of his arguments. "But it is a shame," he insisted, "that at Zionist Congresses, supposed to serve the renaissance of the nation, one hears foreign languages. In this question there can be no compromise. Those among the delegates who don't know Hebrew, must take a teacher and learn." Jabotinsky's admonition apparently was not made in vain. The *Rasswyet* correspondent specifically noticed "the interesting detail" that a considerable part of the debate on the Central Committee's report was conducted in Hebrew.[16] Later, another correspondent (J. Klebanov) stressed that for the first time since the inception of Zionism so much Hebrew was heard at a Congress: "As if people were ashamed in these solemn days to talk a foreign language, as if all of them had taken the vow about which

Jabotinsky spoke so fervently and beautifully—not to speak a foreign language at Zionist Congresses and conventions."[17]

On August 18 (31), Jabotinsky presented his report (also in Hebrew) on "Zionist Cultural Work in Russia." The *Rasswyet* correspondent reported that "around this report there were many rumors and conversations from the very beginning of the conference" and that "everybody looked forward to it with great impatience." Jabotinsky's proposals were:

1. The Zionists in Russia begin immediately with the establishment of a net of kindergartens and model schools, in which instruction will be conducted in Hebrew only.

2. The Zionists begin with the translation into Hebrew and publication of standard literature for children and youth.

3. A special department will be established to direct and administer this work.

In the subsequent discussion, an impressive galaxy of Zionist leaders firmly opposed Jabotinsky's suggestions. Among his opponents were N. Sirkin, I. Grinbaum, Dr. J. Brutzkus, Hillel Zlatopolsky, Dr. J. Klausner, Dr. M. Glikson. Their approach and arguments were different, but they were all strongly, even violently, antagonistic. Summarizing the various trends within this motley opposition, *Rasswyet* divided the opponents into three basic groups:[18]

1. Hebraists who were in full agreement with Jabotinsky, but considered his proposals as utopian.

2. Yiddishists who, out of democratic considerations, were for Yiddish as the language of the Jewish masses.

3. Those who negated any Zionist constructive work in the *Galut*; their most articulate spokesman was Dr. Klausner who argued that, should any truly Hebrew education be possible in the *Galut*, then why should we strive for Palestine?

The debate took up the whole session. Jabotinsky made a strong, point by point, answer to the arguments of the objectors.

Most of them agree, he stressed, that Jewish subjects, which are indeed difficult and complicated, should be taught in Hebrew—why then should they object to Hebrew being the medium for instruction in the much easier general subjects? Answering the question as to how it is possible to teach children arithmetic in a language which is strange to them, Jabotinsky restated his premise that Hebrew kindergartens would be created where children should master spoken Hebrew before they entered school. He cited examples of several European countries where the dissimilarity between the language taught in school and the one spoken at home was as great as the discrepancy between two different languages. He called attention to Zionist schools in Palestine where children had many and various linguistic backgrounds; this, however, did not prevent Hebrew from becoming the sole language of instruction. If it was possible to organize a Hebrew school network in the Arabic environment of Palestine, there was no reason why it should be impossible to establish similar schools in a Russian or Polish environment. Erez Israel, Jabotinsky stressed, does not possess any other magic but one: it fascinates all those who have a national will; and there are, of course, many persons with a similar will in the Diaspora as well. Taking up the argument that Yiddish, as a mother tongue widely spoken in Jewish households, also has national significance and a claim to a place in the national school, Jabotinsky said: the fact that a language is spoken does not make it a national language; the only valid criterion for determining the national language is national tradition, national conscience, and instinct. Jewish children in Russia speak several languages—in accordance with their place of residence—but the cultural future of a nation thousands of years old cannot be determined by the language which this or another Jewish child happens to be speaking. We Jews live in foreign countries and we undoubtedly have to learn their languages, but— like all other nations living in dispersion—we, too, must clearly differentiate between the vernacular and the language of national education. The first is one of the *subjects* taught in school, the latter is the *language of teaching*.

After Jabotinsky's impressive rejoinder, which silenced many objectors, a committee of five was nominated to prepare a resolution; at least three among them were opposed to his ideas. Finally, reports *Rasswyet*, the conference "after a stormy session, by a small majority, accepted Jabotinsky's theses." However, nearly all the recognized leaders voted against them; the majority consisted of "backbenchers," delegates from the provinces. Besides, Jabotinsky's original proposals were considerably diluted.[19] In its final form the resolution said that the Zionists in Russia should "endeavor" to convert Hebrew into a language of education; they must "actively support" the establishment of Hebrew kindergartens and elementary schools; they must "take the necessary steps" to organize

Hebrew teachers; they were to "care" for the systematic publication of manuals and children's literature, and to "help" spread spoken Hebrew. The carefully chosen, deliberately innocuous, and circumventive verbs, supplanting direct action by pious intention, practically nullified the value of Jabotinsky's victory. No special department to implement the resolutions was established; this meant that the Zionist Organization as such would not be directly involved in Hebrew cultural activities; it was specifically stated that the Zionists would work "in contact with the *Histadrut Ivrit* and other Jewish cultural institutions."

The Yiddishist elements in Russia, who feared and hated Jabotinsky's militant Hebraism and accused him of being "Hebrew crazy," fully grasped the true significance of the Vienna resolutions. In an address on "Militant Hebraism," delivered in the St. Petersburg Jewish Scientific and Literary Society, one of the Yiddishist leaders, Israel R. Yefroykin, triumphantly stated: "Jabotinsky was alone in his sincere wish to put the question squarely: if we [Zionists] are for Hebrew, then we must introduce it to the fullest extent both in school and at home. But the Zionists became afraid of this sharp presentation of the problem and voted resolutions which, instead of a categoric imperative to establish [Hebrew] schools, contain merely wishes for the realization of this ideal."[20]

In this, Yefroykin proved to be right. Two years later, Jabotinsky sadly noted the fact that, in violation of the clearly expressed wish of the Vienna conference, the Zionist Organization in Russia had "till now not established one single Hebrew school or published one single Hebrew manual."[21]

In the light of further developments, it can hardly be denied that in the field of the Hebraization of the Diaspora—just as in many other fields—Jabotinsky's vision proved to be both prophetic and realistic. Within a decade after the end of World War I, a widespread network of purely Hebrew schools maintained by the *Tarbut* (Culture) organization was created in Eastern Europe. At the *Tarbut* Conference in Danzig in July, 1928, Jabotinsky was able proudly to state that 80,000 to 100,000 children were receiving their education in the *Tarbut* schools in East European countries; that more than 2,000 qualified teachers were serving in these schools, and that 160 to 180 teachers were graduating annually from the existing eight teachers' colleges; that in Lithuania, 93 per cent of all Jewish children of school age were receiving their education in the *Tarbut* schools.[22]

Jabotinsky was the trailblazer of this flourishing national and cultural development. At the Jabotinsky Memorial Meeting held in London in September, 1941, Dr. S. Ravidowicz, speaking on behalf of the *Tarbut* Association, stated that "all the Hebrew schools and institutions in the Diaspora had to thank Jabotinsky for their existence. Jabotinsky's name would remain ever green in the history of Hebrew renaissance." Jabotinsky himself valued his work in this field more than any of his other achievements. He once told his son Eri: "People usually extol the 'Legion' chapter, but I believe that the main and the most important thing I have ever done, was my struggle for Hebrew."[23]

It took a long time to prove to the Jewish world that the bitter opposition Jabotinsky met with in Vienna was unjustified, and the Vienna experience left a lasting and painful mark in his spiritual memory. Many years later, in a moving article "My Typewriter Speaks," he sadly recalled the hostile atmosphere which surrounded him at the Russian Zionist conference:

> You stand on the platform and move that Hebrew should be introduced as the language to be used in all Jewish schools in Russia, exactly as in Erez Israel. Your audience does not consist, God forbid, of assimilationists. . . . This is a conference of Zionists like yourself. Nevertheless, do you recall the reception given your resolution? "Nonsense!" is heard from the delegates' corner. "Childish!" "Scribe, why do you concern yourself with questions of pedagogy?" . . . You feel that not only do they disagree with you (how could they disagree on such a subject?), but that you annoy them, you provoke anger, and people hate you slightly . . . only slightly . . . but it comes from your own comrades, and is, therefore, ten times as bitter.

Later, in his *Autobiography*, Jabotinsky wrote: "It is difficult to believe, impossible to explain—but I met with derision at a *Zionist* conference. . . . They were not only in disagreement with my resolutions—they did not believe even the facts I had been speaking of. . . . Of course, the conference did not dare to reject such a proposal: it was accepted—with laughter and ironical cheers. I left the conference as a stepchild who abandons a home which he always considered as his own and in which he suddenly has become a stranger. . . . I do not wish to exaggerate. There was a prophet in Israel to whom a son was born and whom he named *Lo-Ami* (Not of my people). Were another son born to me in those days, I would have called him *Ivriani* (I am a Hebrew)."

Jabotinsky plainly regretted that he went to Vienna, where his comrades in the Russian Zionist movement "severed the last bonds connecting him with that naive Zionism."

TEN

IN THE SERVICE OF THE UNIVERSITY

The Appeal of the Hebrew University

At the Eleventh Zionist Congress in Vienna in August, 1913, Dr. Ch. Weizmann submitted a proposal for the establishment of a Hebrew University in Jerusalem, with schools of medicine, law, and political science.* The proposal met with great enthusiasm. The Actions Committee was authorized to appoint a commission for preparatory work for the establishment of a Hebrew University in Jerusalem.[1]

Jabotinsky's mood after the Russian Zionist conference which preceded the Congress was anything but happy. He was deeply hurt and disappointed by the attitude of the Zionist leadership toward himself and his scheme for the Hebraization of Jewish education. He felt that there was no more place for him and his work in the Russian Zionist family.

However, the idea of a Hebrew University appealed to him very strongly. It was part and parcel of his own concept of the Zionist cultural effort. If he failed in the attempt to induce the Zionist Organization to undertake a systematic Hebraization of the Diaspora, he could at least do his share with regard to Palestine. In November, 1913, the Actions Committee met in Berlin and appointed a "Greater Preparatory Commission" for the Hebrew University consisting of all members of the Greater Actions Committee plus Jabotinsky; the "Working Committee," with its seat in Berlin, was composed of five members of the Inner Actions Committee, to whom were added

---

*The idea of a Hebrew University in Jerusalem was first launched in 1901 when the Fifth Zionist Congress in Basel passed a resolution in favor of the project.

147

Dr. Weizmann, Jabotinsky, Wolffsohn, and Ussishkin. Jabotinsky agreed to assume responsibility for the University campaign in Russia.[2] Subsequently, at a session held in Berlin at the end of February, 1914, the Actions Committee appointed a commission for the work in Russia, headed by Jabotinsky, with M. M. Ussishkin, I. A. Naiditch, and I. A. Rosov as members.

Jabotinsky established a special "University office" in St. Petersburg, but he very rarely stayed there. Most of the time he was on the move—lecturing, seeing people, collecting material on the problems facing the University project, raising funds. His letters to the "Working Committee" in Berlin bear eloquent testimony to the great amount of work he did during the first six months of 1914.[3] The net income from his lectures went to the "school fund." No direct fund-raising for the University was as yet envisaged, only preparatory steps for approaching selected wealthy individuals capable of contributing amounts over five thousand francs. Although in some provincial towns this minimum appeared to be too high, prospects looked very promising. In addition to money, Jabotinsky was after medical and other scientific books for the University, and negotiated with the publishing house "Nauka" (Science) in Moscow about publication of scholarly books for the University fund.[4]

He devoted much attention and time to the preparation of a special volume containing material and articles on problems of the Hebrew University, to be published in Hebrew, Yiddish, and Russian. Questionnaires in three languages were sent to Jewish student organizations in Western Europe, inquiring about the number of Jewish students, their countries of origin, the schools they were registered with, university fees, the budget of an average student, existing restrictions on foreign (in particular Jewish) students, etc. Jabotinsky established permanent contact with various Jewish student bodies and was specially interested in *Kadima*, an organization of students at the American College in Beirut. Three weeks before the war broke out, he wrote to Dr. S. Aisenstadt, asking him to contribute to the volume an article on judicial terminology.[5]

University vs. Research Institute

Without neglecting the practical work of propaganda, organization, and fund-raising in Russia, Jabotinsky took an active part in the overall planning of the University. In the spring of 1914, he made an extensive study trip to Central, Western, and Southern Europe inquiring into the problems of organization and budget of the two private universities of Belgium—at Louvain and Brussels—as well as of the Flemish university of Ghent; in Germany he visited for the same purpose the universities of Heidelberg and Tübingen, in Switzerland those of Geneva and Berne; in the Netherlands he investigated the universities of Leiden and Utrecht, and in Italy those of Rome and Padua (the latter was a famous institution of higher learning with a very modest budget).

The main lesson he learned from this study trip was that the type of institution of higher learning as envisaged by Dr. Weizmann and endorsed by the Actions Committee in November, 1913, was not only unsuitable for the vital interests of Jewish youth but was also without precedent in the practice of the universities of other nations. "Dr. Weizmann merely wanted research institutes in which scientists would work and strive to win the Nobel Prize, and not a school in which students would study," Jabotinsky later stated in his *Autobiography*.

Jabotinsky's own vision of the University was different. He wanted an institution of higher learning that would offer a solution to the problem of a large section of Jewish youth which was barred from or discriminated against in the universities of Russia and Western Europe. He wanted a "genuine," regular *Lehranstalt* where professors would teach and students would learn, an institution which the students would leave, provided with the necessary knowledge and diploma that would give them a chance to apply this knowledge constructively in everyday life, whether in Palestine or in the Diaspora.

The fundamental cleavage between the Zionist philosophy of Weizmann and Jabotinsky manifested itself very clearly even at that early period of their Zionist careers. To Jabotinsky, the University was first and foremost an answer to the *Studentennot*, just as the Jewish state had to be an answer to the *Judennot*; both were an urgent necessity. Weizmann resolutely and even scornfully opposed this view. In a letter to the University Committee in Berlin (April 25, 1914), he ironically referred to the wish of "Jabotinsky and other Russian friends to have the University right away; Jabotinsky even has a project for realizing this idea," and he continued:

> Now as for the idea itself and even more that project, I wish to voice my opposition very distinctly and very clearly. Those gentlemen are basing their opposition to the existing project as submitted by me (research institutes) on Russian moods. They want immediately a university because in Russia there is

an emergency. I want to stress with the greatest emphasis that this is a dangerous, a lethal viewpoint. We can utilize the Russian students but only in the sense that we tell the Jews: if we make a serious start, in the future, maybe ten years from now, we may have a university; furthermore, the only earnest beginning is the evolutionary one, via research institutes. This can be proved, supported and defended. I know that it will be less electrifying than the false and seductive project of a fourth-class college which for the same Jews will not have any practical or political value, nor any national significance for us. As the highest intellectual focal point, as a gathering place of Jewish creativeness, the research institute is more than a university. For Palestine itself, for problems of colonization, it is again the research institute and not the college that is decisive.

Dr. Weizmann found it proper to treat the viewpoint represented by Jabotinsky (and fully shared by Ussishkin and Dr. Chlenov) with unconcealed contempt and heavy irony. He said in the same letter:

> I want to be charitable and assume that he [Jabotinsky] cannot be serious—or does he consider me sufficiently stupid or perhaps frivolous that I would engage myself in an undertaking which is designed solely *pour épater le bourgeois!* That can be easily achieved. That is cheap. At the Annual Zionist Conference a declaration can be made that we agreed to open the University in the year of Lord 1917. Let us rather say right away that we are already issuing diplomas, etc. Then the future professors can be shown in cages throughout the *Galuth* in order to collect money. Yet, university this is not going to be, but rather a tremendous shame.

In striking contrast to Weizmann's irritable and even abusive approach to Jabotinsky's proposals, was Jabotinsky's reaction: calm, well-reasoned, and conciliatory. In a letter to the Berlin "Working Committee" (May 5/18, 1914), he wrote: "It is not correct that my formula with regard to research institutes is 'all or nothing.' Rather do I insist that the institutes be placed expressly under the auspices of the University. Should this prove impossible, then we must make a strict division in our collections; collections for the University and collections for research institutes." During his study trip he firmly established the fact that nowhere in the world do research institutes exist at the expense of universities, and he insisted that it was impossible and unfair to collect funds for a university and spend them on research. He bluntly called this a "blind."

Jewish Youth Needs an Alma Mater

The practical work for the University, which Jabotinsky conducted with the utmost intensity, was another source of his opposition to
Dr. Weizmann's scheme.

From the very beginning he was convinced that Jewish communities
everywhere, particularly in Russia where the *numerus clausus* excluded the
overwhelming majority of the Jewish youth from higher studies, would
gladly cooperate in the establishment of an *alma mater* for their youngsters.
In a letter to Dr. Weizmann from Kharkov, dated February 24, 1914, Jabotinsky reported on conversations held with competent persons in three cities—Wilno, Poltava, and Kharkov—which were characteristic of the three
various types of Russian Jewry. They all confirmed what "we knew beforehand," he wrote, that even the most assimilated Jews welcomed the idea
of the Jerusalem University, since this was not a theoretical problem but a
question of the entire future of Jewish youth. What should be done immediately, he went on to say, was to lay the foundation for a real university in
Jerusalem—then Jews "from Dvinsk to Odessa," even the least well-off and
the most miserly, would "make unheard-of sacrifices."

It was Jabotinsky's well-considered opinion that it was vitally essential "in the interests of the University to utilize the present situation of
Jewish students in Eastern Europe." He was, however, fully aware of the existence of an opposite viewpoint (as represented by Dr. Weizmann) that "we
shall not take note of the moment and shall not hesitate to go other ways";
he was even ready to concede that "this too was good and prudent." He
warned, however, that it would certainly be neither good nor prudent "not
to take into account the present feeling and yet to wish to exploit it. *C'est à
prendre ou à laisser*," he insisted.[6] On April 25, 1914, he wrote to Dr. Chlenov:
"I see from Weizmann's letters only one thing: he himself realizes that this
[Weizmann's proposal] is *not* a university; this is why he is all the time trying to prove that the grapes are sour. . . . Not even the name 'University' is
indispensable; it can be supplanted by the name *Ecole Supérieure* or some
other name the Turks would authorize, provided that there should remain
what Weizmann does not want: an establishment for learning."

One of the main arguments against the speedy establishment of a regular university was the premise that it had to be from the very beginning a
first-class temple of learning; since this was an obviously impossible goal for

the near future, research institutes appeared as the only realistic alternative. Jabotinsky was outspoken in opposing this contention:[7]

> Permit me to voice the firm opinion that in no circumstances will we succeed in creating a first-rate university on European lines. For this purpose we shall lack both the material and the spiritual means. To begin with, our University can only be an institution modest in all respects. Do we really hope to attract experienced, first-rate teachers? This is out of the question, if only by reason of the language of instruction. Men of name and rank who would leave a good chair in Europe for Jerusalem will only be an exception. . . . The first generation will consist of efficient but modest teachers (some brilliant exceptions apart)—for the most part younger men who may perhaps later emerge as talented teachers and researchers but who will come to us without great reputations.

If this sober and realistic approach is accepted, Jabotinsky insisted, then the problem of a genuine, regular Hebrew University becomes both simple and more feasible. Taking as a basis the budgets of fifteen European universities, of different sizes and levels, he came to the conclusion that a sum of five million French francs (at that time about $900,000) would be necessary for building and equipment, and that one million francs ($180,000) would be largely sufficient to secure the yearly budget of the University. (Dr. Weizmann argued that even with the amount of two, three, or four million rubles, i.e., of one or two million dollars, it would be impossible to create the University and to secure its existence.)

With regard to the structure of the University, Jabotinsky offered a clearly delineated scheme providing for the establishment within the next three years (by the fall of 1917) of three schools:

1. The first and the most necessary must be the *Medical School:* not less than four-fifths of East European Jewish youth were studying medicine; without a Medical School the Hebrew University would be of no use for most of these young people, and this would greatly affect the contributions for the University so far as Russia was concerned.

2. Then comes the *Philosophical School* (the necessity for which was recognized by everybody so that there was no need to elaborate).

3. The third is the *School of Commerce.* Jabotinsky insisted that "just from the Palestinian viewpoint it is the most necessary of all schools." . . . This is the colonizing school *par excellence*, since the art of colonizing today is primarily the science of economics. This school will exercise its attraction

even outside Palestine, especially in the Orient where business is still the favored career of Jews."[8]

Fighting for a Practical Curriculum

Returning from his study trip, Jabotinsky stopped in Berlin for a session of the University Committee to plead for the repeal of the previous decision providing for research institutes and for adoption of the principle: a university for students. Only one member of the Committee supported this demand: A. D. Idelson, chief editor of *Rasswyet*. Weizmann's original plan was reaffirmed by the majority.

Jabotinsky had to reckon with this decision of the Actions Committee, but he tried to salvage as much as possible of the practical scheme he advocated by shifting the center of gravity of the curricula of single schools from theoretical to practical subjects. He objected to Dr. Weizmann's concentration on research in chemistry, insisted on paying more attention to anatomy, physiology, pathology, and other medical topics instead of natural sciences which would hardly be developed in the near future. In regard to the proposed program of the School of History and Philology, he insisted on a more detailed and concrete specification of the Jewish subjects. Jabotinsky proposed to include in the curriculum:

a) Jewish Law as the most important part of Talmud studies;

b) The Jewish languages of the Diaspora and their literatures. "I am not a Yiddishist," said Jabotinsky, "but to ignore them [Yiddish and Judeo-Spanish] is certainly not the right thing to do";

c) The study of the sociology of the Jewish people must include such topics as: 1. the political, cultural, and economic position of the Jews in Diaspora countries; 2. emigration; 3. Jewish organizations; 4. colonization, particularly in Palestine;

d) Nationality problems, minority and linguistic rights. "I consider this as very important. We intend to educate our students for service to the Jewish national renaissance. But how will they know anything about national equality if they have no knowledge of the nationality problems in various countries?";

e) Bible Exegetics. To Jabotinsky, a Hebrew Philosophical School in Jerusalem without Bible exegetics appeared nonsensical. He admitted that this was a "delicate question," but he asked: "Is it already proven that the orthodox groups and the Mizrachi threaten to raise the same objections against the University as they did against the [Jaffa] gymnasium? . . . They themselves should, however, realize the difference";

f) Out of political considerations, Jabotinsky suggested two more subjects: Turkish history and Turkish philology and literature.

In the School of Commerce, four foreign languages were to be taught: French, Italian, Arabic, and modern Greek, all of them being indispensable for commercial activity in the Near East. With low salaries for the teaching personnel and with hourly fees for the language teachers, the School of Commerce would have a yearly budget of 54,150 francs ($11,000)—the budget of the School of History and Philology was calculated by Jabotinsky at 73,800 francs. This school would, according to Jabotinsky's scheme, be organized as a joint-stock company, with shares of 500 to 2,000 rubles ($250 to $1,000).

In general, Jabotinsky insisted on a much more modest and economical scale of salaries than that which was foreseen in the tentative budget prepared by Dr. Weizmann. Jabotinsky objected to the high salaries which, according to this budget, would have to be paid not to great scholars, prospective heads of the research institutes, but to the average personnel of the University. A yearly salary of 6,000 marks ($1,500) for a lecturer would be an expense the university certainly could not bear, he contended. His insistence on a more modest and realistic budget brought about a considerable reduction of the original proposals. On May 18, 1914, he wrote to Dr. Weizmann: "We like the new budget drawn up by you much better than the previous one, and we think it more likely not to exceed our means."

Postwar Developments

The outbreak of World War I interrupted the work for the University. The University idea, however, survived the war and—of all Zionist projects—was the first to recover and to tread the path of fulfillment. Soon after the liberation of Palestine from Turkish domination—even before the formal armistice—its cornerstone was laid by Dr. Weizmann on July 24, 1918, on the site purchased for the University on Mount Scopus. Jabotinsky attended the ceremony, still in British military uniform; he even edited the Hebrew translation of Dr. Weizmann's opening speech.[9]

The further development of the University went in the direction advocated by Dr. Weizmann, and not in that which Jabotinsky had defended. *The Keren ha'Yesod Book*, edited by Jabotinsky in 1921, in a chapter

"The University," described the official policy of the Zionist Executive in this field as follows:[10]

To call into being a fully developed University at once was considered neither practical nor advisable. . . . We cannot start with final achievements. We have to choose from the various University Departments and Institutes those most suitable to serve as a nucleus for the future complete University. . . . It was decided to begin with the Research Institutes as suggested in 1913–1914 by Dr. Ch. Weizmann and the University Committee . . . and not with teaching facilities. [The article anticipated that these Institutes were] to be transformed as soon as possible and advisable—presumably within a few years—into complete teaching faculties.

There is no evidence in the available minutes of the Zionist Executive, of which Jabotinsky was a member in 1921–23, as to whether he was actively opposing this Weizmann-inspired University policy. His interests were at that time concentrated mainly on different problems: the struggle for the re-establishment of the Jewish Legion and, later, against the Herbert Samuel policy. In addition, the University issue was then largely dormant as an immediate, practical matter. But in 1925, when the University was solemnly "opened" by Lord Balfour without a single teaching faculty, Jabotinsky renewed his struggle against what he considered a travesty of the great University idea. This chapter of his activities will be dealt with in the second volume of this biography.

ELEVEN
ALONE

When, in November, 1913, Jabotinsky took over the work for the Hebrew University, he did it, of course, first and foremost because he believed in the University idea and wanted to contribute to its fulfillment. But in doing so he also seems to have been endeavoring to escape the full impact of his alarmingly growing feeling of estrangement from and loneliness in the Zionist movement in Russia, in which he had been reared. His bonds with the *Rasswyet* group and with the leading circles of Russian Zionism had been slackening since 1911: he "did not like their lack of a definite line of conduct; they were incapable or unwilling to guide the movement" (*Autobiography*). Jabotinsky refused to go to the Tenth Zionist Congress in 1911; for the first time since he became a Zionist, he did not participate either in the Congress or in the traditional pre-Congress convention of the Russian delegates. The convention sent him a telegram: "Your spirit is with us." But the official Zionist leadership opposed and resented most of Jabotinsky's ideas and demands both in the political and the cultural fields as "extremist," "unrealistic," and even "crazy." In the fall of 1912, when this writer visited Jabotinsky in St. Petersburg, he defiantly insisted that his only "crime" was that he launched those "crazy ideas" just "five minutes before everybody sees the light." He said:

"You are a connoisseur of Russian literature and you certainly remember one of Turgeniev's most meaningful poems in prose— the 'Two Quatrains.'[1] It tells the story of a town whose inhabitants—passionate admirers of poetry—were in mourning because for a long period of time no new and inspiring poem was born in their midst. One day, however, a youthful poet, Junius, appeared in the crowded public place, mounted the tribune, and signified that he wished to recite a poem. It was a delightful four-line stanza, full of hope and promise. But when he ended reading, he was met from all sides by hisses, groans, and laughter. The upturned faces of the multitude glowed with indignation; all eyes sparkled with anger; all hands were raised and threatened him with clenched fists. 'Is he turning us to ridicule?' roared angry voices. 'Tear him down from the tribune, the stupid rhymester! Down with the blockhead! Pelt him with rotten eggs, the fool! Stone him! Stone him!'

"Junius plunged headlong from the tribune: but before he reached his house, he heard loud applause, bravos, and cries of admiration. He stealthily returned to the public square and saw high upon the shoulders of the crowd his rival, the youthful poet Julius; and the crowd called out: 'Honor and glory to the immortal Julius! Raise him high in triumph! Honor and glory to the divine poet!'

"Junius approached one of the shouters and humbly asked what the poem was with which Julius so pleased everybody. The man readily obliged—and quoted Junius' own lines, with a few trifling changes which were by no means improvements. Poor Junius tried in vain to establish his authorship. An old gray-headed and wise citizen explained to him the mechanism of public reaction: 'You recited your lines at an unfortunate time. Although Julius merely repeated the words of another, he chose the right moment to do it; hence, his success. Your own consciousness of merit must be your reward.' "

In the light of Jabotinsky's entire political career, this reference to Turgeniev's little poem in prose sounds prophetic. Decried and isolated, he, as Turgeniev put it, "had nothing but his own consciousness of merit to console him and, sooth to say, it consoled him ill enough."

This feeling of lonely bitterness had been growing ever since. Trying to reconstruct the state of mind which dominated him in 1913–14, Jabotinsky wrote in his *Autobiography*:

" . . . There was a revolt in me against my whole life, against my entire past and present. For the first time I realized then that there are some wild creatures for whom there is no place and no refuge even among their own brethren, born from the same mother and the same father: such a human creature must build for himself a tent, a cell, or even less—a stall; but it has to be his very own, belonging to him alone—otherwise he is doomed to peregrinate in a spiritual diaspora, as a lonely wanderer, from one inn to another. Zionism is the name of my atmosphere; in no other could I breathe; yet *this* Zionism is not mine."

Jabotinsky frankly confessed that if at that time he had been asked to define in positive terms what exactly "his" own Zionism was, it would have been difficult for him to give an articulate answer. But "the basic defect of Russian Zionism" ("at that time I did not know the Zionist movement in Western Europe," he admitted) was clear to him: Zionism in Russia did not have "any practical achievements." While Zionist work in Palestine was more or less progressing, the impression produced by the situation in Russia was that there the Zionist leadership "did not care for anything but working out theoretical programs, establishing a *Stellungnahme* [viewpoint] about every important problem—and nothing more." When Peter B. Struve, the editor of the noted monthly *Russkaya Mysl* (Russian Thought), asked him to write an article about the Jewish national movement, Jabotinsky could not help stressing the predominance of theorizing over practical activities. He noticed a characteristic feature in the extensive collective work *National Movements in Modern States*, which appeared in 1910 under the editorship of A. N. Kastelliansky: while the chapter on the Estonians and Letts related the number of national schools created by them, the chapter on the Jews, written by S. M. Dubnov, reproduced eight programs of eight Jewish political parties. . . . "Maybe I am not a serious man, indeed, but to me," said Jabotinsky, "a program has no meaning if it is not immediately being converted into action—no matter whether this action is successful or not: a failure is also a step forward." In this connection Jabotinsky mentioned a conference of "Friends of Hebrew," which at that time took place in Kiev with the aim of promoting Hebrew as a spoken language. Jabotinsky was unable to attend the gathering and sent a letter saying: "Don't take any decision but one: to establish Hebrew schools." M. M. Ussishkin, whom he asked to convey this message to the conference, later confessed that he did not read this particular point to the delegates. "It was not a practical proposal," he argued.

In the field of Russian politics, Jabotinsky advocated an agreement with other national minorities—in the first place with the Ukrainians and Lithuanians; in the leading Zionist circles this concept "encountered open irony and derision." In the field of greater Zionist policy, Jabotinsky felt that "the time has come to return to the Herzlian tradition: I started to write an article 'Back to the Charter,' but did not finish it since in the depths of my heart I knew: nobody will pay any attention."

Hectic work for the Hebrew University for several months stunned this deep spiritual restlessness, which was bordering on despair, and provided some kind of escape. But not for very long. In the late summer of 1914, Jabotinsky's internal crisis reached a climax. "I don't know what I would have done if a world catastrophe had not come. Maybe I would have gone to Palestine, maybe to Rome, maybe I would have founded a party—but in the summer came the world explosion."

It did not come unexpectedly to Jabotinsky. He predicted it with amazing foresight and accuracy in an article called "Horoscope" which appeared in *Odesskiya Novosti* on January 1, 1912: "First item on the list of events in Europe is a great war . . . between two (or more) first-class powers, with all the grandiose madness of modern technique . . . with an incredible number of human casualties and with such financial losses—direct, indirect, and reflected—that for it, it seems, there will be not enough figures in arithmetic." Jabotinsky was not sure whether "the storm will break loose in 1912 or will somehow be delayed for several months," but there was not a shadow of doubt in his mind that such a war was impending.[2]

In a handwritten autobiographical sketch, which was prepared some time in 1934 and was never published, Jabotinsky said: "When the war came, I and nearly all the Zionist leaders in Russia already belonged virtually to separate camps, bearing by mistake the same name 'Zionists' but ready to clash. . . . The real root of the conflict was a basic difference of outlook and temperament —essentially the same cleavage as now."

FIRST STEPS ON THE INTERNATIONAL
POLITICAL SCENE

TWELVE

THE STRUGGLE FOR THE LEGION

An Idea Is Born

The war broke out in August, 1914. Jabotinsky expected this world calamity, and, when it occurred, he felt that something unusually portentous was in stock for the world and for the Jewish people. But he did not see his way clear. His first reaction was to go and to see for himself. He determinedly broke off the settled life he had only recently managed to arrange for his family in St. Petersburg and rushed to Moscow. There he suggested to the editors of the great liberal daily *Russkiya Vyedomosti* to send him as a roving correspondent to Western and Northern Europe; his assignment was to report on the moods and the sentiments produced by the war rather than on the war itself. On September 1st he was already on his way.

Jabotinsky went to Sweden, England, Belgium, and France. In a letter written in 1936 to the Belgian Prime Minister Van Zeeland, he recalled how (on September 27, 1914) when "the heroic Belgian army was retreating from Brussels, Schaerbeek, and Malines in order to re-deploy behind the Scheldt . . . there was, in the Malines post office, as it was being shelled, a Russian journalist—who cried. His unskilled hands, helped by a frightened Belgian post-office employee, were working the telegraph key, transmitting to the entire world the despair of the gallant people of Belgium, whom the 'good neighbor' from Germany was assaulting and murdering with inhuman cruelty."[1] By the time he reached France, the French government had already temporarily abandoned the threatened capital and transferred its seat to Bordeaux. Jabotinsky went to Bordeaux. There, one wet morning, he read in a poster on a wall that, on October 30th, Turkey had joined the Central Powers and begun military operations.

This piece of news radically changed Jabotinsky's entire outlook. His own evidence as to the position he had taken in the first months of the world conflict is rather contradictory. In *The Story of the Jewish Legion*, written in 1928, he states that until that morning in Bordeaux he had been "a mere observer, without any particular reasons for wishing full triumph to one side and crushing disaster to the other." His desire at that time was stalemate, and peace as soon as possible.[2] In his *Autobiography*, which was written in 1934, we find a different emphasis: "From the first moment I hoped and prayed with all my heart and soul for the defeat of Russia. If the fate of the war had depended on me in those weeks, I would have decided: quick peace in the West, without victors or vanquished—but first of all Russia's defeat." Whatever Jabotinsky's initial position, Turkey's entry into the war converted him into a "fanatical believer in war until victory" of the Allied Powers and made this "his" war. It gave final shape and direction to his ever-growing conviction that "where the Turk rules neither sun may shine nor grass may grow, and that the only hope for restoration of Palestine lay in the dismemberment of the Ottoman Empire." He drew the only possible logical conclusion from this premise: whatever the outcome of the war with Germany (at that time he did not predict that Germany would be beaten into unconditional surrender), Turkey would be defeated and sliced to pieces: "stone and iron can endure a fire; a wooden hut must burn, and no miracle will save it."[3]

All this seemed "crystal clear" to Jabotinsky.[4] On November 5th, he wrote to Israel Rosov expounding the idea of offering England—or England and France—"in exchange for certain promises, the extent of which I am not now discussing, to raise a corps of volunteers with the specific task of assisting in the occupation of Palestine." Refusing to estimate how many thousands it would be possible to muster, he stressed that "this is a time when every human penny is highly prized."

It was undoubtedly in this connection that he cabled to his paper in Moscow suggesting a comprehensive tour through the Moslem countries of North Africa to study the effect on the local populations of the Holy War proclaimed by the Sultan. The editor cabled back: "Go ahead."

Jabotinsky's reportages, those from Europe as well as those from Morocco, Algiers, Tunisia, and Egypt, were widely read and much appreciated by the Russian intellectuals. Each of them was not only a literary and publicistic event; it was also a valuable contribution to the understanding and appraisal of the major trends and developments of World War I. Particularly appreciated were his dispatches from North Africa, in which he convincingly and thoroughly demolished the legend of a pan-Islamic revolt against the Allied Powers in response to the "Holy War" appeal of the Sultan-and-Caliph.

The Zion Mule Corps

In December, 1914, still on his North African study trip, Jabotinsky arrived in Alexandria on an Italian ship. There, he heard a British customs official, who was chatting with some officers among his fellow passengers, say: "A few days ago a boatful of Zionists, almost a thousand of them, arrived from Jaffa—the Turks kicked them out of Palestine." Suddenly, for no reason at all, Djemal Pasha, the military overlord of Syria, ordered the Arab police to catch Jews in the streets and to pack them into boats. Later, the number of exiles and refugees rose to 18,000, of whom about 12,000 landed in Alexandria.[5] Among them were merchants, workers, students, doctors, women, and children. At the beginning, about forty second-rate hotels as well as the high-class Métropole Hotel, were rented for them by a local Committee for the Refugees. Jabotinsky joined this Committee and soon became its moving spirit. It was largely thanks to his intervention that the British administration in Egypt agreed to house the exiles in the large quarantine buildings of Alexandria (Gabbari) and allotted for them 170 pounds a day. However, relations among the refugees themselves were strained. They were a motley crowd comprising Ashkenazi and Sefardic Jews,* Bukharians, Moroccans, Georgians, Spaniards; about twelve languages besides Hebrew were spoken in the barracks. Conflicts were many and unpleasant. "In order to stop these quarrels," recalls D. Judelowitz, one of the exiles, "Jabotinsky left the luxurious Regina Palace Hotel and moved to the quarantine buildings. And as if by magic, everything changed and the mixed crowd . . . became a single unit, giving the impression of a group which had been educated in the same orderly way. We called this order amongst the exiles 'the Jabotinsky régime.' "[6] Jabotinsky organized an

---

*Ashkenazim (literally "Germans"), Jews whose forebears hailed from Central and Eastern Europe; Sefardim (lit. "Spaniards"), Jews whose forebears originated in Spain; now applied also to Oriental Jews generally.

autonomous police force from among the refugees—*Notrim*—to maintain order: these *Notrim* formed the nucleus of the first Jewish military unit, whose spiritual fathers were Jabotinsky and Joseph Trumpeldor.

These two men met for the first time in Alexandria though, of course, they had heard of each other much earlier. Jabotinsky devoted several pages of his *Story of the Jewish Legion* to a fine, affectionate sketch of Trumpeldor. When he went to see him and told him of the Legion idea, there was no need to elaborate: Trumpeldor was quick to grasp the essence of a subject, and in a quarter of an hour he gave his reply—it was "yes."

On the evening of the same day, on the 16th of Adar, 5675 (February 23, 1915), eight men, members of the Committee to help the refugees, gathered at the apartment of M. A. Margolis, a leading representative of Nobel's Oil Company in the Orient, who was the committee's treasurer. Besides the host there were present: Dr. Weitz from Jerusalem; V. Z. Gluskin (President of the Rishonle-Zion winegrowers); the agronomist, J. Ettinger; an American tourist, G. Caplan; Joseph Trumpeldor, and Jabotinsky. The latter presented the plan he had agreed upon with Trumpeldor. It was accepted by a majority of five against two, one member abstaining.[7] Those five constituted the Committee for the Legion.

A week later, on March 2nd, about two hundred people gathered in a dim hall of the Mafruza barracks. Jabotinsky, speaking in Hebrew, briefly reviewed the situation and called for the formation of a Jewish military unit to fight for the liberation of Palestine. The response was most satisfactory. About one hundred signatures were put on a piece of paper torn from an exercise book, on which a seven-line resolution in Hebrew was written: "To form a Jewish Legion and to propose to England to make use of it in Palestine." The next day Jabotinsky saw in the Gabbari courtyard three groups of young men learning to march. Further registration progressed successfully: "It sufficed for Jabotinsky to appear in order to awaken the noblest feelings in the hearts of the exiles" (Judelowitz); about five hundred enlisted within a few days.

Then came the great disappointment. When a delegation of volunteers was received by General Maxwell, Commander of the small British Force in Egypt, he told them that he had heard nothing about an offensive in Palestine and that he doubted whether such an offensive was going to be launched at all; furthermore, regulations prohibited the admission of foreign nationals into the British Army. The only suggestion he could make was that the volunteers form themselves into a detachment for mule transport, to be made use of on some other sector of the Turkish front.[8] The delegation did not give any immediate answer to General Maxwell's offer. They had an all-night meeting, at which his proposal was hotly debated. All civilian members of the Committee, including Jabotinsky, felt that the offer must be politely declined. They were not ready to send "the first really Jewish troops in the whole history of the Exile" to "some other front" and they resented the name "mule corps." Talking as a soldier, Trumpeldor disagreed with this attitude. In his view, there was no essential difference between a Palestine front and any other sector of the Turkish front: "To get the Turks out of Palestine we've got to smash the Turks. Which side you begin the smashing, north or south, is just technique. Any front leads to Zion."

Nothing was decided that night. Alone with Trumpeldor on the way back to their hotel, Jabotinsky said: "You may be right; but I personally will not join a unit of that sort."—"I probably will," Trumpeldor replied. Next day, having received a cable from Pinhas Rutenberg who asked to meet him at once somewhere in Italy, Jabotinsky told Trumpeldor: "Joseph Vladimirovitch, I am off to Europe. Should General Maxwell change his mind and agree to form a real fighting regiment, send me a cable and I'll come back at once; if not, I'll try to find other generals."[9]

Maxwell did not change his mind, and in Jabotinsky's absence the four remaining members of the Committee called a general meeting of the volunteers at the Mafruza barracks where they stated that the Committee had dissolved itself and that the volunteers "were no longer bound by their signature to enlist."[10]

This chapter of the Legion, initiated jointly by Jabotinsky and Trumpeldor and endorsed collectively by the Committee of five, was thus closed. Trumpeldor, however, remained firm in his first conviction that even in the form proposed by General Maxwell a Jewish unit would be a great and noble national deed. And when the British military administration in Cairo sent Lieutenant Colonel John Henry Patterson to Alexandria with the mission to try to implement this proposal, Trumpeldor was ready and willing to cooperate. Together, they called a meeting of the former volunteers and exhorted them to enlist in the proposed transport unit. Largely under Trumpeldor's influence they accepted. Toward the middle of April, Jabotinsky received a cable in Brindisi signed "Trumpeldor" and reading: "Maxwell offer accepted."[11] Six hundred and fifty volunteers were formed into a Zion Mule Corps; 562 of them were sent to the Gallipoli front.[12]

Jabotinsky did not join Trumpeldor in the Gallipoli venture and was in no way co-responsible for the creation of the Zion Mule Corps. Itzhak Ben Zvi is, of course, completely mistaken when he asserts that, arriving in Egypt together with David Ben Gurion in the spring of 1915, they found there the first "kernel" of a Jewish Legion, the Gallipoli Legion, "at the head of which was Jabotinsky."[13] Jabotinsky was at that time in Italy and had no connection whatsoever with the "Gallipoli Legion." Ben Zvi is also misrepresenting Jabotinsky's position when he asserts that for Jabotinsky the question whether the unit would be sent to Palestine or to another front "was not important." At that time, Jabotinsky's position was that only the Palestine front was acceptable.

Though he dissociated himself from Trumpeldor's venture, Jabotinsky never opposed or condemned it. His attitude went through a significant evolution from a conditional *post factum* acceptance to a definite admission that he had been wrong in doubting Trumpeldor's judgment.

In an article published in *Odesskiya Novosti* in June, 1916, Jabotinsky still argued that when Patterson put the proposal before the volunteers, "many objections could have been voiced against its acceptance"; but *after* it had been accepted, it should have been "sanctioned and approved."[14] This was still a very hesitant and conditional attitude, a generous condonation rather than an endorsement. It is true that in the same article Jabotinsky also fully acknowledged the "political value of [Trumpeldor's] initiative," stressing the fact that it obtained wide publicity in the world press and put the Zionist cause on the map. But he mentioned this aspect only in passing. He was, however, most outspoken on this point twelve years later in *The Story of the Jewish Legion:*[15]

... One thing I must admit: I had been wrong, Trumpeldor was right. Those six hundred muleteers actually opened up a new avenue in the development of Zionist possibilities. ... All through the first half of the war that mule corps proved to be the only manifestation that somehow reminded the "world," especially Great Britain's military "world," that Zionism could also be "topical," a part of "actuality," and perhaps capable of being transformed into a factor that might prove of some value even under gunfire. ... Trumpeldor was right: though it was in the Jordan Valley that we were victorious, the way through Gallipoli was the right way.

"A Sad Tale of Disappointments"

Jabotinsky left Alexandria early in April, 1915, in order to "try to find some other generals," whose attitude toward the Legion idea would be more satisfactory than that of General Maxwell. He knew, of course, that "generals" do not make decisions of major policy and that he had to win for his plan the understanding and support of the leading statesmen of the Allied Powers. In the summer months of 1915, he tried his luck in Rome, Paris, and London.

Jabotinsky described his experience of those summer months of 1915 as "a sad tale of disappointments and failures."[16] Rome was a failure. Neither the Cabinet members nor the Deputies whom he was able to meet knew whether Italy would get into the war and were therefore reluctant even to discuss the matter. Both Signor Mosca, Assistant Colonial Secretary, and Luigi Bissolati, leader of the Socialists but a great proponent of the war, told Jabotinsky the same thing: "If Italy gets into it, then your idea will be just perfect; come and see us again then and we'll discuss this matter in detail. But now...."

Paris was an even more discouraging failure. The French Minister of Foreign Affairs, Théophile Delcassé, an unimaginative and mediocre diplomat of the old school who still believed in the wisdom of the long-obsolete epigram of Talleyrand's "speech is the best medium for concealing thought," spoke with Jabotinsky in a language from which the words "yes" and "no" had been erased. He was most evasive on each of the questions raised by Jabotinsky. He doubted whether there would be a campaign in Palestine and was not certain who might lead it; he was therefore not interested in the suggestion that a Jewish unit, similar to that fighting in Gallipoli, be included in the French Army.[17]

The hardest failure was London. At the War Office he was told that Lord kitchener, then War Minister, was opposed to any kind of "fancy regiment" as well as to any offensive on the Eastern fronts. This attitude of the then military idol of the British apparently precluded any possibility of further attempts. Jabotinsky tried to meet Mr. Herbert Samuel, who was a member of the Asquith Cabinet and who had already associated himself with Zionism. Dr. Weizmann was ready to introduce him to Samuel, but Nachum Sokolov and Dr. E. V. Chlenov (who as members of the Inner Actions Committee had a decisive say) vetoed the idea.[18]

Here we enter the field in which Jabotinsky suffered his most painful disappointments. It is hardly an exaggeration to state that—with very few exceptions—he was completely alone and isolated in the Zionist world in his struggle for an active Zionist policy and for the creation of the Jewish Legion. This applies in particular to the first six months that followed his decision in Bordeaux to embark upon this struggle. Leading and influential Zionist circles were overwhelmingly and strongly against him and his plans. But even those few, whom Jabotinsky himself found possible to classify as sympathizers, and even comrades-in-arms, were in fact either skeptical or lukewarm and passive.

To the first category belongs Max Nordau. It is rather painful to destroy a noble legend, in the building of which Jabotinsky himself was instrumental. But it has to be done; not even Jabotinsky's own testimony can lend immunity to a patently fictional story.

On November 3, 1914, on his way to Morocco, Jabotinsky stopped in Madrid, where the Grand Old Man of Zionism had been living as an exile from France, in order to present to Nordau his own concept of activist Zionist policy. The account of this conversation in Jabotinsky's *Story of the Jewish Legion*, which was written fourteen years later, creates the impression that, while somewhat "skeptical," Nordau had been, on the whole, in favor of such a policy with all its implications.

There can hardly be any doubt that this account is misleading. Jabotinsky was always a great admirer of Nordau, and he charitably endeavored not to reveal the unflattering truth: that the Zionist political philosophy of the old sage was at that time as unimaginative and superficial as was the philosophy of the entire official Zionist leadership. In a letter to Israel Rosov, written two days after his encounter with Nordau, Jabotinsky sadly reported: "His [Nordau's] opinion is that the Zionists must now sit quietly, not interfere with anything, and only take care of the [Jewish Colonial] Bank." Following this conversation, Nordau himself wrote to Jabotinsky in Cairo: "I hope that the Actions Committee will have sense enough to keep quiet in view of the critical situation of our movement. It can't do any good, but might do a good deal of harm." Jabotinsky, of course, most definitely disagreed. "I do not agree with Nordau; we must now act," he insisted in his letter to Rosov.

Even more pronounced was their disagreement about the idea of a Jewish Legion. In the biography of Max Nordau written by his wife and daughter in 1943 (they were both admirers and followers of Jabotinsky), we read: "In spite of deep personal sympathies [for Jabotinsky], Nordau could see certain objections. Above all, he did not like the name 'Zionist Legion.' At that time, Zionists were among all the warring nations and should not be made to bear the reproach of disloyalty. Zionism as such, moreover, should remain above battle. He also discussed at length with Jabotinsky the impropriety and danger of inciting young Palestinians to take up arms on the side of England. They were Turkish subjects. Turkey had not treated them badly. In a sense it was treason."[19]

Nor was Jabotinsky very successful in his attempt to induce Nordau to support his idea of transferring the Zionist World Headquarters to a neutral country. Nordau wrote to his wife: "Jabotinsky came to bid me goodbye. He begged me to write to Dr. Chlenov via Stockholm and to communicate my opinion that the Actions Committee should be transferred to the United States. [Jacobus] Kann wants it at the Hague; the people in Berlin want to go to Copenhagen or stay where they are." No record is available of Nordau ever having supported this demand. In fact, he even opposed it very resolutely. In 1916, the Copenhagen Zionist Office was delighted to be able to circulate Nordau's statement against a Zionist Coalition Executive; it advocated a Zionist policy bent exclusively on maintaining the unity of the Zionist organization and preserving the existence of the Jewish colonies in Palestine: nothing more could be expected from the Zionist leadership. In an article "Passivism and Split," published in Di Tribune of Copenhagen (April 10, 1916), Jabotinsky called this Nordau statement "a clear and precise program of passivism."

Even more misleading is Jabotinsky's deliberately incomplete account of his attempts at cooperation with Pinhas Rutenberg. As mentioned above, Rutenberg cabled him in Alexandria, urgently suggesting an earliest possible meeting. Toward the middle of April, 1915, they met in a little hotel in Brindisi. Jabotinsky related that "ten minutes' talk was enough to agree on the main subject; though we had never corresponded, we recognized immediately that we had been thinking of the same thing." They agreed that, after a common effort in the interests of the cause in Rome, Jabotinsky should go on to Paris and London and Rutenberg to America to continue there the work for the Legion.

Jabotinsky was charitable enough never to mention the fact that Rutenberg kept his part of the bargain very poorly. When he arrived in America, he indeed wrote a pamphlet on Zionism, in which one chapter dealt with the Legion project. But the publishers of the pamphlet, the *Poalei Zion* Organization, withheld publication of this chapter: David Ben Gurion and Itzhak Ben Zvi, who had both recently arrived in America, were against the idea; so were most of the local leaders. Only a few favored it— among them such outstanding personalities as Dr. Chaim Zhitlovsky, Dr. Nachman Syrkin, Ber Borokhov. When the *Poalei Zion* Party Conference decided that propaganda for the Legion was untimely, Rutenberg submitted and kept silent for more than two years.[20]

With mild reproach Jabotinsky spoke of a third "recruit" he made during this early stage of his struggle. In Paris, he was received by old Baron Edmond de Rothschild.* The "father of Palestine colonization" was enthralled with the news about the Zion Mule Corps. "You must continue at all cost!" he insisted. "See that it becomes a real Legion when the time of the Palestine Campaign comes." Jabotinsky was, of course, thankful for these kind words. But, he confessed, deep down in his heart a small voice asked: "Why I? Why not you? Surely it is easier for you?"

If his stay in Paris was not entirely bereft of positive results, Jabotinsky gratefully recalled, it was but for the fact that he met Dr. Ch. Weizmann who liked the Legion idea and promised his assistance in the work for the Legion: "and a time came when he kept his promise."

With the rest of the Zionist world Jabotinsky was at loggerheads. His contention that, in the best interest of the Zionist cause, the World Zionist Organization must take a clear and definite position in favor of the Allies, and against Turkey and Germany, met with bitter opposition from various quarters. The official position of the Zionist leadership, decided upon at the meeting of the Actions Committee in Copenhagen in December, 1914, was one of strictest "neutrality." This was also the position of the Zionist organizations in the United States and in Russia.

In America, the Zionist leadership practically justified Turkey's decision to enter the war against the Allied Powers. *The Maccabaean*, official organ of the Zionist Federation, wrote editorially in its November-December, 1914, issue about "Turkey a Party to the War":

---

*Baron Edmond de Rothschild (1845–1934), great French Jewish financier and philanthropist who played the leading part in the early pre-Zionist Jewish settlement of Palestine.

We have no doubt that urgent national policy dictated the move. The danger to Turkish interests, should Russia and the Allies prevail over Germany and Austria, must have occupied a large part in this decision. To have remained passive while Russia grew in power in the Balkans would have meant further dismemberment of this much dismembered empire.

When, in December, 1914, Turkey started ruthlessly deporting thousands of Jews from Palestine and wantonly destroying Jewish positions there, *The Maccabaean* (February, 1915) deemed it proper to interpret these acts in such a way as indirectly to make them comprehensible and defensible:

It appears that the Ottoman empire, engaged in elaborate preparations for an invasion of Egypt, found it necessary to order the expulsion of all foreigners, and inasmuch as there were thousands of Jews in Palestine who for one reason or another could not abandon their foreign citizenship, they had to be asked to leave.

Jabotinsky's policies were most unpopular in the leading American Zionist circles. When the New York Yiddish paper *Der Tog* published a report from London about Jabotinsky's negotiations with the British government concerning the raising of a Jewish Legion, *The Maccabaean* (May, 1915) published an editorial under the ironic headline "Jewish Legions Going to Take Palestine." Not content with a statement that "any such action . . . was not in harmony with the expressed policy of the Zionist organization," the editorial described this action as "absurd":

Jabotinsky has no army, and had none. He could not speak in the name of an organized movement. There was no sense in offering England the cooperation of a few hundred undisciplined, unorganized Jews in Alexandria, for England could not consider the offer of such service of any consequence.

Then came an unflattering description of Jabotinsky's personality:

Jabotinsky is not an unknown personage. The characteristics of his public work are well known. He is an orator, a writer, with a peculiar penchant for self-glorification. He has exceptional gifts, but these gifts are vitiated by the fact that their possessor lacks poise, a sense of discipline, a sense of order. Jabotinsky is an "enfant terrible" and no one who knows him would agree that he has the gift of political sagacity or the talent for political organization.

Even less restrained in their criticism were the Yiddish-language papers in America. Characteristic of their manner and style are the headlines of some articles which appeared in these papers. On November 30, 1915, *Wahrheit* published a long article by Dr. Sh. Berstein (then Secretary General of the Inner Actions Committee of the World Zionist Organization) under the title "A Foolish Don Quixote. Jabotinsky's Rotten Arguments for His Tragicomic Legion." In two issues of the Tog (January 9 and 10, 1916), Hirsch Leib Gordon wrote about "The Jewish Legion. History and Criticism of the Bloody Adventure."*

Even more determined was the opposition in Russia. Its most articulate and outspoken mouthpiece was M. M. Ussishkin, whose biographer, Dr. J. Klausner, lists three main reasons for this attitude. In the first place, Ussishkin was afraid of the vengeance of Djemal Pasha, the Commander-in-Chief and ruler of Syria and Palestine; Djemal Pasha could have easily destroyed the whole of the numerically weak Jewish community of Palestine, which for Ussishkin had always been the very foundation of Zionism. Secondly, when the Jews had been expelled from Spain, the Turks had received them cordially and had always treated them well; it was not proper that the Jews should be ungrateful to that nation in its time of trouble and distress. Thirdly, like all nationalist Jews, Ussishkin bitterly hated Tsarist Russia for its anti-Jewish policy, which was aggravated during the war; he could not conceive that the Jews would ally themselves with Russia, which persecuted the Jews, against Turkey, which was fair to them.[21]

In various combinations, this motley array of arguments was characteristic of the mentality of both the leadership and the rank and file of the Zionist movement in Russia. Jabotinsky, only a few years earlier the most popular man in the movement, was now widely considered as an outcast

---

*There was also no dearth of plainly libelous and slanderous attacks. *Di Yiddishe Stimme* of London (November 27, 1916) reprinted under the headline "Jabotinsky Is Asking for Exemption from Military Service" a story from the Russian emigres Socialist weekly *Natchalo* (The Beginning) in Paris to the effect that Jabotinsky, together with four other London correspondents of Russian liberal dailies, had allegedly submitted a "memorandum" to the Russian authorities referring to their "responsible work" and asking for exemption from military service. Jabotinsky had no need to ask for such a privilege: as early as 1903, a Russian military commission at Kherson declared him unfit for military service because of utter nearsightedness. Another Bolshevik journalist, Lourie (who was writing under the pen name Larin) was publishing in the St. Petersburg "folkist" weekly *Yevreysky Mir* (The Jewish World) dispatches from London, in which he alleged that Jabotinsky in his propaganda for the Legion had been acting as a paid agent of the Tsarist régime.

and an irresponsible detractor of the Zionist cause. In the years 1915–17 his name had become unmentionable in the Zionist press. Jabotinsky soon had the opportunity to experience personally the full impact of the hostility against him.

On May 7, 1915, Jabotinsky left London for Stockholm to meet his wife. In Stockholm, he received an invitation from Dr. E. Chlenov and Dr. V. Jacobson, to come to Copenhagen where a session of the Zionist Greater Actions Committee had been called for the month of June. Jabotinsky was not a member of this body, and was not entitled to participate in the session, but Zionist leaders were eager to talk to him privately in advance. They hoped to induce him to abandon the Legion idea which they considered as both wrong and dangerous. Jabotinsky accepted the invitation and had a lively three-hour discussion with Chlenov, Jacobson, and Arthur Hantke—three leading members of the Inner Actions Committee. Their arguments failed to convince him, nor did he succeed in convincing his interlocutors of the justness of his concept. Jabotinsky then offered a compromise solution: the Zionist Organization was to proclaim officially that it was neutral in the world conflict and had nothing in common with any Legion plans; he was to leave the Zionist Organization officially, and to do his work as a private person; he would not interfere with their work and they would let him alone.

This compromise was rejected. The Actions Committee passed a resolution condemning the Legion idea and urging all Zionists to oppose propaganda for the Legion.

Though naturally unhappy to "find himself in a state of war with the entire Zionist Organization," Jabotinsky was not at all prepared to submit and give up. He was determined to carry on. The only man on whose support he could then count in this struggle was Meir Grossman, who lived in Copenhagen as correspondent of the daily *Birzheviya Vyedomosti* (Stock-Exchange Gazette) and at the same time was publishing a Yiddish daily *Di Yiddishe Folkszeitung*. Grossman became interested in the Legion idea. At his initiative, which was eagerly accepted by Jabotinsky, they met in Malmö and immediately found a common language. After his final break with the Zionist Organization, Jabotinsky organized, with Grossman's help, a meeting at which he developed his Legion plan. On Grossman's insistence he agreed, though reluctantly, to speak in Yiddish—probably for the first time in his life. According to Grossman who presided, Jabotinsky "stood the test magnificently: his Yiddish was vigorous, popular, though poor; when he was short of a word, I helped out." The meeting was successful, although the Zionist leaders boycotted it. A second meeting was arranged in Stockholm, where Jabotinsky spoke in Russian (for the benefit of a considerable number of Jewish emigrés from Russia) and Grossman again presided: it was impossible to find any other person of importance who would agree to accept the chairmanship.[22]

The two meetings, though morally successful, did not produce any new adherents or tangible support. Back in Copenhagen, Jabotinsky and Grossman started devising their strategy. Jabotinsky's intention was to pay a visit to Russia, where he hoped to find understanding and support among his numerous friends. Grossman was to remain in Copenhagen and begin the publication of a Yiddish bi-weekly *Di Tribune*.

For the Last Time in Russia

Jabotinsky spent the summer months of 1915 in Russia, visiting St. Petersburg, Moscow, Odessa, and Kiev. His reminiscences of this visit are full of unmitigated bitterness. On the whole, this sentiment is only too well-founded; in some instances it is, however, not fully accurate. It was true that in Zionist St. Petersburg he "was met with stony faces," but it was incorrect for him to say that the Zionist leaders he "did not meet at all," because he was "excommunicated." S. K. Gepstein testifies that, during Jabotinsky's stay in Russia's capital, he had the opportunity of presenting his views to a private gathering of Zionist leaders in the house of his friend I. A. Rosov. He met with fierce opposition on the part of Dr. D. S. Pasmanik; A. D. Idelson and S. K. Gepstein expressed skepticism based on their belief that Germany would emerge victorious from the world conflict and that a pro-British orientation would therefore be suicidal for the Zionist cause. But there was no enmity and no "anathema" attitude. It was a frank and sharp discussion among colleagues and friends. Answering his opponents, Jabotinsky— half-angrily and half-jokingly—said: "In my capacity as a journalist, I have toured almost all West European countries and all of Northern Africa; I have seen with my own eyes the overall situation—and this blacking brush [referring to Pasmanik who had a particularly bristle-like black beard], sitting here in Petrograd—and now peacefully drowsing on the couch!— claims that he knows better! . . ."—"But I am not sleeping at all," protested Pasmanik, "I am listening."—"The better for you; maybe, after having listened, you will understand something," was Jabotinsky's rejoinder. Such an exchange of barbed sallies is hardly indicative of a remote and "stony" atmosphere.

In Moscow, Jabotinsky later gratefully acknowledged, J. A. Naiditch "received him as an old friend, listened to him, encouraged and helped him";[23] all other leading Zionists remained aloof and inimical. The worst reception he met with was in Odessa. There, the entire Zionist life was autocratically dominated by Ussishkin, who loathed Jabotinsky's policies to such an extent that he once deemed it proper to approach Jabotinsky's old mother in the street and to say to her point-blank: "Your son should be hanged." In this home town of his, where not long ago he had been carried shoulder-high, he was now, on Sabbaths and Festivals, called a traitor from the pulpit of the Zionist synagogue "Yavneh"; among the older generation of Zionists there was only one man, Israel Trivus, who had the courage to come to see him in daylight, but even he shook his head and said: "One should never save one's fatherland without an invitation."[24] Even at a small gathering of pro-activist youth, some suggested to "soften or to postpone" propaganda for the Legion; Jabotinsky's reaction was: "You studied Latin in school, so you must know what *non possumus* means."[25]

A happy exception was Kiev, where Jabotinsky was received "like a brother" by the local Zionist leaders, N. S. Sirkin, M. S. Mazor, I. M. Machover, and H. S. Zlatopolski; they called a meeting, listened to his report, approved, encouraged, promised to help as much as they could— and kept their word.

However, Kiev was not indicative of the attitude prevailing in Russian Zionism, which was unmistakably hostile. Jabotinsky's popularity with the Zionists of Russia was at its lowest point, even with the overwhelming majority of the youth. This writer remembers his abortive attempt, in 1916, to break the wall of silence around Jabotinsky and the Legion at least in student circles. He sent to the *Yevreysky Student* of St. Petersburg, the organ of the student organization *He'Chaver*, of which he was one of the founders, an article "Senility," castigating the lack of spontaneous response by young people to the romantic and uplifting Legion idea which, irrespective of its merits, should have had a strong emotional appeal to all those who had not succumbed to the curse of spiritual agedness. The article was published, but provoked no reaction whatsoever. It obviously did not strike a responsive chord in Zionist youth circles.

When Jabotinsky left Russia in August, 1915, he had every reason to feel that, so far as the Jews and the Zionists were concerned, his journey was a definite failure.

More favorable was the attitude of the Russian circles. "My Russian colleagues on the Moscow newspaper received me like a kinsman," Jabotinsky gratefully recalled; and when he announced his intention to go abroad again, Professor Manuilov, editor of *Russkiya Vyedomosti,* was at first opposed to it. "Stay and work with us in Moscow," he suggested. "Why should you go to the West again?"—"The Legion," Jabotinsky replied.—"If so, Godspeed!" said Manuilov, and for the next two years, until the Bolsheviks closed it down, this old, honorable, liberal paper, the pride of the Russian press, enabled Jabotinsky to live in London, to maintain his family—and to do as he pleased.

Utilizing his old journalistic connections, Jabotinsky was able to meet many progressive political leaders, men of stature who, as Jabotinsky put it after his return from Russia, "at the end of the war will perhaps have a direct influence on international political problems." He was shocked by the complete absence of any Zionist political activity in those circles, in whose "political mentality" he could not discern even the slightest trace of any contact with the leaders of Russian Zionism. "Usually they simply have not heard that there is such a thing as Zionism and that the Zionists intended to present some demands" in connection with Palestine.[26]

Jabotinsky also succeeded in establishing valuable contacts with the Russian Ministry of Foreign Affairs. He left Russia the bearer of an "open letter" by the Near Eastern Department of the Ministry, dated August 15, 1915, stating that "Mr. Jabotinsky organized in Alexandria Jewish detachments, which are now fighting at the Dardanelles in the ranks of the British Expeditionary Corps and, according to the reports of the Imperial Ambassador in Cairo, have earned honorable mentions on the part of the British military authorities." The Department asked "all Russian Imperial Embassies, Missions and Consulates, as well as military and civilian frontier authorities, to give Mr. Jabotinsky every possible assistance."

On the Inner Zionist Front

On the way back to London, Jabotinsky broke his journey to see Grossman in Copenhagen. The latter had no good news for him. He was forced to part with his daily paper *Di Yiddishe Folkszeitung:* under pressure from

official Zionist quarters, its financial backers refused further support because Grossman had published an interview with Jabotinsky in defense of
the Legion idea. The Copenhagen office of the Zionist Organization, which
was established in accordance with the December, 1914, decision of the
Zionist Actions Committee, was very much annoyed by this interview. All
Jewish papers were urged not to reprint it, and the Jewish press in America
faithfully abided by this ukase. *Di Tribune* was the only medium through
which Jabotinsky was able to propagate the idea of activist Zionism.

The first issue of *Di Tribune* appeared on October 10, 1915. Jabotinsky
was a regular contributor to this lone organ of Zionist activism. Besides
his literary contributions, Jabotinsky could do little to help Grossman in
the difficult task of editing and publishing a "rebel" organ. He could not
even assist him with the distribution of *Di Tribune:* starting with the second issue, the British censor in his wisdom prohibited the sale of the one
and only pro-British organ in the Jewish press, on the pretense that it
attacked the anti-Semitic policy of the Russian government. Under these
circumstances, Grossman more than once had to pay the printer out of
his own journalistic earnings.

Jabotinsky's first article in *Di Tribune* appeared under the heading
"Activism."[27] The rather modest program formulated in this article contained three demands: 1. Creation of a Zionist Coalition Executive;
2. Establishment of Zionist diplomatic representations in France and Italy;
3. Publication of a Zionist "Blue-White Book" in French. No specific mention was made of the Legion. At that time Jabotinsky was apparently of the
opinion that the prerequisite for any active Zionist policy in general and for
the creation of the Legion in particular was the reform of the Zionist leadership, which had its seat in Berlin and was fully dominated by the so-called
"practical" wing in Zionism. For some time he concentrated on criticism
of the existing state of affairs and the demand for the consolidation of all
Zionist forces.

On November 22, 1915, Jabotinsky addressed to Dr. Weizmann a letter
(written by hand in a still rather awkward English), in which he suggested
the "creation of a Coalition *Leitung* [leadership] of the [World] Zionist Organization including both Practical and Political Zionists, with seat in a
neutral country." The main purposes of such a Coalition leadership were
formulated in the letter as follows: to create permanent representations in
France and Italy; to begin a new diplomatic action in England; to take the

measures necessary to create in England a non-Jewish movement in favor of a British Protectorate over Palestine; to consider the eventuality of need for Jewish troops for service in Palestine. Jabotinsky asked Dr. Weizmann "to take the initiative of a systematic action with support of the two factions of Zionism in England in order to carry out the mentioned tasks."

It can easily be seen that the question of the Legion occupied a rather subordinate place in this set of proposals and was formulated in a deliberately vague and hypothetical manner. As the main theme of the letter appears the demand for a Coalition *Leitung* with a limited but clearly delineated plan of political action. This demand was elaborated upon in a letter "from Dr. W. Jabotinsky" (this was, it seems, the first and the last time that the title "Dr." was used by Jabotinsky) to the editor of the *Jewish Chronicle*, published on December 17, 1915. It was an appeal for a Zionist "Coalition Ministry." Its political premise was that, whatever the prospects of an eventual partition of Turkey, Zionism must be ready to face this eventuality, should it arise: "We must prepare the political and diplomatic ground . . . we must also endeavor to arouse Jewish public opinion."

"Nothing has, however, yet been done in this direction," Jabotinsky stated. "During these fifteen months of war, I have visited England, France, Italy, Holland, Egypt, the Scandinavian States and Russia, and I declare emphatically that nothing has been done. Only in England have efforts been made, but action in England is useless if it is not followed up by a parallel action in the two other Mediterranean Powers, France and Italy. In those two countries absolutely nothing has been attempted. Matters are still worse than this," Jabotinsky insisted. "Not only has nothing been done, but there is not even a plan of action or any intention to act. . . . And I am absolutely certain that while the centre of our organization remains as it now is, the marasmus will continue, the necessary work will be neglected, and we shall lose the favorable occasions that may present themselves."

Speaking of "the centre . . . as it now is," Jabotinsky had in mind the "unilateral character of the Inner Actions Committee," which only represented one of the two fundamental tendencies of modern Zionism. Since the Seventh Zionist Congress there had always existed two currents in Zionism, which had been styled "political" and "practical." The wartime Inner Actions Committee was composed exclusively of the latter. The political Zionists had been reduced to the role of an opposition, deprived of every means of directly influencing the action of the Executive. Jabotinsky's contention was that the maintenance of an Executive which represented only one wing of Zionism, at a time when the movement was in need of all its forces, was "an inexcusable absurdity." Since the present situation demanded that political work be done, "we cannot do without those who represent among us the political principle. . . . If there is in the ranks of Zionism an element capable of resuscitating interest for political action, it is our 'Opposition.' It must be invited to collaborate in the Executive." Jabotinsky was confident that the leaders of the Opposition, if asked for a list of their representatives in a Coalition Executive, would find the means of settling the question among themselves. The seat of the new Executive must be moved to Switzerland.

Jabotinsky did not expect this executive to "perform miracles," but of one thing "he was sure: it will be active. It will reinforce political action in England; it will appoint diplomatic representatives in Paris and Rome; it will prepare the literature necessary for diplomatic and propaganda action; and last but not least, it will remind Zionists all over the world that Zionism lives and fights, and will summon them all to work."

This letter of Jabotinsky's has been related here in some detail, not only because it forcefully expresses his 1915 stand in Zionist affairs, but also because it contains some basic features of the position he took much later in regard to the policies of the Zionist world leadership and to its structure. Then, as later, he put strong emphasis on the *political* aspect of Zionism and demanded priority for a bold activist policy on a world scale. Then, as later, he combated the "unilateral character" of the Zionist leadership which eliminated from collective responsibility and fruitful collaboration an entire sector of the Zionist family; his slogan was a "coalition executive" comprising an equal number of representatives of the two main trends in Zionism.

The response to Jabotinsky's letter was scant and unfavorable. Official Zionist circles in London simply killed it by a conspiracy of silence. The Moscow *Yevreyskaya Zhisn,* organ of the Russian Zionist Central Committee, published a scathing comment in which it sharply protested against Jabotinsky's "methods that are completely unfounded and are lowering the prestige of the Inner Actions Committee, which is just now so necessary everywhere, and in England in particular."[28]

"Alone Against Everybody"

While trying to bring about a change in the structure of the Zionist leadership, Jabotinsky also doggedly continued his lonely struggle for the Legion.

He wrote to both Trumpeldor (in Russian) and Colonel Patterson (in French) who were at Gallipoli, advocating the creation of a Jewish Legion four to five thousand strong, which would be a frontline fighting unit and bear the name "Zion Corps"; as a possible compromise, he suggested that outside of Palestine it could serve as a mule transport unit, but in Palestine as a frontline unit. Trumpeldor's reaction was: "There are many objectionable aspects [in this proposal], but I am in full agreement with the idea as such and I am ready to collaborate."[29] Colonel Patterson assured Jabotinsky of his warmest sympathy for the project and of his willingness to cooperate wholeheartedly.[30]

In British political circles Jabotinsky was able to use the good offices of the Russian Embassy. Apparently on the basis of the "open letter" by the Foreign Ministry in St. Petersburg, the Russian Ambassador in London, Count A. K. Benkendorff, gave Jabotinsky (October 12, 1915) the following letter of introduction:

> Monsieur Wladimir Jabotinsky, correspondent of the "Russkiya Wyedomosti" of Moscow and a wellknown Russian publicist, has done much in connection with the raising of the Zion Corps of Jewish soldiers now fighting at the Dardanelles and is keenly interested in the further recruiting of Jewish troops in the countries of Western Europe. He has been highly recommended to me by the Russian Authorities.
>
> I have, therefore, the honor to recommend Monsieur Jabotinsky to the kind assistance of the British Authorities to whom he may have recourse for the fulfilment of the task which he has set himself.

Through Count Benkendorff, Jabotinsky approached the Laborite head of the British Board of Education, Arthur Henderson. In a letter dated October 19, 1915, the latter wrote that he "has heard with the greatest interest and sympathy" of Jabotinsky's proposal for raising a Jewish Corps for service in the East and that he asked Lord Kitchener to appoint some member of his staff to see Jabotinsky and to learn his proposals in detail; Henderson was confident that these proposals "will be very carefully considered by the Military Authorities." Two days later, Jabotinsky received from Major P. H. Casgrain an invitation to see him at the War Office "with reference to your proposal of raising a Jewish Division." Jabotinsky presented and explained his plan (he, of course, did not speak of a Jewish "Corps" or "Division," but of a Jewish Regiment). But the policy of the British War Office, guided by Lord Kitchener, was at the time unalterably opposed to any offensive in the East; the disastrous outcome of the Dardanelles campaign quite naturally added strength to this aversion.

In London Jewish circles Jabotinsky met with a strong three-pronged resistance.

The official leaders of the Anglo-Jewish community were fixed in their opposition to the very idea of a specific Jewish unit. Their conception of Judaism was a Marrannic one, and they were anxious, in all things and above all things, to hide from the world not so much their Judaism as the fact that on account of it any differentiation should exist between them and the vast majority of their fellow citizens.

No less inimical was the official Zionist leadership. Jabotinsky had against him also the spiritual influence of Achad Haam, who was then living in England surrounded by a close circle of supporters. The whole Legion movement was deprecated as being highly dangerous to the Jews of Palestine and as driving a wedge between the Jewries of the Allied countries on the one hand and those of the Central Powers on the other, and thus definitely splitting up the world unity of the Zionist movement, which the war had so rudely compromised. The only two leading Zionists who supported Jabotinsky throughout were Joseph Cowen and Dr. M. D. Eder, who had in the early months of the war unsuccessfully propagated the establishment of a specifically Jewish unit—though not for Palestine in particular. An enthusiastic partisan of the Legion was also the great Anglo-Jewish writer Israel Zangwill. But Zangwill, though a great moral force, was not an organized Zionist.

More complicated was the position of Dr. Weizmann. At that time he was one of the very few top-level Zionists who realized the vital importance of political work for the entire future of Zionism and Jewry. While working eight to ten hours a day in the Government Laboratory on his chemical discovery, he found time to take active steps in the political field. Jabotinsky highly valued these activities. Complaining that "almost nothing is being done" in the field of Zionist enlightenment on the international political scene, he wrote in *Di Tribune*: "And if it is still 'almost,' it is the personal merit of one man in Manchester. It was his merit that the ground was prepared in certain influential English circles. If it were not for him, we would have had in England the same situation we now have in other countries of the Entente: nothing."[31] When, in April, 1915, they met in Paris, Weizmann declared himself a supporter of the Legion. Jabotinsky ascribed great importance to this support. In the course of a discussion in Rosov's house in St. Petersburg, he said: "There are in our movement two men who ultimately will make all of you revise your 'neutralist' attitude and accept a pro-allied and pro-British orientation; one of the two will do it by violent and furious pressure, the other by quiet, underhand practices." Everyone easily guessed that "the violent one" was Jabotinsky himself; but who was the other one? they asked. "Professor Chaim Weizmann from Manchester," was the answer.[32]

When Jabotinsky came to England, a very friendly relationship developed between him and Dr. and Mrs. Weizmann. He was their guest during the Manchester period of their life. When Dr. Weizmann decided to establish himself in London and temporarily occupied a small house on a side street in Chelsea—3 Justice Walk—they even roomed together (for three months according to Jabotinsky, for six months according to Mrs. Weizmann) and came still closer to each other. "We had a chance now and again to talk at length, and to indulge in some daydreaming," Dr. Weizmann recalled.[33] But, according to Mrs. Weizmann's testimony, her husband could not at that time associate himself openly with Jabotinsky's activities: "he did not consider it possible to antagonize the official Zionist leadership which was dead set against the Legion."[34] Dr. Weizmann frankly admitted to Jabotinsky that he could not and did not care to make his own political work more complicated and difficult by openly supporting a project formally condemned by the Zionist Actions Committee and extremely unpopular with the Jewish population of London. Once he told Jabotinsky: "I cannot work like you, in an atmosphere where everybody is angry with me and can hardly stand me. This everyday friction would poison my life and kill in me all desire to work. Better let me act in my own way; a time will come when I shall find a means to help you as best I can." "Such a time did come, he kept his word, and I have not forgotten it," Jabotinsky gratefully acknowledged in 1928.[35] But then, in the autumn of 1915 and long afterward, Weizmann's sympathy could find no tangible expression, nor could it alter the general atmosphere of irritation and hostility in which Jabotinsky lived.

Most hostile and disappointing was the attitude of the Jewish population of the London East End, in their overwhelming majority emigrants from Russia. They were openly and violently hostile to any suggestion to do military service in any form. While England's youth suffered and died in the trenches, Jewish young men in Whitechapel persisted in continuing "life as usual" and refused to listen to any appeals for enlistment. In unpublished autobiographical notes, Jabotinsky recalled that "everybody's main concern was not to be drafted, and the man who wanted them to join the Jewish Legion was enemy Number One."

When conscription became the law of the land, it was legally not binding upon the overwhelming majority of them, since they were Russian subjects. A special organization called "The Foreign Jews' Protection Committee Against Deportation to Russia and Compulsion" energetically propagated the view that Russian Jews were under no obligation to serve in any shape or form.

The attention of Parliament was drawn to the matter, and after some considerable questioning and debate, Herbert Samuel, who was then Home Secretary, initiated a scheme for the voluntary recruiting of Russian Jews. That plan proved a failure. Very few enlisted in the Jewish War Services Committee, headed by Major Lionel Rothschild who took charge of the scheme. Frustrated and angered by this setback, Herbert Samuel found no better expedient than to announce, on July 6, 1916, in the House of Commons that "any Russian subject" of military age failing to enlist voluntarily in the British Army would be sent back to Russia. This threat, too, failed to impress the East End Jewish youth: not a single Russian "subject" was enlisted as a result of that proclamation. The impression it produced among the non-Jewish British public was the worst possible. Jabotinsky took advantage of the situation so created by calling together the six London correspondents of the Russian liberal and radical dailies; they decided to send a telegram to the War Secretary, Lord Derby, stating that the Home Secretary's latest move with regard to Russian emigres in England was likely to create an undesirable impression among their liberal readers, and they should therefore appreciate an opportunity of talking it over with the Minister. In those years the British government naturally set great store by the attitude of the Russian papers and Lord Derby answered that he had asked the Home Secretary himself to receive them at the House of Commons. At this gathering Herbert Samuel unhappily asked:

"Gentlemen, what else can I do? Those Russian subjects refuse to enlist voluntarily, and resentment is growing against them. Can the government stand by in idleness, watching that resentment degenerate into downright anti-Semitism?"

And looking straight at Jabotinsky, he asked: "What is your opinion, for instance?"

"Sir," Jabotinsky replied, "if you want those people to enlist, why appeal to their fear of Russia? It would be more dignified, and also more practical, to appeal to their own positive national feelings. The government should find out—it is not so difficult— whether there is not some aspect of the war and of victory which could promise them relief and redemption as Jews and offer them a form of service reconcilable with that side of their civil mentality."

Herbert Samuel admitted that he was "very much impressed" by this argument—but evidently only to the extent of officially withdrawing his unfortunate proclamation a few days later; he was not, however, sufficiently impressed to bring Jabotinsky's plan before the Cabinet.

The stalemate thus went on, and resentment in the widest English circles also continued. Anti-Jewish feelings were on the increase; there was even some ugly talk of possible anti-Jewish outbreaks. As early as June 1, 1916, Jabotinsky wrote to Herbert Samuel that friends from the East End had asked his advice whether it would be suitable to organize a unit for local self-defense, as they were sure that anti-Jewish riots must inevitably come: "I think with horror and sorrow of the humiliating effect which both these phenomena would have—the creation of a 'self-defense' *à la russe*, as well as the riots. But I do not know what to reply, the more so, as I have the impression that any advice in these times is likely to be followed. I already bear a responsibility too heavy for private shoulders."[*]

It was this realization of grave responsibility which prompted Jabotinsky to continue his determined efforts to expound the Legion idea to influential political circles in England.

A staunch friend of the Legion idea was Henry Wickham Steed, the editor of the all-powerful London *Times*, to whom Jabotinsky came with an introductory letter from the French historian Seignobos. When the *Times* published an editorial advocating the formation of a Jewish Legion, even the most determined Jewish opponents of the idea looked crestfallen and said to Jabotinsky: "Of course, if the *Times* is on your

---

[*]In fact, anti-Jewish riots took place at Leeds on April 3–4, 1917.

side. . . ." A leading article favoring the Legion also appeared in the influential *Manchester Guardian,* to whose editor, C. P. Scott, Jabotinsky was introduced by Dr. Weizmann. The Liberal M. P. Joseph King underwent an interesting evolution. He started with an attack on Jabotinsky in the House of Commons where he asked the Home Secretary whether he was aware of the fact that "a Russian journalist" was making propaganda in Whitechapel for a Jewish Regiment and whether this journalist had any authority from the government. Jabotinsky thereupon wrote to him: "Sir, before you attack a man and his plans, hear his case." They met and had a long heart-to-heart talk. King was obviously under the strong influence of a Russian Socialist emigré, George V. Chitcherin (destined, in May, 1918, to become Soviet Commissar for External Affairs; in his work for the Legion, Jabotinsky more than once felt his destructive interference); but King responded magnificently to Jabotinsky's argumentation and became a staunch friend and supporter. He brought Jabotinsky in touch with the leading liberal journal *The Nation* and introduced him to a number of M.P.'s, both Liberal and Conservative. The chief counselor of the Russian Embassy, Constantin D. Nabokov, who later became Ambassador and whom Jabotinsky won over for the Legion idea, arranged for him meetings with British Ministers, with the American Ambassador Walter Hines Page, and with the French Ambassador Paul Cambon.

Of inestimable value was the cooperation of Colonel Patterson, who came to London to recover from his illness. It was in the West End Hospital in Dover Street that these two of the three main engineers of the Legion met for the first time. "We became friends at sight . . . and so began a friendship which lasted without a moment's break until the very day of his lamented death," wrote Patterson in the Jabotinsky memorial issue of *Hadar*.[36] The commander of the disbanded Zion Mule Corps was not in the least dismayed by the news that Lord Kitchener was against the Legion. "Realities are stronger than Lord Kitchener," he said, and when asked: "Will you help me?" he answered: "Of course. Come."

The same day he introduced Jabotinsky to Captain Leopold S. Amery, M.P. and one of Lord Derby's Military Secretaries at the War Office. "He knows of our subject," said Patterson; "give him the details."[37] Recalling this first encounter, Amery wrote after Jabotinsky's death: "I was at that time greatly impressed by Mr. Jabotinsky's singlemindedness and fervid enthusiasm."[38] He became Jabotinsky's most energetic and devoted adviser and contact man in government circles.

All this sustained manifold effort was carried on by a single man, a foreigner, who had no organization behind him, no funds or assistance from anyone, and who was surrounded by an atmosphere of intense hostility. He was armed only with the fervent belief in the justness and necessity of the idea he defended; his strong will, personality, and power of conviction were his only weapons. He succeeded in making the Legion an actual issue in government circles. A lively correspondence was carried on between the War Office and the Premier's Secretariat, and in the Propaganda Department there lay a thick file of reports, letters, and press clippings, marked "Jewish Regiment," with a note by Lord Newton: "Important."

During this entire period, Jabotinsky, whose main weapon had always been his pen and in whose well-considered opinion "journalists were, will and must be the world's ruling class," was practically deprived of the possibility to defend and to preach his views in the press. The Copenhagen *Tribune* was but a bi-weekly with a very limited circulation. He was able from time to time to squeeze in a "letter to the Editor" in the London *Jewish Chronicle*. But all other Jewish periodicals were closed to him. *Russkiya Vyedomosti* was, after all, a purely Russian paper whose interest in Jewish and Zionist affairs was very limited. The only paper open to him was *Odesskiya Novosti* where, in 1915 and 1916, he published several remarkable articles, "Back to the Charter," "Orientation," "Letters from a Journey," and others, in which an alert reader can easily discover essential elements of the Zionist philosophy he formulated and defended many years later.

In "Back to the Charter"* (March, 1915) there is clearly discernible the embryo of Jabotinsky's demand for a "colonizatory régime" as the *conditio sine qua non* for the realization of Zionism: "We will never become a majority in Palestine, if we will not beforehand achieve a certain amount of political power over the territory which we intend to settle. Colonization demands a series of preconditions, which can be created only through political power. What is necessary is proper legislation,

---

*Charter, terra employed by Theodor Herzl for the document he endeavored to secure from the Ottoman Sultan authorizing the establishment of a Jewish commonwealth in Palestine.

suitable communications facilities, an administration which is not a hindrance but a help."

In the second, "Letter from a Journey" (June 16, 1916), refuting the current argument that a pro-Allied orientation and the establishment of a Jewish Legion were bound to endanger the existing Jewish achievements in Palestine, he dismissed "three-fourths of all the talk about danger as vain talk." Of course, he admitted,

> nobody can guarantee how much of our positions in Palestine will remain by the end of the war. . . . But this does not mean that the realization of that danger must tie us down. We [the Activists], who are ready to "risk," value the *Yishuv* not less than do the "passivists." We were *Neinsagers* at the Sixth Congress, we fought for the practical work in Palestine, we voted for the new composition of the Inner Actions Committee. But now we have to admit that, trying to "set the stick upright," we had too much bent it over in the other direction. During the last few years the movement had lost its political pathos, and now we pay dearly for it. There is no political swing, we have neither a plan nor men capable of implementing it; those who worked with Herzl have been thrown overboard, and those who are "leading" us now, are politically nerveless.
>
> In the name of many and many I say: *this* we have not foreseen and have not intended. We have never looked upon the *Yishuv* as *Selbstzweck*. Its main value in our eyes was that we saw in it one of the powerful tools of political Zionism. . . . We prized the *Yishuv* as the best of our aces in the political game. But we will not agree to this same *Yishuv* all of a sudden becoming an obstacle to a decisive political game. . . . No, to this we will never agree. The *Yishuv* is an instrument and cannot be anything more than that. . . . It is our political vanguard. And it sometimes happens that for the sake of a common cause the vanguard has to sustain heavy losses. We send them our salute and continue on our way. . . .

It is worth noting that the otherwise penetrating and in many respects prophetic article "Orientation" contained several strikingly erroneous predictions. Jabotinsky foretold that Russia would be one of the outstanding victors in the world conflict and would be rewarded by annexation of the Turkish Dardanelles and of Austrian Galicia; that as a result of this victory the old Tsarist régime would be strengthened; that the Jews of the annexed Turkish and Austrian territories would be deprived (at least for the next thirty years to come) of their civic rights; yet, economically, Jewish merchants in Russia were going to profit because the Dardanelles would be open to their commercial activities.

With regard to Turkey, Jabotinsky had very definite and outspoken ideas, which he formulated in the first book he ever published in English. Insisting that Turkey *est delenda,* he wrote in *Turkey and the War* (pp. 142-43)

Turkey under Turkish rule is doomed to remain backward, unenlightened, barren. This doom is irremovable so long as the Ottoman Empire shall last, and its heavy burden crushes and condemns to death every spiritual bud that sprouts from either Turkish or non-Turkish stalks. The destruction of the Ottoman Empire will be a blessing for both Turks and non-Turks. The latter, independent or placed under the protection of mighty civilizing Powers, will freely develop their long-subdued vitalities; the former, liberated from the oppressive load of Imperial responsibilities, will enter an era of peaceful and productive renaissance. He who wishes Turkey's destruction is a friend, not a foe of the Turkish race.

THIRTEEN

THROUGH DEFEAT TO VICTORY

The Abortive Campaign

By the autumn of 1916 it had become clear to everybody that, if a most disgraceful and dangerous scandal was to be avoided, the Jewish East End must enlist. Jabotinsky and his friends, who had formed a "Committee for Jewish Freedom," decided that the time had come to act and to offer a reasonable and constructive alternative to the equally unpleasant prospects of either being shipped back to Russia or enlisting in the British Army. They issued an appeal, which was widely distributed in London's Jewish quarters. The plan was to collect signatures of men of military age for the following declaration: "Should the government create a Jewish Regiment to be utilized exclusively either for Home Defense or for operations on the Palestine front—I undertake to join such a Regiment."[1] Should a sufficient number of signatures be obtained, it was intended to submit a corresponding petition to the government. The initial financial means for the campaign, which was to be carried through without any governmental assistance whatever, were provided by Joseph Cowen. It was decided to publish in London a daily paper in Yiddish, *Unsere Tribune*, of which Grossman was to be the chief editor. Jabotinsky himself wrote a daily column in English.

Two days after the start of this campaign, Herbert Samuel sent for Jabotinsky, declared that the government was "really grateful" for this initiative, and asked whether the Home Office could be helpful in any way.

"Only in one way," Jabotinsky answered. "Issue an official statement that, if a thousand signatures are collected, the government will form a 'Home and Heim' Regiment. If you do that, I am certain of success."

Samuel argued that it was not for him but for the whole Cabinet to decide such a question. "And you know," he added, "that many Jews—particularly the Zionists—are strongly opposed to the formation of a Jewish Regiment. . . . Can I perhaps help you in any other way?"

Jabotinsky replied in the negative and started the campaign on his own.[2] It lasted a month and, according to Jabotinsky's own outspoken verdict, which can be found in his unpublished autobiographical notes, "ended in riots, disgrace, and failure. . . ." Altogether, the pitiable number of three hundred signatures was obtained. What was even worse, the initiators of the campaign were not even able to make themselves heard by Jewish audiences. When asked by Herbert Samuel whether he could help him in some way, Jabotinsky proudly refrained from asking police protection for the planned meetings. He had every reason to regret this ill-advised pride. The first meeting passed off quietly, for opponents of the Legion were sure that there were police hidden somewhere in the hall, as was customary at recruiting meetings. But they were quick to realize that this was not the case, and at the second meeting some thirty well-organized noisemakers, armed with whistles, easily succeeded in creating an uproar. Wild outcries of "Militarist! Murderer! Provocateur!" interrupted the speakers. Both Jabotinsky and Grossman had their glasses broken and had to retreat through a back door. The same performance, with slight variations, was repeated during the later meetings. Every one of them was the scene of well-planned and ugly obstruction, of clamor, abuse, and scandals. The organizers of the meetings refused on principle to call in the police, and held on stubbornly. Joseph Cowen was a tower of strength and confidence. When Jabotinsky, Grossman, and Trumpeldor reported that at the meetings they were pelted by rotten potatoes, he used to say: "All right, a potato is not a stone, a potato is a plant, and there will be fruits of your labor; we will see to it."[3] But there was no dearth of stones either. "Do you recall the hail of stones that greeted you on the street, and the battered faces of your friends, who dared to defend you against the wild, burning hatred?" Jabotinsky's faithful typewriter pitilessly reminded him.[4] A frustrating atmosphere of failure had already been created in the first week of the campaign. After four weeks they decided to close the campaign and to stop publishing *Unsere Tribune*. Grossman returned to Copenhagen; Jabotinsky remained in London waiting for a "next time."

"Mr. Jug-of-Whiskey"

"Exactly one month after this failure," Jabotinsky recalled, "the first nucleus of the Jewish Regiment was created."[5]

At the end of 1916, a group of one hundred twenty former soldiers from the Zion Mule Corps who, after their unit was dissolved, had volunteered again for army service, arrived in London. Patterson and Amery arranged for all of them to be assigned to the same battalion ("20th County of London") where they were formed into a separate company. Jabotinsky decided to join this nucleus himself and to volunteer for army service—the only one to do so even among those few Zionist leaders who together with him fought for the Legion idea. Before implementing this decision, he wrote to his wife in Russia, asking whether she would approve of such a step. Mrs. Jabotinsky answered by a one-word telegram: *Blagoslovlyayu* (You have my blessing). Later she told a close friend of the family the "pre-history" of this reply.[6] She was, of course, far from happy when she learned of her husband's intention to join the army in wartime. She asked the advice of friends, most of whom were leading Zionists. Each of them said "no." From this she drew the following conclusion: "Everybody will be against him, and he will do it anyway; so why should I, too, be in the camp of those who oppose him? Let him have the satisfaction of acting with my full moral support."

Happy and proud, Jabotinsky journeyed to Haseley Down, near Winchester, where the "20th London" was in training, introduced himself to the Commanding Officer, Lieutenant Colonel Asheton Pownhall, and asked to be accepted for service in the Jewish company. Late in January, 1917, his "status of a free citizen from abroad" ended: he officially enlisted at the recruiting office and received the "King's Shilling"—to be exact, two shillings and sixpence—for his first day as a soldier. Before doing so, he handed to the printers the manuscript of his book *Turkey and the War*.

There was nothing spectacular in his barrack-room record. He served like any other private, "only," he confessed, "I was not as young (thirty-six) or as slim as the others." At first, when his arms ached from the anti-typhus injections, he used to sweep out the barracks and wash the tables of the Sergeants' Mess. The Jewish Sergeant Ephraim Blitstein teasingly complimented him: "Very well washed. If you like I'll ask the Colonel to give you a permanent assignment to wash the tables at our Mess." Very soon, however, Jabotinsky was transferred to the "Russian N.C.O. Class." This, he asserted, happened "not on account of my own classification but only by the Colonel's grace." This promotion, however, did not spare him a humiliating incident, which he good-humoredly reported as follows: When, on Passover, he received the advance copy of his book *Turkey and the War* and was lovingly and proudly patting its red cloth cover in the barracks, the orderly officer—a very young and very red-haired first lieutenant—burst into the room, frowned, and shouted: "Hallo, that man with glasses—open up."—"Open up what, sir?" Jabotinsky inquired. "The windows, you bloody fool!" was the answer.

On the whole, his position in the company was a rather strange one, Jabotinsky admitted. A simple soldier, he was continuously having political interviews with some of the most important British statesmen and military leaders and almost every other day had to go to London. This earned him "a comical reputation" in the battalion. The English sergeants refused to take him seriously as a soldier. On parade, when an orderly would be seen from afar with a brown envelope in his hand, the sergeant would say: "I suppose it's another telegram for Mr. Jug-of-Whiskey." This commonly accepted pronunciation of Jabotinsky's name was easier to articulate; it had a pleasant sound reminiscent of a good drink; and it also paid recognition to his anti-prohibition tendencies.

In May, 1917, Colonel Pownhall decided that Jabotinsky should be given some rank. The obstacle was that there was no vacancy on the roster; but finally he was made an unpaid (acting) lance-sergeant.[7] The following receipt can be seen in the Jabotinsky Institute in Tel Aviv:

No. 222
20th County of London Battalion
(The London Regiment)
Sergeants' Mess
Received from Lance-Sergt. Jabotinsky the sum of
two shillings six pence entrance fee.

Jabotinsky was not much concerned at receiving no pay, for he still was sending occasional articles to *Russkiya Vyedomosti* for which he was well paid.

It took months of hard and patient work to convert the tiny "nucleus of a Jewish Regiment" from a promising possibility into a political and military reality. Jabotinsky was engineering this work from his barracks room at Haseley Down; his right hand in London at this stage was, in the main, Amery.

On the eve of Jabotinsky's joining the army, Amery wrote to him (January 22, 1917): "Since I saw you I have had an opportunity of speaking to people in the War Office, who have promised to look into the whole question again." The next day, on the 23rd, Jabotinsky asked Amery's counsel whether it would be advisable for him and Trumpeldor to make a detailed written proposal to the British authorities and send it to the members of the War Cabinet. Amery's reply was: "I think this is a good idea. If you care to send me a draft of your memo first, I shall be very happy to offer any suggestion as to its form." Two days later Amery wrote on the stationery of the "Committee of Imperial Defence" a long comment of the submitted draft memorandum, suggesting several changes "which you could put in or not as you please." As to the form in which the memorandum should be submitted to the government, Amery advised that it should be sent to the Prime Minister; he recommended that in doing so Jabotinsky should specifically refer to his personal record in this field:

"You might recapitulate that you originally opened negotiations with the War Office and Foreign Office armed with credentials from the Russian authorities, who were favorable to your enterprise; and that you understood at the time that the Foreign Office was not unsympathetic to the idea in view of the political effect in America, but that you [also] understood that the War Office did not at that time consider the matter of sufficient importance to warrant the raising of a special Corps for service in Egypt and Palestine (or whatever was your impression of the views of the War Office and Foreign Office [Amery added in parentheses with his usual dry humor]); then you ought also briefly to mention that, without official encouragement, you undertook a purely personal campaign of meetings in East London, which in the absence of any canvassing or official support did not attract more than a very limited number of volunteers. What I mean is that you ought to briefly put the Prime Minister in possession of the main facts as to your previous efforts to form a special Jewish Corps in this country."

A few days later, Jabotinsky and Trumpeldor signed the final text of the memorandum which Amery undertook to hand over personally to the Prime Minister Lloyd George.

It did not produce immediate results. For some time the matter seems to have been shelved in British governmental circles. Jabotinsky unsuccessfully tried to reactivate it through his political connections. One of them was Mark Sykes, who at the end of 1916 (when the second coalition government with Lloyd George as Premier and Balfour as Foreign Secretary came to power) was authorized to negotiate with the Zionist leaders. Replying on February 14, 1917,to Jabotinsky's letter, Sykes wrote:

"I have thought over your letter very carefully and made enquiries. I think for the moment that it would be best not to press the matter. The military authorities are averse to employing or raising troops whose area of operations is limited, and it would probably be necessary to obtain the concurrence of other powers in the employment of special troops for special purposes in areas in which political considerations were of importance. At the same time I think that the scheme should be kept alive in idea, so that if circumstances prove as I hope propitious it might be proceeded with."

A similar answer came two days later from Amery on the stationery of the "Offices of the War Cabinet":

"I know you must be impatient, but I am afraid you may have to wait a little while yet for any definite decision from the War Cabinet. All the members have had your Memorandum, but they have not yet found the time for a collective discussion of it."

And again, on March 26th, Amery wrote:

"I have tried at intervals ever since I saw you last to get the matter of the Jewish Legion brought before the War Cabinet. But for one reason or another the War Office have so far refused to take an active interest in it, though I do not understand that they are hostile. I am making a further attempt to stir them up today."

It was not before April 13th that Amery was able to give Jabotinsky cautiously some good news:

"Your affair is really making progress at last, and I hope that it will be definitely settled in the next week or two. But, as you know, there are always slips between the cup and the lip and you must not be too disappointed if there are further hitches and delays. Anyhow, you can be sure that I have done my best to help the thing forward and will continue to do so."

And he did. By the spring of 1917, he managed to lay before the War Cabinet the "Jewish Legion" petition which Trumpeldor and Jabotinsky had signed. It was discussed and approved "in principle." The War Secretary,

Lord Derby, was instructed "to discuss the details with the signatories." One bright April morning, Jabotinsky, who was on leave in London, was handed by a messenger from the War Office a handwritten letter signed by General Woodward, Director of Organization. The General wanted "Mr. J." to be so kind as to call at the War Office at 2 P.M. that very day, the purpose being an interview with Lord Derby. Being addressed in the letter as "Sir," Jabotinsky realized that its author did not suspect that the addressee was a mere private in a British infantry battalion. He was inclined to ask Trumpeldor, who was a captain, to replace him; but Trumpeldor felt rather doubtful about his English oratory. So they decided to go together.

At the door of Room 215 they handed in their visiting cards and were immediately admitted. Jabotinsky saluted and introduced Trumpeldor and himself. Though the General's face "betrayed a high degree of astonishment," Jabotinsky humorously related, he did not show any of it in his words. Nor, for that matter, did Lord Derby himself when, five minutes later, they were ushered into the *sanctum sanctorum* of his office: but he was already forewarned by General Woodward who went in first to announce the two unusual visitors. Asked to give some precise details about his Jewish unit scheme, Jabotinsky "reeled off the details automatically": having repeated them so many times, he could have done it half-asleep. The second ministerial question—whether they anticipated a large number of volunteers—was answered by Trumpeldor in his usual matter-of-fact way: "If it is to be just a regiment of Jews—perhaps. If it will be a regiment for the Palestine front—certainly. If, together with its formation, there will appear a government pronouncement in favor of Zionism—overwhelmingly."

After some more questions and answers, the War Secretary thanked the visitors and parted with them, saying that as to the name of the regiment, its badges "and all that," General Geddes, Director of Recruiting, was going to send for them "one of these days and talk it over." When, back in camp, Jabotinsky reported the conversation to Colonel Pownhall, the latter assured him that it was a breach of all the traditions of the British War Office; it was the first time in history that such an adventure had happened to a private soldier.[8]

Echo in Russia

The Russian Revolution of February, 1917, removed one of the strongest psychological obstacles to a clear-cut pro-Allied orientation of world Jewry.

The hated Tsarist régime was no more, and together with it also disappeared the "guilt by association" complex that weighed so heavily on England and France. No longer was it possible to object to the creation of a Jewish unit within the British Army "on the grounds of principle." This changed situation also opened new possibilities for the Legion idea. In a letter dated May 4, 1917, written in Russian,* Jabotinsky wrote that friends in Petrograd were asking him to come to Russia in order to organize among the Jewish youth propaganda for the continuation of the war (defeatist tendencies were dangerously increasing among Russian masses) and for the formation of a Jewish Legion; the British military authorities offered to give him leave of absence or to facilitate his transfer to the Russian Army. Before taking any decision, he asked the addressee and P. N. Milyukov (the leader of the Constitutionalist Democratic Party and later Minister of Foreign Affairs in the revolutionary provisional government) to express their opinion as to the advisability of organizing such a movement among the Jewish youth in Russia.

Either because the answer to this question was in the negative or because his presence was necessary in London where the struggle for the Legion was to last another three months, the project of a journey to Russia did not materialize. This was most fortunate for Jabotinsky. If at that time he had come to Russia, he would have met with a most unfriendly reception. At the Seventh All-Russian Zionist Convention in May, 1917—the first to be called after the Revolution—he personally and the Legion idea as such were still highly unpopular. Among the many hundreds of delegates, only some twenty to twenty-five constituted themselves as an "activist-legionist group," which made a valiant effort to challenge the prevalent anti-Jabotinsky trend. The leaders of the group were M. Grossman, who had recently returned from Copenhagen, A. Babkov from St. Petersburg, this writer and S. Eiges from Rostov on Don, J. Fischer and M. Postan from Odessa. The attitude of the majority was anything but encouraging. When Grossman indignantly mentioned in his speech that the Zionist Actions Committee had forbidden Zionists to enlist for service in the Legion, he was interrupted from the floor by shouts: "And rightly so!" When he said that he was going to send a greetings cable to Jabotinsky, there were shouts: "No! No!" Both Grossman and Babkov accused the Central Committee of having "alienated

---

*The addressee cannot be identified, for the upper part of the letter is illegible.

a talented Zionist leader without even having listened to him." This writer severely criticized in his speech the official Zionist policy of passive neutrality, while Fischer declared that activism was the manifestation of Jewish youth's readiness for self-sacrifice.

The sympathies of the Convention were, however, on the side of the speakers defending the official Zionist line. The Convention's president, Dr. E. V. Chlenov, reaffirmed "the policy of strictest neutrality, which is the only one that is capable of securing the preservation of our position in Palestine and the most important basis of our movement—its unity." With regard to Jabotinsky, Chlenov said: "We all value him and we have not alienated him—he himself has left us, stating that 'there are moments when one has to violate the Torah.' We will be glad to see him again in our midst, but, of course, only as a member of the organization, for whom decisions and instructions of the organization's leading and responsible body are as binding as they are for all of us; we cannot make any exception."[9]

Instead of Jabotinsky, it was Trumpeldor who went to Russia in the summer of 1917. He came with two great projects which he previously expounded to Jabotinsky: the first was *Hechalutz*, the other, a Jewish Army in Russia—not merely a Legion, but an army of 75,000 to 100,000 men—which would go to the Caucasian front and force its way through Armenia and Mesopotamia to Eastern Palestine. Trumpeldor was certain that with Boris Savinkov as Minister of War in the Kerensky government, permission could be obtained to raise such a Jewish Army.[10] On July 25, 1917, Trumpeldor wrote to Jabotinsky from Petrograd: "We are working here all the time and very hard. In the beginning, the Zionists were hostile. Now, theirs is almost a benevolent neutrality." In August, 1917, a "temporary committee of the initial group for the formation of a Jewish Legion" submitted to the Minister of War, Boris V. Savinkov, a memorandum asking the provisional government's permission to begin the recruiting of a Jewish unit. Referring to the precedents of the Zion Mule Corps in Gallipoli and the Jewish battalions then being formed in England, the memorandum stressed that the proposed Jewish unit in Russia should consist of volunteers only; the most desirable front for a Jewish formation would naturally be Palestine, but in view of the community of interests and the unity of the Allied front, the unit would be completely at the disposal of the High Command.[11]

Assent was obtained in the principle. But the collapse of the provisional government and of the entire Russian front made the concrete plan

of a Jewish Legion from Russia obsolete. Yet, the Legion idea remained implanted in the minds and souls of an ever-growing circle of Zionists. Even
in Ussishkin's own domain, Odessa, sentiment for Jabotinsky was rising.
Jabotinsky's nephew, Johnny, wrote to him on April 11, 1917, about the persistent rumors that he was coming to Odessa; almost every day the family
was receiving telephone inquiries about his alleged arrival: "By now, very
many have become sympathetic to your Legion ideas; everybody regrets
that you are not here." At a well-attended All-Russian Conference of the
High School Students' Association held in Odessa in the early summer of
1917, the question of Jabotinsky's policies was hotly debated. B. Weinstein,
who was the chairman, recalls that Ussishkin came to the Conference and
watched the voting procedure "like a hawk": the majority went on record
as welcoming Jabotinsky's action. An open conflict with Ussishkin broke
out over the approaching elections to the All-Russian Jewish Assembly.
Pro-activist youth demanded that Jabotinsky be included in the Zionist
slate in Odessa, and when this was refused on account of Jabotinsky's Le-
gionist activities, many young Zionist propagandists expressed their protest
by asking to be assigned for duty in the provinces and not in Odessa.[12]

In Kiev, the regional Zionist Conference held on December 8-10, 1917,
went on record as urging the Zionist Central Committee to do its utmost
in order to make it possible for Jabotinsky to return to active Zionist work.
In several electoral districts, local Zionist committees, disregarding warnings from above, put Jabotinsky's name at the head of their slates for the
All-Russian Jewish Assembly. In March, 1918, this writer—then a member
of the All-Ukrainian Zionist Central Committee—published in the independent Kiev weekly *Oif der Wach,* edited by M. Grossman, an article "Vladimir
Jabotinsky," which culminated in a strong plea to restore Jabotinsky, who
had proved time and again to have been right in his analysis and prognosis, to a well-deserved and long-overdue position of leadership in the Zionist
movement, which missed him so badly.[13] Early in 1919, *Yevreyskaya Mysl,*
the organ of the Odessa Zionist District Committee, published an article by
J. Fischer "Who Was Right?" devoted to a passionate vindication of Jabotinsky's political vision.[14]

In non-Jewish circles—both friendly and hostile—Jabotinsky was
considered as the incarnation of the new military spirit in Jewry. When,
at the end of 1918, the Russian press published the fantastic report that
"a Jewish Ministry for Palestine" had already been established in London, it

listed Dr. Weizmann as the Premier and Jabotinsky as the Minister of War; Ussishkin trailed a poor third as Minister of Agriculture.[15] On the other hand, when an English anti-Bolshevist expeditionary corps landed at Arkhangelsk in August, 1918, under the command of General Pool, the Soviet press wrote that at the head of one of the regiments was "the notorious Jewish militarist and imperialist Vladimir Jabotinsky."[16]

It's a Long Way . . .

All these encouraging developments belong, however, to a somewhat later period. In England itself, during the first few months following the Russian Revolution, the Legion plan made no noticeable progress toward realization. The term "one of these days" used by Lord Derby proved to be very elastic: it was still a long way to go, and very far from smooth. It was not until June 15th that Amery was able to tell Jabotinsky that "the Legion scheme is now only waiting for the final passage of the Bill in order to be put in hand on a proper scale."

The Bill to which Amery referred had, indeed, a great bearing on the Legion scheme. It provided for Parliament's authorization for the government to enter into conventions with Allied governments whereby the respective subjects of Allied countries be compelled either to return to their native land or to serve in the army of the country in which they were living. This authorization was granted, and it soon became known that the British government was negotiating with Petrograd about concluding such a convention. In Whitechapel, whisperings were heard that this had been "managed" by Jabotinsky and his friends, and the "Protection Society" appealed to the Russian provisional government not to consent to the British proposal. Jabotinsky categorically denied that he had a hand in initiating the British move. But he was no less outspoken in stating that he was not in the least inclined to oppose it—rather the contrary. Asked by the Russian Ambassador in London, K. D. Nabokov, about public opinion, British and Jewish, on the question of conscription for Russian citizens in England, Jabotinsky answered: "Among Englishmen, Gentiles and Jews, there are no two opinions; all agree on conscription. Among the foreign Jews there are two opinions. One is that of the majority in Whitechapel—No. The other is that of my friends and myself—Yes."

The convention with the Russian provisional government was concluded early in July, 1917, and on July 12th, Lloyd George's secretary, Philip Henry Kerr (the Marquess of Lothian, who in 1939 became Ambassador to

the United States), wrote to Jabotinsky on the stationery of the First Lord
of the Treasury:

> With further reference to your letter of July 7th, I have made enquiries
> through the War Office and I am informed that the first steps in connection
> with the organization of a Jewish regiment of infantry have been set on foot.
> I hope you will hear in due course as to the progress of the arrangements.

In the month of August there appeared, one after the other, two official announcements: one dealt with conscription for Russian citizens in
England; the other, dated August 3rd and signed by the Secretary of War,
stated that "arrangements are now nearing completion for the formation of
a Jewish Regiment of Infantry . . . it is proposed that the badge of the regiment shall consist of representation of King David's Shield."

On August 23, 1917, the formation of the Jewish Regiment was officially announced in the London *Gazette*. At the same time it was officially
intimated that a special Jewish name and badge would be given to the battalions of this Regiment.

The assimilationists mobilized all their influence to kill the Regiment.
On August 30th, a deputation headed by Major Lionel de Rothschild and
Lord Swaythling came to see the War Minister Lord Derby and bluntly demanded cancellation of the entire Jewish Regiment scheme, though it was
already endorsed by the government. Lord Derby refused to do so. But he
agreed to deprive the Regiment of the name "Jewish" and promised to send
it, not to Palestine, but "wherever it might be required." This sudden change
of mind provoked an immediate and violent reaction. Patterson resigned
his command, charging a betrayal of his recruits; Captain Amery and Dr.
Weizmann went to Lord Milner who induced Lord Derby to receive a Zionist "counter-deputation" to effect some compromise; and Jabotinsky, faithful to his conviction that "the world's ruling caste are the journalists," rushed
to Henry Wickham Steed, the editor of the *Times,* and told him the story.
Steed curtly promised that "tomorrow the *Times* will tell the War Office not
to play the fool"; and he kept his promise. His editorial gave the War Office
an unheard-of thrashing. It helped.[17] In addition, he sent to Lord Derby a
memorandum, and later a special letter with extracts from the German press
on the importance of capturing Zionism for Germany. Lord Derby replied
that he would do his utmost to form a Maccabean Regiment for service in
Palestine, and that he would put his shoulder to the wheel if he were given

time. Informing Jabotinsky of this exchange of letters, Steed wrote on September 8th: "Don't be too downhearted. . . . You may rely on me to do all in my power to keep the matter well to the fore; and I know that you have some ardent supporters in the Foreign Office and at No. 10 [Downing Street]." Lord Derby kept his promise and told a pro-Legion deputation that the Legion would bear the name "Royal Fusiliers"—until such a time as it would distinguish itself on the battlefield and earn the honorable description "Jewish"; and that it would be sent to Palestine only.

These promises were fulfilled later, after the conquest of Palestine: the "Royal Fusiliers" were granted the description "Judean Regiment" and its insigne was the *menora* with the Hebrew word *Kadima* (meaning both "forward" and "eastward").

Last Skirmishes and—Victory

On July 27th, Colonel Patterson was ordered to come to London and commence the organization of the Jewish Legion. Major General R. Hutchinson, Director of Organization in the War Office, told him, among other things, that "a certain sergeant Jabotinsky would be most useful to him, for he was a very keen worker, and an ardent advocate of the Jewish Regiment." Suppressing a smile, Patterson answered that he had already met Jabotinsky and knew that his assistance would be invaluable; he requested that Jabotinsky be attached to him for duty at once.[18]

Jabotinsky was put in charge of recruitment. Together with three of his comrades in the 20th Battalion, he was transferred to the Recruiting Department headed by General Geddes; they were apportioned three rooms. It was decided that, apart from the general recruiting, an energetic propaganda campaign should be conducted in order to expound to the Jewish community both the moral and the Jewish national value of the Legion. Though initiated and financed by the Recruiting Department, this propaganda was conducted in the name of the "For Jewish Future" Committee, which had been formed by Jabotinsky in 1916.

A poster "To All Jews" was extensively circulated in the East End. It reminded them that the convention between Russia and England was now a fact which "cannot be done away with," and that there were now only two alternatives: "to serve in Russia or to serve here." Every Russian Jew in England was urged to make up his mind and to be prepared "to guard Jewish honor, Jewish prestige and the future of Jewry. . . . If you are prepared to go to

Russia, go in peace. . . . If after calm reflection you come to see . . . that your choice is to remain here, then do your duty as becomes Jewish manhood." Simultaneously, a Yiddish pamphlet prepared by Beilin and Pinsky, who had previously collaborated in *Unsere Tribune,* was mailed in official envelopes, "On His Majesty's Service," to thirty-five thousand addresses of aliens who had so far not enlisted. As conscription regulations permitted a choice between serving in the British and the Russian armies, the pamphlet strongly advocated enlistment in the Legion rather than return to Russia, stressing that Russian military service was far from pleasant.

Jabotinsky amusedly relates the trouble the publication of this pamphlet caused him. One day he was summoned to the Adjutant General's office where he also found Colonel Patterson. The Adjutant General Sir Neville Macready, with a face "wearing an official expression," showed him an English translation of the pamphlet and declared: "I am told that the Russian Embassy is greatly annoyed. This pamphlet is filled with attacks on the Russian Army." Jabotinsky quietly explained that there were no such attacks in the Yiddish text and that the English translation must have been "worse than bad." Besides, he added, he had seen the Russian Ambassador the same day and the day before; they had discussed the Legion, but the Ambassador did not even mention the pamphlet. Jabotinsky suggested to Macready to ring up Mr. Nabokov and verify this statement. Instead, the Adjutant General angrily shouted: "Who gave you the right, Sergeant, to distribute the pamphlet in official envelopes?"

Jabotinsky only "looked at him blankly" (looking is not prohibited, he commented): Macready's own department had given him the addresses, which were an official secret, and supplied him with envelopes. . . . The Adjutant General possessed enough intelligence and sense of humor to realize the absurdity of the situation and burst out laughing. He dropped the charge but, apparently to save his face, said to Patterson: "Send Sergeant J. to your camp at Portsmouth. I hope that he'll show himself to be as good a soldier as he is a propagandist."

Jabotinsky saluted and went out. When, ten minutes later, Patterson appeared in the corridor, he asked: "Sir, when shall I leave for Portsmouth?" Patterson blandly refused to obey his superior's order: "In my battalion I am master, and I want you to stay in London to do the recruiting." Jabotinsky remained in London and, though Macready knew it, he took it in true "sporting" fashion: he made no protest whatsoever and remained a friend of the Legion. Jabotinsky also ascertained that the Russian Ambassador had never heard of the pamphlet and, of course, never protested against its contents. A formal note to this effect was written by the Embassy. Jabotinsky took it to Amery who forwarded it to the Adjutant General with a letter which, Jabotinsky said, "I did not read, but whose contents I could well imagine. . . ."

Besides printed propaganda, the recruiting campaign naturally took recourse to public meetings, too. But this time the meetings were orderly and quiet, even though no police squads were summoned: a group of burly, impressive-looking "muleteers," now in Platoon Sixteen, were present in the hall, and their very presence was sufficient to prevent any attempt at sabotage. The opponents of the Legion were free to deliver the most fiery speeches denouncing Zionism and militarism, but they knew that no rioting would be permitted. And they behaved.

There was, however, no dearth of opposition outside the meeting halls. The official announcement of the creation of the Jewish Regiment had in no way silenced the opponents of the Legion idea. When the British authorities, on July 27th, finally broke up the "Protection Committee," those who supported it transferred their allegiance to another association—the "Russian Committee for Matters of Military Service"—of which Dr. Jochelman was the leading spirit. The object of this Committee was to help Russian Jews, or their families, who might either have decided to go to Russia or who might have elected to serve in England. But the Committee pointedly and purposefully refused any cooperation in matters of enlistment in a special Jewish unit in the British Army. In fact, it was doing its very best to oppose such a course. Dr. Jochelman published a special statement to the effect that his Committee had "nothing whatever to do with the question of the formation of a Jewish Regiment." "But," he stressed, "all the members representing the various Jewish organizations have expressed their unanimous opposition to the formation of a Jewish Regiment, which has been forced upon them without previously consulting the representatives of the Jewish masses, and without regard to Jewish public opinion, which is definitely against the proposal as harmful to Jewish interests." The above decision "has been communicated to the competent [British] authorities."[19]

Even more active were "Mr. Chicherin's boys." Theirs was mostly an underhand whispering campaign among Whitechapel's youth; they were diligently spreading rumors that the Kerensky government already regretted having consented to the British-Russian convention and that the

"Soviet of Workers' Deputies" would soon force it to rescind its decision—
there was therefore no need to worry about any conscription. The boys
should just "sit it out" by refusing any service.

It is difficult to ascertain to what an extent this whispering propaganda was effective. There can, however, be hardly any doubt that the bulk
of the Jewish East End population, even after the official endorsement
of the Legion idea by the government, was strongly opposed to it. The
East End correspondent of the *Jewish Chronicle* (which consistently supported the Legion scheme and could not be suspected of bias) reported
on August 17, 1917: "As to the proposed formation of a Jewish regiment,
it can be said frankly that the mass of Jews will not hear of it. Organized
Jewish labor is opposed to it as violently as are Zionists. . . . They regard it
as a deep grievance that one or two individuals [meaning Jabotinsky and
probably Patterson] have influenced the authorities in that direction. . . .
What is most galling to the Jewish public opinion is the arbitrary manner in which the scheme has been foisted on them." Both Socialists and
Zionists were most outspoken in their hostility. At a conference of various
Jewish Trade Unions it was unanimously resolved that a Jewish Regiment
was undesirable. Several Zionist societies, one of which was composed
mainly of young men, passed a resolution disapproving of a Jewish Regiment; their contention was that if they had to fight, they would do so "as
Englishmen or Russians but not as Jews." On the whole, it appeared that
the overwhelming majority of those liable for conscription had made up
their minds "to serve as Russians" and to return to Russia. *The Jewish
Chronicle* reported that the number of prospective repatriates was above
twenty thousand.

Particularly bitter were the Zionists, whose "recognized and authoritative leaders" still insisted that the formation of a Jewish Regiment "must
prove detrimental to the interest of the Jews in other countries and particularly in Palestine itself." A resolution to this effect was voted by the "Zion"
Association on August 19th. A well-known Zionist veteran, Rabbi Dr.
Samuel Daiches, sent a letter to the editor of the *Jewish Chronicle,* in which
he expressed his protest "as a Jew and a Zionist": "A Jewish regiment is an
absurdity, and a Jewish regiment fighting in Palestine (in a quasi-national
capacity) would be a tragic absurdity."[20]

Even after he won the "battle for the Legion," Jabotinsky remained
for some time the best-hated man in Jewish London. Summarizing

Jabotinsky's experience in the struggle for the Legion, Dr. Weizmann wrote in *Trial and Error:* "It is almost impossible to describe the difficulties and disappointments which Jabotinsky had to face. I know of few people who could have stood up to them, but his pertinacity, which flowed from his devotion, was simply fabulous. He was discouraged and derided at every hand."[21]

For several months, while the Battalion was in training at Plymouth, Jabotinsky continued his recruiting activities at the Battalion's depot in London.* This job was not limited to England only. Innumerable letters were dispatched to the United States, Canada, Argentina, Russia, neutral countries, wherever young Jewish men were to be found. Jabotinsky's own opinion was that "in the main this correspondence bore no fruit whatever—cast your bread upon the waters. . . ." Though soldiers did come from the United States, Canada, and Argentina, he doubted whether this was the result of the work of his little office: "the Legion was making propaganda for itself; the role of its creators had ended." He was even doubtful as to the role he played in the creation of the "38th Royal Fusiliers." One night, on a visit to the Plymouth training camp, watching the low barracks which housed hundreds of young Jewish men, he "lost himself in thought":[22]

. . . The Jewish Legion . . . a dream. So long dreamed, so hardily achieved, and not mine, not built by me, not brought up by me. Just like the story of Aladdin's palace built by spirits. Who is Aladdin? What is Aladdin? Nothing. An accident provided him with a rusty, old lamp and when he wanted to clean it and began rubbing it with a rag, the genie suddenly appeared and built him a palace. The palace stands and will remain standing, but nobody any longer needs Aladdin or his lamp. I wondered. Perhaps we all are Aladdins. Each of our thoughts is a magic lamp which has the power to call up creative spirits. You must only never tire of rubbing. Rub, rub and rub again—until you become superfluous. Perhaps every true creation consists of the creator's becoming superfluous.

---

*Mrs. Vera Weizmann recalls that at that time Jabotinsky had an acute conflict with Major James de Rothschild. The quarrel became so violent that Rothschild shouted at Jabotinsky: "Don't forget, please, that I am your superior in rank and can remand you to a military court." To this Jabotinsky heatedly answered: "Of course, you can send me to a military court, but I beg you not to forget that here, in the Jewish Legion, not you but I am the general." Dr. Weizmann had to intervene in order to reconcile the disputants. (Communicated by I. Trivus.)

Whatever one thinks of the merits of this lofty theory, there can hardly
be any doubt that, at least so far as "rubbing" was concerned, Jabotinsky had
been hard at work for a long and very arduous time. When his "palace" was
finally built—not "suddenly" and not by an obliging "spirit"—and stood
firmly, everybody, of course, enjoyed it and eagerly bathed in its glory:
everybody, friend and foe alike.

In the winter of 1917–18, Jabotinsky was joined in London by his
wife and his seven-year-old son Eri. They left Russia before the Bolshevik
Revolution, but the trip under wartime conditions was long and dangerous.
They traveled via Finland, Sweden, and Norway. On the way, Mrs. Jabotinsky fell ill and had to interrupt her voyage at the Norwegian seaport of
Bergen, there to wait for another boat; later she learned that the boat which
she had left because of illness struck a mine and perished with all hands.[23]
In London, the family saw little of Jabotinsky, his son Eri recalls. They were
very friendly with the Weizmanns, and Mrs. Vera Weizmann devoted much
time to the boy: she introduced him to the English way of life, taught him
table manners; later he heard her saying jokingly that in this she succeeded
with him better than with her own sons.[24]

On the fourth of February, 1918, the Jewish Battalion, with shining
bayonets, marched through the City of London and Whitechapel. Now,
when Jabotinsky's dream became triumphant reality, both the assimilationist Lords and the masses of the East End, who had so bitterly opposed
and reviled him, were ecstatic in their joy and pride. At the entrance to the
Mansion House, next to the Lord Mayor who, dressed in his robes of
office, took the salute from the Jewish soldiers, stood Major Lionel
Rothschild —one of the Legion's bitterest opponents—"looking important
and proud, taking a delight in something he only narrowly failed to destroy."
From the City the Battalion marched to Whitechapel. There, the Adjutant
General, Sir Neville Macready, was awaiting them with his staff.[25]

Describing this "scene unparalleled in the history of any previous British battalion," Patterson added: "Jabotinsky must have rejoiced to see the
fruit of all his efforts"; the same day he had been gazetted to a Lieutenancy
in the Battalion. This rank he owed to Patterson who went to see the Adjutant General and requested him to have Jabotinsky promoted to Lieutenant
in the Corps.[26]

"Quite impossible," objected Macready. "He is a foreigner, a Russian,
and cannot possibly hold a commission in the British Army."

"But, Sir," remarked Patterson, "is not the Tsar of Russia a Colonel in the British Army?"

"He holds honorary rank only," argued the Adjutant General.

"In that case," Patterson replied, "honorary rank will also suffice for Jabotinsky."

The great lesson Jabotinsky learned from the three years of his struggle for the Legion idea, and which remained the foundation of all his further political work, was that "in a public matter, especially in a struggle for an idea, an initiated project develops essentially through failures. One way or another, every setback proves later to have been a step toward victory. Each defeat brings another host of followers, indeed, right from the ranks of the foes of yesterday. . . . After every failure it is necessary to examine yourself and ask: 'Look here, perhaps you are wrong?' If you are wrong, get off the rostrum and shut up. But if you are right, do not believe your eyes: that defeat is not a defeat. 'No' is no answer. Wait an hour and start right over again from the beginning."[27]

Three Controversial Matters

There has been for many years considerable controversy as to whether Jabotinsky's work for the Legion was organically related to the overall Zionist political activities which brought about the Balfour Declaration. As late as 1940, such an earnest and penetrating thinker and scholar as Rav Tzair categorically asserted in his New York Hebrew monthly *Bitzaron* that "Jabotinsky's Legion played no part in the granting of the Balfour Declaration."

Available evidence does not bear out this judgment. While doggedly concentrating his lonely efforts in the British political world on the Legion issue, Jabotinsky never overlooked its organic interdependence with the broader problem of securing England's open support for what at that time used to be called "Zionist aspirations." In all his negotiations with British government personalities and bodies he unswervingly insisted that there was no sense in, and no chance of success for, any attempt to create a Jewish Legion without a corresponding British commitment as regards Zionist aspirations. His insistence at times even threatened to jeopardize the immediate chances of the Legion scheme as such. Amery, Jabotinsky's faithful adviser in his dealings with members of the government whose mentality he knew intimately, had more than once warned him against such a policy. When, in January, 1917, he read the draft of a memorandum which Jabotinsky prepared for the War Cabinet, strongly stressing the connection between the specific Legion aspect and the general attitude toward Zionism, Amery cautiously observed that the way in which this matter was inserted "might a little bit alarm the Foreign Office as too definite in form." He advised to leave out this reference in its original context and to add "an extra sentence suggesting that the success of the recruiting campaign would be especially great if it were possible for the authorities, in sanctioning the Corps, to make use of such language as, without tying down the British Government to a particular form of political settlement for the future of Palestine, would be favorable to Zionist aspirations."[28] Again, on April 3rd, commenting on another memoir which Jabotinsky intended to submit, Amery wrote: "With regard to your letter, the only criticism I should be inclined to make is with reference to the passage on page 4 where you ask for a public promise of a Jewish Palestine. I understand that the question of the future of Palestine has not been settled, and for the British Government to make a public promise of a definite character would raise all sorts of international questions which might delay, if not altogether put off, your project; whereas nothing could do more to help on the views of those whom you represent than the actual fact that Jewish troops had been specifically engaged in the conquest of that country. It is like the question of Woman Suffrage here: by ceasing to bargain about the vote and showing their capacity for patriotic work in the war, they have removed the chief objection to their cause. So, in your place, I would simply say 'the Jewish Regiment fighting in Palestine' etc."

After the victorious outcome of his struggle for the Legion, but before the Balfour Declaration was published, Jabotinsky continued pestering the British authorities by reminders that the success of the Propaganda Bureau for recruitment was largely dependent on the government's general policy toward Zionism. In a letter dated October 30, 1917, *three days before the Balfour Declaration was given its final form and published*, Amery assured Jabotinsky that he had written to Colonel Buchan expressing sympathy with his suggestion: "The work of such a Propaganda Bureau would, of course, be enormously facilitated if the Government would come out with some declaration in favour of Zionism, and personally I hope that will not be long delayed."

After the Balfour Declaration was published, Jabotinsky wrote a heart-felt letter of recognition and gratitude to Sir Ronald Graham, head of the Near Eastern Department of the Foreign Office, whom he described as "an old friend of the Zionist cause who did most to assist Dr. Weizmann in obtaining the Balfour Declaration and me in my fight for the Legion." Graham's reply (November 7th) deserves to be quoted in full:

> Many thanks for your letter and what you say in it. I congratulate you heartily on this important step towards the realization of Jewish aspirations. The Jewish cause is now inseparably bound up with that of the Allies, and they must triumph or fall with them.
>
> I hope you will be given opportunities of further exercising the qualities of energy and capacity which you have already shown in the question of the Jewish Regiment and similar matters and which will make your cooperation extremely valuable.

Both Jabotinsky and Dr. Weizmann basically agreed on the role the Legion played in obtaining the Balfour Declaration. Jabotinsky estimated that "half the Balfour Declaration belongs to the Legion."[29] Dr. Weizmann, who admittedly was never too lavish in sharing glory with others, is reported in a letter by Achad Haam (dated September 4, 1917) to have said in the Zionist Political Committee in London, which conducted the negotiations with the British government: "I built on this foundation [the Legion]."[30]

It has been commonly accepted that Jabotinsky was "the Father of the Legion." However, at a press conference in July, 1933, and later (March, 1934) in a pamphlet *Chaluzischer Zionismus oder Revisionismus* David Ben Gurion made a determined attempt to challenge Jabotinsky's authorship in the Legion idea.[31] He did not question Jabotinsky's subjective honesty when the latter claimed that this idea was born in his mind in Bordeaux after learning that Turkey had entered the war; but this claim, Ben Gurion insisted, must be attributed to Jabotinsky's ignorance: Jabotinsky "did not know that the idea of the Legion preceded the World War and was created not in the Diaspora, but in Eretz Israel." To prove this contention, Ben Gurion quoted two precedents:

1. The *Hashomer* (Watchman) organization, created in 1908.

2. The project of a Jewish Legion submitted in November, 1914, by himself and Itzhak Ben Zvi to the Turkish Commander in Jerusalem, Sakki Bey.

The nature of these two precedents as compared with Jabotinsky's Legion concept deserves careful scrutiny.

The basic characteristics of Jabotinsky's concept were: a) So long as Turkey ruled Palestine, there were no prospects for the realization of Zionism; b) Once Turkey entered the war, she was bound to be defeated and dismembered; c) The Jews must become a partner in the liberation of Palestine from the Turks by forming a fighting force of their own; d) This would put Zionism on the international map as an independent political factor.

None of these basic elements was present either in the *Hashomer* or in the idea of a Jewish military unit in Turkish Palestine.

The *Hashomer* was a valiant and valuable clandestine group of Zionist patriots which was created with the limited aim of taking over from the Arab guards the function of protecting Jewish settlements from thieves and robbers. At that time, such a task was both important and dangerous, and the *Hashomer* certainly deserves, and can be sure of, a most honorable place in Zionist and Jewish history. But there is nothing in common between this local and illegal watchmen's organization, and an official military unit destined to become a factor of international significance.

On the surface, there is, of course, greater resemblance between Jabotinsky's idea and the project of a Legion as submitted to the Turkish authorities: both had in mind a Jewish military unit established with the consent of a belligerent power. But here the similarity ends. Jabotinsky's concept was based on the correct and sound premise that Turkey was an *obstacle* to Zionism; that she must and will be defeated and dismembered; and that the Jews must actively participate in achieving this result and fight on the side of the Allied Powers. Those who, in November, 1914, initiated the abortive plan of a Jewish Legion as a part of the Turkish Army did so for just the opposite—and wrong—reasons. Their reasoning has been formulated by D. Ben Gurion as follows: "It was clear to them that this war would determine the fate of countries and states and that Palestine would sooner or later become a battle-ground for the fighting armies of warring Powers; they decided to establish, with the consent of the Turkish Government, a Jewish Legion for the protection of the country . . . in case of an attack." The meaning of all this is unmistakable: the proposed Legion was supposed to fight on the Turkish side against the Allies; for an "attack" on Palestine could have come from the Allied Powers only. In Jabotinsky's concept, the Allied armies would come as liberators of Palestine from stifling Turkish domination. In Ben Gurion's concept, Palestine Jews had to consider them as aggressors, and a Jewish Legion would have had to defend the country from them together with Turkish troops. It amounted to clear-cut pro-Turkish and anti-Allied orientation, whose results would have been disastrous in more than one respect. It was most fortunate that the original approval by the Turkish military council in Jerusalem, on the basis of which the first volunteers had already begun their training, was canceled by Djemal Pasha, the Supreme Commander of the Turkish Army in Palestine and Syria. Instead of encouraging a Jewish Legion, he instigated severe persecution of Zionism and Zionists; many were imprisoned, others, among them Ben Zvi and Ben Gurion, were deported.

It can easily be seen that there was a fundamental difference between Jabotinsky's Legion idea that materialized, and the Ben Gurion-Ben Zvi idea which did not: the first was based on sound and correct appraisal of the international situation and of the position world Jewry had to take; the second was based on utterly wrong premises. Jabotinsky conceived the Legion as a factor of international significance; a Legion attached to the Turkish Army would remain—even if the Central Powers would have emerged victorious from the war—a purely local Palestinian affair; the Turkish government would have been completely free to reward, to punish, or simply to disregard the Zionist cause for the role this unit played in the war.

Jabotinsky fully realized that Turkey *delenda esse* if Zionism was to be realized. Barnet Litvinoff, Ben Gurion's biographer, on the contrary, testifies that "he [Ben Gurion] and Ben Zvi felt that Zionism, in the way they understood the term, could best be fostered by the complete identification of the Jewish workers with the new progressive forces in Constantinople"; they hoped that they would "one day sit in the Turkish Parliament as the representatives of the Jewish masses in Palestine"; they "remained blissfully unaware of the true character of the [Young Turk] régime . . . blind to all the signs, so clear to European observers, that the régime would not endure."[32]

It was not before the United States entered the war, in the spring of 1917, that Ben Gurion and Ben Zvi realized, as Barnet Litvinoff puts it, that "this was the time to make a special Jewish contribution to the Allied Campaign in the Near East" and "tardily came around to the view that Trumpeldor and Jabotinsky had been right." Reluctantly admitting Jabotinsky's leading role, Ben Gurion and Ben Zvi "sought to contact him, but when they failed, they undertook to work alone," relates Litvinoff.[33] In fact, their telegram reporting the launching of a recruiting campaign in America for the Legion reached Jabotinsky a few days before his departure from England with his Battalion. A message came also from Buenos Aires signed by Vladimir Herman: "English consent obtained." The Greek government had announced that volunteer recruiting would be permitted in Salonica, and a recruiting office had been opened in Egypt itself.[34] Directly or indirectly, Jabotinsky's idea started bearing fruit on a worldwide scale.

The 38th Royal Fusiliers was usually described as a unit formed of "conscripts" who had been pressed into service forcibly, against their will, while the two other battalions—the 39th and the 40th —were composed of volunteers only: Palestinians and Americans. This is only partly true. The Battalion, for the raising of which Jabotinsky was directly responsible, had both volunteers and conscripts. In England itself several hundred enlisted before they were called up. But, Jabotinsky stressed, no difference between the two categories ever made itself manifest. "Tailors"—as the Whitechapel recruits were called—"ultimately became an honorable description, a synonym for first-class soldiers."

The number of volunteers would have been considerably larger since the Adjutant General had granted permission to Jews serving in other units, even at the front, to apply for transfer to the Jewish Regiment (114/ Gen. No. 5767, A.G. 2a of October 10, 1917). Several thousand such applications were made, but only a few hundred men were actually transferred. Jabotinsky ascribed this discrepancy to the influence of the Army rabbis in France who, allegedly under instructions of the Chief Chaplain, the Reverend Michael Adler himself, had been preaching that it was shameful for a "true Britisher" to be banded with "a lot of dirty foreign Jews." A memorandum "re Jewish Legion" submitted by Dr. Weizmann implies that the military authorities were lax in implementing the transfers, fearing a delay in the military employment of the transferees. The fact is that the Jewish unit profited only slightly from this opportunity.

Colonel Patterson who, together with Jabotinsky, did the political spadework for the Legion, firmly believed that much greater results could have been achieved if the official Zionist leadership had not combated and sabotaged Jabotinsky's efforts. In the foreword to the English edition of *The Story of the Jewish Legion* (1945),Patterson wrote:

"Had it not been for the incredible stupidity of the 'Old Men of Zion' who strenuously opposed Jabotinsky's endeavors, I am certain that a Jewish Army of at least one hundred thousand men would have been formed. This was what a high-ranking general at the War Office told me when I was sent for to take command of the 'Jewish Regiment,' as the Legion was at first named.

"What a difference a Jewish Army in World War I would have made! . . . If only Jabotinsky's urgent pleadings had been listened to and a Jewish Army had been created to fight alongside the Allies in the first World War, great evils would surely have been averted and the world would have been quite a different place today. But his opponents, who could not shed their ghetto fears, were too strong for him. Instead of a great Jewish Army a mere Jewish Legion had to suffice, and even this the ghetto men sought to belittle."

WAR, PEACE, AND PRISON

FOURTEEN

WITH THE LEGION IN PALESTINE

Mixed Reception

The 38th Battalion landed at Alexandria on March 1, 1918. Jabotinsky was glad to meet old friends of the "Gabbari" days —the leaders of the Alexandria Sefardic community, who proudly claimed parentage of the unit: "The Zion Mule Corps was our son, the Jewish Legion is our grandson." To this grandson they gave a rousing welcome.

Another enthusiastic reception awaited the Battalion in Cairo. Their encampment was at Helmieh, a village a few miles outside of Cairo, where the Battalion had to complete its training for the front. Drill, bayonet-fighting, grenade-throwing, marching, musketry, and signaling went on from morning until night. It was a full-time job for every officer, but Jabotinsky, in addition to his regular duties as platoon commander, was given one more assignment: to censor letters written by the men in languages other than English. He owed this assignment to the fact that among the officers he was the only one who could read, in addition to other languages, both Hebrew and Yiddish. His duty was to prevent any information of a military nature leaking through the soldiers' private correspondence. He never found anything in the letters that needed censoring, although, he added with a fine sense of humor, in several he "found strong condemnation of the censor himself"; to avoid learning who it was that penned these condemnations, Jabotinsky carefully replaced the letters in the envelopes without looking at the sender's name.[1]

Both Jabotinsky and Patterson considered the 38th Battalion, as well as the 39th and 40th which were being formed in England and in the United States, as the nucleus of a larger Jewish military unit. They were also aware of a strong volunteer movement among the Jewish youth of Palestine and were eager to further it. On March 5th, four days after their landing in Egypt, Patterson addressed a letter to General Allenby, the British Commander-in-Chief, in which he volunteered to commence recruitment in Palestine and to send a recruiting party to make a trip around the Jewish colonies. There was considerable opposition to this suggestion. Allenby's Chief of Staff, Major General Louis Jean Bols, informed Patterson that Allenby was not in favor of building up a larger Jewish military force. Nevertheless, Patterson was invited to come to Allenby's H.Q. situated near the colony of Beer-Jacob;[2] Jabotinsky accompanied him.

He arrived in Tel Aviv on the eve of Passover and found both Tel Aviv and Jaffa "in a state of unbounded enthusiasm." He had to tone down his friends' overenthusiastic estimates of the strength of the Legion and to tell them that so far it consisted of but one battalion. However, this did not weaken their joy at seeing the man whom they had for years considered as the incarnation of the Legion idea. One of the initiators and leaders of the volunteer movement, Eliahu Golomb, later vividly described the excitement that reigned in those days. "The anticipation [of Jabotinsky's arrival] was almost hysterical. We have been waiting for the man, with whose name was connected our greatest dream—the Jewish Army. We expected him to come and fulfil our vision." A petition to the British government to permit the enlistment of volunteers had already been submitted in January, 1918, but no reply had been forthcoming. Its initiators firmly believed that Jabotinsky would be able to "remove the barrier preventing the establishment of friendly relations between us and British authorities." They also expected him to bring about a favorable change in the attitude of the *Yishuv* to volunteering. "The hopes of many of us were concentrated on the person of Jabotinsky. By his political work for the Legion in [English] government circles he did a not unimportant job. His speeches on the political importance of the Legion were helpful in reconciling the leaders of the *Yishuv* with the volunteer movement, and in general in eliminating many doubts."[3]

The leaders of the *Yishuv* were, indeed, far from being reconciled with the Legion idea in all its implications. Their attitude can be judged by several entries in the diaries of one of them, Mordechai Ben Hillel Hacohen,* which were published in five volumes under the title *Milchemeth ha'Amim* (War of Nations). When consulted on organization of a volunteer movement in Palestine, they were of the opinion that "it was too early to decide." Their arguments were basically the same Jabotinsky had had to face two or three years before in London. They were afraid to jeopardize the fate of Jews living in the Samaria and Galilee areas which were still under Turkish domination. They contended that Palestine Jewry who "had been loyal to the Turks throughout the war, certainly cannot and must not form military units amongst its Ottoman youth." Last but not least, they still had "no exact news about the Battalions that are being formed in London . . . on the contrary, we know that many of the national leaders do not approve of these actions, and the Zionist Organization has decided in a way that does not agree with Jabotinsky."[4] They insisted that the initiators of the volunteer movement wait for the impending arrival of the Zionist Commission headed by Dr. Weizmann.** When they met with Jabotinsky in Jerusalem, reports Hacohen on March 27th, "we gathered as friends and chatted away about every possible subject," while carefully avoiding mentioning *the* subject—the question of the formation of a Jewish unit in Palestine. It was Jabotinsky who forced the issue by asking point-blank: "Well, gentlemen, am I going to have to fight you or not?" The reaction was an evasive one, reports Hacohen. "During the discussion, we tried not to upset him, we talked carefully, but he understood our feelings about his military ideas and about his prophecies."[5]

There was nothing personal in this hostility. On the contrary, Hacohen seems to be quite sincere in saying that the hearts of those who opposed Jabotinsky so steadfastly "pained for this precious son, this outstanding personality, this talent without equal, who sacrificed himself for a lost cause on the altar of an idea that is foreign to his people." But they refused to

---

*Mordechai Ben Hillel Hacohen, a prolific Hebrew writer, was one of the founders of the Jewish cooperative movement and President of the Jewish "High Court of Peace" in Palestine.

**Early in 1918, the Zionist Organization was permitted to send a Commission to Palestine in order to assist in the rehabilitation of the *Yishuv*, to act as an advisory body to the British authorities in Palestine in all matters relating to Jews or which might affect the establishment of the National Home for the Jewish people. The Commission left England on March 3, 1918, and arrived in Palestine on April 4th.

understand and to accept his "militaristic ideas."[6] Unwilling—or unable—to fight him openly, they offered an evasive passive resistance of silent disapproval and non-cooperation.

But this resistance could not withstand Jabotinsky's assault. "After Jabotinsky's arrival," recalls Eliahu Golomb, "the arguments for neutrality weakened; it became clear that there was a strong political link between the Allies and Zionism. . . . Some speeches of Jabotinsky strongly impressed the public. Enthusiasm and spiritual exaltation reigned in our midst, while those who had opposed volunteering lowered their heads."[7] Aggressive opposition actually ended. The only hope of those who were still inimical was that by delaying tactics it would be possible to prevent a large-scale volunteer movement along the lines demanded by Jabotinsky, until the arrival of Dr. Weizmann, whom they confidently expected authoritatively to oppose this "militaristic scheme." When the Zionist Commission did arrive, Hacohen was amazed to find out on June 14th that "in Jewish military affairs Jabotinsky has succeeded in gaining influence over Dr. Weizmann, and Major James Rothschild embraced the idea and gave himself over to it heart and soul, with all his power." Having thus received an official stamp, the Legion idea, which only a short time before was labeled as "foreign" to the Jewish people's soul, had now become wonderful and holy. Noting that "youngsters are registering for the Battalion with enthusiasm," Hacohen says: "It is the rebirth of the Maccabean spirit through their descendants."

The Recruitment Campaign

The belief of the initiators of the volunteer movement that with the arrival of Patterson and Jabotinsky official recruitment would soon be permitted, proved to be well founded. On May 5, 1918, Jabotinsky wrote to his wife from Cairo that the British military authorities had finally given in, though he feared that it would take "a hundred years" before everything was settled, and wondered whether "our Palestinian lads will not burst from outrage and impatience." However, things fortunately moved more quickly than he expected, and soon Patterson was able to send out a specially trained recruiting party under the command of Lieutenant Lipsey. Jabotinsky, though a member of the squad, had little opportunity for participating in this campaign, since as early as mid-June his Battalion was already at the front, in the Mountains of Ephraim between Jerusalem and Shechem.

Quite unnecessarily, he belittled his actual share and importance in the success of the recruiting drive. Only in passing did he mention that for three days he was in Jerusalem "delivering addresses, which were quite superfluous."[8] The testimony of one of his listeners at that time refutes his overly modest self-appraisal. J. L. Neiman recalls in his memoirs that at a huge recruiting meeting he attended in Jerusalem several speakers harangued the crowd: "But here is a name strange to Jerusalem—Jabotinsky . . . and after his first few words a hush goes through the audience. The public is charmed by his bright Hebrew, by his expressive elocution, by his fiery words. The meaning of the 'terrible [Legion] idea' is becoming ever clearer; with clearness comes understanding; understanding provokes feeling, and feeling breeds enthusiasm. The meeting ends with stormy applause, and the best sons of Jerusalem, including old men, proudly leave with 'Jewish Legion' badges. That's how Jerusalem first met Jabotinsky."[9]

Similarly, at a recruiting meeting in Jaffa, Jabotinsky could see that the mainstay of the recruiting party were his old friends who had endured with him the black and bitter years of loneliness and disillusionment: "Sasha" Arshavsky, Harry First, Nissel Rosenberg.[10] It was Jabotinsky's spirit that animated the recruiting squad.

However, Hacohen's contention that in regard to raising a Jewish military force in Palestine Jabotinsky succeeded in "gaining influence over Dr. Weizmann" must be taken with a grain of salt. The attitude of the Allenby Headquarters toward the volunteer movement was anything but friendly. When the Zionist Commission headed by Dr. Weizmann arrived in Palestine, friends from G.H.Q. tendered them the "careful" advice to "steer clear" of the volunteers, and at the beginning the members of the Commission showed themselves rather accessible to these counsels. When a mass meeting of all the volunteers was called at Rehovoth, to which nearly a thousand men came, the Volunteers' Committee invited all the members of the Zionist Commission; but none of them came. Jabotinsky was the only Zionist leader who participated.[11] Eliahu Golomb also testifies that "at the beginning the Zionist Commission avoided to manifest a positive attitude toward volunteering. They were strongly influenced by the arguments of the opponents . . . they assisted us and at the same time frustrated us . . . ."[12]

Dr. Weizmann's original reaction to the great success of the recruiting action was peculiar. Eliahu Golomb relates that "in the Legion circles Weizmann allowed himself to express regret that the best and most experienced forces [of the *Yishuv*] went to the Legion"; "Weizmann," says Golomb, "did not see in the Legion the most important deed of our time as we the volunteers and Jabotinsky saw it."[13] Only later, when the volunteers had to leave for military training, did Dr. Weizmann find it possible to attend a grand parade, to present them with a Jewish flag, and to make a moving speech, wishing them success and victory. At that time Jabotinsky was much closer to the heart and soul of the Jewish workers in Palestine than Weizmann. "The Eretz Israel youth adores and deifies the man who has launched the call to his brethren to rise and fight for people and country," wrote Hacohen.

Stating that the volunteers of the Battalion raised in Palestine "adored and deified" Jabotinsky, Hacohen asserts that to the men of Jabotinsky's own Battalion, who joined the unit partly under compulsion and partly because Jabotinsky's speeches "kindled a momentary fire in their hearts," Jabotinsky was a "subject of curses: if something in their present life seems objectionable, they curse him and wish him to be as badly off as they are themselves."

It seems that Hacohen exaggerated in both parts of his statement. There was no dearth of misunderstandings and bad feelings between the Palestinian volunteers and Jabotinsky, whereas the relationship between him and his London "tailors" was far from being as bad as Hacohen described it. L. Sherman, a soldier in the 38th Royal Fusiliers, admits that some of his comrades, in particular those who were conscripts and not volunteers, "were the eternal grumblers and particularly ill-disposed toward Jabotinsky for the creation of the Jewish Legion." He also admits that he himself and his comrades expected Jabotinsky not to be too strict in matters of military discipline and such "prosaic" army requirements as daily shaves, polishing buttons, and shoeshining. They were, however, "sadly disappointed." Jabotinsky, himself a model officer, required of them the strictest compliance with all rules and regulations. "It is to be inferred," cautiously observes Sherman, "that he was not very much pleased with us."[14]

But he was. He devoted to them several fond pages of his *Story of the Jewish Legion* in which he proudly stressed that the name "tailors," at first almost a curse-word, "gradually became an honorable name . . . they demonstrated that they were among the best soldiers in the British Army." They would indulge in "just a little grumbling." But grumbling, in Jabotinsky's concept, was the soldier's only privilege, and even Napoleon called his best men "the old grumblers."[15]

He had nothing but praise for his "tailors." And they themselves gradually made peace with this strange man, who was responsible for their being away from their families and in this strange land of Palestine. The same Sherman relates that they were deeply impressed by Jabotinsky's lecture on Bialik, of whom they had never heard before. The lecture "proved to be a most excellent and inspiring" one. The tailors' judgment was: "Jabotinsky may be such and such . . . but after all he is a wonderful speaker." Another legionnaire, Elias Ginsburg, reports that off active duty Jabotinsky usually "kept aloof and seldom mingled with the 'boys.' In adversity, however, he was a warm and truly devoted friend. When boys in his or any other battalion were in real trouble and needed a defender, Jabotinsky was there to take up the cudgels even when they deserved punishment. Thus long before demobilization he became the favorite of his unit."[16] After his forcible demobilization, his fellow officers and men presented him with an illuminated address, in which they expressed their "deepest esteem" for his services. They particularly stressed that he had "given an example of the true spirit of idealism by personally sharing in all the vicissitudes and dangers through which our Battalion has passed. . . . Your presence in the Hills of Judea and in the Jordan Valley was the expression of the true Maccabean spirit. . . . We pray to God that you may see the fulfilment of your hopes, which are the hopes and aspirations of the Jewish people. You carry with you in your retirement the gratitude and affection of your brother officers, N.C.O.'s and men of the 38th Battalion Royal Fusiliers (First Jewish Battalion)."

War Record

It is not easy to recapitulate Jabotinsky's personal war record. In *The Story of the Jewish Legion* he was not only highly reticent on all matters concerning the role he played in the actual war operations, but he consistently tried to belittle and disparage it. One has to dig diligently into his skillful understatements in order to establish the proper perspective.

Colonel Patterson stressed that, in fact, Jabotinsky was under no obligation to participate personally in actual combat. His linguistic abilities brought him an appointment as liaison officer in General Allenby's Headquarters staff at Sarafend. "However, the moment the Jewish Legion was ordered into the front line trenches, Jabotinsky resigned from his safe staff billet and took his place with his Jewish comrades in the firing line."[17] Speaking in February, 1937, in London at a dinner to commemorate the twentieth anniversary of the formation of the Jewish Legion, Patterson emphasized the fact that Jabotinsky "not only formed the Legion, but served in its ranks. . . . He was an inspiration to all ranks, and as an officer I could say that his courage, his loyalty and his devotion to duty were beyond all praise."

The lull in active military operations that followed the great British offensive of the preceding winter ended in the beginning of June, 1918. Jabotinsky's Battalion, which left Egypt on June 5th upon completing its training, was immediately ordered to the frontline at Shechem in the hills of Samaria, and on June 15th had its baptism of fire. They remained in this area until the middle of August.

Jabotinsky described this period as "comparatively quiet" and the military activities they were conducting as "small warfare." Patterson, whose judgment in military affairs can be trusted, gives a somewhat different picture. He stresses that the Battalion's front wire "was actually a few hundred yards down over the crest of the hill on the Turkish side. . . . We at once assumed a vigorous offensive policy; our patrols were pushed out every night down into the valley. . . . Our aggressive policy thoroughly scared the Turks, so much so that they never once attempted to come anywhere near our front."[18]

Jabotinsky himself admitted that there were "two dangers to face during these months": night patrol duty and the seven days' watch at Abouein.

The story of the night patrols was told in Jabotinsky's usual impersonal way: "Eight to twelve men would go out under a lieutenant" —deliberately omitting to mention that he himself was a lieutenant and had to lead some of these night parties. The pronoun he employed most is "they," and only occasionally the word "we" slipped into the narration. But even in Jabotinsky's own studiously "light" and often ironical description of these "excursions" one can easily detect that they were anything but a picnic. They included a climb to the enemy's hill, sometimes to within two hundred feet of his observation post, and then back again down the hill for a two hours' climb—both very often under enemy fire. "It would be a most beautiful sight. . . you would feel really flattered—if you could set your mind on it," Jabotinsky commented dryly.

Another danger spot was Abouein. Though it was actually in No-Man's Land, it had been included in the line of Jabotinsky's Battalion, and each week a new platoon was being sent there to occupy it for seven days. Jabotinsky and his platoon were repeatedly assigned to this duty, and even in his restrained narrative it emerges as a difficult and highly dangerous task. In a letter to his wife he described in a light vein the seven days of Abouein "as a delightful week," adding that "it seems that both the military authorities and the soldiers were satisfied with me." He sent his wife a diary he had been keeping in this deserted village where he occupied an empty harem, and a caricature of himself for the benefit of his son Eri.[19]

In the middle of August, 1918, the Jewish battalions were sent to the Jordan Valley—one of the deepest spots in the world—which in summer is a purgatory. Patterson writes in his book that no white battalions (except for cavalry) were ever made to remain there for more than a couple of weeks: the Jewish Legion stayed there for five weeks.[20] Jabotinsky's Battalion had the sad privilege of being stationed at Mellahah—the most desolate and malaria-stricken spot in the entire Jordan Valley. The Battalion paid dearly for this privilege. When it arrived in the valley, it consisted of eight hundred men; when the great offensive started five weeks later, there remained but five hundred and fifty; when they returned to Ludd, no more than a hundred and fifty remained, and of thirty officers there were only fifteen left. Over twenty men were killed, wounded, or captured. The rest were down with malaria; more than thirty of them died.

On September 19th, Jabotinsky's Battalion, together with two companies of the Battalion headed by Colonel Margolin, was assigned the task of capturing both sides of the ford across the Jordan known to the Arabs as Umm Es Shert, and thereafter advancing far beyond the Jordan. The first attempt to gain the ford failed. Then Jabotinsky's company "was ordered to make the second attempt . . . and achieve the purpose at all costs." Lieutenant Barnes was in charge while Jabotinsky was second-in-command, but the main operation was entrusted to him. The operation was completely successful. Allenby reported that "on the night of 23rd September the Jewish battalion captured the Jordan ford at Umm Es Shert."[21] Jabotinsky's personal conduct was described by Colonel Patterson as follows: "Never shall I forget the keenness with which he led the machine gun section when we made our attack on the Umm Es Shert ford over the Jordan. He was the first man to reach the historic river and thereupon immediately placed his guns in a strong position to resist any counter-attack by the Turks."[22] Jabotinsky himself, however, spoke of his record during the Jordan operations in rather ironical terms. In a letter to his wife he highly praised the conduct of the men of his company, and added casually: "My main exploit was that on the way to Es Salt I requisitioned a horse from a Bedouin."²³

Jabotinsky's Battalion was one of the first to enter Trans-Jordan. "This march into Transjordan was the most difficult I have ever experienced," he later recollected. Man after man would fall out and throw himself down, with mouth wide open, unable to drag himself farther.²⁴ When Jabotinsky returned to Jerusalem, he was completely exhausted. The first two weeks he was in bed and asleep most of the time, Miss Bella Berlin told this writer.

Before leaving for the Jordan front, Jabotinsky wrote, on a simple sheet of paper, a farewell to his wife—the last will of a man going into battle from which he may never return. It is too deeply intimate a human document to be made public. Sh. Ben Baruch (Sh. Schwarz), who has seen it, briefly reports that it touched upon two subjects only: the first was a moving expression of his feelings toward his life companion, saying in prose what he eventually put in so masterful a poetic form in his exquisite "Madrigal"; the second dealt with the education of their son Eri—without giving any instructions as to this topic, he only asked his wife to see to it that Eri should know Hebrew.²⁵

Jabotinsky went through these months of actual warfare unscathed. In a letter to his mother and sister, dated December 13, 1918, he wrote: "I, too, have been in the field, commanded first a platoon and then was second-in-command of a company, and was neither killed nor wounded."²⁶ But he did not escape injury. While on night patrol on the Nablus-Jerusalem front, he knocked a knee against a stone wall or a wire fence; it started bleeding, but he paid no attention to this slight injury, and the knee seemed to have healed. On July 24th he attended the ceremony of the laying of the foundation stone of the Hebrew University on Mount Scopus and for this solemn occasion he put on tight-fitting riding breeches. His knee started bleeding again, his temperature rose to 102°, an abscess formed, and a minor operation had to be performed. "I did not squeak and was only biting my lips, like a hero," he jokingly wrote to his wife. "Jerusalem was full of rumors about blood infection, somebody was inquiring whether the bullet had already been extracted, somebody probably wrote to Egypt that I was wounded—in short, if you in London hear that I was killed, I beg you not to believe it. . . ."²⁷ There was certainly nothing serious in this little mishap, but Miss Bella Berlin, who was nursing

Jabotinsky on this occasion, recalls that it was quite a painful and unpleasant incident; Dr. Jacques Segal, who treated him, feared complications; for some time Jabotinsky walked with a limp.[28]

Struggling for the Legion's Survival

In the early autumn of 1918, the entire territory of Palestine was liberated from the Turks. The Armistice with Turkey was officially signed on October 31st. The battered remnant of Jabotinsky's 38th Battalion under Colonel Patterson took over the "Line of Communication" duties. Colonel Margolin's Battalion (mostly American volunteers) soon joined them. The 40th Battalion, consisting predominantly of Palestine volunteers, which was deliberately kept—allegedly for further training—in Egypt, also forced its way to Palestine early in December. By the beginning of 1919, the three battalions numbered over five thousand men, about one-sixth of the entire British Army of Occupation. Jabotinsky, who had always considered that the main purpose of the Legion was not so much its immediate participation in the war as its remaining as the garrison of Palestine after the war, had every reason to be satisfied with this state of affairs. He saw that the very presence of these Jewish units was sufficient to preserve peace and order in the country. The Arabs of Palestine were exposed to violent anti-British and anti-Jewish propaganda, but not the slightest disturbance occurred.

There were also ambitious plans for expanding the Legion. On August 11, 1918, Jabotinsky optimistically wrote to his wife that "Allenby definitely decided to form a Jewish Brigade and make Patterson a General. We expect it any day. . . . I still believe that we will have a Division as well—if . . . the Turks will not collapse before that, something I wholeheartedly hope for." The Turks did collapse about six weeks later. But the plans to build up the strength of the Jewish battalions were not discontinued, and they were all connected with Jabotinsky. Late in October, 1918, he wrote to Mrs. Jabotinsky that Dr. Weizmann wanted him to go to America and to Salonica. He decided to decline both offers. A third offer was to go to Russia: this one he did not decline, though he was reluctant to undertake such a mission. But, he added, in the present circumstances "any recruitment for the Jewish Legion, be it in Salonica, Russia or elsewhere, must apparently be thrown into the ashcan."[29] Nevertheless, as late as September, 1919, he wrote to Dr. M. L. Streicher in Tiflis, welcoming the idea of enlisting Caucasian Jews in the Legion and promising that everything possible would be done in order to obtain the consent of the British authorities.[30]

Six months later, plans for the expanding of the Jewish Regiment by recruiting in Palestine or by enrolling young men from abroad were again presented at a meeting of the Zionist Commission on March 25, 1920. On this occasion Dr. Weizmann said: "The only capable man for this task is Jabotinsky. He knows the ropes and has a name. He ought to go to London for this purpose." Dr. Eder concurred: "The press in London must be influenced. Jabotinsky is the only man who can work in the matter of the Jewish Regiment." Even M. M. Ussishkin, who had been hostile to Jabotinsky throughout, agreed that the latter "must go to London." It was decided that Jabotinsky was to leave for London together with Dr. Weizmann.[31] Yet this decision was not carried out: a scant two weeks later, dramatic events intervened.

The status of the existing Jewish battalions started deteriorating much earlier.

The anti-Zionist British military authorities were eager to demobilize Jewish soldiers at the earliest convenience. Dr. M. D. Eder, Acting Chairman of the Zionist Commission, reported on December 31, 1918, seven weeks after the general Armistice, that "demobilization had already begun to a smaller extent."[32] Greatly perturbed, Jabotinsky proposed at the meeting of the Commission, held on January 6, 1919, that a cable be sent to London asking that "the organization there use its best endeavors to prevent anything being done that would accelerate the demobilization of the Jewish Regiment, which should be kept in existence as long as possible." The majority decided to postpone consideration of the cable.[33]

In the meantime a new and important problem had arisen. Among the American legionnaires, many expressed the desire to be discharged in Palestine with a view to settling there permanently. In a cable to N. Sokolov, dated January 15, 1919, Jabotinsky insisted that "such discharge should not take place until the Zionist Commission will be able to give them land and work." The same applied to the demobilization of the Palestinian volunteers. First on the demobilization list were students and farmers. This would entirely disband the Palestinian Battalion "at a time when students cannot proceed to European Universities and farm workers cannot find work." The only alternative to immediate discharge was, however, re-enlistment for two

years, something Jabotinsky considered "also undesirable from the stand-
point of colonization." He therefore asked Sokolov to obtain facilities for
individual Jewish soldiers to apply through regimental channels for exten-
sion of service in Jewish battalions until peace was signed, and added: "We
understand that a considerable number [of legionnaires] intend to present
such applications. Consider the matter urgent, as otherwise a great increase
of the number of unemployed is to be feared."

Apparently no such energetic action as was demanded by Jabotinsky
was taken in London; nor was the Zionist Commission very active in dealing with the problems of the legionnaires. At the meeting of the Commission on January 6, 1919, it was reported that men of the Jewish Regiment
complained that the Commission "did not seem sufficiently interested in
them and that it was delaying in taking any action in their favor."[34]

It was probably at least partly due to this inaction that the mood of
the legionnaires began changing. The war was over. Their willingness to
settle in Palestine and to help build the country was not immediately and
constructively utilized; "many of them decided that there was no purpose in
just wearing khaki, and began to demand demobilization."[35]

Jabotinsky was alarmed by this tendency. It seemed clear to him that
the post-Armistice period was the most important in the Legion's service, and he was dead set against the clamor for speedy demobilization.
At a series of informal discussions held by the Executive Committee of
the Zionist Commission with the representatives of the Palestine Jewish
community in February and March, 1919, Jabotinsky reported that of the
4,500 men in the three battalions, about 3,000 (mostly Palestinians and
Americans) were willing to be discharged in Palestine. In a circular he
issued in February and distributed unofficially, Jabotinsky insisted that
those who had chosen to be demobilized locally were advised that "it is
in their own interest to remain in the Army until the status of Palestine is
definitely decided upon and the Zionist Organization is able to begin the
work of systematic colonization. . . . Every Jewish volunteer must realize
that the mission of the Jewish battalions in Palestine is much more important now than it ever was before."[36]

Unrest among the soldiers was greatly intensified by the independent
action taken by the Commander of the 40th Battalion, Lieutenant Colonel Fred Samuel, who started discharging or granting indefinite leave to
any legionnaire who could produce an employment certificate. Jabotinsky

reported to the Zionist Commission that this practice had resulted in great demoralization. "Soldiers were coming in dozens [to the Zionist Commission] begging for [employment] slips," which "were given loosely." Non-Palestinian soldiers saw in this an unfair privilege for the local volunteers. On the other hand, there was unrest among the Palestinians themselves: "because when certain individuals get leave and others do not, men will grumble about favoritism."

Jabotinsky therefore insisted that the Colonels be advised by the Commission not to issue any more indefinite leaves to individuals and to withdraw those already issued. He was glad to be able to report that appeals made to those who were so discharged, were not made in vain: many soldiers who had handed in their slips had withdrawn them, stating that they wished to remain in the Battalions. Jabotinsky was confident that Palestinians "would overcome this temporary illness." However, he was not dogmatic in regard to individual discharges and dealt with each specific case on its merits. He agreed, for example, that Itzhak Ben Zvi and David Ben Gurion, who were "very useful," should remain with their Battalion; at the same time he advised that Shmuel Yavnieli and Berl Katznelson "had better be discharged: they were of no use whatever as soldiers, and there was much need for them as very valuable and important leaders of the new workers' party [*Akhdut ha'Avodah*] here." Recalling specifically that Yavnieli (in 1909) had brought to Palestine hundreds of Yemenite Jews, Jabotinsky insisted that though both Yavnieli and Katznelson "did not wish to leave, it would be well if these two men could be discharged." As a rule, however, Jabotinsky suggested that submitting application for leave be discouraged completely.

Continuing his efforts to convince the Jewish soldiers that their clamor for immediate demobilization was both unfounded legally and unfair morally, Jabotinsky wrote under the pen name "Altalena" in *Haaretz* of July 16, 1919, that legally the legionnaires had volunteered to serve in the British Army until "the cessation of hostilities," and that the interpretation of this phrase was to the effect that it was equivalent to the "end of the war." In other words, the legionnaires were obligated to serve until the actual signing of peace with Turkey. Even more cogent, insisted Jabotinsky, were moral considerations:

I am not going to touch upon the duty of the legionaries to the Jewish people or to Palestine. I speak about a fundamental ethical principle. The majority of our legionaries enlisted in 1918. It was not their fault, because they were only then permitted to join the Jewish Legion. . . . At any rate, it is a fact that they enlisted last year, whereas there are in the country thousands of English soldiers who took part in the desert campaign and have not seen their families in England for two or three years. There are even some who belong to the year 1915, and there are hundreds of them if not thousands. They are all anxious to go home, but they are obliged to wait because the army is still needed and there is a shortage of ships. The Jewish legionaries have been here for only a year or less, and for the most part they had no share in the sacrifices which the British soldiers made for the liberation of Palestine. If these British soldiers should see that the Jewish legionaries demand from the government to give them, the newcomers, a thousand or two thousand berths on the ships and thus keep out an equal number of soldiers who fought at Gaza and took part in the capture of Jerusalem, they will consider the Jewish demand as unjust and deprived of feeling for the brotherhood of men.

At a big meeting of the representatives of the American and Palestinian volunteers, together with workers' spokesmen, held at Petach Tiqvah in the summer of 1919, Jabotinsky endeavored to make the legionnaires "listen to the voice of their people and land." He warned them gravely that the most important period of the Legion's existence was just beginning: a gigantic campaign of pogrom propaganda was being carried on. Its instigators firmly believed that neither the British nor the Indian troops would lift a finger to protect the *Yishuv*. The only force they were afraid of was the Jewish Legion. In these circumstances, how did anybody dare speak of demobilization?

This warning availed little. Not that the majority of the delegates to the Petach Tiqvah conference did not recognize, at least theoretically, the necessity of preserving the Legion. But they bitterly resented Jabotinsky's statement that "those who now abandon the Legion are traitors to their people," relates Eliahu Golomb. Nor were they pleased with Jabotinsky's blunt statement that while the Zionist Commission was not trying to prevent any legionnaire from leaving his Battalion, he—if he had the power to do so—would have done his utmost not to let them go; "but I have no such power, and I say to all those who want to leave [the Legion]—*skatertyu doroga* [a contemptuous Russian expression meaning both 'nobody is keeping you' and 'good riddance']."[37]

All this was highly unpopular with the delegates. They were antagonized rather than impressed by Jabotinsky's exhortations. Jabotinsky

himself did not blame the legionnaires alone for this attitude: "Had they
been convinced, as I was, that there was danger lurking, they would
themselves have demanded to be retained. . . . But there were people in
the *Yishuv* who 'reassured' them. They were told that the man who had
been warning them of danger was himself a newcomer to the country and
knew nothing of the true situation; they, the 'reassurers,' however, were
local inhabitants; they knew the Arab and were emphatically positive that
he would never start a pogrom—this was ten months before the pogrom
in Jerusalem! For the Americans, however, this was naturally a powerful
argument. Who talks of the danger? An 'outlander'! Who says 'We need
no forces'? The men on the spot. Consequently. . . . Within a short while
after the meeting at Petach Tiqvah, only two of the three battalions remained, then only one—the Palestine volunteers—and then only a part of
that." In the spring of 1919 there were 5,000 men in the Legion; one year
later, only 300 to 400 remained.[38]

Advocate of the "Mutineers"

The anti-Zionist attitude of the British military authorities found
the Jewish soldiers a convenient and defenseless victim. Discrimination
against, and unfair treatment of, the legionnaires was becoming increasingly widespread and vicious. The volunteers, in particular the Americans
and Canadians, who had come to Palestine with high expectations, were
deeply affected by this attitude. They started clamoring for speedy demobilization and repatriation.

We have seen that Jabotinsky determinedly opposed and combated
this cry for demobilization. But he could not help admitting that the soldiers had ample grounds for dissatisfaction. They lived for months in an
atmosphere of insults and provocation. The majority bore this burden with
patience and dignity: but in two cases it led to a clear breach of discipline by
outraged groups of American volunteers. In the first case, fifty-five Cana-
dian and U.S. volunteers of the 38th Battalion, and in the second, forty-four
of the 39th, refused to do their military duty. They were accused of mutiny
and remanded for trial by Court Martial.

According to King's Regulations, a soldier remanded for trial by
Court Martial had the right to request the help of an officer to act as
his "friend" at the trial. The accused American volunteers petitioned

Jabotinsky to act as their advocate. He had a lawyer's diploma, but had never appeared in a court of law; yet not this was the reason which made him not at all anxious to defend the men. He felt that they should have carried out their duties faithfully to the end, even though they had well-founded grievances against authority. As Jabotinsky himself put it: "When one is on guard at a time of danger—which was our task in Palestine—one dare not be trapped by provocation." Still, he agreed to undertake this unwanted and onerous task. In a letter written two days after the mutiny of the fifty-five he insisted that their rebellion was brought about by "the same general causes that had destroyed the original enthusiasm of the Jewish volunteers and deprived their work and their sacrifices of any idealistic content." He, Jabotinsky, had always endeavored to pacify the soldiers and had demanded from them unconditional discipline, but now "the water reached the mouth [a traditional Hebrew expression meaning that human patience and capacity for suffering were exhausted], and I cannot accuse these soldiers."[39]

The trial of the fifty-five took place at Kantara on July 29–30, 1919. According to Colonel Patterson, Jabotinsky "pointed out a fatal flaw in the charge sheets, with the result that the charge of mutiny failed and the Court had to be dissolved." The original charge sheets were withdrawn and a new court convened. This time the men were arraigned on the lesser charge of disobeying an order. Even on this lesser charge they were savagely sentenced to various terms of penal servitude ranging from seven years downward.[40] They were all amnestied four months later.[41]

No less severe were the sentences imposed the following month on the forty-four mutineers of the 39th Battalion, whom Jabotinsky defended before a Court Martial at Sarafend: they ranged from two to seven years' penal servitude. For twenty-eight of those who were sentenced up to five years, sentence was commuted to one year; actually they served only six months. Fourteen legionnaires, whose sentences were heavier, addressed the following letter to Jabotinsky:

Sarafend, August 23, 1919

Lt. V. Jabotinsky, Counsel for the Accused of the
39th R.F. at FGGM. Sarafend, 23 August 1919.

Sir,

We, the undersigned, hereby authorize you to apply on our behalf to H.M. the King for obtaining our pardon, in which petition we beg you to state all our grievances and sufferings as Jewish soldiers.

(14 signatures)

Jabotinsky was always of the opinion that the cause of the legionnaires was not their personal cause but should have been of concern to the entire organized *Yishuv* as represented by the *Vaad Zemani*,* whom he accused of indifference and inaction in dealing with the problem of administrative persecution of the Jewish soldiers. In a letter dated July 5th, he complained that the *Vaad Zemani* "had been doing nothing to change the anti-Semitic attitude towards the [Jewish] soldiers, which had been gradually spreading on all army levels."[42]

In accordance with this concept, Jabotinsky approached the *Vaad Zemani* with the request that a petition be sent in the name of that body to King George V, asking for a pardon for the sentenced Jewish soldiers. The motion to this effect was carried. Characteristically enough, the Zionist Commission decided that "it could not endorse such a petition and will not consent, if requested, to forward it on behalf of the *Vaad Zemani*."[43]

Compulsory Demobilization

Jabotinsky had no illusions as to the attitude of the British military authorities in Palestine toward Zionism and the Legion. Yet he was loath to believe that the systematic mistreatment of Jewish soldiers and manifestations of open hostility toward Jewish ideals in Palestine by certain members of General Allenby's staff could be the expression of Allenby's own policy. He therefore addressed to the Commander-in-Chief the following letter, which Patterson quotes in full:[44]

Sir:

I was the initiator of both the Zion Mule Corps and the actual Jewish Battalions. Today I am forced to witness how my work is breaking into pieces under the intolerable burden of disappointment, despair,

---

Vaad Zemani—Provisional Council—of Palestine Jews was first elected at the Preparatory Assembly held at Petach Tiqvah on December 31, 1917.

broken pledges, and anti-Semitism, permeating the whole administrative and military atmosphere, the hopelessness of all effort and of all devotion.

The common opinion is that you are an enemy of Zionism in general and of the Jewish Legion in particular. I still try to believe that this is not true, that things happen without your knowledge, that there is a misunderstanding, and that the situation can yet improve.

In this hope, as the last attempt to stop a process which threatens to impair forever Anglo-Jewish friendship throughout the world, I beg you to grant me a personal interview and permission to speak freely. This letter is entrusted to your chivalry.

(Signed) V. Jabotinsky

This was, undoubtedly, an unusually bold step on the part of a humble lieutenant, and guardians of military etiquette had every reason to hold up their hands in holy horror at the audacity of it. Yet Jabotinsky's seeming boldness or "naiveté" was not without reasonable foundation. Only a few years before, members of the British Imperial War Cabinet thought it good policy to hear his views when he was still wearing the uniform of a simple soldier. He could not imagine that Lord Allenby, to whose chivalry he entrusted his letter, would prove less accessible and straightforward than the British Minister of War, Lord Derby. He felt confident that even if he were deviating from ordinary routine, it was for a good purpose and would not be counted against him.

In this he was badly mistaken. Patterson tells an almost incredible story of how the British General Headquarters handled Jabotinsky's request, and to what devices they resorted in order to trick, and to get rid of, the "rebellious" officer.[45]

It was known to Allenby's staff that Jabotinsky was at the time staying in Jaffa, and that he was to be found almost daily at the house of Yechiel Weizmann, a brother of Dr. Weizmann. About a week after he had sent his letter to the Commander-in-Chief, a Staff Major G.H.Q., Egyptian Expeditionary Force (a Jew, according to Jabotinsky's evidence), appeared in Jaffa and took up his quarters in the same house where Jabotinsky's friend was living. When the inevitable meeting took place, the Staff Major who, by the way, knew Jabotinsky well, remarked that the Commander-in-Chief had received Jabotinsky's letter, and would probably send for him one of these days, but that in the meantime it would be well if Jabotinsky stated his grievances then and there to him. "You can speak to me openly as to a friend," said the Major, "I have some influence at G.H.Q., and I shall be glad to assist in righting any wrong done to Jews." On hearing this, Jabotinsky unhesitatingly explained the situation both in its effects on the Regiment, and on Jewish aspirations in Palestine. The result of this "friendly conversation" was a mendacious report written by the Staff Major to the Deputy Adjutant General at G.H.Q., E.E.F. Some time afterward, by a mere chance, Patterson saw a copy of this report and, he testifies, "so far as it referred to Jabotinsky, it was practically untrue from beginning to end." Jabotinsky was, among other blackening features, described as a "Bolshevik." If the responsible authorities at G.H.Q. knew of the method adopted to lure Jabotinsky into the "friendly conversation" which served as a pretext for this gross libel on his character, it certainly reminds one of the "good old days" when governments had recourse to *agents provocateurs*, Patterson comments indignantly.

These responsible authorities did not even take the trouble—before taking any action against Jabotinsky—of submitting to him the secret report for his verification, and such explanation or refutation as he might give, though it is strictly laid down in the King's Regulations that all adverse reports must be shown to the officer whose reputation is affected. The officers at G.H.Q. were evidently too eager for a document compromising Jabotinsky to abide by either the most elementary rules of fairness or by their own military code; they swallowed the report with avidity without any reference to Patterson, Jabotinsky's superior. Instead, an official letter from the Deputy Adjutant General dryly stated that "the Commander-in-Chief has his own duly constituted advisers on matters of policy, and is not prepared to grant an interview to a Lieutenant of the 38th Battalion Royal Fusiliers to discuss such matters."

From this moment on, G.H.Q. lost no time in getting rid of Jabotinsky. They knew that he had volunteered for the Army of Occupation (Report to Headquarters, Ludd Area, July 30, 1919) and were not at all eager to have him in active service. On August 9, 1919, a telegraphic message numbered LD 140 was sent to the 38th Royal Fusiliers stating:

Lieut. Jabotinsky [is] given option of local demob or demobilization in U.K. Please reply as early as possible which he accepts.

Jabotinsky had, of course, no intention to get demobilized, be it in Palestine or elsewhere, and did not make use of the "option." Then, on August 29th, Patterson received the following urgent message:

38th Royal Fusiliers
LD 153
Reference my D. 93/154 of 20/8/19 Lieut. Jabotinsky should proceed forthwith to homeward Kantara. Authority DAG GH 2 No A (D) 65 dated 2-8-19. Please comply with Para 806 Demobilization Regulations. Report Departure.*

Since Patterson was very short of Jewish officers, and stood much in need of Jabotinsky's services in the Battalion, he wrote and protested against the latter's demobilization; but the only result was the following peremptory memorandum, signed by a Staff Officer:

A direct order was conveyed for Lieut. Jabotinsky to proceed to demobilisation Camp Kantara forthwith. If he has not already gone, this officer will leave for Kantara by rail today. Non-compliance with this order will lead to disciplinary action being taken. Please report departure.

As a result of this piece of Prussianism, Jabotinsky had to proceed to Kantara, where with lightning speed he was demobilized.

He wrote a protest to the Army Council, which Patterson forwarded with his own views on the case. The appeal was lengthy; the following passages were, however, the most striking:

With the deepest reluctance and regret I must say that I consider this action shows ingratitude. I do not deserve it at the hands of the British Authorities. From the first days of the War I have worked and struggled for British interests. . . .

Against this I know of no facts which could justify the attitude taken up by G.H.Q., E.E.F. I have never heard of any complaint or censure of my conduct as

---

*This and previously reproduced documents are available in original. Mr. Gershon Agron, editor of the *Jerusalem Post*, who kindly put them at the disposal of this author, explained in a letter dated November 10, 1954, how he had "come by these papers": "Towards the end of my service in the 49th Battalion, early in 1920, I marked time in the Orderly Room while waiting for local demobilization, and I had an interesting time going through files. I heard then that on the Battalion's being dispersed, the files would go to Hounslow, in England, the seat of the Royal Fusilier Regiment. I also knew that after some time they would all be consigned to the flames in Hounslow. So I borrowed these papers for safe keeping—and a good thing, too."

Officer or Man; I have never been informed or even given a hint that anything in my activity could be objected to.

My compulsory demobilization under these conditions will throw a slur on my name. I consider it unjust. I request that it be annulled, and that I be reinstated in my well-earned position as an Officer of the Judeans.

A reply to this appeal was never received and it is not known whether it ever reached the Army Council.

Jabotinsky tried to appeal to London. He approached both the Foreign Office and the Colonial Office. On October 9, 1919, the former answered that "as the question at issue appears to be one of military discipline, on which this department is not competent to express any opinion, your letter has been referred to the War Office with the request that your case may be examined." The answer of the Colonial Office, signed by L. S. Amery on October 16th, was more sympathetic but not much more helpful: "I was very sorry indeed to hear from you that the military authorities in Palestine demobilized you in so summary and ungracious a fashion. I don't suppose that anything could be done now to remobilize you." But, Amery added, "I think the least the War Office could do would be to show their recognition in some way or other of your services in the creation of the Jewish units and have written to urge this upon them. Meanwhile I know, in your keenness for the cause, you will be concentrating all your efforts on the future."

Amery's urging resulted in the War Office's decision to bestow on Jabotinsky the Medal of The Most Distinguished Order of the British Empire (M.B.E.). It was not a very high distinction, and Jabotinsky, still outraged by the slur thrown upon his name, was most reluctant to accept this decoration. Informed by Colonel Patterson of this attitude, Amery, on February 27, 1920, asked Patterson to forward to Jabotinsky a letter in which he wrote: "I can quite understand that you feel sore at the unsympathetic treatment which, I gather, you received from some of the military authorities you had to deal with." Yet, he asked Jabotinsky to regard this fact "as a transitory and incidental vexation" and not to let it obscure in his eyes the fact that the permanent view of his services "held by the British Government is that which is embodied in the decoration officially recommended by the War Office and approved of by His Majesty the King."

Amery asked Colonel Patterson to "support in writing" his plea to Jabotinsky. But, forwarding the letter, Patterson added only two lines: "My dear Jabotinsky, you see what Amery says. Do what you think best."

Jabotinsky accepted the decoration.* Ten years later he indignantly returned it to the British government after having been barred from returning to Palestine in 1930.

Jabotinsky joined the Legion when he was thirty-six years old, having spent all his life prior to that as a civilian, and after two years of military schooling and service he returned to politics and literature: he had thus only about two years of "military career" as against decades of civilian endeavors. Nevertheless, Patterson, an old soldier of long service, stressed that "Jabotinsky never lost his . . . upright, soldier-like bearing, which he maintained with inborn ease to the last day of his life. . . . No one who came in contact with the man could have been in any doubt as to his military past."[46]

An authentic account of the five years (1914–19) of the struggle for, and life with, the Legion can be found in The Story of the Jewish Legion.** Jabotinsky himself saw in this account a "story," not a "history" of the Legion: it was not based on documentary material, which "a wanderer like myself" was unable to gather and to have at hand. "I have only recorded my personal memories, probably with all the faults which this kind of literature involves: subjective evaluation, sometimes an error in a date or a name, and too much of the 'I.'"

On the whole, these personal memories are singularly one-sided: affirmative and lavishly laudatory; critical judgments are conspicuously few and are classical examples of masterful understatement; in the entire picture light overwhelmingly prevails over shadows. All this is, of course, deliberate. Jabotinsky admitted that there were during those five years "many unpleasant details, bitterly unpleasant, often repulsive." But he chose to overlook them, though he realized that by doing so he made the story he was telling "much too

---

*Arab rulers seem to have had a highly exaggerated notion of Jabotinsky's military position and rank. Itamar Ben Avi relates that King Feisal of Iraq whom he met in the home of James de Rothschild spoke of "General Jabotinsky, the first general of the Jewish Army," and that Abdallah, Emir (later King) of Transjordan, told him in Amman that he considered Jabotinsky a Field Marshall When Ben Avi related this to Jabotinsky, the latter "burst into a fit of laughter." Both Feisal and Abdallah "did not like him [Jabotinsky] possibly, but both of them respected him certainly," comments Ben Avi.—"Jabotinsky the Fearless." Bnei Zion Voice, September, 1940.

**First published in Russian in 1928, The Story of the Jewish Legion has been translated into Hebrew, Yiddish, English, Spanish, Ladino, Italian, and German.

smooth, too pretty": almost all the personages he spoke about appear "good, all as brave as lions . . . everybody who assisted you appears like a perfect man." And he asked himself: "Have you forgotten the troubles, the humiliations, which you had to endure—and just from those heroes whom you have tendered so much praise?" The answer to this question is characteristic of Jabotinsky's general approach to life and history: "The memory is an autonomous organism, and a petty one. It attracts tiny details, especially unpleasant ones. . . . That is why we have been vouchsafed a controlling apparatus which we call 'taste.' " It was this keen sense of taste that prevented Jabotinsky from dwelling on negative and unpleasant aspects of his struggle for the Legion. To him, the Legion movement and the Legion were a truly noble part of Jewish history: "The trifles which mar the smoothness of its features can interest only hostile gossips." Even "the most beautiful epochs of world history had their ugly stains," but by omitting them we in no way distort the fundamental truth. Seeking support for this lofty philosophy, Jabotinsky quoted from Goethe's autobiographic *Dichtung und Wahrheit*: "Not lies nor colored descriptions, but truth—yet truth cleaned of its offal." To him, this was "the only true form, the only worthy garment, in which the truth should appear before the world."[47]

Personal Problems

There was no lack of financial worries during the period of Jabotinsky's service with the Legion. Besides the necessity of maintaining a standard of life befitting an officer of His British Majesty's Army, he had to provide for a wife and son in London. On October 25, 1918, he wrote to his wife that he was transferring through a bank the amount of £160 ($750 at the 1918 rate of exchange), which he had borrowed by mortgaging his officer's pay. His financial relations with the Army were "most indefinite," he reported. His nominal pay was eleven shillings and sixpence *per diem* (at that time about $2.50) "plus half a dozen allowances which are sometimes due and sometimes not." These additional allowances he received as compensation for a special journalistic and propaganda engagement, to which he had been assigned by the Army. He informed Mrs. Jabotinsky that he was "preparing a message to the War Office urging the clarification of my personal status in regard to rank, office and pay . . . should this not be settled by the New Year, I will leave for England and try to find journalistic work there. From here it is impossible to earn anything but pennies." In the meantime, the department for war propaganda among Jews in the British Ministry of Information apprised Jabotinsky that his *per annum* pay had been retroactively fixed at £350 ($1,662 at the 1918 rate of exchange), but that his engagement was terminated. Jabotinsky consented to this arrangement with the proviso that his officer's pay should not be deducted from this amount, as his official instruction had been to the effect that he must "write articles without severing connection with the Jewish Regiment," so that he had been doing double work all the time.

It was probably in order to substantiate this claim that on November 26, 1918, Colonel Patterson gave him the following certificate:

In the Field,

26. 11. 18.

This is to certify that Lieut. V. Jabotinsky of the Battalion under my Command was ordered by G.H.Q. E.E.F. to write articles for publication whilst retaining his connection with this Unit.

In accordance with the above order, Lieut. Jabotinsky has maintained his connection with the Battalion throughout the period from its landing in Egypt up to the end of the recent offensive, acting as a Platoon Officer, both at the Training Depot and at the Front. During the last Offensive he was acting for a time as Second in Command of a Company in "Patterson's Column" in the Jordan Valley.

During his absences from the Battalion he was doing important propaganda and recruiting work for the Jewish Battalions.

The necessity of borrowing, and the absence of certainty as to his being able to provide a decent livelihood for his family, weighed heavily on Jabotinsky's mind. Once, when his wife mentioned something about her financial difficulties in London in which some well-intentioned but tactless friends had been trying to help out, he gave vent to a long pent-up bitterness:[48]

I am also weary of being a poor relation. Oh, my darling, how I suffer because of it, and how I suffer when I think that people dare to render us services, and that all this is falling on your shoulders, with all this pride of yours. I swear that we are going to be rich! I consider my public work done. If there were in Russia a press, I would this very day resign and start getting rich. I have no ambitions and interests besides this one. Since there is no place to go and I still hope to obtain from the War Office the possibility of securely holding out till the end of the war, I am staying here and making politics. Yet, because of these politics I will not spend here—and anywhere— one single day needlessly.

While stationed in Palestine, Lieutenant Jabotinsky remained faithful to his traditional admiration for women. On page 119 of *The Story of the Jewish Legion* an alert reader can find two statements: describing the success of pretty Jewish nurses whom Colonel Patterson brought along to the races at the Raffa camp, he says that the *Yishuv* "had both strong men and good-looking women," and that "Colonel Patterson believes that nobody may deprive an Irishman of his position near a young woman." There were many good-looking girls around Jabotinsky, and an Odessan certainly was second to none in his determination not to be pushed aside in the presence of the sweet sex.

From the conversations this author had in Israel with several ladies who lived in Palestine in 1918–19 and belonged to the circle of Jabotinsky's closest friends, he gained the impression that the names of several young girls and women were at that time connected with the popular and charming Lieutenant of the 38th Royal Fusiliers. In Jaffa, he was a frequent and welcome guest in the house of the Russian Zionist veteran Eliahu Berlin, who had two daughters, Bella and Nina; he often stayed with another leading Zionist of Russian origin, Bezalel Jaffe, with whose young daughter Mirra he was very friendly. In Jerusalem, Mrs. S. O. Gorodetzky and Dr. Helene Kahan were often seen in his company, together with several others. Just as had been the case in Russia fifteen years earlier, there was much talk about these friendships.

Mrs. Jabotinsky apparently heard something about the friendship which developed between her husband and the sisters Berlin, and jokingly inquired about this "flirtation." Jabotinsky answered that he had already sent her "a detailed report" about "the damsels Berlin" from Jerusalem, where they had been nursing him during a month-long illness resulting from an abscess on the knee—at first both, and then Bella, the elder sister, alone: "They are both very nice indeed. The older one is an interesting girl of about twenty-five, redhaired; the younger is about twenty-two and is of a more housewifely kind. I am very friendly with both of them, and one does not interfere with the other, since the older is in Jerusalem and the younger in Jaffa. Now, when Galilee is liberated and I will have to visit it often, I would prefer that a third one should be available in Haifa. You have nothing to fear from our flirtation, it is on the level. But, with my natural honesty, I must confess that the hindrance lies not with me—I have more than once complained to you about the damned position of a 'public personality' who must always be as above suspicion as Caesar's wife."[49]

FIFTEEN

PALESTINE 1919—
PUBLIC AND PRIVATE AFFAIRS

The Zionist Commission

Jabotinsky never considered the Legion as an isolated function in the totality of Zionist political effort. It was therefore only natural that in Palestine, while still on active duty with his Battalion, he devoted much of his time and energy to political matters—first in the service of recruitment and later on behalf of the Zionist Commission which arrived in Palestine almost simultaneously with him.

The Zionist Commission, as originally constituted early in 1918, was to include representatives from the Allied countries. Not all of the original members of the Commission arrived in Palestine, and some stayed but a relatively short time. The biography of Dr. Eder reports that "in the autumn of 1918, Dr. Eder was the only member of the original Zionist Commission who remained in Palestine . . . assisted by Commander Bianchini and, for a time, by V. Jabotinsky."[1]

In fact, Jabotinsky actively cooperated with the Zionist Commission from the very start. During the first several months, his relations with Dr. Weizmann were excellent. The latter was doing his best to introduce him to the highest British authorities in Palestine. His relations with James Rothschild were also very good, on the whole. Only once did they have a sharp conflict, which for some time actually interrupted their collaboration; peace was finally restored by Dr. Eder. Relations with Dr. Eder himself were invariably cordial.[2]

241

With the end of the war, Jabotinsky's connection with the Zionist Commission became closer and steadier. On October 25, 1918, he reported to Mrs. Jabotinsky: "I am now working for the [Zionist] Commission." On December 3rd he wrote to his mother and sister in Odessa: "I am now a member of the Zionist Commission."[3]

In the letter to his wife Jabotinsky stressed that the philanthropic activities of this body were of no interest to him. "But I intend," he wrote, "to work out with the help of some local people as it were a Helsingfors program for Palestine, since I am afraid that the London Zionists are ready to rely on the good will of the benevolent [British] authorities without any conditions and guarantees."

It is questionable whether the label "Helsingfors program" could be attached—even for the sake of analogy—to the concept which Jabotinsky had in mind and later advocated. The program, which was formulated at the Third All-Russian Zionist Convention in Helsingfors in November, 1906, dealt with the internal self-organization of Russian Jewry and with its demands to the Russian government. The main emphasis of Jabotinsky's program for Palestine was, on the contrary, on the international aspect, on the role of world Jewry, and on its relationship with the Mandatory Power which had to be appointed by the Allied Powers. In an address delivered by Jabotinsky at the conference of delegates of Palestine Jewry (*Moatzah Erez Israelith*) held on December 18–23, 1918, in Jaffa, he stressed that the promise of a Jewish National Home contained in the Balfour Declaration was given not for the sake of Palestine Jews but to world Jewry. "The Jaffa assembly actually speaks, not on behalf of the present Jewish minority in Palestine, but on behalf of millions of Jews throughout the world, on behalf of all those who will come, who are yet to come." In all matters of the administration of Palestine, a decisive voice must belong to the Jewish people as a whole. The Powers would appoint Great Britain as a Trustee with the task of assisting the Jewish people in building a national home. The Trustee would appoint a Resident who would, however, act "like a King in a constitutional state" and be assisted by an Executive Council, which would control the police force and all matters pertaining to public security and order. The Zionist Congress, as the Parliament of World Jewry, would delegate its representative in the capacity of a Deputy Resident; all members of the Executive Council (with the exception of a Minister for Arab affairs) would have to be appointed in accordance with a slate submitted by him.

Non-Jewish groups would be given broad autonomy in matters of religion, civil status, education, social assistance, and internal jurisdiction. Abroad, the Zionist Organization would represent Palestine Jewry before foreign governments and act as the representative of world Jewry in its relations with Palestine.[4]

An "Outline for the Provisional Government of Palestine," which was drawn up by the *Moatzah* and submitted to the Zionist world leadership for their consideration in presenting the Jewish case before the forthcoming Peace Conference, incorporated several essential features of Jabotinsky's scheme. As summarized by a report in *The Maccabaean*, the "Outline" demanded that Palestine should be recognized as the Jewish National Homeland, "in the affairs of which the Jewish people as a whole shall have a determining voice." While both Arabic and Hebrew were to be recognized as official languages, "the name of the land must be Eretz Israel, and the Jewish flag—the flag of the country."[5] The similarity between these demands and Jabotinsky's concept is farreaching. However, the official "Statement of the Zionist Organization Regarding Palestine," which was submitted to the Peace Conference on February 3, 1919, did not contain the basic demand that the whole Jewish people have a voice in the affairs of Palestine.

The discrepancy of political views between Jabotinsky and the official Zionist leadership started developing much earlier. On the personal plane, relations with Dr. Weizmann were still most cordial. On August 11, 1918, Jabotinsky wrote to his wife that Dr. Weizmann had been "nice" to him, and added: "He rendered great services to the Legion—and the Legion rendered great services to him." But politically they started driving apart. Jabotinsky grew increasingly apprehensive of the political situation in Palestine and critical of Dr. Weizmann's conciliatory and appeasing policies, while the latter apparently disapproved of Jabotinsky's methods of dealing with the British authorities. A few days before Dr. Weizmann's first departure from Palestine (September 18, 1918), Jabotinsky took over from him the task of representing the Zionist Commission before the Palestine administration. In his memoirs, which were written more than three decades afterward, Dr. Weizmann asserted that this transfer of political representation was but a "theoretical" one, and that relations with the British were merely "nominally in the hands of Jabotinsky"; actually "it was [Dr.] Eder's authority which expressed itself in the [Zionist] Commission." Praising Dr. Eder as "a model of patience and forbearance" and stressing that "he always gained his point by persuasion and never resorted to threats or bluster," Dr. Weizmann said: "Unfortunately the same could not always be said of his political colleague." Though "he was familiar with all the necessary languages, speaking fluent French, English, Hebrew and German, possessed great eloquence and a high degree of intelligence," Jabotinsky "seemed to be entirely devoid of poise and balance, and, what was worse, of that mature judgment so urgently required in that small but very complex world."[6]

This belated attempt to minimize Jabotinsky's political stature in Palestine and to construe a clash of personalities between him and Dr. Eder is not supported by any evidence. The Zionist Commission, of which Dr. Eder was then Acting Chairman, appointed Jabotinsky head of its political department on January 6, 1919, months after Dr. Weizmann's departure from the country; it apparently had full confidence in his ability to fill this position.[7] Dr. Eder's biography emphatically states that during Jabotinsky's term of office Eder "was on excellent terms" with him.[8] In order to substantiate the statement that Jabotinsky "lacked poise and balance" in his dealings with the British authorities, Dr. Weizmann related the following episode: on the eve of his departure, he saw General Clayton, the political officer, and the latter asked him to "impress upon Captain (!) Jabotinsky that things would be much easier if he would fix definite hours each day at which to call upon him to transact business, and not to walk in on him at all hours of the day and night!" This remark apparently greatly alarmed the President of the Zionist Organization; he thought that it "did not augur well for my successor"; he "tried to impress on Jabotinsky the need for caution and naturally warned Eder" who "promised to keep an eye on things."[9]

Irrespective of the question as to whether there was cause for alarm, Dr. Weizmann, when reporting this episode, must have been misled by his memory, for the two protagonists of the story were absent at the time it was supposed to have happened. Here are the chronological data:

1. Dr. Weizmann left Palestine on September 18, 1919, so that the conversation with General Clayton must have happened on September 17th.

2. The Zionist Commission arrived in Palestine on April 4, 1918. The official history of the war records: "The Chief Political Officer, Br.-General G. F. Clayton, carried out the duties of the Chief Administrator until the 16th April (1918), when he was succeeded by Major General Sir A. W. Money."[10]

3. Between mid-June and at least until the end of September, 1918, Jabotinsky had been almost continuously at the front, first in the mountains and later in the Jordan Valley.

Simple chronology makes it impossible that General Clayton should have become "an easy victim" (as Dr. Weizmann compassionately called him) of Jabotinsky's "zeal and ardor." This on the surface minor and trivial discrepancy can, however, be considered as characteristic of the fundamental difference in the appraisal of the political situation—and in the reaction to it—between Dr. Weizmann and Jabotinsky.

Jabotinsky felt strongly that the prospects of the Zionist cause were being systematically undermined by the openly anti-Zionist British military administration, whose policy was not properly opposed by the Zionist leadership. This administration was filled from top to bottom with confirmed opponents of the official British policy of the Jewish National Home. They considered this policy to be an inadmissible folly and openly demonstrated their utter hostility and contempt for the Jews and their national aspirations. Growing Arab impertinence was deliberately fostered by government officials.

Characteristic of the almost pathological anti-Jewish attitude of the British military authorities is a little-known episode, in the last stage of which Jabotinsky played a dramatic role.[11]

Shortly after his arrival in Palestine, when the Turkish Army occupied a part of the country and the frontline was very close, a British detachment occupying a hill overlooking the Jewish colony of Petach Tiqvah* noticed one night in one of the houses lights moving from one window to another. Suspicious as they were of everything Jewish, the officers at once decided that signals were being transmitted to the enemy. They surrounded the house, which belonged to Israel Rosov, a veteran of Russian Zionism, and arrested his younger brother Raphael. The latter's explanations that the "suspicious lights" were simply a lamp burning on the second-floor balcony, which he occasionally took to another room when he needed a book or a cup of tea, were not believed. He was thrown into prison and charged with spying on behalf of the Turks—a charge involving capital punishment.

---

*Petach Tiqvah had been conquered by the British forces early in November, 1917; it was reoccupied a few weeks later by the Turks who stayed there for about a month, and was then recaptured by the British in December.

British officers testified that they had observed Rosov moving the lamp up and down, so as to signal to the enemy across the lines.

The absurdity of the accusation was obvious. It should have been clear to everybody in his right senses that a leading Russian Zionist family could not be involved in pro-Turkish espionage. But mistrust of Jews and animosity against Zionists blinded the British military administration. Dr. Weizmann, who had known the Rosovs long and intimately, interceded with British Headquarters in Egypt. But the decisive blow to the entire structure of the charge against Rosov was dealt, in a most dramatic way, by Jabotinsky. When the actual trial started, he walked in in the middle of the proceedings, wearing his officer's uniform, went straight up to Rosov who was sitting manacled on the bench of the accused, and embraced and kissed him. The prosecutor and judges could not possibly condemn as a spy a man with whom a British officer so demonstratively associated himself, without involving this officer in that criminal affair. The whole charge collapsed like a house of cards under the psychological impact of Jabotinsky's gesture.

Warnings

Jabotinsky tried repeatedly to warn Dr. Weizmann and the Zionist Commission of the impending danger.

As early as November 12, 1918, he wrote to Dr. Weizmann, who had left Palestine about two months before and was expected back soon:[12] "The local situation is not good. Precedents are being established that will later be used against us. Everything that is now being done here against us will serve as a precedent. I never thought that our National Home will emerge by miracle. But we believed in one thing: that the [British] Government will conduct in Palestine a clear policy earnestly aiming at the establishment of a Jewish National Home, and that when the British Administration will take over, there will be equality between Jews and Arabs." There was no such equality, Jabotinsky insisted; and he substantiated this statement by a series of striking factual examples of discrimination against Jews in the municipalities and against the Hebrew language, coupled with favoritism toward the Arabs and their anti-Zionist propaganda.

The second letter, dated January 22, 1919, is even more outspoken.[13] Describing the situation in the country, Jabotinsky wrote:

. . . Arab impudence is growing daily. No forty-eight hours pass but some inciting speech is heard in Ramleh, concluding in a call to the "Arab sword". . . . The Palestine authorities are acting in a manner which clearly tells the Arabs that the [Balfour] Declaration need not be fulfilled. . . . The Administration's attitude is assuming the character of a systematic [anti-Zionist] attack organized by the lower officials, while the higher ones let them do as they please. . . . The proposals formulated in your last telegram—if they have not been altered—are no more suited to the situation, because the most essential thing is omitted: there is lacking the demand that the Palestine Administration be appointed in accordance with a slate submitted by us. I do not believe that this is so difficult to attain. . . . But even should this demand be rejected, I would consider it as unforgivable if we would not submit such a demand. It seems as if you were handing the British a certificate of faith in their intention of choosing people who are favorable to us. You have no right to give such a certificate, knowing well as you do that we are surrounded by enemies here and that the Foreign Office has not lifted a finger to remedy the situation. . . . The fact that the Foreign Office is getting accustomed to the idea that the Zionists will digest everything, diminishes the value of your demarches.

"I consider it my duty," Jabotinsky stressed, "to warn you that if all this exceeds certain limits, I shall be forced either to resign altogether or to see to it that the cry of Palestine shall be heard in Europe. . . . Forgive the bitterness of my letter, but I did not participate, in my youth, in the organization of self-defense in order that I should now sit quietly and complacently watching while the Arabs have it drummed into their ears that *it is possible* [italics in the original] to get rid of us if they only give us a hard enough kick."

To the Zionist Commission, of which he was appointed chief political officer, Jabotinsky repeatedly tried to convey his apprehensions. Two days before sending Dr. Weizmann his second letter, he voiced "a pessimistic view" and "thought that the main fault lay in the undefined position of the [London] British Government . . . [which] did not sufficiently instruct its administrators here of its intention to make Palestine the National Home for the Jewish people. If this were done at once, the Arabs would adopt another attitude towards us." He requested the delegation of Palestine Jewry, which was being sent to the Zionist Conference in London, to inform this gathering of the Arab agitation and "to press our leaders to take more energetic steps with the British Government."[14] At the end of February, he again submitted to the Commission a special insistent report on the political situation. He stressed that "the Balfour Declaration had the effect of excellent propaganda in the Allied countries, but the promises therein contained had not been fulfilled; the Jews were not accorded even equality of promise with the Arabs . . . and the situation had developed in such manner that the Arabs believed that the British would welcome massacres of the Jews." He proved his analysis by citing several specific cases of anti-Jewish actions and pronouncements by British officials and officers.[15]

On March 12, 1919, at the request of the Commission's Acting Chairman, Commandant A. L. Bianchini, Jabotinsky gave a detailed survey of the political situation in the country. Fifteen of the thirty-five pages of the official minutes of this meeting are devoted to this survey; it gives a truly alarming picture—abundantly substantiated by facts, figures, and names— of a most vicious Arab anti-Zionist propaganda, which was being tolerated and indirectly encouraged by the attitude of the British administration. He quoted chapter and verse from bloodthirsty articles in the Arab press, leaflets, speeches, and private utterances which were bound to lead to anti-Jewish outbreaks. Most of this propaganda stemmed from the conviction of the Arab agitators that this anti-Zionist action was fully in line with the general policy of the British rulers. The Arabs firmly believed that the authorities "would not at all be angry if they could produce a strong anti-Zionist manifestation of a kind that would enforce European attention . . . they would not be so sorry if anti-Jewish excesses happened in the country."

At that time Jabotinsky was "convinced that this belief of the Arabs is a mistake . . . that the authorities do not want any excesses, and are prepared to suppress them, should anything break out." This was "obvious" to him. But, he insisted, "this is not at all obvious to the Arab masses: on the contrary, the general attitude of the Government, as well as the conduct of some of its agents, is most apt to suggest to the Arabs that a pogrom would be welcomed; and in the presence of a large stock of firearms in native hands and of an energetic pogrom propaganda, such official attitude cannot help leading to trouble with an almost mathematical certainty." Unless "the government changed this general attitude, the population's attitude would continue forever. It was not of importance to us whether the Arabs would be able to kill three women, one or more: important to us was to have no trouble whatever in Palestine. . . . What was necessary was to make the Arabs realize once and for all the firm attitude of the government."

Discharged

The last-mentioned two reports to the Zionist Commission were submitted by Jabotinsky when his connection with this body had already been severed: he had been summarily discharged by Dr. Weizmann both as a member of the Commission and as head of its political department.

By the end of 1918, the Zionist Commission counted twelve members, among them Jabotinsky. Very soon, however, the Commission was apprised by a letter from London, dated January 8, 1919, that the appointment of six names on the original list, among them Jabotinsky, was "authorized only as experts and advisors, not as members of the Commission."[16] A month later, on February 7th, the Zionist Inner Actions Committee headed by Dr. Weizmann reconstituted the Zionist Commission. In the new list Jabotinsky's name was completely omitted. This was the first *capitis diminutio*.

Then came the second. Before Dr. Eder left for London in January, 1919, Jabotinsky was officially given the title of Chief Political Officer of the Commission. However, when the new Acting Chairman, Dr. H. Friedenwald, and Mr. Robert Szold, the newly appointed member of the Commission, arrived in Palestine in February, 1919, the latter brought with him a short letter from Dr. Weizmann, in which Jabotinsky was instructed to hand the political department over to Mr. Szold. Mr. Szold told this writer that, though "Jabotinsky had had no previous notice, he nevertheless turned over his files, and assisted his successor."[17]

This new set-up put an end to the "Jabotinsky era" in the Zionist Commission. On February 26th, Commandant Bianchini announced that "Lieut. Jabotinsky had resigned [this was obviously a face-saving formula] and was about to proceed to England." As mentioned above, Jabotinsky presented at this meeting and at the following (March 12th) an extensive survey of the political situation and outlined the measures to be taken. The minutes of the latter meeting devote fully thirty pages to this survey. The next meeting of the Commission, on March 18th, was, as Jabotinsky later put it, "the first in which Dr. Friedenwald and Mr. Szold participated, and the last at which I was present."[18] A perusal of the minutes of twenty-seven meetings of the Zionist Commission in March-July, 1919, failed to discover any mention of Jabotinsky's name.

The régime of Dr. Friedenwald and Robert Szold lasted five months, until July, 1919, when both left Palestine.* In September, M. M. Ussishkin, a staunch and implacable adversary of Jabotinsky from the Legion times, assumed general control of the Zionist Commission. S. D. Salzman relates that during the Jerusalem period "Jabotinsky never met Ussishkin," though in Russia they were very close both politically and personally. In the years of Jabotinsky's struggle for the Legion their ways parted so radically and sharply that there apparently was no mending of the rift, not only in public matters but in private relations as well. Jabotinsky, who ordinarily had a "white memory" in regard to attacks directed against him personally, never forgot and never forgave what Ussishkin had said to his mother in 1915 to the effect that her son deserved to be hanged; and Ussishkin was not a man to forget an old grudge. Being in control of the Zionist Commission, he was, of course, able to frustrate Jabotinsky's every attempt to influence the work of this body.

It would be misleading to assume that, while working with the Zionist Commission, Jabotinsky was interested in matters of high policy only. In fact, he busied himself with numerous everyday problems and needs of the *Yishuv* and of the Jewish battalions. In January, 1919, he reported to the Commission that the colonists of Motza complained of the cattle plague and asked for serum.19 In March, he drew its attention to the situation of lace-making schools for girls in Tiberias and Safed; he also spoke of the difficulties facing students wishing to go to Europe to complete higher studies. He was particularly keen on all matters, big and small, concerning the legionnaires. He complained about the absence of comforts for the soldiers of the Jewish battalions, such as paucity of paper and stationery, of tobacco and recreation facilities; it was, he said, mainly the fault of the *Yishuv*, and he insisted that a Soldiers' Home be established in every township and center. It was also necessary to issue weekly bulletins for Jewish soldiers in both Hebrew and English, which would supply them with general Jewish information as well as with news concerning the Jewish battalions.[20]

---

*Jabotinsky later spoke derisively of this practice of haphazard appointments by the London Executive: "There have been cases during the last three years when such appointments were held by gentlemen paying their first (and very short) visit to the country. . . . The results of this system of government by tourists are well known."—"The Task of the Actions Committee." *Jewish Chronicle*, January 28, 1921.

Even after his separation from the Zionist Commission, Jabotinsky continued his intercessions on behalf of the legionnaires. On May 27, 1919,he wrote to the Commission that the volunteers from America were complaining that the British government was not paying support to their wives, while the wives of other soldiers in the British Army were receiving it, and insisted that the Commission must actively intercede in this matter. In May and again in November, 1919, he approached the Zionist Commission on behalf of thirty former soldiers of the Zion Mule Corps, who intended to settle in Palestine and to establish a colony of their own. In June, 1919, Jabotinsky asked the Zionist Commission to enable the legionnaires to participate in the elections to the projected Constitutional Assembly.[21]

Private Resident of Jerusalem

In February, 1919, Jabotinsky was discharged from the Zionist Commission; in August of the same year, General Allenby discharged him from the British Army. From then on, he had no official standing whatsoever in the *Yishuv*. He was just a private resident of Jerusalem, holding no office, position, or trust, without any authority except that bestowed on him by his personality, energy, talent, and devotion. These qualities proved to be sufficient to make him the dynamic center of Jewish spiritual and political life in the country. There was hardly a single field in which his initiative and influence did not make itself felt.

At Jabotinsky's initiative, a series of lectures on law and sociology was arranged for Jerusalem's intelligentsia; among the lecturers were Palestine's leading legal authorities. Jabotinsky, too, lectured every fourth Sabbath on his specialty—the rights of national minorities. Other topics were: Bialik's poetry, the theory of the state, England, the women's suffrage problem. The underlying idea of these lectures was to train for the future Jewish state a body of prospective civil servants, diplomats, and political leaders, versed in the basic problems of modern statehood. To Jabotinsky a Jewish state was not a distant and vague ideal, but a closely impending reality, which might, as it did, find the Jewish intelligentsia unprepared for the job. He tried to fill the gap created by centuries of statelessness.

Among youth his influence was great, and they responded eagerly to his every appeal for public service, in which he was the first to give a personal example. The winter of 1919–20 was particularly severe. An unusually deep snowfall covered the streets of Jerusalem.[22] Arab propaganda immediately capitalized on this phenomenon of nature, alleging that the Muscovite Jews had brought the curse of frost and snow from the steppes of Russia to annoy and to harm the Arabs. Many houses were so blocked by snow that their inhabitants could not get out; they stayed home and waited for help. Ziskind Abramowitz, at that time a youngster, later recalled that, sitting at the window of his room in one of the poorer quarters of the city, he "noticed from afar a familiar figure, wearing thigh-high boots, carrying a long hoe, with a heavy sack on his back." He recognized Jabotinsky who told him: "Why are you remaining at home when hundreds of families are prisoners in their houses? Come out and let's help them."[23] Jabotinsky organized groups of youngsters who, under his personal direction, started clearing the snowed-in sidewalks behind which the Jerusalemites were marooned, going from house to house, and distributing bread and other victuals among the stricken population.[24] There is a picture of Jabotinsky, wading knee-deep through the snow, laden with food parcels.

Jabotinsky's relations with the Sefardic youth groups (*Halutz Hamizrachi*) were very friendly. He was already then a convinced admirer of Sefardic Jewry and deplored that so little attention was being paid to this precious branch of the Jewish people.

In the cultural field he devoted much attention and time to improving the pronunciation of the Hebrew language which used to be spoken in a rather careless and slovenly way. At a gathering of Hebrew teachers in Jaffa, he elaborated for over half an hour on the necessity to be more careful in using the *shva-nakh*. Even such Hebraist zealots as Mordechai Ben Hillel Hacohen refused to understand why Jabotinsky was "making an issue" out of a matter "that is not worth a penny; *shva-nakh*—a burning problem, indeed!" Hacohen scornfully commented. At the same time, he admired Jabotinsky's "ability to keep a packed hall in suspense for over half an hour on such a subject."[25] In the summer of 1919, Jabotinsky was elected to the Board of Directors of the newly created society *Sefatenu* (Our Language) and delivered a series of lectures on problems of Hebrew. The chairman of the youth organization *Herzlia* stated in the press that under the influence of Jabotinsky's speech in *Sefatenu*, his organization decided henceforth to deal with the authorities in Hebrew only.

Jabotinsky had ambitious plans for establishing a grand publishing house, with branches in all the big centers of Europe and America; more than once he would even describe in detail the shape, color, and lettering of the signs that were to hang over all these offices and shops. When people mockingly asked him how a serious man could indulge in such fanciful dreams, he would reply: "Who was more serious than the prophet Ezekiel in his time, and yet even in exile he 'played' with the memory of the Jerusalem Temple, and in his fantasy he even made a drawing of it up to the least detail." This publishing dream-house of his was in the first place to serve the Hebrew school, producing atlases, maps, primers, and text books; blocks, ABC's for the composition of words, ABC's in pictures; translation of children's literature from other languages. De luxe editions of the *Tanakh*, of the Psalms, and of the five *Megilloth* were also among his dearest projects. With all this in mind, he convened a group of leading Hebrew writers, submitted his plans to them, listened to their suggestions, weighed and discussed all possibilities.[26]

Jabotinsky attached great importance to securing proper representation and influence of the *Yishuv* in Zionist affairs. The proper relationship between the *Yishuv* and the World Zionist Organization, as he saw it, was as follows:[27]

> The Zionist Congress and the *Yishuv* are two distinct bodies. It is not good that they are separated, neither would it be good if one were to annul the other. Often enough, in the near future, will the *Yishuv* have to defend its views against those of the Congress. . . . "Faithful but free," this is how an enlightened Jew once described his relations with orthodox Jewry, and I think that this formula perfectly fits the relations between [Zionist] Congress and the *Yishuv*. . . . They will always reach a compromise, but a compromise is not possible if both sides do not agree beforehand to [a system of] compromising. First of all the *Yishuv* must find its true face, fix its shape, express itself. . . .

Led by this perception, Jabotinsky considered the self-organization of the *Yishuv* as one of the most pressing problems. The existing "Provisional Committee of the Palestine Jews" (*Vaad Zemani*) was a very imperfect and obsolete representation. It was therefore proposed to convene in July, 1919, a democratically elected *Asafah ha'Myasedeth* (Constitutional Convention), which would lay the foundations of a permanent organization and representation of Palestine Jewry. This seemingly self-evident idea had, however, provoked opposition in several quarters. "The leaders of the different factions . . . were intimidated by the proposed Constitutional Convention," wrote Gershon Agronsky, the Palestine correspondent of *The Maccabaean* (January, 1920). "Jabotinsky stood out almost alone for the minimum rights of the Jewish minority in Palestine . . . for their right to plan their constitution. . . . The majority was disinclined to follow Jabotinsky."[28] It was in vain that Jabotinsky urged in *Haaretz* to "disregard all the existing political parties in the country* and solely to care about one single thing: the organization of the community" and reminded "all those who are interested in building up and organizing [it] that there is no justification for hesitancy." Agronsky saw in this hesitancy a characteristic feature of "the 'waiting for' Weizmann period."

Jabotinsky was a most outspoken opponent of this sterile "waiting for" system in all fields of Zionist work in Palestine. At the meeting of the *Vaad Zemani* on December 22, 1919, a major political discussion took place between Dr. Weizmann and M. Ussishkin on the one side, and Jabotinsky on the other.[29] The latter accused the official Zionist leadership of not taking into consideration the political proposals submitted by the December, 1918, assembly of Palestine Jewry, and insisted that these proposals be made the foundation of a bold and far-reaching Zionist program to be put before the Allied Powers "without any compromise or concession whatsoever." **He was sure that if such a program originating in Palestine were presented, it would be accepted by the Powers. The same, he insisted, applied to the reaction of the Jewish people. Dr. Weizmann has said that an essential precondition for the success of Zionist work was that America give all the money needed. But it was wrong to think that it would be enough to send a delegation to America: the Zionists were not the only ones who were asking for money. There were similar demands for the needs of Jews in Eastern Europe, Russia, etc. If the Zionists were asking for money in order

---

*Jabotinsky had little understanding and sympathy for the Party system in Zionism. M. Shertok (Sharett), who at that time saw much of Jabotinsky, told this writer that when he joined the newly established *Akhdut ha'Avodah* Party, Jabotinsky was very disappointed. He expected to enroll him in a different formation, the idea of which he then cherished: a non-partisan group or club, embracing Zionists of various convictions, who would agree on one point only—that the emphasis must be put on the political aspect of Zionism (*Doggesh Medini*). He later published in *Haaretz* an article entitled "Doggesh Medini."

**S. D. Salzman relates that when Jabotinsky proposed to publish Herzl's *Judenstaat* in Hebrew and English (volunteering to do the English translation himself), the Zionist Commission emphatically turned down this suggestion. They considered it not "statesmanlike" to revive the Jewish state issue; their attitude was one of apprehension: "What will the Gentiles say?"

to build a homeland, others appealed to the sense of charity, begged for immediate help to the needy. The only way to "get all the money" in America was to combine both aspects, to show that the upbuilding of Palestine will eventually bring help to all those for whose sake appeals for charity were being made. The colonization scheme, submitted by Ussishkin, did not do justice to this necessity. What was wanted was a truly comprehensive plan of large-scale mass settlement. Voicing his surprise that Dr. Weizmann had omitted mentioning the demand for a Jewish Army, Jabotinsky said: "There will be an Army in this country, and it is imperative that this Army, even though it may wear British uniforms, be Jewish in composition and spirit. . . . I beg our leaders to accept two decisive elements of the success of the Zionist cause—the Legion, and a grand-scale program."

Both Ussishkin and Weizmann were most emphatic in rejecting Jabotinsky's approach. They were ready to favor the demand for a Legion. But Ussishkin refused to endorse a large-scale settlement plan: "We are not going to wage propaganda for a program, which we know beforehand cannot be implemented. . . . Not hurriedly, as the Exodus from Egypt, will the country be built, but by slow immigration, as it was the case after the Babylonian Exile." Dr. Weizmann went even further and denied the very possibility of offering the suffering Jewish masses a hope of rescue in Palestine:

> We cannot base our plans upon the sad events that occurred in Russia. There is no territorial program in the world capable to satisfy the present needs of the Jewish people. It would be possible to make propaganda along the lines suggested by Jabotinsky only if we could put such a program on a scientific basis, proving its feasibility. But this is out of the question. . . . I haven't got the courage to come to the Jewish people and submit a large-scale program when I know beforehand that it is not practical. . . . Zionism cannot be the answer to a catastrophe. . . . We advance slowly.

Continuing this discussion in the columns of *Haaretz*, Jabotinsky revealed the fundamental difference between his own and the Weizmann-Ussishkin concept of Zionism. His emphasis was, then as later, on speedy mass immigration as the solution to *Judennot*: "Zionism is the answer to the lie called *Galut*, or else Zionism itself is a lie. . . . Zionism's aim is the creation of a sanctuary for the Jewish people in the Land of Israel; this is Zionism, and nothing else. In the face of the abyss of blood and fire, we shall submit a maximum program. . . . If we erect a giant building, many from among our People will be attracted and support us. But if we aspire to build but a humble hut, they will not come. The completion of the building was first estimated to take fifty or twentyfive years, but now we are compelled to accomplish it in a much shorter time."[30]

While official Zionist leadership determinedly opposed Jabotinsky's approach and demands, the leaders of organized labor in Palestine at that time were very near to his program. The relationship between them and Jabotinsky was nevertheless a contradictory, even a paradoxical, one. Fundamentally, they had very much in common. D. Ben Gurion was most outspoken in stressing to this writer that, in regard to most of the controversial issues, he and most of his colleagues in the *Akhdut ha'Avodah* leadership were in 1918–20 more pro-Jabotinsky than pro-Weizmann. They fully shared his demand for the preservation of the Legion, his insistence on mass immigration and on the idea of Greater Zionism, as well as his criticism of the British administration and his opposition to the official Zionist leadership. There were times when they were "more anti-Weizmann than Jabotinsky himself." But, Ben Gurion explained, while agreeing on the aims and scope of Zionism, ready to cooperate in the struggle against external and inner obstacles, they never really felt spiritually akin to Jabotinsky. Their attitude toward the Legion, though identical on the surface, was different in substance. Eliahu Golomb, one of the labor leaders and himself a legionnaire, formulates this difference in a way which, though obviously unfriendly to Jabotinsky, is nevertheless basically correct: for Jabotinsky, he said, the Legion was important primarily as a political phenomenon, a factor that would have to be taken into consideration by the forthcoming Peace Conference in Versailles; for the labor leaders, the Legion was the expression of their "longing for personal fulfilment and Jewish participation in self-liberation." According to Golomb, it was because of this difference that Jabotinsky was "unable to conquer the hearts of the volunteers, though they appreciated his activities and abilities." They joined the Legion with the idea of returning as soon as possible to their work and of strengthening the labor movement in Palestine. Jabotinsky, on the contrary, concentrated on the Legion as such.[31] Another labor leader, Berl Katznelson, also a legionnaire, stressed that the trouble with Jabotinsky was that "he did not at all think of other matters—colonization, etc.— the Legion was the only thing that counted." And still another labor leader and one of the first promoters of the volunteer movement, Rahel Yanait Ben Zvi said: "He [Jabotinsky] did not demand human elation, he did not care who was serving [in the Legion], while we demanded idealism, and the pick and salt of our [Labor] Movement joined the Legion."[32] According to Golomb, this was the reason why the labor leaders among the volunteers felt themselves closer to Weizmann, whose attitude toward the Legion was aloof, than to Jabotinsky, who had created it. As Golomb put it, Weizmann "knew how fully to appreciate the spiritual motives and longings of the volunteers' movement."

There is, no doubt, much exaggeration in all these statements about the alleged indifference of Jabotinsky to "all matters but the Legion" and about his alleged disregard for the spiritual values and motives in the volunteer movement. Jabotinsky was deeply and actively concerned with the problems of mass immigration, colonization, organization of the *Yishuv*, Hebrew, etc. Himself a volunteer, he was certainly more qualified to understand and to appreciate the greatness and beauty of the volunteers' spiritual impulses than those who had been watching them from outside. But there is no denying that he was unique in the intensity of his realization of the crucial role the Legion was destined to play in the entire development of all other aspects of the Jewish national effort in Palestine. Very few matched his single-mindedness of purpose and dedication, and among those who did not, there was a humanly understandable, vague resentment against his "maniacal insistence" on the all-pervading importance of the Legion.

It must, however, be taken into account that most of the statements quoted above were made much later than 1919–20, at a time when animosity against Jabotinsky in the labor ranks—animosity generated by quite different causes and motives—was at its peak. They largely represent a *post factum* rationalization of an attitude which was in fact not at all unfriendly, much less hostile. While differing in some respects, the leadership, and even more the rank and file of Palestine labor, were fond of Jabotinsky, respected him highly, and treated him accordingly.

Back to Journalism

In April, 1918, the British military administration started publishing a weekly *News from the Holy Land* (later renamed *Palestine News*) in English, Hebrew, and Arabic (the Hebrew edition appeared under the name *Hadoshoth MeHaaretz Hakdusha* —News from the Holy Land—and later as *Hadoshoth Haaretz*). It was printed originally in Jerusalem and later in

Cairo. Jabotinsky actively collaborated in the Hebrew edition and occasionally wrote articles on Zionism for the English edition.

In March, 1919, Jabotinsky reported to the Zionist Commission the administration's suggestion that the Commission buy up all the three editions
of the *Palestine News*. His advice was to accept the proposition. In regard to
the Hebrew paper, he said that the necessary financial means would be provided by his friend Itzhak Goldberg, a wealthy and generous veteran of Russian Zionism; its organization would be secured as soon as his old publisher,
S. D. Salzman, who was then detained by G.H.Q. in Egypt, would arrive in
Palestine.

Of these three projects only the first materialized. In June, 1919, permission was received to transfer the *Hadoshoth Haaretz* from Cairo to Jerusalem and to convert it into a daily; later Jabotinsky obtained from General
Storrs permission to change the name to *Haaretz* (the request to change it
to *Eretz Israel* was refused). The administration of the publication was in
the hands of S. D. Salzman. Dr. Turov was appointed editor, but he soon resigned and Dr. S. Perlman took over as acting editor. Jabotinsky was invited
to join the editorial board and to write at least three articles a week.

Dr. Perlman told this writer that he deeply enjoyed collaboration with
Jabotinsky, who used to come daily for several hours to the editorial offices
and, besides writing his own articles, actively participated in all editorial
and even technical work. His articles were appearing over his full signature, or initials, or various pen names such as Altalena, A.T., etc. They dealt
with a wide variety of subjects: Zionist policy and problems of education
(he raised for the first time the question of mixed Arab-Jewish schools and
of the need for teaching English); Hebrew law and reform of the Hebrew
language; land questions and literary criticism; translations of Gabriele
d'Annunzio's and Joséphin Soulari's poetry; Sefardic Jewry and Herbert
Samuel; the necessity of preserving the existence of the Jewish battalions,
and the urgency of self-organization of the *Yishuv*.

Haaretz had no fixed political line of its own, and Jabotinsky was free to
write as he pleased. However, some of his articles provoked violent opposition. When Jabotinsky insisted that Jewish economy in Palestine must be
based not solely on agriculture but also on industry, one of the *Hapoel Hat-
zair* leaders, Shlomo Schiller, "almost fainted from indignation," Dr. Perlman recalls.[33] There was also much resentment of Jabotinsky's criticism of
Dr. Weizmann's and the Zionist Commission's policies. At a meeting called

in the house of Mordechai Ben Hillel Hacohen, an attempt was made to restrain Jabotinsky's freedom of expression. The answer was: "I shall write what I deem right; the only man who is entitled to make any corrections is Dr. Perlman." And, indeed, the latter stated, Jabotinsky gave him *carte blanche* in this respect and never objected to the alterations made by him, whether stylistic or political. Dr. Perlman admitted that the Hebrew style of Jabotinsky's articles was in the beginning often far from perfect—one could feel that they were mentally translated from another language; but they were easier to correct than articles written by old-timers of Hebrew literature: sometimes the vocabulary or grammar was faulty, but not the construction of the sentences. In almost every article, Jabotinsky used to leave a few blank spaces for expressions he was not sure of, to be filled in by Dr. Perlman or the chief translator and copy-editor of the paper, Masham, whom he called the "living encyclopaedia of the Hebrew language." Most of the articles were written at home in the early morning hours. The winter of 1919–20 was exceptionally cold and the apartment was unheated, so that Jabotinsky had to wear gloves and galoshes. The article ready, he would leave for the printingshop saying: "Now I am going to the *Heder*."[34]

There was, of course, a lot of trouble with the censorship which was unduly strict, and more than once Jabotinsky had to intervene personally in order to salvage some important article or piece of news. Despite all these complications, Jabotinsky loved *Haaretz* dearly, and greatly enjoyed working for the paper, which had become his pet child. His salary was scant and so was his standard of life; but he always was cheerful, Dr. Perlman recalls.

Family and Friends

Since he had left Russia on September 1, 1914, it was the first—and the last—time that he lived uninterruptedly (except for short trips to Egypt) in one country for almost two and a half years: from April, 1918, to the end of August, 1920. He was alone during the first fifteen months; in July, 1919, he was joined by Mrs. Jabotinsky and his son Eri; later, his mother, sister, and nephew arrived from Russia. The entire family was reunited after years of separation.

How did Jabotinsky live as a private individual during these twenty-eight months spent in the Jewish homeland? What was his mode of existence? What occupied him besides his public activities?

For about a year, being almost permanently on the move, he had no fixed residence. When in Jerusalem, he used to stay at the headquarters of the

Zionist Commission or at Dr. Eder's house. In Tel Aviv, he was a welcome guest at the home of Bezalel Jaffe or of Eliahu Berlin. In the late spring of 1919, his old friend S. D. Salzman arrived from Russia. For a time they roomed together at the Hotel Amdursky in Jerusalem's Old City, opposite David's Tower. Since both Jabotinsky and Salzman expected the arrival of their families, they rented an apartment in the house of Levi on Jaffa Road, opposite the Russian Compound. The house was a three-story building; the top was occupied by Van Vriesland (Treasurer of the Zionist Commission) and on the ground floor lived Jabotinsky's friend Mark Schwarz; Jabotinsky got the middle floor and stayed in this apartment until his imprisonment in April, 1920. "The inhabitants of the house lived as one big family," Salzman recalls.

The arrival of his wife and son was a great event in Jabotinsky's life. Anticipating it, he wrote tenderly to Mrs. Jabotinsky from Lydda on June 15, 1919: "The apartment will be cleaned for your arrival. . . . You wrote to me twice that Eri is longing to see me, but 'much less to see Palestine.' Who taught him that? Yet, I myself want to see him much more than any country or any miracle in the world—with the exception of his mummy."

Jabotinsky met his family at Port Said, where they took ship for Jaffa. The first few weeks they lived in Tel Aviv in the apartment of Eliahu Berlin on Hashachar Street near the Herzl Gymnasium "as in a bivouac," recalls Eri. Jabotinsky had to leave them alone almost immediately after their arrival in order to go to Kantara where he was to defend the fifty-five "mutineers" of the 38th Battalion. "My poor ones," he wrote from Kantara on July 29th, "what a fine welcome have I arranged for you in Palestine! How ridiculously, idiotically unlucky are we—as if all this [the trial] could not have happened two weeks earlier or two weeks later!" He was full of concern for the well-being of his family: "How do you feel here? Annele, my darling, take care of yourself and of your kidney, don't bend: better wait for me or for my orderly. How is Eri? How is he getting acclimatized? How is the chameleon he caught?"

Jabotinsky promised his wife that "the [Jerusalem] apartment will be cleaned." It was. But the furniture was rather scant, in particular in the beginning. Eri recalls that when his mother was presented with a small working table by his father, she jokingly boasted that all their "movable property" consisted of this table and of the horse Jabotinsky then possessed in his capacity as a British officer. The apartment was large: six rooms, of which two were occupied by Salzman.

On the whole, Mrs. Jabotinsky was pleased with Jerusalem. "She would have been quite satisfied," Jabotinsky wrote to Rosov on February 28, 1920, "but she is suffering from some rheumatic pains. She is already able to make herself understood in Hebrew— in a rather funny manner; Eri speaks fluently." Coming from London, the boy also spoke English fluently, and Russian was his mother tongue.

Jabotinsky's sister and mother left Odessa shortly before the advent of the Bolsheviks early in 1920. They arrived in Palestine in March; Johnny, the son of Mrs. Jabotinsky-Kopp, had come earlier—in December, 1919.

Jabotinsky was overjoyed to be reunited with his mother, whom he had not seen since 1915. According to Salzman, she was then, in spite of her advanced age, "an intelligent, courteous, orthodox lady who always knew how to calm down her big son. . . . Jabotinsky showed much reverence for his mother, always obeyed her, and his filial obedience was touching. . . . His replies to her were full of love and respect, and the same was true in regard to his sister. At every occasion he would say: 'Let us first of all hear the opinion of the women,' meaning his mother, wife, and sister."

Life was difficult in the Jerusalem of those days. Many essential commodities were lacking; domestic help was unobtainable. Jabotinsky refused to be daunted by these everyday hardships. "Let us be a mutual-aid cooperative," he used to say, and everybody would be mobilized to help in the household. He himself would put on an apron and do his bit, cheerfully saying that this was one of the few trades he had learned in the Army. The house was old, with insufficient water, light, and facilities; the furniture was dilapidated, and even chairs were rather few; the guests had to take turns in drinking tea because there was not enough crockery. But all this did not prevent the Jabotinsky house from becoming a preferred meeting place for the intelligentsia of the country. They used to gather there once or twice a week—mainly veterans of Russian Zionism, but also Sefardic Jews and *Sabras;* there was no party distinction—left-wingers and right-wingers, orthodox and freethinkers were equally welcome and equally enjoyed the spiritual climate of the house. The "official language" was Hebrew; whoever forgot the rule and spoke another language had to pay a fine into a National Fund box, which was in the custody of nine-year-old Eri. "Exemption" was granted only to Mrs. Jabotinsky who had just started to study Hebrew, and to those guests who did not know the language. The conversation was quite informal. Sometimes musical evenings were arranged when songs (chiefly Hebrew folk songs) were sung; when in the mood, Jabotinsky lustily joined the chorus. Among the habitués were Trumpeldor, Dr. Joseph Lurie, Dr. M. D. Eder, Dr. Jacques Segal, Dr. I. M. Rubinov of the *Hadassah,* Dr. S. Perlman, and also officers of the Legion: Patterson, Margolin, Samuel. Very cordial were the relations with Pinhas Rutenberg, whom Jabotinsky nicknamed the leader of the "non-Zionist Party in Zionism," while Rutenberg called Jabotinsky the leader of "the stubborn among the Jews."[35] Jabotinsky also took a friendly interest in young Moshe Shertok, who had then returned from his service in the Turkish Army and was rooming on the ground floor of the house. Introduced by Dov Hoz and Eliahu Golomb—labor leaders and soldiers in the Jewish Regiment—Shertok showed Jabotinsky his translations of modern poetry into a beautiful Hebrew and enjoyed the latter's translations from d'Annunzio and Soulari.[36] High English officials also were frequent guests, among them General Storrs, the Governor of Jerusalem, who later wrote in his *Orientations:* "No more gallant officer, no more charming and cultivated companion could have been imagined than Vladimir Jabotinsky."[37] Storrs was pointedly friendly toward the entire Jabotinsky family. Eri recalls that, when he once fell ill, Storrs paid him a visit and said: "When you are well again, come to see me at Government House and I will show you your country."[38]

Jabotinsky himself deeply enjoyed the pleasure—unusual for him—of being a family man. Patterson, who on innumerable occasions was Jabotinsky's guest at his home in Jerusalem, believes that "the years spent by Jabotinsky in Palestine were the happiest in his life"; his home was "the centre of Palestine life at its best and brightest; never was this devoted husband and father more happy than when leading his family in the singing of both Hebrew and Russian folk songs."[39] His intention to leave Palestine and to start "getting rich," which had found so passionate an expression in his letter to Mrs. Jabotinsky in October, 1918, proved to be just a passing mood. On March 28, 1920, he wrote to I. A. Rosov: "On the whole, I have no wish whatever to leave. I feel very well here and think that here I can arrange my life better than in any other country." He maintained a lively correspondence with friends and supporters abroad: with Meir Grossman, whose faithful and ardent collaboration in the struggle for the Legion he gratefully remembered; with I. L. Greenberg, the editor of the *Jewish Chronicle,* who supplied him with valuable information on what was happening in the London political world; with Joseph Cowen in London as well as with the veteran Russian Zionist leaders Hillel Zlatopolsky and Itzhak Naiditsch in Paris; with C. P. Scott, the editor of the *Manchester Guardian,* who often utilized Jabotinsky's reports on the situation in Palestine.

At the same time he worked hard on his Hebrew. His plans included a thorough, and not merely superficial, study of the Talmud and of other basic sources of Jewish religious tradition: one cannot, he argued, write a truly good Hebrew without having absorbed the spirit of the Talmud in its original tongue (which is largely Aramaic). Already at that time he dreamed of preparing a manual of Hebrew for adults and a detailed atlas of Palestine. S. D. Salzman believes that it was then that the idea of his "Samson" novel started maturing in his mind, for he had been making extensive notes on that topic, and showed much interest in the names of men and women of the period of the Judges.

The Tel Hai Tragedy

In October, 1918, an Anglo-French agreement was concluded which divided the provisional administration of occupied enemy territories (O.E.T.A.) into three zones: South (Palestine north to Acre and east to the Jordan) under a British administrator; North (the Syrian coast) under the commander of the French detachment; and East (Trans-Jordan and the interior of Syria) under one of Faisal's officers. Between September and December, 1919, British forces were completely withdrawn from the French and Arab zones. Meanwhile, Arab unrest in the area situated on the frontier between the French and the English zones was growing. Armed raids by Bedouins became a common event. Though not aimed directly against the Jews, they nevertheless created an atmosphere of tension. The four Jewish settlements in Upper Galilee (Metullah, Kfar Gileadi, Tel Hai, and Hamara), where neither French nor British authority had as yet been firmly established, felt endangered. In December, 1919, attacks by Bedouins were reported from Kfar Gileadi and Tel Hai (Joseph Trumpeldor, who returned from Russia in October, 1919, was among the Tel Hai colonists). *Kuntress,* the organ of *Akhdut ha'Avodah,* published an appeal to workers to go to Upper Galilee in order to defend the endangered Jewish positions in that area.

In an article "Metullah and Deschanel," published in *Haaretz,* (January 22, 1920), Jabotinsky gave a different appraisal of the situation. He did not believe that Arab raids were of far-reaching and lasting political significance, so far as the future of Palestine's northern frontier was concerned. He was convinced that with the election of the strongly nation-alistic Paul Deschanel as President of France, the French government would take care of Arab intransigeance. In a later article under the title "Upper Galilee," published on February 28th, Jabotinsky elaborated on this thesis stating that "it is not within our power to put an end to what is going on in the French zone in Upper Galilee." He insisted that, if the purpose of the announced mobilization for Galilee was the actual defense of the Jewish positions in that area, it was devoid of any real importance. If, however, the purpose was again to demonstrate the Jewish right to Upper Galilee by go-ing there and if necessary by dying there, then the mobilization appeal did make sense. At the same time he stressed that now, when the war was over, it must be taken into account that the political influence of martyrdom had considerably diminished.

The question of defending the four exposed Jewish settlements in Upper Galilee was put before the session of the *Vaad Zemani,* which as-sembled on February 22, 1920. Notwithstanding the obvious urgency of the matter, it was only on the third day of the session (February 24th) that it came up for consideration. Jabotinsky was not a member of the *Vaad Zemani,* but he was invited to attend the meeting in which M. M. Ussishkin, then Chairman of the Zionist Committee, and delegates of the Tel Hai colonists also participated. He made a strong appeal to the representatives of organized labor to recall all their comrades from the endangered colonies in Upper Galilee. The gist of his speech, which he summarily transcribed from his notes into his diary the very next morning and published five years later in *Rasswyet* (March 18, 1923), was as follows:

V. Jabotinsky makes an urgent appeal to the labor organization to summon Trumpeldor and his comrades to come back from that part of the country. A systematic defense of the northern settlements is under the present conditions impossible. There are in Tel Hai about fifty people, among them several women; the number of Arabs is estimated at several thousand, and the Arabs are well armed. Under these circumstances it is doubtful whether the envisaged relief group will be able to come through, even if it would not be burdened by carts and provisions. But, as was already rightly stressed by Mr. Ussishkin, the main difficulty lies not there. It is a basic strategic rule that no advance must be made as long as communication (with the advanced force) has not been secured. Otherwise, it is impossible to organize a regular delivery of provisions. If a detachment that is not heavily laden could eventually be smuggled through the Arab bands, this would be completely impossible for carts with heavy sacks, which would have to be sent every week. Such an attempt will therefore inevitably result in a tragedy, or, at the best, in the defenders of the northern colonies being captured and abused by the Arabs. The labor leaders should not reckon with the enthusiastic mood of the youth and not with the mood of this assembly [*Vaad Zemani*]. Any hopes for a quick succor by the [British] Government are problematic; everyone knows the British complacency in such matters. And the hopes for a strong action on the part of the Zionist Commission are certainly absurd.* Trumpeldor and his comrades must be recalled while it is not too late to do so.

Any other course, Jabotinsky insisted, would be irresponsible. He reminded his audience that at the beginning it was asserted that two hundred men would be able to secure the defense of the Jewish positions in the Galilee. That was, of course, simply ridiculous: with such forces it would be absolutely impossible to hold the area; they would be exterminated to a man. Now people spoke of five hundred men. But this number, too, would be unable to hold Galilee. An attempt to do so would also be politically nonsensical. The Zionists had always demanded that the British authorities be responsible for safeguarding every part of Palestine's territory. There was no purpose in trying to defend the Galilee settlements separately from the British.

None of the speakers at that meeting of the *Vaad Zemani* attempted to refute these arguments on their merits, Jabotinsky recalled eleven years later. But they all, including Ussishkin, rejected his stand. It was overwhelmingly decided that defense of Upper Galilee was a matter of national honor, and that men and money must be mobilized.

Jabotinsky had no illusions whatsoever in regard to the seriousness and effectiveness of this *Vaad Zemani* decision. "The influence of this body," he wrote in 1931, "was at that time even smaller than the influence of the *Vaad Leumi* nowadays"; he did not count on the Zionist Commission either. The only body he expected to take action was the workers' organization. Its representatives in the *Vaad Zemani* did not accept his suggestion, but "they have answered my plea with respect and honor, since the relations were

---

*D. Ben Gurion told this writer that at this juncture Jabotinsky turned in the direction of M. Ussishkin and contemptuously exclaimed: "On whom are you relying? On that man? . . ." Ussishkin grew pale.

then as yet not so poisoned,"* and they asserted that the defenders of Tel Hai "can be and will be helped."[40]

In fact, next to nothing was done within the next few critical days. Jabotinsky lived then at the house of Bezalel Jaffe on Rothschild Boulevard, in the very center of Tel Aviv. On the morning of February 25th he eagerly looked for some signs of mobilization: there were none. The situation did not improve in the course of the afternoon and of the following few days. Between February 24th and March 1st, i.e., between the day when the *Vaad Zemani* took its decision and the day when Trumpeldor and his six comrades fell at Tel Hai, "numerous volunteers who registered before the *Vaad Zemani* meeting to go to Upper Galilee and to defend Tel Hai and Kfar Gileadi, received neither the order nor the opportunity to go there," Jabotinsky later recalled.[41]

In an attempt to correct this sweeping assertion, D. Ben Gurion later insisted that, on February 26th, nine men had arrived in Kfar Gileadi, and thirty-five men and girls on the 28th. Among the latter "some were armed, others not."[42] However, even with this correction, it can hardly be doubted that for all practical purposes the decision of the *Vaad Zemani* and the pledge of the labor leaders remained an ineffective gesture. Such reinforcements as reached Kfar Gileadi and Tel Hai did so in a spontaneous, unorganized way, unarmed or scantily armed.** Their arrival certainly did honor to the volunteers' spirit of national duty and sacrifice which Jabotinsky never doubted. What he did doubt and vigorously questioned, was the capability and preparedness of the organized *Yishuv* as represented by the *Vaad Zemani,* the Zionist Commission, and even the labor leaders to do their duty and to make this sacrifice worth while. In this respect his doubts were unfortunately only too well founded. All those who pleaded and voted for the defense of Upper Galilee did pitifully little to remedy in time the admittedly critical situation. The only "action" they bestirred themselves to make was to dispatch a "commission" of six (Dr. M. Eder, Leib Jaffe,

---

*In a conversation with this writer, Mr. Ben Gurion stressed that though the labor leaders disagreed with Jabotinsky in the Tel Hai debate, they did not even for a moment doubt the integrity of his motives, his patriotism, and bravery; this disagreement had at that time not in the least affected their friendliness and their respect for him.

**In the same conversation, Mr. Ben Gurion admitted that practically very little could have been done for the Tel Hai defenders: arms were scarce and difficulties of communication tremendous.

M. Smilansky, Sh. Hefter, J. Baratz, and E. Golomb) "to look into the situation." When this commission finally arrived on March 1st in Ayeleth Haschakhar (20 kilometers—12.4 miles—from Tel Hai), it was already too late: the same day came the news that Trumpeldor and six of his comrades had been killed and that Tel Hai and Kfar Gileadi had to be evacuated.

Behind Jabotinsky's seemingly "heartless" insistence on timely evacuation of the Upper Galilee positions was his realization of the inevitability of such an outcome and his eagerness to save the precious lives of those who were heroically determined to defend them and if necessary to die there. Jabotinsky knew too well the pathetic inefficiency of the leaders of the *Yishuv* in all matters demanding quick and determined practical action of military or semi-military character. As a man with some military experience, he could not indulge in wishful thinking and seriously believe that they would be capable of organizing speedily, of arming and transferring to Upper Galilee even the utterly insufficient cadres of two hundred, let alone five hundred, men. And he fully realized that speed was of the essence, that the fate of the four settlements was going to be decided not within months or even weeks, but within days. It was most improbable that anything like adequate help could have been dispatched in such a short time. The Upper Galilee outpost was therefore bound to be left in the lurch, without even a fighting chance to fulfill its mission, and doomed to perish. Jabotinsky's mind revolted against this thoughtless and irresponsible sacrifice of Trumpeldor and his comrades; and in this he was undoubtedly right.

More controversial appears his analysis of the general political situation. The faith he had put into Paul Deschanel's régime as a bulwark against Arab aggressiveness was hardly well-founded and was not borne out by subsequent events. On the other hand, his contention that the ultimate settlement of the boundaries of Palestine would not be influenced, let alone determined, by Bedouin raids proved to be absolutely correct.

Where Jabotinsky's judgment seems to have failed him was in his minimizing appraisal of the "political value and political influence of martyrdom in our days" (article "Upper Galilee" in *Haaretz*, February 22, 1920). There can hardly be any doubt that the sacrifice of Trumpeldor and his comrades was not in vain. At a memorial mass meeting for the heroes of Tel Hai, held in the courtyard of the Jerusalem *Bet Haam* (People's House), Jabotinsky himself stressed that "their death gives us the right to claim this area." If it was not directly instrumental in determining the frontier delineation in the Upper Galilee, it was only because the fate of this area had been predetermined by other factors. Yet, its "political value and political influence" in Zionism and Jewry proved to be both powerful and lasting. The legend of Tel Hai and Trumpeldor belongs among the most potent and cherished forces in the Jewish liberation movement, and Jabotinsky himself admitted it by naming the youth movement he created and loved above all *Brit Trumpeldor;* the fund established to finance all activities of *Brit Trumpeldor* and of the Revisionist Organization was named "Tel Hai Fund."

Jabotinsky was deeply affected by the tragic death of Trumpeldor and his comrades. The memorial article he published in *Haaretz* read like a poem in prose, Dr. Perlman recalls. Eulogizing the great moral stature of the Tel Hai defenders, he wrote:

> Six of that seed lie buried between Tel Hai and Kfar Gileadi, Jews and Jewesses by the Grace of God. . . . These were the heroes who knew no retreat, these were the maidens true unto death: there are still the like of them in Israel; the whole country, from Metullah down to the Sinai Desert is strewn with such bones.
>
> Rain and dew fall upon you, ye hills of Upper Galilee, Tel Hai and Kfar Gileadi, Hamara and Metullah. *Ein davar* [it does not matter], you were ours, you will remain ours.

While in the jail of Acre, Jabotinsky wrote a "Song of the Prisoners of Acre" in memory of Trumpeldor, in which he said:

> . . . From generation to generation
> No holier blood was shed
> Than the blood of the tillers of Tel Hai.
> Between Ayeleth and Metullah stands a lonely grave.
> It is the blood of one who guards the boundary of our land—
> A one-armed hero.

SIXTEEN

DEFENDER OF JERUSALEM

Encounter with Brandeis

In march, 1919, Jabotinsky was convinced that the British authorities did not want any anti-Jewish excesses and were prepared to suppress them, should anything break out. In the summer of the same year, he no longer had this confidence. He began to suspect strongly that the military administration was not at all loath to see a "little pogrom," which would show the British home government that the Balfour Declaration simply could not be implemented and that the Arabs were determined, and capable, to stop the "menace" of further Jewish immigration to the country. It was in vain that he had been trying to convey the full impact of these apprehensions to the Zionist leadership both in Jerusalem and in London and to stir them up for action.

Jabotinsky, therefore, eagerly looked forward to the visit, in July, 1919, of Justice Louis D. Brandeis, member of the Supreme Court of the United States of America and leader of the American Zionist Organization. He expected to find understanding and support from this distinguished and influential visitor.

These expectations did not materialize. Brandeis noticed the unfriendly, often hostile attitude of some of the highest British military authorities toward Zionism and was, of course, concerned and perturbed by it. But he was loath to believe that this attitude had developed into a fixed pattern, a system, which was endangering the very prospects of the Zionist cause and even the physical safety of the Jewish population.

269

When Jabotinsky met Justice Brandeis, he told him plainly that the administration's policy was bound to result in anti-Jewish outbreaks and did not shrink from using the word "pogrom." This was a notion that was inconceivable to Brandeis in regard to a territory under British rule. He was a firm admirer of the British political tradition and he simply could not imagine that such a thing could ever happen "in the shadow of the Union Jack." When Jabotinsky told him: "We of Russian origin are like hunting dogs who can smell blood from afar," Brandeis answered: "Why do you quote examples from Russia? This is not Tsarist Russia. This is a territory occupied by an Anglo-Saxon Power. It belongs to a completely different world. I do believe in British justice." When Jabotinsky continued explaining the looming danger and insisted that steps should be taken to prevent it before it was too late, Brandeis replied coldly: "Sir, I can only see that we do not speak a common language." To this Jabotinsky retorted: "Your Honor is certainly an excellent judge, but you don't possess a bit of political understanding if you cannot see what is taking shape under your very nose."

This exchange of darted remarks is being reported here on the authority of the late Mark Schwarz, to whom Jabotinsky related the memorable conversation almost immediately after it had taken place. Mr. A. Remba recorded Schwarz's evidence in his unpublished study "Jabotinsky the Defender and Prisoner." Mr. Robert Szold, who was present at the Brandeis-Jabotinsky meeting, did not confirm this report and only stated that "Brandeis listened attentively to Jabotinsky's exposition of the [political] situation." However, he admitted to this author that Brandeis "did not take to Jabotinsky." There undoubtedly was a clash of personalities, which left its mark on all their further relationships, opened a rift between the two men, and kept them apart almost until the end of their lives.

The situation in Palestine remained tense and menacing. The British administration persisted in encouraging the Arab anti-Zionist drive. Jabotinsky denounced this Arab-British conspiracy in an article in *Haaretz* of March 28th. For the past two years, he wrote, there had been a tendency to bring about events in Palestine which would prove to London that Mr. Balfour's declaration must be abandoned. This tendency had brought the country to its present state. Jewish public opinion, however, should not exaggerate the danger, Jabotinsky insisted. The aim of the anti-Zionist forces is a sinister one, but "they may be able to achieve it only if we, Jews, continue to be silent. We have made an unparalleled mistake in having kept quiet." Jabotinsky expressed hope that "this will teach us a lesson. England possesses a sound and deep public opinion, and it is on our side. But public opinion is a tribunal which does not interfere in the dispute unless one comes and states his case. If we do it, we shall win. If we fail, we are bound to lose."

The entire concept of Jabotinsky's Zionist political strategy is clearly recognizable in this early credo. However, it was not followed by the Zionist leadership in either Jerusalem or London. The situation was growing ever more tense and explosive.

First Haganah Commander

At the end of 1919, Jabotinsky called a conference of Palestine Zionist leaders with the participation of Pinhas Rutenberg, Moshe Smilansky, and representatives of the labor groups, to discuss the creation of a self-defense force. Its necessity was unanimously recognized. The discussion revealed, however, a fundamental difference of approach between Jabotinsky and the labor representatives. The latter contended that the self-defense organization must function as an underground body. Jabotinsky was opposed to this concept. He insisted that self-defense in the Land of Israel dare not be like self-defense in other countries—a clandestine body. It must come into the open, so that even in England its existence should be known. Even if there were arrests among its members, it would pay off because of the political significance of such a course. According to evidence given by Pinhas Rutenberg to the military investigation commission, which was appointed by the military authorities after the April riots, this conference decided that for political and practical considerations, the self-defense body should not be a clandestine one; Jabotinsky was asked to organize the manpower for it, and when a sufficient number was enlisted, the authorities must be approached with a request to legalize and to arm the Self-Defense Corps.

After the conference, Rutenberg left for Galilee. When he returned, he learned that Jabotinsky had already organized the first three to four hundred men. Rutenberg further testified that with the situation becoming increasingly grave, "we decided to obtain arms and requested all those among the Jewish population who possessed arms to hand them over to the Self-Defense." "I was not at the time in Jerusalem," continued Rutenberg, "but I know that Jabotinsky had informed Col. Storrs of the existence of the Self-Defense Corps."[1]

The nucleus of such an organization was already available. A few months before Passover of 1920, a group of youngsters had spontaneously decided to establish a clandestine unit named *Haganah* (Defense). After a few weeks of propaganda and underground recruitment, the first *Haganah* group started on rifle-drill under the guidance of a sergeant, a legionnaire from America.[2] But these were small and poor beginnings only, lacking a reasonable chance of growing into a genuine defense force. What was needed was dynamic, expert, and authoritative leadership. They turned to Jabotinsky. He accepted.

It seems important to establish the fact that he did so with the knowledge and on behalf of the Zionist Commission, which was at that time headed by Dr. Weizmann and M. M. Ussishkin. In June, 1920, when already in Acre, Jabotinsky bluntly reminded the Zionist Commission (through Dr. Eder) that "the Self-Defense had been created and organized at the request of the Zionist Commission and with the help of its funds." Dr. Eder fully confirmed this claim and added that "he himself had already stated to Col. Storrs and in the presence of the Committee of Inquiry that the [self-] defense had been organized on the instructions of the Zionist Commission and with its consent."[3] In his evidence at Jabotinsky's trial, Colonel Storrs testified that he asked Jabotinsky, when the latter first urged the arming of his men, "whether the Zionist Commission sent him to speak in their name"; the answer was that "he was not sent but that his action had the countenance of the Commission"; the next day Storrs "met with Dr. Eder who corroborated the accused's statement."* Pinhas Rutenberg shared this task with Jabotinsky, but the main responsibility, both politically and organizationally, rested with Jabotinsky. His military background and great popularity with the youth made him the only man qualified for leadership. He thus became the recognized head of the *Haganah* both by appeal "from below" and appointment "from above."

---

*This and all the following references to the trial of Jabotinsky are based on two sources: (1) The official, very imperfect, minutes of the trial; and (2) A typewritten (single-spaced) eighteen-page memorandum "Proceedings of the Trial of Lieut. Jabotinsky" compiled by Dr. M. Eliash, head of the Zionist Commission's Legal Department, who acted during the trial as "Prisoner's Friend." At the end of the memorandum, Dr. Eliash states that it was "copied from my notes taken during the proceedings and correct to the best of my belief."

In order to build up the cadres of the *Haganah*, Jabotinsky addressed several youth meetings. Not content with propaganda, he started organizing the defense machinery. In March, 1920, he invited one of the youthful initiators of the *Haganah*, Jeremiah Halperin, and, addressing him as "Sir," offered him the position of aide-de-camp in the organization and training of the *Haganah* groups in Jerusalem. "The 'Sir' did it," recalls Halperin. "I had never been called thus until then." He eagerly accepted the offer.

The most urgent job was to get arms. An Armenian arms-runner in the Old City supplied them—at a high price. The arms were deposited in Jabotinsky's and Halperin's apartments, which were the first two *Haganah* armories. Eri Jabotinsky recalls that once his curiosity was aroused by a heavy sack which had been brought to their house by one Zvi Nedava (one of the *Haganah* men) and had been hurriedly put under the bed; he untied the sack at the first occasion, pulled out a gun, and was sternly upbraided by his father.[4]

Haganah units held arms-drills every night; on Saturdays and holidays, hikes were organized and field-drill, grenade-throwing, etc., were taught. Nearly every morning between six and eight, a parade took place in the playground of the Laemel School or at the Bet *Haam* in Zichron Moshe quarter, and Jabotinsky would personally take the rollcall and lead the drill. Fully realizing the explosiveness of the situation, he sternly instructed the men to "guard their tongues, to obey their commanders and not to yield to provocation." His prescription was: "If an Arab walks up to you and insults you, do not answer; never strike first; but if he hits you once, hit back, and twice as hard."[5]

Jabotinsky was very fond and proud of the *Haganah* youth. When Shabtai Djajen, Chief Rabbi of the Sefardic community of Rumania, then on a visit in Palestine, came to see him, Jabotinsky asked him: "Has Your Honor seen a sunrise in Jerusalem?" "No," answered the Rabbi. "Then I shall be very happy to show it to you," said Jabotinsky, and they agreed to meet the following morning at five in the center of the town. After a lengthy walk over boulder-strewn trails, they approached a clearing, where they could see rows of young men drilling and engaging in field exercises. It was a cloudy morning, and the sun had not yet risen, but Jabotinsky said to the Chief Rabbi: "I invited Your Honor to come and see how the sun rises and shines over Jerusalem—here it is! Look and see: the sun rises!"[6]

True to his concept that Jewish self-defense in the Land of Israel must not be a clandestine affair, Jabotinsky conducted the *Haganah's* activities in the open. Elias Ginsburg who, together with other non-commissioned officers recently demobilized from the Jewish Legion, was in charge of the training of the Corps' recruits, states that "it was an open affair, well known to the authorities. A few days before the Moslem festival of Nebi Moussa (Prophet Moses), regular military manoeuvres were staged by the Self-Defense Corps at the foot and on the slope of the Mount of Olives, the seat of the Government, and British officers 'reviewed' our movements through field glasses. . . . The official attitude toward the self-defense organization not only did not appear to be negative but seemed paternal to a degree."[7] Colonel Patterson also testifies that Jabotinsky "had organized the Self-Defense Corps with the full knowledge of the authorities, many weeks before the outbreak . . . his first act on taking command was to inform the authorities of the existence of the Corps, its arming and its purpose."[8]

At the subsequent trial of Jabotinsky, Colonel Storrs admitted that a week before the outbreak of the riots Jabotinsky came to his headquarters urging "the strong desirability of forming a body of Jewish special constables to whom the Government should issue arms," and stating that "he could produce a number of men, the number they wanted." Under cross-examination by Jabotinsky, Storrs "could not remember precisely" whether Jabotinsky had been speaking to him of "his boys with arms" and whether "he gave him to understand or informed him that he would arm these boys when he could." Jabotinsky tried to refresh Storrs' memory and reminded him that he twice—once in the presence of R. Howes, Commander of the Jerusalem police, and P. Rutenberg, and the second time in the presence of Rutenberg and Colonel Bramley—stated that "he was arming the Jewish population to protect themselves": "You asked me, is it true that you arm the Jewish population, and I said yes." Storrs replied again that "he does not remember these conversations." But he did not try to deny the correctness of Jabotinsky's statement, and R. Howes, who followed Storrs on the witness stand, testified that "he himself heard the accused stating that he provided arms for the Jewish Defense Corps." The witness was "sure that the Jewish Defense Corps was discussed as a thing that was already in existence and he himself knew of it in his professional capacity"; he knew that its object was "the protection of Jews against attacks by Arabs; of its methods he knew only that they were doing drill." Witness Dr. Isaak Max Rubinov, Director of the American Zionist Medical Unit, also testified that he was present when Colonel Storrs asked Jabotinsky: "You got in arms?" and received the answer: "Of course, we have arms." Storrs himself could not help admitting that he "never thought of conspiracies" in connection with the work of the organization headed by Jabotinsky, as well "as the openness with which the situation was discussed." Under further cross-examination, Storrs corroborated Jabotinsky's statement that "he was giving his men special training against answering [Arab] provocations." He likewise confirmed that he had received "a telephone message of the O.E.T.A. [Occupied Enemy Territory Administration] asking him who were the Jewish Army manoeuvering on the Mount Scopus," and that "he might have said half-seriously to Dr. [da Sola] Pool that he met the other day some of Jabotinsky's Army."

There can be no doubt that "Jabotinsky's Army" was an open affair. The British administration had categorically refused to issue arms to "Jabotinsky's boys," but they knew of their organized existence and of their being armed.

As the Nebi Moussa week, coinciding with Easter and Passover, approached, persistent rumors were in circulation that during this week a large-scale pogrom à la russe would be staged. The intelligence service of the Self-Defense Corps got hold of an Army circular received by every battalion, which was to be read not only to officers but to sergeants as well, and which started with the following sentence: "As the Government had to pursue in Palestine a policy unpopular with the majority of the population, trouble may be expected to arise. . . ."[9]

The Jews were determined not to let themselves be caught napping. For the purpose of defense, Jerusalem was divided into four sectors, each in charge of a commander responsible to Jabotinsky, who had established his headquarters in a central place on Jaffa Road. However, among the *Haganah* leadership, there was a far-reaching divergence of opinion as to the strategy of the defense.[10] Local leaders, supposed to be experts in Arab mentality, claimed that the Old City with its long-established Jewish population was not in danger. They argued that Arab animosity was directed only against the new immigrants, the "Muscovites," and not against the old *Yishuv*, which was not at all pro-Zionist and had no political or national aspirations. Jabotinsky resolutely discarded these quibbles. His contention was that during a pogrom the rabble rules, and not the politicians; the rabble will first of all attack the weakest and most defenseless spots; they will make no distinction between Jew and Jew and will strike wherever they can. He insisted that particular attention be paid to the defense of the Old City. Yet, it was very difficult to organize such a defense against the violent opposition of this quarter's Jewish population, which was strongly opposed to Zionism and to modern ways of national self-assertion. They had been openly voicing their determination not to let the irreligious and impertinent *Haganah* people entrench themselves in the Old City; this would bring disaster in its wake. Synagogues, the only place where the *Haganah* might have set up its positions in the Walled City, were closed to them, and no owner of a private house would admit a *Haganah* squad. Some orthodox Jews threatened to hand over to the police any *Haganah* man who dared patrol their streets. The best Jabotinsky could do under these circumstances was to concentrate *Haganah* units near the Wall, in the hope, should the need arise, of putting them into action from their positions in New Jerusalem. This disposition, as we shall see, was frustrated by the British authorities.

The Nebi Moussa festival came. Thousands of pilgrims started converging on Jerusalem. On April 4th, the crowd, inflamed by anti-Jewish speeches, started attacking Jewish passers-by and Jewish stores. Soon Jewish blood was shed and the mob rushed into the Jewish quarter to kill and to pillage, shouting: *El Dowleh ma'ana*—"the government is with us." Instead of assisting the victims, the Arab police either adopted a passive attitude or joined the attackers. The pogrom lasted two days and resulted in five Jews and four Arabs killed, and 211 Jews and 21 Arabs wounded; two Jewish girls were raped.

At the outbreak of the riots, *Haganah* Headquarters were established in the house of the Zionist Commission, where two rooms on the second floor had been "requisitioned" for that purpose: the inner room was for Jabotinsky and the other for his aide-de-camp, Halperin, who had to receive messages from liaison men and intelligence agents. One of the latter excitedly reported that at a recent Arab meeting it had been decided to assassinate Jabotinsky in his house the very same night. Halperin went to Jabotinsky's room and relayed the message. "Sir," Jabotinsky angrily retorted, "I have instructed you to bring me verbal messages only when they are really important and permit no delay. . . ."[11] Jabotinsky changed night into day, Salzman recalls. At noontime, he would come home, snatch a short nap, and return to the command post, giving instructions and receiving reports from the guards posted in the dark alleys of Jerusalem, on the roofs, and behind hedges.[12]

Immediately after the outbreak of the riots, Jabotinsky, in accordance with the previously established disposition, dispatched to the Jaffa and Damascus gates two *Haganah* companies, which were posted nearby in New Jerusalem. But they found the gates closed to them and held by British troops whose rifles, bayonets, and machine guns "were directed not against the pogromists but against Jews who wanted to penetrate the Old City and to bring help." Nobody was allowed to enter or to leave.[13] The Jews of Old Jerusalem paid dearly for their anti-*Haganah* attitude. In a letter to the London *Times*, published in 1921, Jabotinsky rightly stated that in the Easter, 1920, riots "the only part of Jerusalem affected by the riots was the Walled City where, owing to the old-world character of its Jewish inhabitants, no local self-defense could have been organized; all the other quarters of the City were guarded by Jewish patrols, with the result that not one casualty occurred there."[14]

Arrest

Hardly was the pogrom over when the British administration started reprisals against the Jewish defenders of Jerusalem. On April 6th, at 7:50 P.M., a house on the North Jaffa road, called *Ravakiah*—a kind of bachelors' abode—was entered by police headed by Captain Jansen. According to Jansen's evidence given during Jabotinsky's subsequent trial, arms (three rifles, two revolvers, and 250 rounds of ammunition) were found in the house and impounded; nineteen *Haganah* members who were stationed there under the command of Elias Ginsburg were arrested.

"On being questioned," testified Captain Jansen, the arrested men "stated that the arms did not belong to any individual, but gave witness to understand that they were communal property belonging to members of the Zionist Commission." The following morning, April 7th, the witness paid a visit to the Zionist Commission where "people connected with the Commission . . . gave him the impression that the arms belonged to a Defense Corps and that the accused [Jabotinsky] was the leader of that Corps." Around 11 A.M. a British military police officer arrived at the offices of the Commission and asked for Jabotinsky, saying that he had a warrant for his arrest. The late Israel Rosov, who was then in the office, invited the officer to wait until Jabotinsky could be found and went straight to Jabotinsky's apartment, where he found him sound asleep on the couch. Rosov woke him up, told him the story, and added: "If you would like to sleep a while longer, we will tell the officer to call again in the afternoon." "No," was the reply, "I am coming right away." Jabotinsky got up, washed, and went along with Rosov. When they arrived at the Zionist Commission, the officer was still waiting.

"I came to find out who is in charge of the *Haganah* in Jerusalem," he said.

"I am," said Jabotinsky without hesitation.

"I have a warrant for your arrest."

Jabotinsky replied calmly: "I have a few urgent matters to settle at home. Would it be all right if I came to the police station at two o'clock?"

"Do you give your word as a gentleman that you will come?"

"Yes."

On the way home, Jabotinsky was anxious to prevent his mother from learning of this sudden arrest and thus to spare her grief. He therefore invited a few friends to join him at a farewell dinner, pretending that he was leaving for Jaffa. Among those invited were Van Vriesland and Mark Schwarz who lived in the same house, as well as Rosov and Pinhas Rutenberg. They gathered around the dinner table and Jabotinsky joked and made fun so as not to arouse his mother's suspicions. When dinner was over, his wife packed a little suitcase; he took leave of his family and arrived at the police station at two P.M. sharp as promised. Dr. M. Eliash of the Zionist Commission's Legal Department accompanied him.[15] Before his arrest, Jabotinsky ordered Halperin to send away from the building every man carrying arms, and to warn anyone entering that the British police might raid the place; he also asked Halperin to act as aide-de-camp to Pinhas Rutenberg to whom he had transferred command of the *Haganah*.[16]

The nineteen *Haganah* members who had been arrested the previous day were taken to Kishleh, formerly a Turkish prison, converted into a police station and a place of detention. The next afternoon, through the paneless windows, they saw Jabotinsky arrive together with Dr. Eliash. After several hours Dr. Eliash reappeared without Jabotinsky. Later, the detainees learned that what Jabotinsky told the authorities in effect was:[17]

"The Self-Defense is not and never has been an illicit organization. You knew of its existence, practically sanctioned it. The arrested men committed no crime. You have no charges against them, except that arms were found in the house they were in. They should be released forthwith. But if you consider them guilty, I, too, am guilty, because I am their leader. If you persist in holding them, you should arrest me as well."

The British authorities obliged Jabotinsky. He was arrested on the spot and taken to the Kishleh police station. For five days, up to his trial, Jabotinsky was held in solitary confinement and was forbidden to have any contact with his nineteen comrades under the same roof. They were all guarded by soldiers of an Indian Lahore regiment who received strict orders to this effect. The nineteen and Jabotinsky were taken for exercise at different times so that they should not meet. This arrangement was probably made in order to prevent Jabotinsky from "briefing" his comrades.[18] Mrs. Jabotinsky and her sister-in-law were permitted to visit him. When the latter suggested that they should bring along his mother, Jabotinsky objected: he did not want the old lady to be upset by the sight of the prison and to have to ascend the steep staircase leading to his cell. It was only later that she learned from *Haaretz* of his imprisonment, insisted on seeing her son, and somehow managed to climb up the steps.[19] Dr. S. Perlman, who also visited Jabotinsky in Kishleh, remembers that Jabotinsky received him "without undue show of sentiment." They swapped jokes; Jabotinsky was gay, cheerful, laughed much and heartily. At the time of Jabotinsky's arrest, Dr. Perlman was in Alexandria. There he met Dr. Weizmann who was on his way to London with a letter from Lord Allenby to the British Prime Minister, Lloyd George. Dr. Weizmann was perturbed by rumors about a planned bomb attempt on General Bols (in connection with Jabotinsky's arrest) and asked Perlman, who was about to return to Palestine, to convey to Rutenberg the request "to restrain the boys"—at least until after his audience with Lloyd George. When Dr. Perlman delivered the message, Rutenberg cryptically said that "*now* we have nothing to fear." He intended to accompany Perlman on his visit to Jabotinsky, but changed his mind at the last moment.[20]

Jabotinsky first met his nineteen comrades when all prisoners were brought for interrogation to a large, stable-like room with scanty military office furniture. They were surrounded by Arab guards with Turkish lashes in their hands, and had to face, in addition to a few local British officers called in as witnesses for the prosecution, an Australian captain as judge and an Arab secretary. At the order of the Judge, the secretary started the investigation by addressing Jabotinsky in Arabic: "What is your name?" There was no answer. The question was repeated in French: *Votre nom, Monsieur?* No answer either. Finally in English: "Will you please tell me your name?" No answer.

The Captain lost patience, banged on the table and angrily shouted: "Why don't you answer?"

Turning to the Judge, Jabotinsky said quietly but firmly:

"Your Honor! I shall not answer a court secretary who belongs to the tribe of the murderers whose attacks upon innocent people, coupled with pillage and raping, are still going on beyond these walls. Furthermore, I shall answer no questions unless they are asked in Hebrew, my language, the language of the Land of Israel and the language of my nineteen comrades."

"There are no nationalities in this Court; there are only officials," the Captain sternly admonished him.

"If this is the case, I shall not reply to this official," was the composed answer.

"Take him out of the room," ordered the Judge.

This was quickly done. But the remaining prisoners firmly clung to Jabotinsky's policy. The Court adjourned. Two hours later they were summoned again; a Jewish sergeant, speaking English and Hebrew, was in the secretary's chair and his opening question to Ginsburg, the first in line, was in Hebrew: *"Mah Sh'meicha?"* (What is your name?).

Hebrew and English became the languages of the investigation.[21]

The Jews of Jerusalem learned that Jabotinsky and his comrades of the Self-Defense Corps were committed for trial, on Sabbath, April 10th. The same day, three hundred-eighty members of the Defense Corps who had not been arrested, signed a petition to the Court declaring themselves at one with the twenty arrested men and asking to be tried together with them. Simultaneously, in all synagogues signatures were collected under a petition expressing full solidarity with Jabotinsky and stating that, although the signatories had not been in a position to participate in the Self-Defense Corps, they would have done so, had it been possible. The Chief Rabbi of Jerusalem, Rabbi Kook, was the first to sign the petition and authorized its signing on the Sabbath by others. Two thousand five hundred Jews signed, among them three hundred women who stated that they had been urging their husbands, brothers, and sons to join the self-defense. The petition was submitted to the Military Court, but was disregarded.

Trial and Sentence

Jabotinsky was arrested on April 7th. On April 8th, Lieutenant Colonel P. L. Beedy, commanding the 8th Brigade and all British troops in Jerusalem, appointed a "Field General Court-Martial on Active Service," consisting of a major and two captains. The trial of the nineteen *Haganah* members, who had been arrested in the *Ravakiah* house, took place on April 10th. Jabotinsky was summoned as a witness and assumed before the Court full responsibility for the creation and arming of the *Haganah*. When he had completed his evidence, he was escorted back to his cell; he had no knowledge of the Court's verdict against his comrades, who were sentenced to three years' hard labor.

Two more days passed. On April 12th, at 2:30 P.M., Jabotinsky was brought to court and handed five charge sheets, three of which carried with them the death penalty. He asked that the trial be postponed until the morrow of the 14th in order to give him an opportunity to study the charges and to prepare his defense. This plea was refused. The trial started the next morning at 9. The accused was thus totally unable to communicate with his witnesses or retain counsel. Applying two months later (on June 14, 1920) to the D.A.G. of the British Army for review of the proceedings of the Court, the English law firm of Devonshire, Golding, and Alexander in Cairo, stressed the "amazing rapidity" with which the arrest, trial, and conviction of Jabotinsky and his comrades had taken place. "This must be unique in the history of English Criminal Law," they wrote. The other peculiarity of the proceedings stressed in the plea was their absolute secrecy: "A Court Martial is an open Court and is only closed for particular evidence and in exceptional matters. We have never known a Court Martial of the Military Court to sit throughout as a close Court, and to rule at the outset that it is a close Court." Another extraordinary circumstance was the fact that the Court was sworn in without the mandatory question of objection to the judges being put to the accused, and the Court refusing even to record this omission: the Court insisted that no Rules of Procedure were incumbent upon it, since the law procedure applicable to Courts Martial did not apply to Military Courts. It was not until later in the trial, when the defense produced a book of standing orders of O.E.T.A. wherein it was expressly said that Military Courts were to be ruled as near as possible, *mutatis mutandis*, by the rules applying to Courts Martial, that the Court agreed to record this important circumstance. But when Jabotinsky stated that he did have personal objections to some of the judges, one of whom was a member of the O.E.T.A., "which was undoubtedly interested in and connected with that case," the Court decided that they "did not think" that the rule concerning objections "applied in that case."

The legal position of the prosecution was an embarrassing one. Originally they intended to charge Jabotinsky with organizing and arming a Jewish Self-Defense Corps, a deed he was ready to admit and to bear the legal consequences for it. But it turned out that none of the penal codes applicable in Palestine—that is, neither the Ottoman code nor British military law, nor any proclamation of the British military administration—contained any article prohibiting organization of self-defense units or distribution of arms for self-defense purposes. The administration therefore took recourse to ransacking the Ottoman Penal Code, which they considered as still valid in Palestine, to trump up the most fantastic charges against the accused.

The first two and the last of the five counts on which Jabotinsky was indicted were of "factual" nature:

1. (a) That in contravention of Proclamation 57, he was in possession of fire arms, to wit, three rifles, 250 rounds of ammunition, and two revolvers found in a certain house, on the 6th April.

(b) That in contravention of the same Proclamation he was in possession of a revolver handed over by him to the Military Governor of Jerusalem on the 4th April, the first day of the disorders.

2. That he in contravention of Proclamation 36 was in possession of Government property, to wit, three rifles and 250 rounds of ammunition found in a certain house on the 6th April.

5. That he in contravention of Article 58 of the Ottoman Penal Code, became aware of the carrying of destructive appliances in Jerusalem, to wit, three rifles and two revolvers, and failed to communicate this directly to the Government, with an evil intent and without good excuse.

Jabotinsky, who conducted his own defense, with Dr. Eliash acting as the "Prisoner's Friend," was able to prove that on charge 1 (a) and charge 2 he had been "already acquitted by a competent court, namely, the Military Magistrate," and raised a "plea in bar of trial."* Most reluctantly, the Court

---

*It is unfortunately not clear either from the official Court minutes or from Dr. Eliash's account who this "Military Magistrate" was, and at what time this acquittal had taken place; the author was unable to find other sources which would clarify this important point.

accepted the plea and agreed to consider Jabotinsky as already acquitted on these two charges.

What remained were charges 1(b) (possession of a revolver), 3, 4, and 5; charges 3 and 4 were formulated as follows:

3. That he in contravention of Articles 45 and 56 of the Ottoman Penal Code, did arm the inhabitants of the Ottoman Dominions against each other with the evil intent of bringing about rapine, pillage, devastation of country, mutual homicide, etc. and that as a result of this action disorders came to be.

4. That he in contravention of Article 58 of the Ottoman Penal Code, framed a conspiracy with more than two people with the execrable thought and the evil intent of bringing about the crimes mentioned in charge 3.

Jabotinsky pleaded "Not Guilty" to all these charges.

With regard to charge 1(b), he established beyond any doubt the fact that Proclamation 57 referred to had been issued on April 5th, while he (and Rutenberg) surrendered their guns to Colonel Storrs at his demand on April 4th.

Charge 3, he claimed, was thoroughly disproved by prosecution and defense witnesses alike. In reply to the question whether he thought the accused likely to have the evil intentions ascribed to him in these charges, Colonel Storrs, who had been summoned by the prosecution, said that he had known Jabotinsky for a year and a half and that he "does not consider him personally a man likely to pursue specifically any of the evil objects mentioned in the charges"; however, he qualified this statement by the comment that he considered the accused "capable of embarking upon a course of actions which may lead to them [to evil objects]." While stating his belief that Jabotinsky had "great influence with the Jewish young men, especially over the advanced youth," Storrs admitted that he "used that influence especially to steady the most excitable temperaments." Colonel B. H. Waters-Taylor, Chief of Staff O.E.T.A., summoned by the defense, declared "most definitely that he does not think that the accused was a person likely to start an organization with the intent to lead to rapine, pillage, etc., etc., as stated in the charge sheet; were he of an opinion that accused is a likely person to have the intention ascribed to him, he would have arrested him a long time ago." In his defense speech, Jabotinsky appealed to the Court "to consider all the evidence produced: not a single witness has ever proved, tried to prove, or hinted at his being possessed with the execrable thought and evil intention, attributed to him . . . [while] the basis, the *sine qua non* of that charge, is the intention, the evil thought to bring about the terrible consequences enumerated in Art. 56 of Ottoman Penal Code."

In regard to charge 4 Jabotinsky insisted that there could be no question of "conspiracy," because everything he did was done with the knowledge of all the authorities concerned: O.E.T.A., Military Governor, Public Security. Evidence given by Colonel Storrs, R. Howes, Colonel Waters-Taylor, and Dr. Rubinov fully substantiated this statement. Replying to charge 5, Jabotinsky established that Article 58 of the Ottoman Penal Code, on which it was based, was "only applicable to dynamite or bombs or similar destructive appliances and is utterly inapplicable to three rifles and two revolvers found in a certain house, and to the failure to report them which was brought as a charge."

Having expertly disposed of the legal aspect of the accusation, Jabotinsky stressed the moral and political background of his actions. Dr. Eliash's account contains a detailed report of Jabotinsky's defense plea, from which some excerpts are quoted below.

Stating that he "assumes the responsibility of having organized the Jewish Self-Defense Corps for purposes of defending Jews from attacks," Jabotinsky stressed that

he had unfortunately been through pogroms before and knows that the only thing that saved the Jewish population was the Self-Defense. . . .

Article 56 [on which charge 3 was based] deals with criminals who arm bands or robbers and assassins for the purpose of bringing about murder, rapine, and devastation of the country. It was sufficiently proved that the only purpose for which he caused certain arms to be shifted from place to place, was for self-defense of the Jewish population against assaults, and the only article of the Ottoman Penal Code applicable to this action was Article 42, which justifies any action taken for the purpose of self-defense and exempts self-defense from any conception of crime.

Quoting the statement ascribed to him by Col. Storrs that he would welcome a chance given to the Jews to account for some of their assailants, Jabotinsky stated that this was part of a lengthy conversation. During this conversation, Col. Storrs tried to explain to him the glory, perhaps from the point of view of Christian morals, of death caused by injustice, and the moral attainments of innocent victims. In reply to that, he [Jabotinsky] explained to Col. Storrs that the impression made on the world by the fact that Jews in Jerusalem were allowed to die like dogs without being given a chance to defend their lives, would be horrible.

. . . And then the moral point of view. . . . What would the world think . . . if such among us who knew of the dangers threatening our people—dangers that, unfortunately, have only too cruelly materialized —the insufficiency of protection and the unreliability of the police recognized by the Administration—if such among us who knew of all that, would have remained silent and inactive and allowed their aged womenfolk and children to be murdered without an attempt at manfully defending them.

Jabotinsky conducted his defense with skill, firmness, and quiet dignity, without undue excitement or provocation. His purpose apparently was not to pose as a hero and to achieve the glory of martyrdom, but to prove the baselessness of the accusation and to justify his and his comrades' action. But the Court was obviously determined not to be influenced by legal or moral argument. Replying to Jabotinsky's plea, the prosecutor, Captain E. P. Quigley, said that "although the intention ascribed to accused in charge 3 was not proved by any evidence, evidence was not necessary in view of the fact of his [Jabotinsky's] collecting arms." When prosecuting the accused for inciting the population, "he did not have in mind the Jerusalem population or the Jerusalem events, but the news of his [Jabotinsky's] arming the Jews may have incited, for instance, the Arabs of Beersheba and brought trouble there." In the prosecutor's opinion, legitimate self-defense "applied to individuals only and not to a body. . . ." He thought it was "a conspiracy though he had no evidence to prove it." In conclusion, Captain Quigley found it necessary "to express his regret that it should have been his duty to prosecute a man of Lieut. Jabotinsky's standing and reputation, of crimes so grievous. . . ."

After the prosecutor's speech, the Court informed Jabotinsky that now he would be removed to the place of detention. This was too much even for one of the Court members, Captain S. C. Kermack, who bestirred himself to correct this statement and asked the accused to wait outside the courtroom "so as not to disclose the Court's set mind of finding him guilty," Dr. Eliash commented. It was only after some time that Jabotinsky was ordered taken back to the Kishleh police station.

He stayed there until April 19th, when sentence of fifteen years' penal servitude was read to him. An exactly similar penalty was meted out to two Arabs convicted of raping Jewish girls during the riots. He was found guilty on charges 1 (b), 3, and 4 (charge 5 apparently could not be sustained even by that Court). To the sentence was added a rider providing for his deportation from Palestine after expiration of the penalty.

"Heptameron" and "Moscobiah"

On the day of his sentence, Jabotinsky was transferred to the so-called "Moscobiah Prison" in Jerusalem. There he finally joined his nineteen comrades who had been tried and sentenced before him. Elias Ginsburg, one of the imprisoned, vividly describes this reunion scene:[22]

"Very soon the door opened and Jabotinsky emerged from the dark corridor into the cell, asking with a smile: 'May I join your company, honorable convicts?' When told that his comrades' sentence was three years of hard labor, he burst out laughing: 'Your sentence compared to mine is just a punishment for sucklings; I got fifteen years of hard labor and expulsion from the country when I am through serving. That is real stuff.' The intention of this tirade obviously was to bolster the morale of his depressed friends; its immediate impact, however, was anything but beneficial. The strained nerves of some of the convicts broke down: at least two of them . . . collapsed and wept hysterically. Jabotinsky vigorously harangued his fellow prisoners:

" 'Hey, you men, be ashamed of yourselves. The whole thing is a joke, a nasty joke in a big game of chess. We are checked today, we will checkmate tomorrow. Fifteen years I am supposed to serve. But I assure you, neither you nor I will stay here for even fifteen weeks.' "

He succeeded in cheering up his men, Ginsburg reports. During the week spent in "Moscobiah," he found ingenious ways of keeping up the spirits of the prisoners, mostly by an inexhaustible flow of story-telling, each story being full of dramatic suspense and of equal interest to the various ages and intellectual levels of his nineteen listeners. One of them later gave this week the name of "Heptameron."

The prison was a veritable dungeon. The cell was situated about three to four meters below street level, with moist and moldy walls. Besides narrow strips of matting on the dirty floor, there was no furniture: no beds, chairs, or benches, no table; a large pail stood in the corner for "hygienic" uses. At 7 A.M. and 5 P.M. the prisoners were taken to the washroom for a few minutes. During the first three days they had no fresh air; on the fourth day they were taken for a fifteen-minute walk.[23] Notwithstanding his officer's rank, Jabotinsky was allotted no privileges. He wore the same prison garb and was subject to the same conditions. The prison barber cropped his hair. Together with the others, he refused the prison food and demanded Kosher soup; when they did not get it, they lived for seven days on Arab bread spread with some finely cut onions. They were deprived of all their personal belongings, candles, combs and books. Their spirit, however, remained unabated: "Every new drop of poison we swallowed with a smile during those seven days," Jabotinsky recalled.[24]

On the evening of the eighth day, they heard in the corridor the sound of many boots, one of which "squeaked in a very aristocratic manner." The outer door of the cell opened, and the sound of an English voice was heard pronouncing Jabotinsky's name. Recognizing the voice, Jabotinsky raised himself on his mattress and asked: "Is that Colonel Storrs?" "Shalom, Adoni," (Greetings, sir), was the answer. They shook hands and Storrs asked Jabotinsky to come with him without bothering about his belongings— the guard would bring them. "There is nothing to bring," Jabotinsky dryly answered. Promising his friends to let them know what happened to him, he followed Storrs to another cell, about twice the size of the one he had just left; it had an iron bedstead with a mattress, and a table with a small paraffin lamp. Indicating "all this splendor with a gesture full of magnanimous grandeur, as though he were the lord of the castle welcoming guests on the threshold of the most historic hall," Storrs told Jabotinsky that this cell was for him personally. He even volunteered to go to Jabotinsky's flat and to bring all the belongings Jabotinsky was lacking (he did not want to send a policeman in order "not to frighten the ladies"—Jabotinsky's wife, mother, and sister), and instructed a young lieutenant, who was with him, to produce "at once, if you don't mind!" two chairs, a washstand, and a somewhat more presentable dining table. "Lehitraot, Adoni" (See you later, sir), said Storrs, departing hastily.

Half an hour later Storrs was back, and not alone. He brought with him Mrs. Jabotinsky and, acknowledging that "this was against all the rules," explained apologetically that "this room badly needs a woman's hand." Then the guard staggered in laden with two suitcases; later, somebody brought chairs, jugs, a washbasin, and a tray, on which were several plates of food and a bottle of wine labeled "Rishon." Storrs left, promising to return in an hour to take Mrs. Jabotinsky back. Asked by Jabotinsky what was going to become of his friends, Storrs magniloquently said: "Don't worry about them. I shall do all I can for them, too." As soon as he went away,

Mrs. Jabotinsky laughingly deflated Storrs' pompous promise: "What has he got to do with it? An order came from London that you were to be treated as political prisoners. . . . And tomorrow morning you are all being sent to Cairo where they are preparing 'apartments' (as Storrs himself put it) for you at the Kasr-el-Nil Barracks."

In the morning Jabotinsky shaved for the first time in eight days, and put on his own clothes, throwing the prison garb under the bed. In the corridor he found his former cellmates, also shaved and in their own clothes, the British authorities having decided to consider all of them as political prisoners. Together with them, however, were the two Arabs convicted of rape. The Jewish prisoners went out into the street in formation, four abreast, in accordance with the rules of marching inherited by the Self-Defense Corps from the Legion; behind them, though keeping a little distance, came the two Arabs.

Although it was still early, and no one in Jerusalem had been informed that Jabotinsky and his comrades were being sent to Egypt, the station was packed to capacity and the crowd enthusiastically shouted *Hedad* to them. The administration found no other day but the Sabbath for transporting the prisoners. Efforts to induce the authorities to postpone the departure until Sunday were of no avail. In order to be able to say farewell to her son, Jabotinsky's old mother was forced—for the first and last time in her life—to travel on the Sabbath. Mr. Shertok overheard Jabotinsky saying proudly: "My wife is a soldier's wife, my mother is a soldier's mother, my sister is a soldier's sister; and I hope that my son will be a soldier's son."[25] A space was cleared to enable Jabotinsky to take leave of his mother, and a special first-class carriage was put at his and his wife's disposal; they had a pleasant lunch in the dining car in the company of Major Smolley, who was in charge of the "party," and his adjutant.

At Artuf and Shorek stations, small groups of Jews greeted the train. In Lydda, "half Tel Aviv" gathered and hundreds of hands started waving handkerchiefs and caps. The military police did nothing to prevent the last four hundred Palestine volunteers, stationed at Sarafend, three miles from Lydda, and still wearing the uniforms of the Jewish Legion, from appearing in full strength; they were headed by Colonel Margolin in person, who stood at attention.

Shortly before sunset the train arrived at Kantara on the Suez Canal. From here, Mrs. Jabotinsky went to Cairo accompanied by Major Smolley, while the prisoners were retained at Kantara according to instructions. Led by Major Smolley's adjutant, they again went into formation—with the two Arabs again lagging behind—and arrived at the prison barracks. Full of good intentions, the adjutant whispered to the Corporal in charge of the prison that Jabotinsky was "in a special category." However, the latter apparently interpreted this recommendation as necessitating the strictest and most severe supervision, and assigned to Jabotinsky the darkest and narrowest cell in the whole barracks—without a bed, a chair, or a window. The good Corporal did it reluctantly and with a heavy heart. Looking around in all directions to see whether anyone was listening, he said with great sadness in his voice: "That is what one gets for fighting for one's country. I come from Ireland, sir."

In the night he came back and asked Jabotinsky whether he would like to take a walk. The offer was gratefully accepted. Then the Irish Corporal, an admirer of those fighting for their country, whispered into Jabotinsky's ear that behind the barbed-wire fence there were some Jewish soldiers who wished to speak to him. The visitors proved to be Jabotinsky's former "clients," American volunteers, whom he had defended before the Court Martial on charges of mutiny. Thanks to his efforts, they had received relatively light sentences and were serving their term in Egypt; in the meantime an amnesty had been granted. Most of them left for America, but these men had decided to stay on in Palestine and, having learned that Jabotinsky was in Kantara, had come secretly to tell him that—as Jabotinsky himself put it—"there was nothing to say, and anyway, it could not be expressed." With trembling voices they said to him: "Sir, it breaks our hearts to see you here. . . ."[26]

SEVENTEEN
THE PRISONER OF ACRE

Life in Acre

The administration's decision to send the convicted men of the Self-Defense Corps to Egypt to serve their sentences was the first attempt to deport Jews from Palestine, and the precursor of the deportation to Eritrea and Kenya of the *Irgun*, Stern group, and Revisionist suspects in 1941–47. This move was blocked by Lord Allenby who declared that he did not want to have any "Palestine criminals" on Egyptian territory; the prisoners were brought only as far as Kantara, on the Egyptian frontier; from there they were sent back to Palestine via Haifa. Their destination was the fortress of Acre, which the British converted into a prison.

From Kantara to Haifa, Jabotinsky traveled in a first-class compartment. At the Haifa railroad station, where he and his comrades arrived toward evening, they were welcomed by a large crowd singing *Hatikva* and shouting: "Long live Jabotinsky! Long live the Jewish Legion! Long live the *Haganah!*" Food, rugs, and pillows were handed to the prisoners.[1] According to a report by Winston Churchill in the House of Commons, Jabotinsky "walked from the [railroad] station to the civil gaol, which is quite near, and spent the night in separate quarters."[2] There he received a delegation of local Jewish leaders headed by Selig Weizmann (uncle of Dr. Weizmann) which, *inter alia*, happily informed him of the impending appointment of Sir Herbert Samuel as the High Commissioner for Palestine. Jabotinsky's reaction was, however, significantly unenthusiastic. He said to the delegation: "Gentlemen, I am afraid that this appointment may prove disastrous

291

to our interests in Palestine. . . . A good 'goy' would be now better for us.
. . .A Jew's hands will at best be tied by his supercautiousness. . . . He will
find himself in an awkward position unless he is supremely courageous."[3]

Next morning the prisoners were taken by train to Acre, and then, in
a motor ambulance, transferred from the station to the fortress, where, as
Churchill reported, Jabotinsky "was handed over to the civil authorities by
the British officer escorting him." He entered through a narrow bridge that
spans the deep moat separating the fortress—a medieval structure with
one side toppled down into the sea—from the prison, mounted the narrow
winding steps up to the top floor, and found himself in the living quarters assigned for the *Haganah* culprits. They consisted of six cells, without
doors; five of them had but a bit of matting as furniture; the sixth—a large,
dusty room with a high ceiling and brown tiled floor—had a big table, a
few wooden benches, and a small kerosene lamp. On the wall were posted
Prison Rules instructing the wardens to treat the prisoners politely, and in
case of mutiny—to shoot at their legs.

At the beginning, the transfer to Acre caused consternation in Zionist circles. They contended that the Acre prison, an old Turkish building,
was notorious as one of the worst jails in the world. They also argued that
there Jabotinsky would be cut off from Jewish surroundings.[4] These apprehensions turned out to be exaggerated. The detainees were considered and
treated as "second divisional" (political) prisoners. While far from comfortable, the quarters assigned to them were quite habitable. Answering
repeated inquiries by Brigadier General Colvin in the House of Commons
on June 29th, Winston Churchill gave a fairly accurate description of the
conditions of Jabotinsky's imprisonment:[5]

> He [Jabotinsky] is confined in Division 2 [simple containment], and is in
> separate quarters. He is allowed to wear his own clothing, and has his own bedding.
> Any food he wishes may be sent to him. He is allowed exercise in the open every two
> hours under supervision, and is given facilities for bathing, and medical treatment
> by a doctor from outside the prison if necessary. He has facilities for reading and
> studying. His wife visits him twice a week, and he is allowed interviews with Zionist
> friends at any time.

The prisoners had arranged their living quarters as follows: of the three
cells facing the sea, the smallest was chosen by Jabotinsky as his sleeping
quarters; two others had to house fourteen of his comrades; in another

cell, facing the Acre plain, the remaining five were lodged. The last two cells were to serve as kitchen and washroom. Jabotinsky was elected "commander," and it was decided that each of the twenty inmates would have to take turns in mopping the floor, serving the food, and washing dishes. The "commander" firmly insisted on his "inalienable right" to share equally with others the task of cleaning the premises and dishwashing; he was particularly proud of "not having broken a single dish in the process."[6]

The attitude of the prison administration was stern but fair. There was no chicanery on the part of Captain Andrews, the Chief Warden, and the prison guards, once they had found out who their wards were, became quite friendly. They would even violate the rules by leaving their rifles in a corner while sitting down with the prisoners for tea and cake. Except for strong drink, there were no restrictions as to the food the prisoners were allowed. A special committee to take care of their needs was organized in neighboring Haifa by Selig Weizmann under the chairmanship of Dr. Hillel Yoffe; the Zionist Commission allocated the necessary funds for this purpose. A certain Shisha, the only Jew living in Acre, catered for the prisoners. Jabotinsky later jokingly commented that, when they had been liberated, Shisha went into mourning.[7]

Though officially allowed to see her husband only twice a week, Mrs. Jabotinsky visited him daily, sometimes even twice a day, usually accompanied by her son Eri. Abandoning their Jerusalem apartment, they took quarters in the Hotel Herzlia in Haifa, traveling to Acre either by car or by train. For Jabotinsky, it was the first opportunity in years to devote much time to his son; he taught the boy Roman history, using the text book of Charles Seignobos, the noted French historian, and had long talks with him on a variety of subjects.[8]

There were no restrictions on visiting by friends and admirers, and many of them took advantage of this liberality. Jabotinsky was rather exasperated by the abundance of guests. "Visiting me," he used to complain, "has become a kind of fashionable pastime for Palestine Jewish society."[9] Friends and opponents alike were eager to pay homage to the "Prisoner of Acre."* Even those of his visitors who did not belong to Jabotinsky's partisans were deeply

---

*The noted American-Jewish philanthropist Nathan Strauss cabled to Jabotinsky: "What can I do for you?" Jabotinsky asked Salzman to cable back: "Thank you." S. Salzman, *Min ha'Ovar*, p. 292.

impressed by him. Miss Henrietta Szold wrote from Jerusalem on June 21, 1920, that she had never sympathized with Jabotinsky's ideas—"he is militant and aggressive." "But when one listens to him, they [these ideas] assume charm as well as cogency. My visit to him will be a memory I shall always want to recur to."[10]

Jabotinsky kept himself busy during the ten weeks of his imprisonment. He translated into Hebrew several Sherlock Holmes stories: he firmly believed that the power of observation, stress on logic, inventiveness, and courage featured in this kind of literature would be both interesting and useful to Jewish youth. He also worked on a translation of Omar Khayyam's *Rubaiyat*, and wrote a poem, "The Song of the Prisoners of Acre," in memory of Joseph Trumpeldor. His major occupation, however, was his translation of Dante's *Divine Comedy*. Shortly before his arrest, the publishing house of A. I. Stiebel in America had asked him to undertake this translation; the fee was £2,000. While in Acre and in need of funds, Jabotinsky asked for, and received, an advance of £500. He worked hard to fulfill his obligation. But, as he wrote to S. D. Salzman ten years later, the assignment "surpassed my knowledge of Hebrew; I had to compose first a dictionary of rhymes."[11] Nevertheless, he succeeded in translating several stanzas. Itamar Ben Avi, an exacting connoisseur of Hebrew, says that it was done "in one of the most exquisite Hebrew styles it was ever my privilege to read."[12] At the same time, Jabotinsky frequently lectured to his comrades on a wide variety of topics, general and Jewish alike: on Ireland, the Negroes in America, Chekhov and Gorki, Herzl and Achad Haam (the latter's theories he called "milk-and-water Zionism"), the policies of Weizmann and Ussishkin, which he severely criticized, etc. There were also less serious occupations. For two hours a day, sports were practiced: in the large central room the prisoners ran, jumped, and played football. An orchestra was formed, with plates, washing bowls, forks, spoons, and even benches as instruments. Hebrew, Yiddish, Russian, and English songs were often chanted.

During the first weeks of imprisonment, spirits were high and the mood confident. Shortly after their arrival in Acre, they learned that Field Marshal Allenby had reduced Jabotinsky's sentence from fifteen years to one year, and those of nineteen others from three years to six months, without hard labor. This drastic reduction was, no doubt, a half-hearted admission that the first sentence had been a legal and moral monstrosity. But neither Jabotinsky nor Jewish public opinion was ready to accept such a lame gesture as either just or satisfactory. The London *Jewish Chronicle* said editorially on May 7th:

> Public opinion will argue that either the first punishment was deserved, in which case its swift and summary reduction almost to vanishing point is inexplicable, or that it was not merited, in which case there was clearly a serious failure of justice. The mere curtailment of the sentence cannot obviously settle the matter, for it exonerates neither Lieut. Jabotinsky nor his judges, being one of those unsatisfactory compromises which pleases nobody.

Two weeks later, a *Jewish Chronicle* editorial insisted that

> the question now is whether the sentence should not be wiped out altogether. . . . A man like Jabotinsky would be more useful if definitely enlisted in the service of Palestine regeneration than if left to nurse a serious grievance in gaol.

In the same issue of the paper there appeared an interview with Jabotinsky, which is characteristic of his mood at that time:

"I don't regret anything I have done. I am happy to be imprisoned for such a cause as defense of unprotected Jews against blood-thirsty hooligans. I have been in my life many times in prison, but that was in Russia. I would never have imagined that one day I should be imprisoned in Palestine, and by British officials, and the hardest sentence of all should be inflicted upon me by them. . . . I am not ashamed of my sentence. I am proud that we Jews can show the others that we are not natives with whom anyone can do as he likes. . . ." Referring to the Military Court that imposed the sentence, he said: "These judges will no longer judge me, but I should be able to judge them."

Worldwide Repercussion

At that early stage, it looked as if Jabotinsky's hope to be able to exchange places with his judges was to materialize soon and thoroughly. Jewish and non-Jewish public opinion in Palestine, England, the United States, and in many other countries seemed to have strongly and wholeheartedly endorsed the cause of the "Prisoners of Acre," as Jabotinsky and his fellow prisoners came to be called, and no effort seemed to be spared in order to obtain their release and vindication.

Jerusalem's Jewish community learned of the sentence imposed on Jabotinsky and his comrades on the evening of April 19th. Shocked to their depths with horror and indignation, the Jews— Sefardic and Ashkenazi alike—closed their shops. *Haaretz* of April 20th described the situation in the city: "Since early today, the Jews of Jerusalem and all the suburbs have gone silent. . . . All the schools, institutions, shops, etc. are closed. Nobody on the streets; no trading, no newspapers, nothing. A total strike." Around noon, the authorities ordered the shops to reopen and the pictures of Jabotinsky to be removed from the windows. Later, police started to confiscate the pictures and threatened those whose shops would remain closed with a fine of £50 (about $230). The *Vaad Zemani* and the Rabbinate proclaimed the 26th of April a day of general strike, fast, and mourning, with the sounding of the *Shofar* in all the synagogues of the country. As manifestation of the unanimous support by Palestine Jewry for the "Prisoner Jabotinsky," the *Akhdut ha'Avodah* Party appealed to all parties to put his name at the head of the respective slates they would present at the forthcoming elections to the *Assefath ha'-Nivkharim* (Assembly of the Elected). This appeal was published and supported by all papers, with the sole exception of *Doar Hayom*, which was then the organ of the Zionist Commission.[13] Jabotinsky's name was the first on every slate throughout the country.

On April 28th, the *Vaad Zemani* addressed a memorandum to General Bols expressing the "feeling of wrong and embitterment aroused by the pogrom in Jerusalem and the arrest and sentencing of the members of the Self-Defense." The memorandum stated that the Jews of Palestine "will not rest until the following demands have been granted to them:

"1. The liberation of the sentenced members of the Self-Defense, Jabotinsky and his comrades, and a review of their trial.

"2. The appointment of a representative commission of inquiry, to investigate the pogrom in Jerusalem and the manner of its preparation."

A few weeks later, the *Vaad Zemani* telegraphed to Allenby complaining that Jabotinsky and his comrades were still imprisoned. Allenby answered that he regretted "not to see any reason to revise the verdict of the court."

On behalf of the Zionist Headquarters, the English law firm of Devonshire, Golding, and Alexander in Cairo appealed to the Advocate General at the Allenby General Headquarters for a review of the Court proceedings against Jabotinsky and his comrades. The appeal was rejected.

Efforts to obtain the liberation of the "Prisoners of Acre" came not only "from above"; the general public and various organizations were no less eager and active.

In every Jewish settlement there circulated (in English and Hebrew) a petition to Lloyd George, then Prime Minister of Great Britain, which described the detention of Jabotinsky and of his comrades as "national humiliation" and demanded their "immediate release and the immediate revision of the trial."[14] Thousands of signatures were collected under this petition. The Convention of the Akhdut ha'Avodah Party appealed to the British Labor Party for Jabotinsky's release. The organization of demobilized soldiers in Palestine cabled Lloyd George, requesting the release of Jabotinsky; they also cabled to the Chairman of the Association of British Demobilized Soldiers, asking the Association to intervene to the same end.[15]

Excitement about Jabotinsky's plight was not limited to Palestine.

When the news about that vindictive sentence reached London, a storm of public indignation was aroused. Patterson recalls that a leading British statesman, on seeing the telegram announcing the verdict, was heard to remark: "The Military in Palestine must have gone mad."[16] In an interview with the Director of the Jewish Correspondence Bureau, Dr. Weizmann revealed that everyone at the Allied Conference at San Remo (April, 1920) to whom he spoke about the Jabotinsky case (including Lloyd George's secretary, Philip Henry Kerr) "was very upset that a man like Jabotinsky should be tried in such a cruel way."[17] In the House of Commons, the Secretary for Foreign Affairs, the Lord Privy Seal, the Secretary for War and Air, and the Secretary for the Colonies were flooded on April 27th, 28th, and 29th, May 3rd, 4th, and 11th with parliamentary questions from Lieutenant Commander Kenworthy, Mr. Killey, Lieutenant Colonel Asheton Pownhall (Jabotinsky's former commander in the 20th London Battalion), Colonel Wedgwood, Robert Cecil, and Brigadier General Colvin. The questions repeatedly put by them were: 1. Would any appeal be allowed? (Kenworthy); 2. Would an inquiry be made "as to the circumstances which had caused such a sentence"? (Pownhall); 3. "Is this Mr. Jabotinsky the same gentleman who raised the Jewish Battalion?" (Kenworthy); 4. "As this [Acre] prison is reserved for felons, will he [Lieutenant Jabotinsky] be transferred elsewhere, pending the consideration of the sentence?" (Colvin); 5. "Are we to understand that a precisely similar sentence to that passed on Mr. Jabotinsky was passed upon Moslems for the rape of Jewish women?" (Lord Cecil); 6. "Were instructions sent to see that he [Lieutenant Jabotinsky] was properly treated in prison?" (Wedgwood).[18]

The British government was obviously embarrassed by this unpleasant affair. Churchill, who had to reply in the name of the government to most of the questions, for weeks dodged a straight reply. His standard answer was that he was awaiting "further telegraphic report from Lord Allenby on various points, including especially the case of Lieut. Jabotinsky" (April 27th). It was not before June 29th, when the first indignation had somewhat quieted down, that Churchill found it advisable to give an exact report on the conditions of Jabotinsky's imprisonment in Acre.

The reaction of the leading organs of the English press was also very strong.

In a leader entitled "The Mandate for Palestine" (April 27th), the *Times* called the verdict an "apparently vindictive punishment. Lieutenant Jabotinsky is well and honorably known in this country. . . . It is true that, since the end of the war, he has made journalistic attacks upon the British Administration in Palestine—a crime that may well seem to the objects of his criticism to merit a lengthy term of imprisonment." The *Manchester Guardian* wrote editorially on May 3rd: "If Mr. Jabotinsky was in possession of firearms, if he organized a Defense Corps and even used it (which, however, he is stated not to have done), there is *prima facie* evidence that he may have been perfectly justified, owing to the failure of the military authorities to discharge their proper duties."

The entire English press in London, as well as the provincial papers, prominently and sympathetically featured a report by the Jewish Correspondence Bureau, released by Reuter's Agency, in which it was stressed that "Jabotinsky is to the Jews what Garibaldi was to the Italians." The London *Daily Herald* on April 24th added that Jabotinsky had "much influence on Jewish public opinion throughout the world, and his imprisonment was bound to create consternation."

The consternation predicted by the *Daily Herald* proved to be both worldwide and strong, in particular in the United States.

A cablegram from New York received by the London Jewish Correspondence Bureau vividly described the Jewish reaction to Jabotinsky's sentence:

> Jewish public opinion in the United States has been deeply stirred by the news of the sentence of 15 years' penal servitude passed in connection with the Jerusalem disorders on Lieutenant Vladimir Jabotinsky, the Zionist leader and founder of the

Jewish Legion. All the Jewish papers there devote leaders to the sentence, which they describe as an insult to the Jewish people.

The London *Evening Standard* (April 28, 1920) published this cable under the heading: "American Appeals for Man Who Founded the Legion." *The New Palestine*, the official organ of the Zionist Organization of America, wrote editorially on April 30, 1920:

> London newspapers are calling Vladimir Jabotinsky "The Jewish Garibaldi." He deserves this distinction and will wear it nobly.... He is taking the consequences of his act without a whimper, without a whine, content that he sought to serve, to save. [The editorial expressed the hope that] Jewish intervention on his behalf will be in keeping with his own dignity. No one would resent more than Jabotinsky the whining plea that he must be forgiven because "he didn't mean to do it," and that he be spared, for pity's sake, the hardships of imprisonment. . . . He must be released because he was right.

An extraordinary American Zionist Convention, held in New York City on May 9th and 10th, unanimously "went on record in identifying itself and standing sponsor to the cause of Jewish self-defense in Palestine, as personified by Lieut. V. Jabotinsky." A resolution voted by the Convention, hailing "the gallant efforts of Lieut. Jabotinsky," said: "We look forward to his complete vindication and his speedy return to active participation in the rebuilding of Palestine."[19]

A Major Policy Problem

Protests and demarches, both in Palestine and in England, did not produce the expected results. Those forces that had been responsible for the pogrom in Jerusalem and for the sentence on the city's defenders were not ready to yield, and proved to be sufficiently powerful to maintain this attitude. It was becoming increasingly clear that only a bold frontal attack against the entire military regime in Palestine, which would reveal its shocking inefficiency and wickedness, could break the deadlock. The case of the "Prisoners of Acre" had to be made a major policy problem and to become a point of departure for a grand-scale Zionist political offensive.

Neither the *Vaad Zemani* in Palestine, nor Gentile friends of Zionism in England, nor Zionist organizations in various countries could, of course, authoritatively launch such an offensive. Major policy problems were the prerogative of the Zionist Executive in London and of the Zionist Commission in Jerusalem. Neither was prepared for a major political move. Their line was to avoid a showdown. The situation did not, in their view, warrant any "dramatic gestures." This attitude was reflected in the manner in which the official Zionist leadership dealt with the Jabotinsky case.

They had systematically and deliberately played down the case. Dr. Weizmann asserted that this was in accordance with Jabotinsky's own wishes: "I was in Palestine at the time of the arrest of Jabotinsky. The matter was then not considered a serious one, and Jabotinsky himself asked that I should do nothing."[20] In fact, Dr. Weizmann was not in Jerusalem when Jabotinsky was arrested on April 7th; he arrived on April 10th, and immediately left for Egypt with a police escort, so that he had no opportunity to be asked by Jabotinsky to "do nothing." It is also most unlikely that Jabotinsky would ever have uttered such a wish; nor could the attitude of the *Yishuv* possibly be interpreted as "not a serious one." What seems to be accurate is that Dr. Weizmann faithfully abided by the "do nothing" precept. According to his own statement, it was not before the Allied Conference in San Remo that he "cabled to London" in connection with the Jabotinsky case. This writer was unable to find the text of this cable in the Central Zionist Archives in Jerusalem. Its content can, however, be guessed from the interview published on April 26th in the *Manchester Guardian*. In that interview, Dr. Weizmann, while stating that the sentence on Jabotinsky "amounts to judicial murder," found it proper to admit that "technically he [Jabotinsky] is guilty,no doubt":

> He organized the Jewish Defence Corps against an occurrence which the British assure us would never occur. It did occur. In any case, it is monstrous to give this man, who was guilty, if of anything, of the political offence . . . such a sentence as that given to the two Arabs who were proved guilty of raping Jewish women.

Dr. Weizmann condemned, only the vicious severity of the sentence; he was ready to grant that Jabotinsky was "guilty of the political offence." He upheld this apologetic position also at the twenty-first annual Conference of the English Zionist Federation: he did not so much as mention the responsibility of the British administration for the Jerusalem pogrom; neither did he, even by implication, justify Jabotinsky's action. He merely asked the Conference that they "shall respectfully appeal to the Mandatory Power to undo the injustice which has been committed on one of our best men, on Vladimir Jabotinsky." It was "a blot on British justice," he said, "that this man should remain a day longer in the prison of Acre. We respectfully pray the Prime Minister to set Jabotinsky and his colleagues free at once."[21] This was exactly the kind of a pro-Jabotinsky plea against which *The New Palestine* editorial had warned: "The whining plea that he [Jabotinsky] must be forgiven because 'he didn't mean it,' " and not a manful demand that "he must be released because he was right."

Also far from firm and consistent was the attitude of the official Zionist leadership in Palestine as represented by the Zionist Commission. We have seen that when the Military Court's verdict became known, the *Vaad Zemani* together with the Rabbinate proclaimed April 26th as a day of mourning and protest to be observed by the entire Jewish community. However, on April 25th, the Conference of the Principal Allied Powers at San Remo assigned the mandate for Palestine to Great Britain. When news of this decision reached Palestine, the Zionist Commission ordered that the day of April 26th be converted from a manifestation of protest and grief into a jubilant festivity. In Jaffa and Tel Aviv, this order was disregarded by the Jewish population: a general strike was proclaimed and three protest meetings were held, at which rabbis and leaders of all political parties spoke. But in Jerusalem—the seat of the Zionist Commission and of the Palestine government—and in the colonies not a word of protest was uttered and a joyful mood reigned.[22]

Jabotinsky and his Acre comrades deeply resented this easy switch from sorrow, anger, and protest to jubilation and festivity. The Leftist *Kuntress* (organ of *Akhdut ha'Avodah*) wrote on May 14, 1920, that they were "in a very depressed mood." They were angry "not so much against the accusers and inciters, as against the Jewish community that had betrayed them." This mood found its expression in a passionate appeal to Palestine Jewry not to let their case be sidetracked and dragged on indefinitely.

The "Prisoners of Acre" issued two proclamations. The first was in the name of the Self-Defense Corps as such (its style reveals the authorship of Jabotinsky). It contained merely a demand for the revision of the trial and for the punishment of those responsible for the events of Nebi Moussa.

The second was a "Letter to the Jewish Community" written in Jabotinsky's personal name—though, he stressed, his attitude was "shared by most of my friends in Acre."

Directed against the entire official Zionist policy as represented by
Dr. Weizmann, this message accused Palestine Jewry of having forgotten
the "Prisoners of Acre":

The *Yishuv* has forgotten us and the lessons of our imprisonment. True, they
read articles dedicated to us; they buy pictures and sometimes even send cables;
but you all know that all these vanities are of no value—for you do not continue
our struggle. You received from Dr. Weizmann and from the Zionist Commission
instructions not to persevere in the struggle, to "pacify" the people.

Jabotinsky insisted that it was "an unparalleled crime to comply with
these instructions," which proved that the official Zionist policy did not
profit from the bitter lessons of the recent past: "we did neither learn, nor
forget."

Weizmann has never understood the political position in the country, never
realized the significance of previous events as precedent for the future; during those two
years of continuous pogrom he had stifled the outbursts of protest until the
impudence of our enemies grew and ripened and took deep roots, and we became
hefker [ownerless property] in their eyes. During last Passover he saw for himself
the results of his tactics—but even after the slaughter he did neither learn nor
forget. And now he is continuing his blind policy that is bound to bring us ever
greater damage.
. . . The Zionist Commission knows and sees the situation: it also knows
the value of promises, statements, agreements which are lacking real guaranty.
And while knowing the terrible damage that these tactics of silence, this lack of
complaints from Palestine have caused us until now, they have converted a day of
fasting into a day of jubilation, banned the protest meetings and sent cables full of
rejoicing all over the world, without even making a single allusion to the national
mourning.

Jabotinsky bitterly complained that Jewish public opinion still did not
realize what had to be done in order "to put an end to this moral shame."

If we demand the elimination of this criminal foreign [British] Administration,
we must first of all get rid of our own [Zionist] Administration who committed the
lowest of all crimes: they abandoned their wounded wards in order to go and to
dance *mayofis* before the murderer.
And where is the young generation? And the Parties that pray morn and eve
for struggle and revolution [referring to the Socialist parties]? I do not understand

them. I do not understand any of you at all. And it only pains me that in my lack
of understanding I have trailed behind me into prison these young sufferers who
believed in me.

Both proclamations were hectographed and widely distributed all over
the country. They caused quite a stir and a lively discussion. Several leading personalities of the *Yishuv*—among them Eliezer Ben Yehuda, Professor
Nachum Slouscz, Dr. Joseph Klausner—defended the traditional policy of
caution and moderation. In labor circles, on the contrary, Jabotinsky's fervent appeal found much understanding and sympathy. *Kuntress* wrote: "We
confess the crime committed by Palestine Jewry who for two years treated
this question [of defense] with "so what?", hoped for miracles and did not
plan concrete actions, did not understand the value of the Jewish Battalions and did not give them moral support so that they might remain in the
Army until after peace is signed. . . . We confess the crime committed by the
Battalions themselves who did not foresee the events, did not realize their
own value. . . . They called the man who forecast what was to be expected an
impostor—him who warned us of what would happen."

Obviously embarrassed by the attack from the prison, the Zionist
Commission started negotiating with Jabotinsky.

At the meeting of the Commission on June 4th, Dr. Eder gave a report
on the conversation he had with Jabotinsky in his jail cell: on behalf of all
his co-prisoners, Jabotinsky demanded that all over Palestine protest meetings be organized, which would demand the removal of those responsible
for the riots and the immediate liberation of the prisoners; these protests
should be transmitted by the Zionist Commission to the governments and
newspapers of Europe and America. The Commission, for its part, would
have to demand from the British government at least the immediate liberation of the Acre prisoners. Jabotinsky warned that "if the prisoners were
not released, they had resolved to go on hunger strike, and were prepared
to resort to even more desperate expedients."

Of the three members of the Commission who took part in that
meeting, two (Dr. M. Eder and Dr. A. Ruppin) voted for the acceptance of Jabotinsky's demands; M. M. Ussishkin, the Chairman, voted
against. At the meeting held five days later, a characteristic discussion arose regarding the wording of the cable to be sent to the British
Prime Minister in the name of the Commission. The draft submitted

by Jabotinsky contained the following words: "They were sentenced for deeds which were not only authorized by ourselves, but . . ." Dr. Eder manfully defended this sentence. The majority, however, was "opposed to so strong an expression," record the minutes, "feeling that the word 'authorized' could do harm to our political situation." It was decided to use the word "endorsed." The cable sent to Lloyd George read in its final form as follows:

> Jabotinsky and twenty comrades now seven weeks in prison for an attempt to save the lives and honor of Jewish men, women and children. They were sentenced for deeds which were not merely endorsed by ourselves but would be approved not only by every Jew but by every person of honor. Most earnestly we appeal to you to have this great act of injustice rectified, to order the immediate liberation of these men so unfairly sentenced.

The cable was signed by M. Ussishkin, Dr. M. Eder, Dr. A. Ruppin, and Bezalel Jaffe.[23]

Meanwhile, the prisoners decided to carry out their intention of going on hunger strike. On June 6th, they officially notified the Governor of Haifa and Captain Andrews, Commander of the Acre garrison, that—unless set free before June 14th—they would begin an indefinite fast. Jabotinsky was against this move, but when the proposal was accepted by the majority of his comrades, he promised to go along.[24]

The news of the impending hunger strike spread rapidly through the country and caused quite a stir. The prisoners were flooded with letters beseeching them to rescind their decision. On the eve of the day designated for the strike, they had the visit of two delegations: one from *Akhdut ha'Avodah,* and one representing the entire organized Jewish community. Both delegations used every conceivable argument to dissuade the prisoners from their "fatal and futile" step. The decisive intervention, however, seems to have been that of Rabbi Kook, who sent a moving letter to Jabotinsky.[25] Jabotinsky answered that he and his comrades were deeply grateful for the sentiments expressed in the letter and, yielding to it and to the insistence from many other quarters, decided to call off the strike. On June 14th, the Zionist Commission cabled to Zionist Headquarters in London: "Acre prisoners decided to give up hunger strike." The deadlock continued.

Amnesty and After

However, the days of the military administration in Palestine were numbered. Soon after the San Remo decision, Sir Herbert Samuel, a Jew and a Zionist, was appointed High Commissioner to institute a civil government.

On June 22nd, the Jewish Correspondence Bureau reported that Sir Herbert Samuel was going to signalize his entry into office by proclaiming an amnesty for those—Arabs, Christians, and Jews alike—who had been sentenced in connection with the riots in Jerusalem; the amnesty was to include Jabotinsky.

When the High Commissioner arrived in Palestine on June 30th, his intention to amnesty Jabotinsky with his comrades and the two Arabs on the same level became a certainty. There were reasons to believe that Jabotinsky and some of his colleagues would refuse to be amnestied, especially in this combination. The Zionist Commission requested Selig Weizmann to use his influence with Jabotinsky to induce him not to reject the amnesty. He visited Jabotinsky in Acre together with Yechiel Weizmann and Mrs. Jabotinsky. When they left at midnight, the prisoners started discussing the issue; by 2 a.m. the majority decided— against Jabotinsky's advice—to accept the amnesty.[26]

On July 8th, Herbert Samuel arrived in Haifa, where he solemnly declared that amnesty had been granted to all those imprisoned in connection with the Jerusalem riots. The same morning, Captain Andrews announced to the prisoners the news of their pardon with a string attached: they were to be brought back to Jerusalem under guard. Jabotinsky balked. He told the Captain in the name of the entire group that they would go back as completely free men, or they would not budge from jail. He won. The same night all prisoners were released unconditionally.[27]

They spent the first night in a Jewish house in Acre. Early Friday morning, many friends arrived from Haifa, insisting that Jabotinsky must spend the first Sabbath of his regained freedom amongst the Haifa Jewish community. He accepted the invitation. The Hotel Herzlia, where Jabotinsky put up, "was literally covered with flowers," recalls Uri Kessary. In the evening, a mass meeting took place on the flat roof of the Hotel Halprin, in the very heart of Arab Haifa. According to Uri Kessary, many believed that Jabotinsky's speech at this meeting had been "the boldest, the mightiest speech of his life: he criticized, he foamed, he was full of anger; he warned against the illusions about a Jewish High Commissioner, whose Commission of Appointment was written in English."[28]

Interviewed about his plans by a *Jewish Chronicle* correspondent, Jabotinsky said that he proposed to leave immediately for Jerusalem to reorganize the Jewish Self-Defense Corps, which, he hoped, "will not be needed again." He also expressed the hope that recruiting for the now very small Jewish Battalion would soon be allowed: "And here also I have to do work." Turning to politics, he said: "It is some slight satisfaction to know that those men who were so glad of the opportunity of getting rid of me [meaning the military administration] and who had the foresight to order my deportation after fifteen years, have now themselves been compelled to leave the country which they so signally failed to understand. I only hope that Sir Herbert Samuel will not commit the same mistakes as his predecessors."[29]

On Monday, July 12th, Jabotinsky left by train for Jerusalem. His son Eri remembers that on the way some ingenious pickpocket had managed to cut out the pocket of his trousers together with the wallet, leaving Jabotinsky without a cent. He arrived at 6:30 P.M. An immense crowd gathered at the railroad station to greet him; "all Jerusalem" was there. British police, mounted and on foot, maintained order. Before Jabotinsky could step down on the platform, dozens of hands lifted him shoulder-high and carried him bodily to the *Hadassah* car that was waiting for him. Later that evening, about three thousand persons gathered in the courtyard of the Laemel School. Jabotinsky arrived together with his mother, wife, and sister. Exemplary order and complete silence reigned among the crowd, giving way to a mighty roar of *Hazak ve'Ematz* (Courage) while he mounted the rostrum.

Several speakers representing the *Haganah*, the Zionist ruling bodies, and the central institutions of the *Yishuv* greeted Jabotinsky and his comrades. In the name of *Vaad Zemani*, Dr. Jacob Thon made a moving appeal to Jabotinsky: "You, Jabotinsky, had been the creator of the Jewish Legion. At a time when the whole world had turned away from 'militarism,' you came to the Jewish masses and instilled in them the military spirit, which you considered to be the need of the hour. You demanded order and discipline from us—and for this we owe you gratitude. Now, we expect that you, in turn, will show an example of order and discipline in our ranks and that you will join us in the great work ahead." A letter from Rabbi Kook was read, in which the leader of religious Jewry sent to his "beloved brothers led by Jabotinsky, the hero with such a great soul," his heartiest greetings to this feast of the joy of their freedom. He expected them to become "the messengers of peace tidings for all of us."[30]

There was in many of the greetings, enthusiastic and sincere as they were, an undertone of concern and uneasiness: what would Jabotinsky's attitude and line of conduct be now that he was liberated? Was he coming back to freedom in a mood of bitterness and frustration, eager to square accounts with those Zionist leaders whom he had so vigorously attacked from his prison cell, or was he prepared to disregard the past and to cooperate loyally and wholeheartedly with the leading institutions of the *Yishuv* and of the Zionist Organization? And what would his attitude be toward Sir Herbert Samuel whom the entire *Yishuv* hailed as a second Nehemiah, come to establish the Third Jewish Commonwealth, and about whom Jabotinsky was known to have uttered some frankly critical remarks?*

In his concluding speech at the Laemel School meeting, Jabotinsky dispelled these apprehensions. He undoubtedly did much thinking, soul-searching, and arguing with himself during the three days that followed his release. There is, of course, no way of knowing what was going on in his mind in these critical days between Haifa and Jerusalem; but it seems to be a reasonable conjecture that he had to wrestle with a great temptation.

He was returning to liberty as a universally recognized and acclaimed national hero: his popularity was at its peak. There was a strong temptation to utilize this position for a determined attempt to smash the present Zionist leadership, whose policy in his opinion had been a complete and dismal failure, and to assert himself as the bearer of a new policy. It was probably just the easy obviousness of this enticement that made Jabotinsky discard such a line of conduct. He was loath to speculate for politcal purposes on the halo of a hero and a martyr; it would be a cheap and vulgar speculation, one not to his taste. He decided against such a course and, with the "extremism" that was so characteristic of him, chose the diametrically opposite one: the course of all-out loyal cooperation with the dominant forces in Palestine and Zionism, putting his energy and reputation at the disposal of a common effort.

---

*It is significant that in his *Memories* (London, 1945), Herbert Samuel managed not even to mention with one single word the Jewish Legion, the 1920 riots, Jabotinsky's sentence and its subsequent quashing.

This was a decision difficult to reach. But having decided upon such a course, he expressed it clearly and forcefully in his address at the Laemel School meeting.

He deliberately minimized his and his comrades' "prison suffering" and stressed that they came not as critics but as allies whose purpose was "peace and work." The time had come for the constructive work of building. While referring ironically to the Court that convicted them and to some Jerusalem officials, he reiterated his faith in British justice, which would clear them from the charges. He paid glowing tribute to the new High Commissioner, whom he described as a man "embodying the best in the Jewish and in the English people" and as "the noblest gift the Jewish people had ever received." Insisting that full support must be given to Sir Herbert Samuel, he stressed that this attitude also implies "constructive criticism." He even found a good word for the "courteousness shown by the Arabs in the Acre prison" and stated that "incitors and assailants were not typical of the Arab people." Speaking confidently of great problems and hopes, Jabotinsky stressed the necessity of "vigorous discipline."[31]

There was nobility in this display of goodwill and of eagerness to discard old grudges, to work in harmony, to serve actively after months of enforced isolation and idleness. When he arrived in London seven weeks later, the *Jewish Chronicle* correspondent who interviewed him noticed that Jabotinsky[32]

certainly looks none the worse for, and does not show any sign of dampened or chastened spirit by reason of prison experiences of which, as a matter of fact, he speaks very lightly, dismissing the episode with a shrug of the shoulders. Few men who have been sentenced to fifteen years' penal servitude, even when afterwards reduced to a few months' imprisonment and subsequently amnestied, would have got over the shock so completely and so quickly. Mr. Jabotinsky is burning with the zeal and energy, of which he seems to have an inexhaustible supply, to take his rightful part in the re-building of our nation in Palestine. "The past is past," he observed, "the dead are dead, let us look forward to the living future. That is all we need to worry about."

The only exception from this almost benign mood was his attitude to the manner in which he and his comrades had been liberated. In a conversation with the correspondent of the London *Jewish Chronicle*, immediately after their release from Acre, Jabotinsky said:[33] "The fact that an amnesty was granted, which in itself implies that we were considered at fault, certainly cannot satisfy our demand for justice; but that the instigators of the whole pogrom should also have been pardoned at the same time, proves that the new High Commissioner is willing to place us of the Self-Defense Corps on the same standing as those who caused the whole trouble. It is thus impossible for us to let the affair stand as it is."

He acted accordingly. "When I came from Acre to Haifa," he told the Twelfth Zionist Congress in August, 1921, "I was mad. I telegraphed [Sir Herbert] Samuel: 'Don't make this mistake! Better leave me here in Acre, but don't put me on the same level with a blackie.' " (Answering interruptions from the floor, Jabotinsky explained that he had in mind moral blackness, and not the color of the skin.) Knowing that just at that time an international Zionist Conference was sitting in London, he told himself: "All my friends are there, they will surely understand in what position I am being put by Samuel, they will protest."[34] On July 10th, he cabled from Haifa to London:

> Please communicate to the Conference: notwithstanding my protest, Mechutan [code name for the High Commissioner] issued amnesty and included pogrom instigators. Wording of the proclamation makes no difference between us and them. This forces myself and my friends into irreconcilable local opposition. You know at whose request I had undertaken my work. Now I am denied retrial and placed by an authoritative Jew on the same level as pogrom makers. I apply to the Conference for defense of my honor and demand energetic protest and action. I shall consider approval or even silence about this insult in any address from the Conference to Mechutan as abandonment of my defense by the Zionist Organization and shall draw the only logical consequence. Don't commit the terrible mistake of forgetting that justice is more important than sham harmony and that our meekness about official blunder and injustice had already proved itself fatal to both Administration and Zionism in Palestine.

In his Congress speech, Jabotinsky stressed that he "loyally addressed [this cable] not to his personal friends, but to the Chairman of the London Conference, Mr. Louis D. Brandeis," who "put the cable in his pocket and did not show it to the Conference."

It is true that the London Conference did not voice any protest against the improper way in which Jabotinsky had been liberated and that his cable had not even been conveyed to the Conference. However, in fairness to Justice Brandeis, it must be stated that the cable, the original of which the present writer has seen in the Zionist Archives in Jerusalem, was not addressed to Brandeis personally or to the Chairman of the Conference, but to "Zionburo London," which is the cable address of the Zionist Headquarters. Whoever was responsible for not communicating Jabotinsky's message to the Conference, it was not Brandeis. It is to be regretted that, still smarting under the insult of the year before, Jabotinsky mistakenly ascribed to Brandeis an action incompatible with his moral stature. There was hardly much understanding and sympathy between the two men, but from that to suppressing an appeal for help was to go a long way down, and Brandeis was not a man likely to do that. It is strange that none of Brandeis' friends and supporters at the Twelfth Congress so much as tried to correct Jabotinsky's assertion and that nothing was attempted after the Congress.

Jabotinsky's insistence on the unacceptability of the amnesty as final settlement of his and his friends' case was by no means based only on outraged pride. At a reception organized by the Jerusalem Jewish community on July 13th, he emphasized that the prisoners of Acre were sentenced for "banditry" and that, legally, this conviction still stood. There was, of course, the possibility of an appeal in England, but legally there was no appeal against an amnesty. The High Commissioner wrote him that, having amnestied them, he had no other possibility to give them satisfaction; should they, however, strive for the annulment of the verdict, he would support their demand.

It was in the main with this purpose in mind that Jabotinsky left Palestine on August 20, 1920, to arrive in London on September 1st. Somewhat in contradiction to his previous stand, he recognized in an interview with the *Times* correspondent that in releasing the prisoners of Acre and in restoring to them their civil and political rights, Sir Herbert Samuel "did a wise and noble thing"; he added, however, that "amnesty should not preclude the revision and quashing of unjust sentences, and that is what we shall demand."[35] Four weeks later he addressed an official letter to Dr. Weizmann in the latter's capacity as President of the Zionist Executive, stating that he had employed the first month of his stay in London in obtaining legal advice and was now satisfied that action aiming at the formal annulment of his and his comrades' sentence and at obtaining "legal satisfaction for their unlawful imprisonment . . .

can and must begin." He then raised the delicate question of financing such an action:[36]

> As the organization and arming of the Jewish Self-Defense Corps had been undertaken at the request of the Zionist Commission, I now have the honor to ask you kindly to confirm that the Executive is prepared to finance the Action, the cost of which naturally cannot and should not be borne by ourselves.

Jabotinsky asked for a written reply. Three days later, he was informed by the Acting Political Secretary of the Executive that his letter was "receiving attention."[37] A copy of it was sent to the Zionist Commission in Jerusalem in order "to ascertain their view."[38] Apparently without waiting for reply from Jerusalem, the London Executive on October 19th stated that it was "willing . . . to support Mr. Jabotinsky if he applies to the Army Council . . . to the best of their ability." But in a letter dated November 15th, the General Secretary of the Zionist Commission informed London that "anxious as this Commission is that the matter should be fully cleared up in accordance with the wishes of Mr. Jabotinsky and his friends, we can take upon ourselves no financial responsibilities in this respect." Upon receiving this reply, the London Executive on December 31st explained that the promise of support given on October 19th "did not mean financial support of any kind."

The correspondence summarized above makes strange, almost incredible reading, but every one of the quoted letters is on file in the Central Zionist Archives in Jerusalem. Both the Zionist Commission and the Zionist Executive bluntly refused to finance a legal action by men who had defended Jews in Jerusalem at their direct request, had been sentenced and imprisoned for that, and were now trying to upset a defaming verdict.

True to his philosophy of never taking "no" for an answer, Jabotinsky proceeded with the legal action on his own responsibility. On December 21, 1920, he engaged the London law firm of Whitebook and Storr, paid them out of his own pocket on account of Counsel's and Solicitor's fees an advance of £50, sent the receipt to the Treasurer of the Zionist Executive, and asked for reimbursement. In the meantime, Dr. Weizmann started negotiating with Jabotinsky about his joining the Executive, and under these circumstances it had obviously become impossible to persist in refusing him financial assistance in his legal action.

The action was successful. In March, 1921, the official Reuter's Agency published a communiqué that, "after reference to the War Office in London and consultation with legal authorities," the Commander-in-Chief in Egypt had "quashed all the proceedings of the military court held in Jerusalem in April 1920, for the trial of Lieutenant V. Jabotinsky and nineteen others, who were charged with being concerned in the disturbances which took place in Jerusalem in that month."[39] As a face-saving device, the communiqué added that "an exception is made with regard to the conviction of Lieut. Jabotinsky having a revolver in his possession"; but no legal or other consequences were drawn from this somewhat nebulous statement. Together with his nineteen comrades, Jabotinsky had won his case.

TRIAL AND ERROR OF COALITION VENTURE

EIGHTEEN

IN THE ZIONIST EXECUTIVE

First Steps in London

Jabotinsky arrived in London with his wife and son on September 1, 1921. He was met by a large number of enthusiastic admirers. Representatives of all major London papers interviewed him. The impression he made was described by the *Times* (September 10th): "Jabotinsky is a thickset, clean-shaven, dark man of medium height. His personality suggests great energy, and his appearance is youthful for a man who has been connected with such great events."

In the name of his liberated prison comrades and in his own, Jabotinsky expressed gratitude "to all those in England—journalists and politicians—who defended us during our imprisonment, and particularly for the powerful intervention of the *Times*," and he added: "I am glad to state that we left our prison as true and devoted friends of England, and as staunch admirers of British justice as we had been ever before."[1]

Jabotinsky's first efforts were devoted to quashing the Military Court's sentence; in this he was successful. But uppermost in his mind was the necessity of saving the Jewish Legion from final disbandment, and its possible revival. He said in his very first interview with the correspondent of the *Daily Express*: "While I am here, I am going to do my best to further the cause of the Jewish Regiment. I feel convinced that if Palestine were garrisoned by a Jewish regiment as an official part of the British Army, much good would be done."[2]

Profoundly convinced as he was that re-establishing the Legion was of paramount importance, Jabotinsky realized that under the then prevailing conditions this task could be undertaken only through the instrumentality of the governing bodies of the World Zionist Organization. In wartime it had still been possible to conduct the crusade for the creation of the Jewish Legion practically singlehanded, without help from, and indeed against the strong opposition of, the Zionist leadership. The situation in 1920–21 was different. The Zionist Organization was then considered and treated by the British government as the representation of world Jewry in all matters concerning Palestine. No individual political action had the slightest chance of success, and Jabotinsky had no intention of building a Zionist political machinery of his own. Upon his release from Acre, he made up his mind to integrate himself fully and unreservedly with the collective Zionist effort, and when he came to London, he acted accordingly. He was willing and eager to cooperate wholeheartedly in every major aspect of this effort.

The first Zionist body to seek Jabotinsky's active cooperation was the *Keren ha'Yesod* (Palestine Foundation Fund), which had been created by the Annual Zionist Conference held in London in July, 1920. The amount required for the building of the Jewish National Home was fixed at £25,000,000 distributed over five years. The national levy of the *Ma'aser* (tithe), deeply rooted in Jewish tradition, was held up as an example. The new institution was conceived as a non-partisan, all-Jewish fund, formed for purely constructive colonization purposes.

The initiators of the *Keren ha'Yesod*, Messrs. I. Naiditch and H. Zlatopolsky—old friends and admirers of Jabotinsky—invited him to collaborate in the launching of this new Fund and in directing its activities. He joined the Board of Directors and was put in charge of the Press and Propaganda Department. Jabotinsky felt strongly about the importance of the Fund and became its ardent patriot. "Jabotinsky set to work with all the energy and talent he was blessed with by the Almighty," recalled Naiditch in 1930. "The standard work on the *Keren ha'Yesod*—'The Keren ha'Yesod Book'—was prepared by him. There was no branch of Zionist activities in Palestine that was not dealt with in this book. As the editor, Jabotinsky went over every single article in this collective work with the utmost care and invested much of his ability in this book, which has become the very basis of the *Keren ha'Yesod* activities."[3]

It was typical of Jabotinsky that his name as editor does not appear on the cover; throughout the 187 pages of the text—even in the chapter dealing with the Legion—the most attentive reader would be unable to come across

Jabotinsky's name at all, though the anonymous editor had been most lavish in mentioning dozens of names connected with the preparation of the
book and with the various fields of Zionist work. A brief introductory note
stresses that "while pursuing the task of welding the various articles into
one coherent scheme, the Editor has not thought it desirable to subdue the
expression of individual tendencies and sympathies. Obviously the chapter
on 'Agricultural Colonization' could only be efficiently written by a believer
in the supremacy of the plough, that on 'Industrial Possibilities' by an adherent to the rather opposite school of economic thought, and that on 'Cooperation' by a supporter of socialistic ideals. As in Zionism, so in the *Keren
ha'Yesod* and in this 'Keren ha'Yesod Book,' there is room for all shades of
opinion."

The "Great Cabinet" Vision

Devoted as he was to the *Keren ha'Yesod* work, Jabotinsky saw in it
merely one aspect of a much larger problem which the Zionist movement
had to face and to solve.

In the speech made in Jerusalem after his release from Acre, he pledged
himself to active cooperation with the then Zionist leadership. But he was
far from being satisfied with both the policy and the composition of this
leadership. He felt strongly that the Zionist movement had to have a decisive influence on the appointment of any future High Commissioner of
Palestine; that it had to oppose vigorously the anti-Zionist practice of the
Palestine administration; that without the re-establishment of the Jewish
Legion there could be no security for Zionist colonization. He accused the
Zionist Executive, formed at the London Conference, of having failed to
realize the vital importance of those demands. He was also opposed to the
narrow base on which it had been established: organized Palestine *Yishuv*
was not represented, and the work was largely concentrated in the hands of
a very small circle of "irreplaceable persons." Jabotinsky's views on the state
of Zionist affairs were shared by a group of London Zionists; some of them
had fought together with him for the Legion idea in 1915–17; others were
old friends, who had recently arrived from Soviet Russia. They were known
as "the opposition group."

Jabotinsky came to London with a vision of a new, broad, and truly
representative Zionist leadership. In his speech at the Carlsbad Congress
in August, 1921, he said: "What I wanted . . . was an attempt to create a

Great Zionist Cabinet." The Great Cabinet, as Jabotinsky visualized it, had to be based on a limited but clear program which had been agreed upon by Dr. Weizmann and himself. Speaking at the Congress in Dr. Weizmann's presence, Jabotinsky categorically denied that the agreement they reached was based on "mutual concessions":[4]

> I would never have come to Dr. Weizmann and demanded concessions on his part, as I would be unable to offer any counterpart, for I was not making any concessions. I went to Weizmann (after Messrs. Naiditch and Zlatopolsky did me the honor of believing that they need me in the *Keren ha' Yesod*) to ask him: "I haven't seen you for a long time; during this time many things have changed; maybe now we are in agreement?" Had Weizmann said that we were not in agreement, I would never have dared to demand concessions from the leader of Zionism. I think that Weizmann, too, would never have undertaken to demand concessions from me. We have, however, established that we did agree, because life had brought him and myself to certain changes.

The agreement, as Jabotinsky related it to the Congress, comprised four essential items:

1. Should the time come for "a big change on the Mount of Olives" (meaning the appointment of a new High Commissioner), the Zionist Organization was to demand the right to have its say.

2. Concerning the Legion, "there was no need of an agreement, because in this question Dr. Weizmann and myself have cooperated for several years."

3. In any reorganization of the Zionist Commission, the Palestine *Yishuv* must be represented.

4. Reconstruction of the Executive along the lines indicated above.

Negotiations about reconstruction seem to have started soon after Jabotinsky's arrival in London. Late in November, 1920, the *Jewish Chronicle* reported that the Zionist Executive had "entered into a compact with the opposition group of which Mr. V. Jabotinsky is the leader." The terms of compact as reported by the paper largely coincided with those actually agreed upon.[5] There were, however, within the opposition group itself considerable doubts as to the wisdom of abandoning their independent position and entering the Executive.

Before finally joining the Executive, Jabotinsky asked the advice of a group of close friends who for years had shared his views and participated in his battles. Joseph Cowen invited to his house Dr. M. Schwartzman, I. M. Machover, M. Grossman, and Jacob Landau. At this gathering, Jabotinsky reported that he and Dr. Weizmann had come to a full agreement on the main actual problems of Zionist policy and work; that he would be able to enter the Executive together with Cowen and Richard Lichtheim, who both adhered to this program; that a sufficient budget was going to be secured for the work of his department; and that he hoped to be able to work in full harmony with Dr. Weizmann and exert the necessary influence on the entire Executive.

Cowen, Schwartzman, and Machover were in favor of joining the Executive; but Grossman and Landau strongly disagreed. They warned that, without an organized political force behind him, Jabotinsky would be practically at the mercy of the then dominant Zionist coterie. Jabotinsky accepted the majority's opinion.[6] He was eager "to do things," to shoulder collective responsibility. To justify his action, he published in the *Tribune* an article, "Two Paths," in which he argued that there were two possible paths to be followed in politics: one was to tear down a fortress by an assault from without; the other was to conquer it by working from within. He had chosen the second, for he believed it to be the only practical and expedient one. This belief in the possibility of "conquering from within" was based largely on the renewed friendship and harmony with Dr. Weizmann. The latter, however, seems to have had a peculiar notion about the part Jabotinsky was to play in the new set-up of the Executive. When Leon Simon, one of the staunchest Zionist "minimalists" in Weizmann's closest circle, remonstrated with him about the "extremist" Jabotinsky being allowed to join the Executive, he received a reassuring reply: "He will eat out of my hands!" Sir Leon later dryly commented: "The event proved that Weizmann misjudged his man."[7]

Yet, at that time relations with Weizmann appeared to be harmonious, almost idyllic. The main difficulties came from the London exponents of the "Brandeis group," Julius Simon and Nehemia de Lieme. On January 20, 1921, they addressed a letter to Dr. Weizmann and Nachum Sokolov, in which they strongly objected to Weizmann's agreement with Jabotinsky. Their contention was that by this "private pact" Dr. Weizmann "bound himself privately, without consultation with them, to an arrangement which destroyed any prospect of a homogeneous Executive with themselves as members." They also protested against the fact that, according to the agreement, "the Jewish Legion was to become an accepted and important part of

Zionist policy."⁸ Simon and de Lieme therefore announced their resignation from the Executive.*

The first immediate result of the attempt to create a broader Executive was thus the narrowing of its base. Neither were Jabotinsky's earlier attempts in other directions much more successful. In his Congress speech he reported that several leading Zionists were approached: "Please come, we shall work together. The Organization is undergoing a grievous crisis; we are facing tasks that cannot be handled by one single group alone, we are in need of all political and business forces; we shall unite, we shall divide the work between various departments, and thus find a way. But from all sides I have, unfortunately, received the same negative answers. A gentleman from Paris wrote: 'I will not work with such a clique as you are.' Similar answers came from the others."

The vision of a truly "Great Cabinet" collapsed. The plan narrowed down to a partial reconstruction of the Executive. This took place at the meeting of the Executive on March 2, 1921, which the official minutes describe as "the first meeting," meaning that a completely new body had been established. According to the minutes, Dr. Weizmann "submitted a scheme for the formation of a Provisional Executive" and announced that "the Presidium (Mr. Sokolov and himself) were to call on Messrs. Cowen, Jabotinsky and Lichtheim to cooperate with them and to form together with them an Executive having externally a provisional character, but exercising internally the rights and duties of an Executive of the [World Zionist] Organization." Both Cowen and Jabotinsky had specified the points on which agreement providing for their joining the Executive was based, and "all present expressed their concurrence with this view," state the minutes. "Dr. Weizmann thereupon declared that the Provisional Executive was formed."⁹

In the new set-up of the Executive, Jabotinsky assumed important and responsible tasks. Together with Dr. Weizmann and N. Sokolov, he headed

---

*This was, however, not the only reason for their resignation. There were also other, more fundamental, differences. The "Brandeis group" claimed that the "political phase" of Zionism was basically over and that the entire strength and pathos of the Zionist Organization must be concentrated on practical colonization work in Palestine. This work, they insisted, had to be conducted primarily by private initiative and private capital; they accordingly opposed the prevailing role which was ascribed to national capital as represented by the *Keren ha'Yesod*. Already at that time they suggested that prominent non-Zionists be invited to occupy key positions in the conduct of Zionist affairs.

the Political Department. He was also in charge of the Publicity Department, which at the same time functioned as the Press and Propaganda Section of the *Keren ha'Yesod*.[10]

The "Great Cabinet" Jabotinsky dreamed of did not materialize. Yet he
was not ready to give up this dearest hope of his. At the Twelfth Congress
he made a last ardent appeal "to every one who sits here and is capable of
doing something for Zionism: let's build bridges to each other; there is work
for all of us. Besides viewpoints on which we disagree, there still are those
on which we do agree. Let's work together.... Then, maybe we will succeed
[in establishing] what we have once ruined: the Great Cabinet of all those
who accept the foundations of historic Zionism, who possess sufficient tol-
erance to compile a program which would be satisfactory to everybody and
for which we all would be able to work."

This certainly sincere and well-meant, but somewhat naive appeal, was
of no avail. The Simon-de Lieme group refused to rejoin the Executive;
nor were the absent Nordau and Rutenberg ready to lend their names and
cooperation. The appeal in itself is, however, characteristic of Jabotinsky's
1921 mentality: he passionately wanted an all-embracing Zionist unity and
apparently firmly believed in the possibility of a program which would be
"satisfactory to everybody." This belief is the more surprising since both
Jabotinsky's personality and his past experiences had certainly made him
the least likely man to preach this kind of ideological vagueness and to expect people to respond to such preachings.

In the Zionist Executive, Jabotinsky worked hard, both in the Political Department and in the *Keren ha'Yesod*. Until the end of 1920, the entire family lived in Hotel London on Lancaster Gate; later they took a small
apartment at Stafford House, Maida Hill West. When in London, Jabotinsky
always was at his desk at 75 Great Russell Street precisely at 9 A.M. He also
traveled extensively on behalf of the Executive. There was little opportunity
for taking care of his physical well-being. A lunch, hurriedly snatched at the
nearest "Lyons" tea shop; nights spent in hotel rooms; innumerable meetings
and appointments, with no time for relaxation and physical exercise—all this
could not fail to affect Jabotinsky's robust constitution. In September, 1922,
he was forced to consult Professor Goldstein in Berlin, who found no organic
deficiencies—"heart, lungs, liver and all this is in ideal condition," Jabotinsky
wrote to his sister from London; the diagnosis was: "nerves and overfatigue...
too corpulent, which increases fatigue." Goldstein prescribed "rest and sports

... for at least six weeks not to come to the office and not to attend meetings, not to travel on railroads, and not to live in hotels." Jabotinsky took a four weeks' leave of absence from the office—"I could not afford six weeks"—and "every morning I am now taking a bus and going out of town till 4 P.M."[11] This brief rest cure helped. When, one month later, Jabotinsky came to Palestine, his nerves were again in perfect order and there was no trace of overfatigue.

Haganah vs. Legion

As could be expected, Jabotinsky devoted much of his time and work in the Executive to the problems connected with the security of Palestine Jewry. In this field, he had first of all the task of combating, and disposing of, the dangerous scheme of creating a "mixed Arab-Jewish Force."

A Middle East Conference held early in March, 1921, in Cairo and Jerusalem under the chairmanship of Winston Churchill rather reluctantly endorsed Sir Herbert Samuel's scheme of a Jewish-Arab force, based on voluntary enlistment and kept up at the expense of the Palestine government.

When reporting on Sir Herbert Samuel's project at the meeting of the Zionist Executive at which Jabotinsky's entry in the Executive was ratified (March 3, 1921), Dr. Weizmann did not express any opposition to it. Jabotinsky, on the contrary, saw great dangers in this scheme. His contention was that very few Jews and very many Arabs would volunteer for service in such a body and that the Jews "could not and would not remain in a mixed militia, just as little as in a mixed police force." The result would be a militia mainly composed of Arabs, which of necessity would be anti-Jewish and anti-Zionist. It would mean "the creation of a pogrom army."

The minutes record Dr. Weizmann as stating that "the arguments of Mr. Jabotinsky were very weighty; the dangers he had described did exist and the attention of Sir Herbert Samuel would have to be drawn to them." This view was endorsed unanimously.[12]

Continuing his "offensive" against the High Commissioner's "mixed" militia plan, Jabotinsky urged the Executive on May 6th to cable a request to Sir Herbert Samuel "not to proceed with the militia scheme," and to state frankly that the Executive "could not take the responsibility for encouraging the Jews to join the [mixed] force if it was established."[13] Two weeks later he was able to report to a special meeting of the Political Committee, in which Lord Rothschild, Sir Alfred Mond, and Major James Rothschild also participated, that he had received a letter from Winston Churchill stating that the latter was in communication with the High Commissioner with a view to the modification or abandonment of the Mixed Defense Force scheme.[14]

The plan of an Arab-Jewish militia was, indeed, abandoned, at least for several years to come. The field was thus cleared for the positive counterplan: the Jewish Legion. Jabotinsky obtained the support of the Zionist Executive to the following three proposals dealing with "Military Force in Palestine," which were to be submitted to the British government:

1. The 38th-40th Royal Fusiliers ("Judeans") as formed in 1917 should continue to form part of the British Forces in Palestine.

2. Recruiting of Jewish volunteers should be reopened until their number reached at least one-half of the proposed total strength (7,700) of the British garrison.

3. It was assumed that, by appealing to the patriotism of the *Halutzim*, a sufficient number could be induced to enlist at a pay of one Egyptian pound per month for privates, two pounds per month for sergeants, etc. Apart from the difference of pay there should be no disparity between the recruits in the proposed force and in any other British troops in Palestine. Only single men would be enlisted, so that family allowances would be out of the question.

These three points were unanimously accepted by the Executive. There was, however, in Jabotinsky's original resolution one more point: it stated that, beginning with the year 1922–23, the Zionist Organization should undertake to contribute toward the upkeep of the "Judeans" a sum sufficient to cover enlisted men's pay. This essential proviso was rejected even by such staunch friends of the Legion as Joseph Cowen and Dr. Eder. Jabotinsky pointed out that without it the resolution "was rendered of dubious practical value . . . the Government would reply that the Arabs could make the same offer" of supplying men without providing for their pay. He was outvoted. He admitted nevertheless that it was imperative for the Executive to submit the three proposals even in their imperfect form.[15]

The controversy about financing the Legion scheme was not the only one threatening the unity of the Zionist effort in this field. Gradually, another controversial issue started emerging: *Haganah* vs. Legion.

Jabotinsky was the first commander of the *Haganah*, and it was in this capacity that he became the "prisoner of Acre." He could hardly be suspected of indifference or unfriendliness to this body. In fact, he was most eager to contribute actively to its development. After the Jaffa pogrom of May, 1921, Moshe Shertok and David Hacohen, who at the time lived in London and were connected with the *Haganah* in Palestine, decided to establish a fund to buy arms for the *Haganah*. Their first visit was to Jabotinsky, and his was the first check they received—for £25 ($120). At that time, it was a considerable amount and, knowing that Jabotinsky was both overgenerous and far from being financially secure, they hesitantly asked him: "Isn't it too much?" "I can do it," he reassured the two young men, vaguely referring to some "fund for publication of books" that allegedly was at his disposal.

Yet this interest and sympathy for the *Haganah* did not prevent conflicts. Jabotinsky did not consider a clandestine self-defense body as an adequate answer to the problem of the *Yishuv's* security: he insisted that it must be viewed and treated as part and parcel of the overall Zionist political effort to re-establish the Jewish Legion. The chances for the success of this effort seemed good. He felt strongly that everything must be subordinated to the supreme goal of re-establishing the Legion, and rejected any "competition," any device likely to be offered as a substitute, thus preventing the concentration of all Zionist effort on the struggle for the Legion.

Haganah leaders viewed the situation in a somewhat different light. After the Jaffa pogrom in May, 1921, Eliahu Golomb, then the head of the *Haganah*, wrote to Jabotinsky from Palestine that the campaign for the re-establishment of the Legion was bound to be a protracted one, while what was needed was "the immediate strengthening of our defense means." Even if the Jewish battalions were revived, it was possible that in a case of emergency they would be "far away at a time when we need them for action. . . . We must have the initial means of defense at hand, so that help should not come too late." Therefore, insisted Golomb, efforts on behalf of the Legion must not prevent a sustained effort to provide arms for self-defense. Hundreds of workers could be "converted into a secret army" and "the question of arms is now not less important than the question of the Legion."[16]

This approach was unacceptable to Jabotinsky. He was, of course, no "enemy of the *Haganah*," as his opponents claimed; but he was becoming increasingly apprehensive of its being put to the fore. On the other hand, *Haganah* "patriots," without being adversaries of the Legion, resented Jabotinsky's deprecation of the *Haganah's* decisive value. Basically, it was a difference of emphasis rather than of principle. Yet both sides persisted in stressing their points of divergence rather than the points they had in common. The dispute grew both in scope and intensity, creating conflicts and bitterness which were not at all warranted by the merits of the controversy. There was sad irony in the fact that precisely the leaders of organized labor in Palestine—in their majority former legionnaires—had become Jabotinsky's most outspoken opponents in this field.

The first showdown occurred at the session of the Zionist Actions Committee in Prague in July, 1921, two months after the pogrom in Jaffa. Jabotinsky energetically pressed his point that the prerequisite for the security of the *Yishuv* and for the progress of Zionist work in Palestine was the restoration of the Jewish Legion, which must be a constituent part of any British garrison in the country. D. Ben Gurion quotes from Jabotinsky's speech the following relevant excerpts:[17]

> We have the money, we have the men, but we are confronted with an Iron Wall: the anti-Semitic attitude of British officialdom. The key for this is to be found in the military situation. Samuel, to be sure, wants to protect the Jews from pogroms, but he is dependent on his General. That General, on the other hand, is thoroughly familiar with the psychology of his men. He therefore is not too keen to defend the Jews. The only way out, therefore, is not to make defense depend on the British military: we need Jewish soldiers.

"The question raised by Jabotinsky now becomes the center of discussion," reported the *Jüdische Rundschau*.[18] It was discussed for three full days. Some of the opposition stemmed from pacifist convictions; its proponents relied on achieving friendly relationship with the Arabs. Others were opposed not as a matter of principle, but out of practical considerations. Their view was most articulately voiced by D. Ben Gurion:[19]

> We need a Jewish Legion. We support the Zionist Executive in its positive efforts in that direction; but we don't know whether we shall have a Legion. I for one am sceptical. I do not doubt our moral right to raise a Jewish Legion in Palestine. Our right to Palestine is that of a nation, not of a minority. We therefore must protect our rights by our own efforts. The question is merely as to how this is to be done. In this respect I do not agree with Jabotinsky. He believes that only a Legion is able to protect us. I, however, am not certain of protection by a Legion—even if it were to consist only of Jews—so long as it is not under Jewish command, but that of an English General.

Together with other labor representatives, Ben Gurion therefore pleaded the case of self-defense as the most realistic and effective way to guarantee the security of the *Yishuv*.

Replying to this argument, Jabotinsky said:[20]

The Jew is always bent on substitutes; this is why he believes in self-defense, in arming the *Yishuv*. I warn you not to do it. Do not place arms in the hands of Jewish adolescents who know no military discipline. Arms are only for adults who are under military command. A Jewish self-defense of 10,000 men will stir up the Arabs more than 2,000 Jewish soldiers would. The only way is to renew the Legion. Without the Legion, a colonization of Palestine is not possible. . . . I am not one of those radicals who demand a Jewish Force under the command of *Va'ad Leumi*. A few thousand Jewish soldiers are a force—even though under British High Command and within the British Army.

Jabotinsky spoke for two hours and stressed again that for him "the question of defense is decisive. . . . In his opponents' speeches he noted the absence of any concrete plan how to do things differently, and described the arguments advanced by them as 'literature,' which was up against harsh facts. He demanded that the Actions Committee take a resolution enabling him to stay on in the Executive and carry out his plans."[21] The last argument, which implied that, should his Legion demand not be accepted, he would be unable to remain in the Executive, apparently played an important role. Adolf Böhm, an avowed opponent of Jabotinsky and of the Legion, says in his authoritative *History of the Zionist Movement:* "Taking into account the frame of mind of the masses, most leaders yielded to the pressure of Jabotinsky who was at that time celebrated as a national hero. Even the labor representative, Ben Gurion, approved of the Legion idea, though he spoke of it in a somewhat sceptical manner."[22]

The Actions Committee decided to "authorize the Executive to take such steps as may be necessary to secure the re-establishment of the Judean regiment formerly operating in Palestine."

At the Twelfth Zionist Congress in Carlsbad (August, 1921), Jabotinsky also devoted a considerable part of his long speech to a spirited defense of the Legion. There was only scant overt opposition to the Legion idea from the Congress rostrum. Nehemia de Lieme made a few pointed, critical remarks, and Ussishkin reasserted his traditional opposition to the Legion. The latter, however, wisely refrained from making of this stand a "Cabinet issue." All he said was: "The Legion—that's a thing you either do or don't do; but you don't discuss it. In my opinion, my friend and opponent Jabotinsky yesterday made a mistake in discussing this question in detail. However, anyone coming here and speaking against the Legion would make an even bigger mistake."[23]

But behind the scenes, there was much excitement. The special correspondent of the *Jewish Chronicle* reported from Carlsbad that "the question of the Jewish Regiment threatened to cause serious contention . . . but sensing trouble and realizing the mood of the Congress on the one hand, and the firmness of Mr. Jabotinsky on the other . . . the leaders behind the scene took Mr. Ussishkin's advice that the less said about the subject the better for all concerned."[24] The battle for and against the Legion was therefore going on mostly in the closed meetings of the Political Commission. Mr. Shertok who, though not a delegate, was allowed to attend these meetings, told this writer that in his zeal for the Legion Jabotinsky was then ready to sacrifice the illegal *Haganah* for the sake of the restoration of the "Judeans." At one of the meetings, Jabotinsky, in Shertok's words, "artificially conjured up antagonism between the *Haganah* and the Legion." When the meeting was over, Shertok reproachfully asked him why he had done it. Jabotinsky bent his knee and made the gesture of breaking a stick over it: "I will thus break them [the *Haganah*], even for the sake of a remotest hope for the establishment of the legion."[25] This episode can, however, hardly be interpreted as characteristic of Jabotinsky's true attitude toward the *Haganah*. Only two months before the Congress, he wrote in *Di Tribune* that he "did not think that *Haganah* could be considered as a permanent institution," but "if there should be no other way, we will, of course, have to accept it."[26]

In 1922, with prospects for the revival of the Legion becoming ever dimmer, Jabotinsky's interest in the *Haganah* increased considerably. But here again, his concept of the nature and function of this body clashed with that of the *Haganah* leaders. He insisted—just as he had done in 1920 when the Self-Defense Corps had been initiated in Jerusalem—that Jewish self-defense in Palestine must not be a clandestine body; it could serve its purpose usefully only if legally recognized by the Palestine government. In August, 1922, at the Annual Zionist Conference at Carlsbad, he told Golomb that the only acceptable form of the *Haganah* was "legal defense, sanctioned by the government"; *Haganah's* clandestine activities endangered the political status of the Zionist Organization. Golomb came to the conclusion that it was "hopeless" to change Jabotinsky's attitude and he wrote to his friends in Palestine that Jabotinsky was harming their work "behind the scene"; his "only consolation" was that "at present, Jabotinsky lacks any influence"; he therefore believed that the *Haganah* leadership had "no interest in reaching an understanding with Jabotinsky on methods of our work."[27]

Nevertheless, when Jabotinsky visited Palestine in October, 1922, his relations with the *Haganah* were still very cordial. Since *Haganah's* intelligence had reported that an attempt on Jabotinsky's life was planned by the Arabs, he was guarded day and night by *Haganah* sentries. The *Haganah* Command arranged for him a special clandestine review of about fifty of its *Mefaqdim* (officers); fully armed, they carried out military exercises, which he watched hidden behind a curtain.[28] At the same time he was trying to obtain *Haganah's* legalization. He met Sir Wyndham Deeds, Chief Secretary to the Palestine government and the only pro-Zionist high official in Samuel's retinue, and suggested that the government sanction the organization and training of the *Haganah* units in the towns and in the colonies; in return, the Zionist Organization would do its best to induce the Jewish population to surrender its arms; these arms would be held in custody—as was the case in the colonies—of trustworthy persons. Deeds liked these proposals.* Informing Dr. Weizmann of his conversation with Deeds, Jabotinsky wrote on October 18, 1922, that it was of the greatest importance that the person whom the government would appoint as chief instructor for the *Haganah* (and who would be, of course, subordinate to Major General Sir Henry Tudor, Commander of all British forces in Palestine), should enjoy the confidence of the Zionist Executive; as possible candidates, he named Colonel Margolin, Colonel Patterson, and Major June. He insistently warned that if the matter of *Haganah's* legalization were not settled, a big scandal was inevitable, for the clandestine import of arms would then continue, and this was bound to end in a spectacular failure.

After his return to London, Jabotinsky submitted the scheme which he had discussed with Deeds to a meeting of the Zionist Executive. This scheme implied that, in return for legalization, the *Haganah* would surrender illegally held arms. Nachum Sokolov, who was in the chair, put a preliminary question: "But would the *Haganah* heed our decision?" Jabotinsky confidently stated: "They will deliver everything they will be told to."

---

*Sir Wyndham was a great admirer of Jabotinsky. In 1919, when he was British High Commissioner in Constantinople, he asked S. Salzman, who was on his way to Palestine, to give his regards to Jabotinsky and to tell him that when they met in London, Jabotinsky "said something that was not true": "I asked Jabotinsky whether there were among the Jewish people more men of his kind, and he answered that there were thousands of them. Tell him, please, that till now I have not found a single Jew who would be equal to him." S. Salzman, *Min ha'Ovar*, p. 259.

M. Shertok, who attended the meeting as liaison officer on behalf of the
Haganah, "begged to differ": the *Haganah* people, he said, were no obedient
tools of the Zionist governing bodies; they considered themselves responsible for the *Yishuv's* security and had a sense of duty of their own; should
they feel that what was decided here was not right, they would not obey.
Informed of this conflict, Eliahu Golomb on November 21, 1922, wrote to
Shertok from Palestine that he fully approved of the stand the latter had
taken: "We will not agree to sacrifice our real strength, if ever so small,
on the altar of Jabotinsky's illusions. . . ."[29] The Zionist Executive accepted
Jabotinsky's proposal to demand the legalization of the *Haganah* as a distinct, systematically trained body, with discipline and hierarchy of its own;[30]
the question of surrendering arms was left open. Among the *Haganah* leadership, animosity against Jabotinsky was strong and growing.

Going Along

When, in March, 1921, Jabotinsky joined the Zionist Executive,
he was almost pathetically eager to make a success of this experiment
of broader Zionist cooperation. He was therefore doing his very best to
go along with the Executive's traditional policy, sometimes apparently
against his own feelings and better judgment.

On April 6, 1921, together with Dr. Eder, Joseph Cowen, and Richard
Lichtheim (who were then the only Executive members present in London), he signed a "report on the present situation," which was circulated
among the members of the Actions Committee. The report contained a
rather complacent appraisal of the political situation in Palestine, which
could hardly have fully corresponded to Jabotinsky's opinion: "During the
past year the situation has on the whole improved in our favor. There can
be no doubt that the High Commissioner Sir Herbert Samuel is friendly
disposed towards us and is doing all in his power to assist our progress."

It must not be forgotten that all these encouraging commonplaces
were dispatched to the Actions Committee members exactly twenty-five
days before the pogroms in Jaffa, Tel Aviv, Kfar Saba, and Ain Hai, and
the attacks on Petach Tiqvah, Hadera, and Rehovot. Sir Herbert Samuel's
administration had not only failed to protect the Jews from attacks, but
halted the landing of Jewish immigrants in Jaffa, and on May 14th Samuel announced the complete suspension of immigration pending revision
of the existing legislation.[31]

It is easy to imagine Jabotinsky's reaction to these developments. But his loyalty to the body he then belonged to prompted him to do things he undoubtedly regretted for the rest of his life. Together with other Executive members then in London, he was responsible for the decision to withhold statements to the general press on the May pogroms and to issue statements to Zionist Federations and the Jewish press only.[32] As Jabotinsky himself formulated in his draft of a telegram to Herbert Samuel, the Executive "did all they could to keep up the confidence of the Jewish people in his [Samuel's] statesmanship."[33] In an interview published on May 20th in the *Jewish Chronicle* he went even farther. In his eyes, he said, "the main culprit responsible for the Jaffa events is the Jewish people themselves: it has failed in the acid test which, with the irony in which Providence sometimes indulges, is money." When hearing all the protests against the Palestine administration, the Zionist Commission, the London Zionist Executive, the British government, he "cannot help asking the same question: 'You, who protest, have you done your duty?' "

This kind of public statement is obviously reminiscent of Dr. Weizmann's rather than of Jabotinsky's political mentality.

Within the Executive, however, he continued pressing for a more active political line. At a meeting held on June 17, 1921, he insisted that "it was incumbent on the Executive to set forth its attitude in a clear and unmistakable manner vis-à-vis the British Government and the Jewish public, who were everywhere losing confidence in the Zionist Organization. It should be made clear to the British Government that the Government of Palestine must get rid of all anti-Semitic elements among the higher and lower officialdom; that the connection between Palestine and Egypt must cease, that no high official must be appointed to the Palestine Administration who was not an adherent of the policy of the Jewish National Home; finally, that the defense of Jewish life and property in Palestine must be safeguarded under all circumstances. . . . Unless the British Government accepted these demands, they [the Zionist Executive] could not carry out the Mandate over Palestine and . . . might be forced to take the consequences and resign."

The general lines of Jabotinsky's suggestions were accepted and he was asked to draft the statement accordingly.

Having entered the Executive, Jabotinsky did not sever his relations with Meir Grossman, whose *Di Tribune* continued its sharp criticism of Dr. Weizmann and his policies. They did not meet often, but when Grossman once teasingly said: "Now that you belong to the 'Government,' you would never dare to appear on the same tribune with me," Jabotinsky's reaction was: "I will, whenever you ask me—and without 'preliminary censorship' of the speech you would make."[34] And he kept his promise. On May 25th he presided at a meeting held under the auspices of *Di Tribune*, at which Grossman made Dr. Weizmann responsible for all the shortcomings of the Zionist cause and demanded his resignation.[35] This obviously put Jabotinsky, a member of Dr. Weizmann's Cabinet, in a most awkward position. The next day he sent the following cable to Weizmann in New York:

> Yesterday at a meeting under my chairmanship the main speaker [Grossman] insisted on your abandoning leadership at [the forthcoming] Congress. This suggestion [was] made without previously informing me. I rejected it in [my] closing speech, declaring [that] you [are] indispensable.* Considering, however, that the fact of its being made under my chairmanship might be misinterpreted, I intended to tender you my resignation, but, colleagues refusing acceptance, I place myself in your hands, reaffirming confidence in your loyalty to [the] agreed program of [the] new Executive.

Dr. Weizmann accepted Jabotinsky's apology, and the incident had no further repercussions. According to Grossman, Jabotinsky later, on the eve of the Twelfth Zionist Congress, tried to persuade him to close down *Di Tribune* and to publish a statement that since the new Executive was now conducting a satisfactory policy, he and his friends were abandoning their opposition. Grossman refused.

At the Congress, Jabotinsky loyally and vigorously defended the Executive's policies against the criticism of de Lieme and Simon, who were the spokesmen of the Brandeis group. His speech was expected with great impatience.

The official minutes of the Congress report that when Jabotinsky mounted the rostrum, he was met by "protracted, stormy acclaim and applause," that he was at least a dozen times interrupted by "strong applause," and that at the end he was rewarded by "great and sustained

---

*According to a *Jewish Chronicle* report, Jabotinsky said that "to attribute all the causes of the situation to the errors of one or two men, was a superficial point of view. . . . As long as Zionism needed diplomacy and statesmanship, Dr. Weizmann must remain its leader." *Jewish Chronicle*, June 3, 1921.

acclaim and applause."[36] Nevertheless, his speech at this Congress can hardly be counted among his best Congress performances. Whether it was because it was delivered in German—a language he at that time had not yet mastered completely—or because he still did not feel at home in the new situation and pleaded a cause which was largely Dr. Weizmann's, his speech lacked a central idea, unity of purpose, and that touch of greatness which was so characteristic, for instance, of his address at the Fourteenth Congress in 1925. It was largely polemical in its contents and style. Explaining why he had abandoned his intention "not to utter at this Congress one single word in a language other than Hebrew," he frankly said: "There is only one reason that forces me to speak German. If I were to defend myself, I would do so in Hebrew, irrespective of whether there are delegates who would not understand me. But I intend to *attack*, and I intend to attack just such gentlemen who don't understand Hebrew. It is not fair to assail people in a language they don't understand."[37]

And attack he did. The polemical methods he used, though effective and fair, were not always in the best of taste, and those who had opposed and disliked him were hardly inclined to change their attitude. Delegate Davis Trietsch made a formal motion "to exempt from formal discharge the speech of Jabotinsky, a motion for its being struck from the Minutes being about to be made." The majority decided "to move the previous question."[38] But the very fact of the motion being made was characteristic of the mood of a certain section of the Congress. Reporting on "the personal element" in the Congress picture, the special correspondent of the *Jewish Chronicle* wrote: "Jabotinsky has a large following, but. . . his position as a member of the Executive may not be unchallenged, though his eventual triumph may be regarded as certain."[39] Jabotinsky himself seems to have been not at all so sure of such an outcome. "The Congress is nearing the end of its deliberations, but I still don't know anything; there is still hope that I will be thrown out [of the Executive]," he wrote to his sister on September 13th.

He was not "thrown out," but was overwhelmingly re-elected as a member of the Executive. Georg Halperin, who at that time was close to Zionist ruling circles, told this writer that Dr. Weizmann then considered Jabotinsky as his most likely successor in the leadership of the World Zionist Organization.[40]

Discovering America

The first ten years of his public life Jabotinsky spent in Russia; during the next decade he became familiar to almost every Jewish community on the European continent and to almost every Jew in Palestine. American Jewry, however, had known him only by name, and to him the American continent was an unknown quantity. The opportunity to "discover America" presented itself soon after the Carlsbad Congress, when he was asked to join the first *Keren ha'Yesod* delegation to the United States. Other members of the delegation were N. Sokolov, A. Goldstein, Professor Otto Warburg, and Colonel J. H. Patterson. He left London on November 5, 1921.

Strangely enough, Jabotinsky remained unimpressed by the United States. In a letter to Mrs. Vera Weizmann, he wrote on January 16, 1922: "America is a dull country. Thus far, I haven't seen here anything, for the sake of which it would be worth while to cross the ocean. It is true that Zionists and meetings prevent one from seeing the entire perspective, so that there are perhaps wonders which have not been shown to me. But I am somewhat bored and beginning to get tired." It was only on his subsequent visits to the United States (in 1926, 1935, and 1940) that he learned to see and to appreciate "the entire perspective," which had remained hidden from him during his first visit. But even in 1921–22 he had learned much from his American experience.

This experience included a first-hand study of the *Keren ha'Yesod* principle of *Maaser* (tithe) as applied by the Mormons. One of the *Poalei Zion* leaders, Meyer L. Brown, visited Mormon settlements in the state of Utah and talked with their apostle who demonstrated and explained to him their machinery of enforcing the biblical tithe. "You, Jews, preach the *Maaser*, and we, Mormons, implement it," he proudly stated. Brown published in the *Poalei Zion* paper *Di Zeit* an article describing what he had learned from the Mormons. Apparently impressed by this description, Jabotinsky approached Brown for additional information, and they agreed that Jabotinsky should make a study trip to Salt Lake City, which he did; he also secured abundant literature on Mormon life and organization.[41] It was not an easy task to introduce the exacting tithe taxation to the American Jews, who at that time were far from realizing the scope of Palestine's needs and demands. But Jabotinsky unrelentingly pressed for it. Dr. Mordecai Soltes, who in 1921 was Chairman of the *Keren ha'Yesod* in Arverne, Long Island, recalls that when Jabotinsky met with the Chairmen of the various *Keren ha'Yesod* sections, he strongly emphasized that they "should not accept ordinary contributions, but think in terms of *Ma'aser*." One of the immediate results of this approach, relates Dr. Soltes, was that when he explained Jabotinsky's stand to a man who originally offered five dollars, the latter contributed five hundred dollars.[42]

In addition to collecting funds for the *Keren ha'Yesod*, the delegation was supposed to combat the opposition against the *Keren ha'Yesod* idea which was expected from the Brandeis-Mack group in America.

Jabotinsky accepted this aspect of the assignment without any hesitation. He had no pleasant recollections of the two occasions on which his path had crossed that of Justice Brandeis: in February, 1919, and in July, 1920. But besides this personal element of dislike, the two men were at that time far apart in some basic matters of principle.

When the Annual Zionist Conference convened in London in July, 1920, Jabotinsky was still in Palestine and was unable to follow its deliberations closely. He was therefore only superficially conversant with the main issues which were discussed there and, in particular, with the controversy on the methods of the building up of Palestine as between the "Americans," led by Brandeis, and "Europeans." All his sympathies, however, belonged to the second camp. It comprised all his friends and represented the "good old values" of both Russian and Palestinian Zionism as against a more "businesslike approach of the American newcomers." A "political Zionist" *par excellence*, Jabotinsky was also bound to oppose the disregard for any further Zionist political work which was voiced by Brandeis at the meeting of the American delegates to the London Conference. "Politics," said Brandeis, "may now be banished; certainly politics may go into suspense . . . to my mind, practically the whole of politics is to proceed efficiently in the building-up of Palestine."[43]

All this inevitably prejudiced Jabotinsky against the entire concept of the Brandeis group; it made him overlook completely its positive elements—in the first place its emphasis on the importance of private initiative and private capital, which were then not less than in the following years neglected in favor of "national capital" as a factor of Palestine colonization. His association with the *Keren ha'Yesod*, which was the main bearer of the idea of national colonization, also contributed to his shutting his mind against the Brandeis program as a whole.

It is in this context that we must read Jabotinsky's private letters from America, which are full of disparaging remarks about the Brandeis-Mack group. While his opinion about the efficiency of the official Zionist leadership in the United States was far from flattering, "the Mack group is even more incapable," he wrote to Mrs. Vera Weizmann on January 16, 1922. He was still more outspoken in a letter to I. Trivus: "The Brandeis group does not possess even one per cent [of the strength] which is being attributed to it in Europe. Even from the political viewpoint—contrary to my expectations—our people [adherents of the Weizmann Executive] are stronger than that group."[44] Possibly because of this low assessment of the opposition's strength and nuisance value, and possibly because of his ardent desire to promote peace and not war in the movement, Jabotinsky during his stay in America abstained from any factional strife. Moreover, he did his very best to further conciliation and unity in the Zionist ranks.

This attitude came as a great surprise to the Zionist leadership in the United States. When Jabotinsky left America after seven months of arduous work, *The New Palestine* wrote in a farewell editorial that before his arrival

the name of Jabotinsky had been used as a slogan for all that was pugnacious, aggressive, daring, with a dash of military pepperiness. He was heralded last year as the audacious usurper, who had made conditions which Dr. Weizmann had to agree to, succumbing to the forcefulness of the unrelenting Jabotinsky. Mr. Jabotinsky was regarded as the evil genius of the *Keren ha'Yesod*.

The real Jabotinsky, whom American Zionists got to meet, disproved the legend that preceded him:[45]

When the history of Mr. Jabotinsky's visit to America will be revealed [wrote *The New Palestine*], it will be found (wonder of wonders!) that it was he who did his utmost to attain that for which every Zionist is longing, the peace of which so many speak, and so many hope will soon be consummated. He was as soft as the softest. No faint whisper of peace passed him by, but he at once pursued it to its lair. All his efforts were in vain. But he persisted to the last hour of his stay in this country. So the legend of the swashbuckler, the usurper, has been exploded.

In regard to the main purpose—the collecting of money—Jabotinsky's letters from America were full of confidence in the success of the delegation's mission. As early as December 18, 1921, he wrote to his mother and sister: "I am working hard, but I don't feel tired, since it is only office work that wears me out. I hope to collect a lot of money." Seven weeks later he wrote to I. Trivus that the delegation expected to collect nine million dollars, and said: "There isn't here [in the United States] any backwoods dump, from which it would be impossible to get money for Palestine. . . . Nine million dollars are to be found just in the street—not from the rich or the assimilationists, but from our own people—the average *baleboss*. Our task is to approach him and not to wait till he will come to us. I am using the word 'approach' not in the ideological but in its simplest meaning. We must organize systematic canvassing of Jewish homes, and there is the rub. The local leaders believed that it would be possible to do the job through meetings and banquets. . . . We successfully pressed for a new scheme based on canvassing of homes, etc. We will see."[46] At a meeting of 3,500 canvassers held in New York in April, 1922, on the eve of the beginning of a $3,000,000 campaign in that city, at which every group assigned to a certain section paraded with its placards, Jabotinsky recalled the organization of the self-defense in Jerusalem two years before: at that time, too, the volunteers had gathered, bearing placards announcing the sections of the city they came from. Pressing the analogy further, he said that the more volunteers there were for the *Keren ha'Yesod* in America, the less would there be need of self-defense in Palestine. "Go out and get it," he called upon the volunteers.[47]

Meyer Weisgal, who at that time was in the center of Zionist activities in America, describes Jabotinsky as the best speaker of the delegation: Professor Warburg was no speaker at all, Nachum Sokolov was anything but impressive in his public speeches, A. Goldstein's "main oratorical effects were still limited to Kishinev pogrom dramatics—amongst them Jabotinsky stood out as a speaker of Aristide Briand's stature."[48] He usually traveled together with the friend of his Legion days, Colonel J. H. Patterson. Describing their tour of the Middle West, *The New Palestine* (January 27, 1922) wrote that with their appearance "an element of romance has come into the more or less prosaic life of the Jews in the large centers of the Middle West. . . . These two men represent the aggressive and militant aspect of the Jewish National restoration. Their appeal is meeting with the response which the personality,as well as the cause of these two men, merits."

The Yiddish and Anglo-Jewish press of that period was full of glowing accounts of Jabotinsky's *Keren ha'Yesod* speeches. At the solemn reception for the delegation he was the last speaker—a place always reserved for the

most impressive performance. Introduced by the Chairman, Samuel Unter-
meyer, as a "militant Zionist" known the world over as the "Jewish Garibaldi," Jabotinsky, according to a press report, delivered "an incisive address,
full of hammer blows and punctuated with crescendoes"; he "fearlessly
detailed the many and great problems confronting Zionists—the political
difficulties, the Arab situation, colonization, immigration, the Legion, etc.
The answer to all these, he maintained, was *Keren ha'Yesod*. 'Begin the work
today,' was his striking conclusion." According to another press report, his
speech "has made a deep impression on all those present; he charmed everybody." Other reports stressed his "faultless English," his ability "to make
the people warm and enchanted."[49]

A. Tulin, who was very friendly with Jabotinsky and saw him practically every day while he was in New York, also stresses this endearing feature
in Jabotinsky's relations with people he had to deal with:[50]

Jabotinsky was very simple and sincere in his approach to all men and women
alike; but he was courtly at the same time. Sokolov described him to me once as the
gentleman *par excellence* in the Zionist movement. My own observation confirmed
this description as correct. He was the most chivalrous man I have ever known.
I think it is a fact that every woman who ever worked for him as secretary fell
hopelessly in love with him at the distance which he always kept between them.
They could not help it—when one considers Jabotinsky's unvarying warm courtesy
and politeness coupled with his great personal charm and brilliance.

Jabotinsky spent about seven months in America and on behalf of the
Keren ha'Yesod visited fifty to sixty towns. Tulin describes Jabotinsky during his stay in America as "indefatigable in furthering his Zionist mission
in which he would not and could not be deterred by setbacks and discour-
agements." He once expressed his philosophy on this subject to Tulin, when
the latter made some pessimistic remarks about the sodden indifference of
the American Jewish masses to Zionist appeals for national renaissance, by
telling him that one day, while walking with his grandfather, they passed a
mud puddle. The grandfather stopped, pointed out the mud puddle, and said:
"My son, do you see this mud? It is dirty, isn't it? But out of mud you can
make bricks and with bricks you can build beautiful palaces." Tulin calls this
story "mythical," yet, he says, it fully expressed Jabotinsky's "faith and basis
of action all through the time that I knew him until his death." While working hard, Jabotinsky also knew the art of relaxing. "He loved music, beauty,

charm and gaiety," Tulin recalls. "Very often he would rout me out of bed late at night after he had returned from some gruelling speaking engagement, and would cajole me into dressing and going with him to some high class nightclub; there we would sit at a table in a corner until the early hours of the morning over a bottle of light wine, watch the young people dance and at the same time discuss philosophical subjects."

Jabotinsky was the main speaker at the solemn opening of the Conference of former legionnaires and Jewish soldiers in the American Army held in Philadelphia on May 20–21, 1922. His speech, which contained the basic elements of the future ideology of the *Betar* and the *Brith ha'Chayal*, was enthusiastically received by the delegates. Jabotinsky was elected by acclamation an honorary member of the American Jewish Legion.[51]

When Jabotinsky left the United States early in June, 1922, the official organ of the Zionist Organization of America wrote editorially that during his stay he "impressed his personality upon a large number of American Jewish communities and upon Zionists in general. . . . He leaves behind him here a host of friends who know him at his real value, and who appreciate his self-abandonment for the sake of the Zionist cause. We are infected by the contagion of his spirit. He gave himself to Zionist service without stint. He has enhanced his value to the movement, and is freed from false reputation which had preceded him in this country."[52]

Family Problems

In a letter to Mrs. Vera Weizmann from Kansas City, Missouri, (January 16, 1922) we read: "Ania writes that at the end of December she and Eri spent a day in your house. How do you find Eri's speech?"

Behind this seemingly casual inquiry lies a pathetic story of almost twelve years' struggle on the part of the boy's parents against a deformity with which he had been born and which ever since had been weighing heavily on their minds.

Eri, their only child, was born with a harelip and a cleft palate. It was a hard blow to the young parents. Jabotinsky wept bitterly on his mother's shoulder, saying that "Ania is the unhappiest mother in the whole world." When the child was four months old, the noted Odessa surgeon, Dr. Silberberg, operated on the lip in order to make proper feeding possible; when he was twelve months old, the cleft palate was operated on. Both operations improved Eri's condition only slightly.[53]

In the summer of 1918, when Mrs. Jabotinsky and Eri lived in London, the boy underwent one more operation. On August 11th, Jabotinsky wrote from Jerusalem: "Only now have I learned of Eri's operation. . . . Oh, my little dove, let this be your last torture, and Eri's as well. When it will be possible, take a picture of him and send it to me. . . . I also hope that there will be no more nasal accent. But, of course, we will have to wait a long time. . . . When the war will be over—even if in Palestine everything will be just wonderful—you will stay in Europe as long as will be necessary to put Eri straight in every respect. Well, God be praised—and you be praised! You are a piece of iron wrapped in silk—and I adore both the iron and the silk and I am starved for both." To his eight-year-old son, he wrote (in printed Russian letters): "My dear Eri, you are a brave lad. Look after mummy and take care of her and of yourself. Give her as many kisses for me as there are hairs on the crown of your head. Papa."

From the medical viewpoint, the operation was completely successful. All purely anatomical obstacles to normal speech had been eliminated: and, still, the boy was heavily handicapped in his elocution.

His parents never gave up hope of correcting his speech so that it would be completely normal. Since there was no organic cause for the remaining defects of enunciation, they started looking for other devices. They heard of a professor in Berlin who was noted for his spectacular successes in this field. On June 10, 1921, Jabotinsky wrote to his sister (from Kissingen) that in about three weeks Mrs. Jabotinsky and Eri were going to Zehlendorf, a suburb of Berlin: Professor Gutzman promised "in two to three months to normalize Eri's elocution." On July 25th, Jabotinsky reported: "Eri is taking lessons and making progress in pronunciation."

The treatment proved completely successful. When this writer met Eri in Berlin in 1923, there were but very slight traces of nasality in his speech; later, they disappeared completely.

Jabotinsky was very fond and proud of his son. In September, 1923, he wrote from Berlin: "He is a delightfully good boy. Ania and I are in love with him, and it seems that so is everybody."[54] Hebrew was the only language father and son spoke with each other. Very early, Eri showed exceptional aptitude for mathematics. Jabotinsky pretended to be shocked by this to him "inexplicable" predilection of his son, since he himself was completely lacking in interest and understanding for this branch of human knowledge and professed to despise it. But in 1927, when Eri obtained fourth place among five hundred contestants in a competitive examination at the Paris Ecole Supérieure, he boastfully described it as "a very important event in the history of the twentieth century."[55] Two months later, he wrote to his sister: "Eri is a very good lad and a very sensible one; and I think that he will arrange his life both reasonably and well in respect to Palestine." Apparently referring to his sister's suggestion that Eri should settle in Palestine at once, he wrote: "This is his business, not ours. As it seems, he is just now not eager to go to Palestine: this settles the question."[56]

Jabotinsky's confidence in his son's leanings proved to be well founded. He was almost the sole Zionist leader whose son followed in his father's footsteps—a source of deep satisfaction to him.

Jabotinsky's mother and sister occupied a great and revered place in his mind and soul. There was nothing he would refuse them. The sole limit he gently but firmly put on them was that they should not try by remote control to influence his worldly affairs and to advise him how to arrange his life.

Yet they apparently too often did just that, overwhelming him with endless suggestions, almost every one of them aimed at his immediate return to Palestine.

A long letter from London (September 29, 1922) is largely devoted to a spirited self-defense against such loving but ill-advised attempts. It gives a revealing account of the many suggestions he had to reject, and of the reasons that motivated his refusals:

My very dears, I am objecting to "advice" not because I am spiteful, but because it is *always* impracticable. For example, Tania cabled me to America: "Come directly to Palestine." Impracticable: in order to get a "service ticket," I would have to be officially delegated by the *Keren ha'Yesod* Board, and for that I had to come to London. A second example: "Start building a house [in Palestine]." Impracticable: before beginning to build a house with cash, I must get insured —this is much more important; and before starting to build a house on credit, I must pay off my debts since otherwise there will be no credit. A third example: "Settle in Palestine." Impracticable: I have no job there and cannot earn my livelihood. A fourth: "Become a lawyer." Impracticable: a man of forty-two cannot take up a profession he hates. Fifth: "Establish a publishing house in Jerusalem." Impracticable: the book market is now concentrated in low currency countries, so that no book published in Palestine can command a ready sale. Sixth: from the latest letter: "Now, the main activities of the Zionist Organization will be concentrated in Palestine, and therefore . . ." Impracticable: in the first place because your information about the new state of affairs in Zionism is inaccurate, and even the [British] Government is insisting that the Jewish Agency remain in London; and in the second place, because the Congress elected me not to administer colonization and agriculture, but to conduct propaganda, etc. And so it is with all other matters.

For God's sake, do not get offended because of all this. I am saying it not as a reproof, but in order to clarify things. It pains me that an impression is being created that every letter from Jerusalem contains some concrete proposal concerning my displacements, settlement, or in general some changes in my mode of life, and I apparently reject all of them. The truth of the matter is simply that my life is a very complicated one, and it cannot be directed from afar, and not even from the adjacent room. My very dears, I beg you to drop these attempts. The question as to when, how, where I shall go, settle, do, or what I shall wear, can be solved by myself only, and all the rest is just unnecessary vexation both for you and for me.

While rejecting any interference with his plans, he himself was invariably full of solicitude for his sister and her son Johnny. The latter studied engineering at Lausanne and his budget was secured by Jabotinsky. When Johnny once hinted that this year he might not continue his studies, Jabotinsky balked: "I don't want to hear such things; my budget is calculated on the basis of a nephew in Lausanne."[57]

He knew that his sister had never ceased to mourn for the high school for girls she had been forced to leave behind in Odessa, and longed for an opportunity again to head a similar school. Palestine with its high currency was too expensive a country for such a project, and he could not even dream of financing it there. Germany, where the currency was low and where in the early thirties a large Russian-Jewish colony had gathered, was a different proposition. "Berlin is now a second Odessa," he wrote to Johnny. "There are in Berlin 300,000 Russian Jews and they hate the German schools. If there would be established an 'Ostjüdische Töchterschule, Frau Jabotinsky-Kopp,' with Hebrew, Russian and German languages, or at least a Kindergarten, it would attract many pupils, and it could be organized cheaply and quickly." Should Johnny's mother "agree in principle," Jabotinsky was ready to start the necessary *démarches* immediately.[58]

Mrs. Jabotinsky-Kopp was reluctant to leave Palestine, and the project died in its infancy. It was, however, only one of the many manifestations of Jabotinsky's eagerness to please her and to help her to rebuild her life.

NINETEEN
"THE PACT WITH THE DEVIL"

The Jabotinsky-Slavinsky Agreement

In his speech at the Twelfth Zionist Congress at Carlsbad in September, 1921, Jabotinsky referred to the old charge against him that his pro-Allied propaganda during World War I practically made him an associate of the reactionary and anti-Semitic tsarist government. Replying to this charge, Jabotinsky rephrased the famous saying of the great Italian patriot and revolutionary, Mazzini (*Noi faremo l'Italia anche uniti col Diavolo*), and said: "In working for Palestine I would even ally myself with the devil." The official stenographic *Protokoll* records that this statement was followed by "lively approval and applause" of the delegates.[1] But Jabotinsky very soon learned that, in the specific climate of Jewish political life, an attempt to apply this much applauded patriotic precept was a highly unpopular and thankless undertaking.

During and immediately after the Congress, Jabotinsky became involved in one of the most heated and painful controversies of his eventful public life. Its background was determined by two basic trends of his political credo.

The first was his active and friendly interest in Ukrainian national aspirations. In Russia, Jabotinsky had written often and competently about the Ukrainian problem; he was widely known and appreciated by Ukrainian patriots, many of whom had in the meantime become closely associated with the Ukrainian nationalist government headed by Simon Petliura. The acute deterioration of Jewish-Ukrainian relations caused by bloody

341

pogroms perpetrated by Petliura's armies in 1917–20 (it is estimated that during Petliura's rule over the whole or parts of the Ukraine 897 pogroms took place) was a source of serious concern to Jabotinsky. A second element in Jabotinsky's political credo was his firm conviction that the only effective remedy against pogroms was, always and everywhere, Jewish self-defense organized in conjunction with the state authorities.

It is against this background that one must view the contents and the outcome of Jabotinsky's encounter with an old friend, Maxim Antonovitch Slavinsky, who in August, 1921, came to see Jabotinsky in Prague and later in Carlsbad. A staunch liberal and a sincere and active wellwisher of the Jews, Slavinsky closely cooperated with Jabotinsky during the 1907 elections to the second Russian Duma in the Rovno district of Volhynia. A devoted Ukrainian patriot, Slavinsky had been active in the Ukrainian national movement in all its manifestations and was at that time Chief of the Extraordinary Diplomatic Mission of the Ukrainian Democratic Republic to the Republic of Czechoslovakia.

Slavinsky's first encounter with Jabotinsky took place in Prague on August 30th in the presence of the Ukrainian Minister to Berlin, Roman Stockyi. In a report to his government Slavinsky wrote: "As good old friends, we have considered in principle the problem how to improve adverse Jewish public opinion with regard to the Ukrainian cause."[2] At the time of Slavinsky's visit, this government was in exile in Polish Eastern Galicia. Yet is was still keeping an army of about 15,000 men, fully equipped and well fed, in two military camps, not very far from the Russian border. The Treasury of a great Western Power financed that expensive establishment, as well as Petliura's administrative and diplomatic machinery. It was obvious that the Western Powers still expected to utilize Petliura's armed forces for fighting the Bolshevik régime in the Ukraine; it was known that a new invasion was planned for the spring of 1922.[3] This prospect, of course, implied the danger of new pogroms. The problem was whether this danger could be prevented.

Such was the situation when Jabotinsky and Slavinsky met in Prague. The following is Jabotinsky's authentic account of this meeting, exactly as it was given by him to a few friends; it was taken down by Nahum Levin, and the text was later approved by Jabotinsky himself.[4]

Slavinsky was asked: "How could you and Professor [Michael] Grushevsky, and [Andrey] Nikovsky, and so many others whom I always knew as honest democrats—how could you tolerate all these pogroms without rebelling against Petliura?"

Slavinsky bowed his head and tried to explain the reasons for their failure; it was, of course, a most unsatisfactory explanation. Yet Slavinsky, in his turn, also put a question to Jabotinsky, to which the latter could give no satisfactory answer.

"Why," asked Slavinsky, "are you Jews so hard on Petliura while you forgive General Allenby and your own Sir Herbert Samuel? Petliura had to deal with thirty million Ukrainians, in a country twice the size of France, and his army consisted of unruly bands. Allenby had seventy thousand well-disciplined troops against a handful of Arabs, and yet he did nothing to stop the pogrom in Jerusalem a year ago [April, 1920], and the organizer of the Jewish self-defense was sentenced to penal servitude; and only a few months ago the Jewish High Commissioner, Samuel, under very much the same conditions, allowed the May pogroms [in Jaffa] to last almost a week, with about 100 Jewish victims, while the soldiers were ordered to use sticks instead of rifles. Yet you Jews have not 'rebelled' against Allenby or Samuel or the British."

Jabotinsky answered in the way one usually replies in such cases, mentioning the Balfour Declaration and the great difference in the number of victims. But of course it sounded rather lame.

Slavinsky then went on to say that the main question was what could be done in the next spring when the Ukrainian troops would again have to cross the border and to occupy the border towns containing Jewish communities. What if those troops would again prove as "unruly" as before? What, he asked, could one advise the Ukrainian Nationalists to do to prevent further pogroms? Should they issue a proclamation to their troops? Should they threaten the offenders? They had already tried all this, without result. . . .

Jabotinsky replied that, of course, proclamations must be issued and offenders threatened with severe penalties, but that this would be of little help without the establishment of a Jewish gendarmerie composed of Jews, commanded by Jews, well-armed, and authorized to garrison the occupied towns. It was not to take part in any fighting. Its only concern would be to defend the peaceful population of the towns under Ukrainian occupation.

Slavinsky asked for time to submit the suggestion to his government. Jabotinsky's sole condition was that the government view this suggestion as his own and that it was in no way committing any organization with which he was connected.

Slavinsky went to Galicia to see his chief, while Jabotinsky consulted some leaders of Russian and Ukrainian Jewry who were then in Prague (among them V. Tiomkin, I. Trivus, M. Schwarzman, Y. Machover, Y. Suprassky). Eight approved of the plan and three rejected it; Jabotinsky, however, insisted that, although eight endorsed the plan, the entire responsibility was to be his own. He never formed a committee. He was sure he could raise both men and the money.

A second meeting between Slavinsky and Jabotinsky took place on September 3rd; a third, on September 4th. At the latter, held at the Olympia Palast Hotel in Carlsbad, an agreement was reached and signed. At these two encounters, Slavinsky was the only representative of the Ukrainian camp. According to his report, at the final meeting was present "among others, also Colonel Patterson, who very warmly supported the cause and pledged to help it."[5] Jabotinsky and Slavinsky, the signatories, undertook "to use their best endeavours, each one within the sphere of his personal influence," to put into effect a plan whereby a Jewish gendarmery, properly armed, manned, officered, and maintained by Jews, would be attached to the Ukrainian Army and, whilst "proceeding in the immediate rear and not taking any part whatsoever in military operations," would take over police duties and ensure the safety of the population in those towns and settlements, containing a Jewish population, which might be occupied by the Ukrainian Army.[6]

Some of Jabotinsky's friends whom he consulted in Carlsbad and who had no basic objections to the idea of Jewish police units with the Ukrainian Army, nevertheless argued that Petliura's government did not represent any real political or military force and could hardly be considered a real partner to any agreement providing for large-scale action; they warned that no tangible advantage for Ukrainian Jewry was likely to result from the agreement; the only certain result would be a storm of indignation and abuse against Jabotinsky himself.[7] Jabotinsky's reaction to these warnings was: "I am not completely sure about the 'practical results.' But if there is at least the tiniest chance that this agreement is capable of preventing or alleviating a new wave of pogroms, it is worth a try. And so far as attacks and abuse are concerned—you know, I do not care in the least."

However, as early as November 24, 1921, in a letter from New York to the Zionist World Executive in London, Jabotinsky was forced to admit regretfully that "the whole matter seems to be nothing more than a newspaper controversy." According to the agreement, he explained, "it was the duty of Slavinsky's Government to establish a Jewish Police; then I should have considered myself under obligation to give them, in this respect, all my assistance. But I gathered from Slavinsky's letters of which the last was written on October 20th, that an organized action of his government was not intended for the present." Jabotinsky quoted from this letter the following face-saving passages: "We can depose the Bolsheviks any day, but we are afraid of doing it because our diplomatic and financial rear in Europe is not yet sufficiently prepared, and without this rear we risk a prolonged anarchy."

Slavinsky's assurance that Petliura's government was able to "depose the Bolsheviks any day" was no doubt an empty boast. Its "diplomatic and financial rear in Europe" never became strengthened and stabilized. There was some talk about its army moving into the Ukraine in the spring of 1922. In the meantime, however, the policy of the Western power whose treasury had been financing this army and which was encouraging Petliura's interventionist plans, underwent a radical change; Petliura and his government were quietly dropped as a possible card in the European political game—his subsidy was withdrawn and his Army had to be disbanded. This was a development which Jabotinsky apparently could not foresee in August, 1921. The Jewish gendarmery provided in the agreement with Slavinsky thus did not come into existence for the simple reason that the invasion of the Soviet Ukraine by Petliura's army did not take place and there was no need, fortunately, for the protection of the Jewish population from the danger of pogroms.

Stormy Repercussions

What did "come into existence" was the predicted flood of indignation and abuse, as soon as the news of the agreement appeared in the press through Ukrainian indiscretion. It was immediately labeled as "an agreement with the pogromist Petliura." Anti-Zionist elements eagerly seized the opportunity to brand a Zionist leader as "Petliura's ally." Particularly active were the Socialist journalists. In Zionist ranks, too, there was considerable bitter criticism of Jabotinsky's action, and again the most violent in their denunciations were the Leftist groups. Though two of their own leaders (Abraham Revutzky and Shlomo Goldelman) had been Ministers in Petliura's cabinet, the *Poalei Zion* were most vocal in the demand that the Zionist Executive or the Actions Committee take drastic action; that they disavow, censure, or force Jabotinsky to resign from the Executive. In a letter to the Executive, Jabotinsky found it "characteristic that the only people who seem to be concerned with the whole business are the *Poalei Zion*. . . . Slavinsky's government fights the Bolsheviks and the Poalei Zion are afraid that their Socialist rivals might accuse them of friendly contact with the Zionist Executive, one member of which is supposed to be in friendly contact with an anti-Bolshevik government."[8]

On November 14, 1921, the Zionist Executive cabled to Jabotinsky in New York: "Slavinsky question arousing strong feeling in Eastern Europe. Send full report, copies documents." Jabotinsky cabled back on the 20th: "Mailing Slavinsky material, intend no concession to misguided public feeling."

The question of Jabotinsky's agreement with Slavinsky was first raised at a meeting of the Actions Committee, December 27 to 30, 1921. In the absence of Jabotinsky, at that time on a *Keren ha'Yesod* mission to America, the Actions Committee limited itself to a statement that "Mr. Jabotinsky has conducted negotiations and made agreements without having obtained the consent of the Executive and without having informed them of the steps undertaken." The Actions Committee, the statement continued, "declines all responsibility on behalf of the Zionist Organization for these negotiations and agreements and resolves that the Executive should ask Mr. Jabotinsky on his return from America to justify his action, and report to the Actions Committee at its next meeting."[9]

In the meantime a storm broke loose in the Zionist press and among leading Zionist circles.

The London *Jewish Times* (November 30th) demanded Jabotinsky's immediate resignation, pointing out that the name of Petliura was associated with some of the worst pogroms and that any agreement with him would be thoroughly repugnant to the Jewish conscience. The *Poalei Zion* of America cabled on December 3rd to the World Zionist Executive in London: "Demand Jabotinsky's immediate withdrawal from America and exclusion from the Executive on account of the scandalous Petliura agreement." The American Yiddish press was divided on this question: while the *Zeit* and the *Tagblatt* demanded Jabotinsky's resignation, the *Morning Journal* and the *Day* defended his action. Zionist public opinion in Europe, so far as it found expression in the reaction of its recognized ruling bodies, was, on the contrary, united in violent condemnation of

Jabotinsky. The Council of the English Zionist Federation and the annual conference of the Netherlands Zionist Federation demanded his resignation.[10] *Jüdische Rundschau*, the organ of the Zionist Organization in Germany, which at an early stage had taken a rather understanding position, later yielded to the prevailing feeling and claimed that "temperament and fantasy had misguided Jabotinsky into a grave political mistake."[11]

Particularly excited were the numerous Zionist emigrés from Russia and the Ukraine. They formed an inter-territorial "Federation of Russian-Ukrainian Zionists," which was officially recognized by the Zionist Executive; the seat of its Central Committee (*Merkas*) was Berlin. On November 23, 1921, Dr. Victor Jacobson, a member of this Central Committee, wrote to Richard Lichtheim, who at that time was Jabotinsky's colleague in the Zionist Executive: "The Russian *Merkas* . . . is very much afraid that . . . Russian Zionists will be exposed to great dangers." The same concern for the fate of their comrades in Russia induced the *Merkas*, one week later, to ask the Zionist Executive to get in touch with Leonid Krassin, the Soviet Ambassador in London, apparently in order to forestall possible persecution of Zionists in Russia. Lichtheim informed Dr. Weizmann of this request. The latter's political secretary, Leonard Stein, answered that "Dr. Weizmann declines to touch this matter."[12]

The Judgment

Jabotinsky himself reacted with studied equanimity to the violent and often openly malicious controversy. Absorbed by his grueling work for the *Keren ha'Yesod* in America, he wrote to his mother and sister from New York on December 18, 1921: "You have probably heard of a new storm raging against me for my agreement with Slavinsky. But here in America I don't feel it. I am being received everywhere with respect and ovations. Many articles against me are being published, some more are in my favor. I do not read any of them. I am used to all this, and it is not even interesting."

Urged by a friend not to let himself be provoked by press attacks, he answered: "Don't doubt me. I will not yield to any provocation. It is simply ridiculous to think of my resignation. . . . I will not only not resign, I will not even get angry and start calling names. When the barking will calm down, I will publish two articles written in an academic style. The first will be on the 'Usefulness of the Gendarmery' and the second on 'The Executive and Local Politics.' "[13]

Jabotinsky wrote not one but several articles on the first question. His basic "philosophy" in matters concerning the safety of the Jewish population in areas affected by armed conflicts was formulated in a succinct manner as follows: "Wherever there is danger of pogroms, because of a conflict between two or more non-Jewish armed camps, I recommend an agreement to form a Jewish gendarmery with any side that will only agree to establish a Jewish gendarmery. A Jewish gendarmery with the White Army, a Jewish gendarmery with the Red Army, a Jewish gendarmery with the Lilac and the Pea-green Army, if any; let them settle their quarrels, we shall police the towns and see to it that the Jewish population shall not be molested."[14]

Elaborating upon the second topic (i.e., the Executive and local politics), Jabotinsky insisted in the letter to I. Trivus that it was impossible "to implicate the Executive of a worldwide organization in problems of self-defense in the Ukraine or of recognition of Yiddish as an official language in Lithuania. On the other hand, it is equally unthinkable that I, because of my being a member of the Executive, should forego the right to care for the [Jewish] self-defense in South-Russia— *especially I, [when it comes to] self-defense and South-Russia!*—or [M.] Soloveitchik, even if he would leave his position as Minister of Jewish Affairs in the Lithuanian government, would stop caring for the Jewish autonomy in Lithuania. . . . I therefore think that the only possible solution of this problem is to leave everything as it is."

The *status quo* in this field was based on the political resolution No. VIII of the Carlsbad Congress. It laid down the principle that all political work in the Diaspora countries was to be conducted under the exclusive jurisdiction of national organizations (*Landesorganisationen*) or Federations which were to be in this respect independent of the leading organ of the World Zionist Organization. Jabotinsky therefore insisted that the agreement with Slavinsky was a matter on which only the Zionist Organizations of Russia and the Ukraine were entitled to pass judgment. Zionism in these countries was banned by the Soviet régime. A substitute, however, existed in free Europe: tens of thousands of Zionists from Soviet Russia and the Ukraine fled to Germany, Poland, France, Czechoslovakia, Belgium, England, etc., and lived there as refugees. Almost in every country separate groups of such refugees existed, which were united in an interterritorial "Federation of Russian-Ukrainian Zionists."

Jabotinsky submitted the controversy to this body. On September 7–11, 1922, a Conference of Russian-Ukrainian Zionists met in Berlin.[15] Jabotinsky presented his case in full, with all the pertinent material. A large majority of the delegates, among whom were several outstanding leaders, was ready to endorse and justify his action. A small subcommittee, of which this writer was a member, was nominated to formulate a suitable resolution. Anxious to secure the widest possible backing by the delegates, the subcommittee formulated the motion in rather general terms. When the draft was shown to Jabotinsky, he indignantly declared that it was unacceptable to him and that he would reject it, unless it were drastically strengthened. Angered by this threat, this writer heatedly said: "Please, don't blackmail us!" To that Jabotinsky haughtily answered: "You know, Yosif Borisovitch, I prefer your written style to your verbal pronouncements." Young and fresh as this writer was at that time, he defiantly retorted: "This can be very easily arranged, Vladimir Yevgenyevitch; we can limit our relationship to correspondence only, and never speak to each other." Jabotinsky looked at him with an unexpected twinkle in his eyes and said: "Let's not rub it in. Let's see what we can do with this damned resolution of yours."

After that, an agreed resolution was easily hammered out. It stated that "having heard the explanations of V. E. Jabotinsky and having acquainted itself with the documents relating to the project of an understanding signed on the 4th September 1921 by V. Jabotinsky and M. Slavinsky," the Conference has arrived at the followed conclusions:

1. The negotiations with Slavinsky were conducted by Jabotinsky privately and exclusively in HIS personal capacity as an individual, Slavinsky being fully aware at the time that Mr. Jabotinsky did not with regard to this question represent either the [Zionist] Executive, or any other body of the World Zionist Organization, nor the Russian-Ukrainian Zionist Organization.

2. In accordance with resolution No. VIII of the Twelfth Zionist Congress, the Conference holds that the judgment in the above mentioned question comes in its essence within the scope of the Zionist Organization of Russia and the Ukraine.

3. While the Conference of Russian-Ukrainian Zionists abroad is not entitled to speak in the name of their comrades in Russia and the Ukraine, it deems it, nevertheless, to be the duty of its conscience as Zionists to declare, in the name of the Russian-Ukrainian Zionists abroad only, that on the basis of explanations and documents submitted:

a) Jabotinsky's mode of action and intentions were undoubtedly of a neutral character, i.e. in the sense of non-interference in the fighting forces of the Ukraine or in the military action of the Soviet authorities [who were combating the Jewish pogroms];

b) While rejecting every suggestion as to the anti-moral nature of Jabotinsky's action, the Conference declares that Jabotinsky was actuated in his action exclusively by the apprehension as to the fate of the Jewish population which had previously more than once been subjected to pogroms and butcheries during the military operations in the Ukraine.

4. The Conference holds the view that it is essential that V. E. Jabotinsky should continue his fruitful Zionist activities in the position occupied by him.

It is easy to see from this carefully worded resolution that the Conference did not go into the question of the *merits* of the agreement: no approval or disapproval of its *contents* was expressed. What the Conference did was to exonerate Jabotinsky from the accusation that he interfered into Ukrainian political affairs, thus jeopardizing the neutrality of the World Zionist Organization. The resolution also fully recognized the integrity of Jabotinsky's motives and the importance of his remaining an active force in a responsible position in the World Zionist Organization.

The Last Straw

Jabotinsky's adversaries doggedly continued their efforts to keep the "Slavinsky affair" alive.

When the Actions Committee met in Berlin in January, 1923, several members, representing the parties of the Left (Messrs. Rubashov, Mereminsky, Kaplansky) demanded from the Executive the promised report.[16] M. Soloveitchik, replying on behalf of the Executive, stated that:

1. According to the resolution adopted by the Twelfth Zionist Congress at Carlsbad, Diaspora politics come within the competence of the local Zionist Federations and not of the World Executive or the Actions Committee.

2. The Slavinsky affair therefore belonged to the sphere of the Russian-Ukrainian Federation, with its seat in Berlin. The latter had examined all the pertinent documents and found that Jabotinsky had acted in his private capacity and was actuated entirely by humanitarian motives.

3. The Executive is satisfied with this procedure and recommends that the Actions Committee regard the matter as settled.

However, the Leftist representatives were not prepared to drop the matter. Some claimed that their friends and comrades had suffered under the Soviet government in consequence of the Slavinsky agreement. They insisted that, whatever the view of the Russian-Ukrainian Central Committee in Berlin, it was not the view of other Russian-Ukrainian Zionists, whether in Poland or America. Finally, they threatened to abstain from voting the resolutions of the Political Committee without Jabotinsky's statement in justification of his action.

Anxious for a vote on the political resolutions and apparently sure of his ground, Jabotinsky declared that he was willing to appear before a special commission appointed to investigate the Affair. The seven members appointed to this Commission were Messrs. I. Grinbaum, Z. Rubashov, R. Weltsch, L. Reich, Rabbi Brodt, and Senator Rubenstein.

However, at the next morning's session (January 18th), Grinbaum read a letter from Jabotinsky stating that, as he had resolved to resign from the Executive and to leave the Zionist Organization, there was no purpose in appearing before the special Commission. The representatives of the parties of the Left immediately interpreted this move as proof that Jabotinsky simply "shirked the ordeal of appearing before the Commission." They declared that, since he had now withdrawn from the Zionist Organization, they would drop their demand for any inquiry into this affair, but should he return, they would immediately renew their demand. A motion was adopted that under these circumstances "the Actions Committee, as far as it is concerned, considers this matter as settled."[17]

Jabotinsky categorically rejected the allegation that his resignation had anything to do with the Slavinsky affair. The statement of the Executive in this matter was assured of the endorsement by the Actions Committee. On the other hand, no Actions Committee resolution in this question could influence his position toward either the Executive or the Zionist Organization.[18]

The Bolshevik Bogy

One of the main arguments of those who attacked Jabotinsky's agreement with Slavinsky was the allegation that because of it Zionists were bound to be persecuted in Soviet Russia. Jabotinsky resolutely dismissed this argument. In a letter from New York, he wrote on December 18, 1921:[19]

Soviet reprisals fail to impress me. I don't believe that they will come to pass, but even if they would, I cannot take them into consideration. I don't understand how is it possible to reckon with 100 arrests and 10 executions when a man dreams—with or without reason—to prevent, at least partly, 10,000 deaths from pogroms. If it is in the cards that Sapir [Dr. J. B. Sapir, popular Zionist leader in

Odessa, of whom Jabotinsky was very fond] or X be imprisoned, I would regret it very much—but let him be under arrest. He is not the first one to be imprisoned. This approach, I feel, will vex you, but I will not forswear it. When I conducted my propaganda for the Legion, people also tried to frighten me by [prospects of] pogroms in Palestine.

Jabotinsky proved to be right in his skepticism as to the alleged inevitability of anti-Zionist reprisals in Soviet Russia. It is true that the Jewish Communists had eagerly taken advantage of this opportunity to assail and denounce Zionism. *Emes*, the Yiddishlanguage organ of the Jewish Section of the Communist Party (*Yevsektziya*), published an article with huge headlines: "The Zionists Are Plunging a Knife into Revolution's Back. Jabotinsky Has Aligned Himself with Petliura to Wage War Against the Red Army." A few days later an article appeared in *Zhisn Nazionalnostey* (Life of Nationalities), the official Russian-language organ of the Commissariat for National Minorities, appealing to the Soviet Government "to liquidate the Zionist counterrevolutionary hydra" in Russia and, first and foremost, to put an end to the legal existence of the Jewish sports organization *Maccabi*. The article specifically quoted paragraph 3 of the Jabotinsky-Slavinsky agreement which mentioned *Maccabi* members as prospective recruits for the local militia destined to protect the Jewish population of Soviet towns and hamlets occupied by the Petliura army, and stressed: "It seems that Jabotinsky heavily counted on the *Maccabi* membership in his project of collaboration with Petliura."

Zionist and *Maccabi* circles were deeply perturbed by these attacks. But the Soviet authorities proved themselves less apprehensive than their Jewish agents. Engineer Itzhak Rabinovitch, a leading Russian Zionist, who at that time headed the *Maccabi* organization in the Soviet Union, related how the matter was handled at this critical juncture.[20] He was summoned to appear before the dreaded *Cheka* (political police, later GPU), where he had a long but inconclusive discussion on Zionism, revolution, pogroms, Bolshevism, Jabotinsky, Petliura, and similar subjects. Finally, Rabinovitch suggested that the entire matter be submitted for investigation and decision to another high Soviet body—the War Ministry's Division for Sport and Military Preparedness of the Youth, to which *Maccabi* was directly subordinated. The suggestion was accepted, and in a few weeks Rabinovitch appeared before a special committee of three, headed by the *Politruk* (Political Instructor) of the Division, Comrade Valnikov. The hearing did not last long: the members of the Committee had never seen the inciting articles in the *Yevsektziya* press. To them the entire subject was an episode that concerned Galicia where the Petliura army was stationed. In the meantime the few Petliura detachments which had invaded Soviet territory had been decisively beaten. Rabinovitch had a relatively easy job. He simply stated that, legally, the whole affair had nothing to do with the *Maccabi* organization; Jabotinsky was not the head of the *Maccabi* in Russia and signed the agreement with Slavinsky without consulting that organization. But, says Rabinovitch, "I did not want to hide behind purely formal considerations and was ready to clarify the issue on its merits." He dared to make it clear to the Committee that Jabotinsky's intention was "to save Ukrainian Jews from a new slaughter in case Petliura succeeded in at least temporarily occupying some Ukrainian towns with a Jewish population. . . . I am telling you quite openly: if I were in Jabotinsky's place, I would have acted exactly as he did. You have thus a moral right to try me before a court."

After thorough deliberation and analysis of the full text of the agreement, the Committee exonerated the *Maccabi*. Moreover, it concluded that "it appears improbable that the agreement between Jabotinsky and Slavinsky was motivated, on the Jewish side, by counter-revolutionary intentions; it can be surmised that it has been caused exclusively by the fear of pogroms and further slaughter." "This was the favorable outcome of the enraged hue and cry raised by the *Yevsektziya*," concludes Rabinovitch; "nobody got hurt."

Perhaps even more significant was the reaction to the Jabotinsky-Slavinsky agreement of the non-Marxist Labor Zionist Organization (*Zeirei Zion*) which existed clandestinely in the Soviet Union.

In April, 1922, a secret *Zeirei Zion* Convention had taken place in Kiev. It was attended by about seventy delegates, mostly from the Ukraine. One of the questions before the Convention was the Party's attitude to Jabotinsky's action, which had for some time been hotly debated by various local groups. Three participants in this Convention—Joseph Ariel, now Israeli Minister to Belgium, David Bar Rav Hoi, *Mapai* member of the *Knesset*, and Baruch Weinstein, now a member of the General Zionist Central Committee in Israel—have kindly shared with this writer their recollections of the handling of this issue. They were members of the delegation from Odessa, Jabotinsky's native town, and ardent defenders of his policies. They found much understanding and support on the part of the delegates from the Podolia region and from several other delegations. It is Mr. Ariel's recollection that, had it come to a vote, their position would have been approved by about one-half of the delegates. After a lengthy discussion, the question was referred to a Political Committee, which had to submit a draft resolution. Mr. Weinstein was entrusted with the drafting of the text. The tenor of his draft, Mr. Weinstein recalls, was that, considering the circumstances under which the agreement with Slavinsky was concluded, the Convention approved of Jabotinsky's action.

As Weinstein was about completing his draft, the Convention room was invaded by *Cheka* agents who arrested all the participants. Weinstein managed to tear up the draft, but he was not able to swallow or otherwise to destroy the scraps; the *Cheka* thus succeeded in piecing them together, securing evidence of the Party's presumed attitude to the Jabotinsky move.

The delegates knew that the evidence was in the hands of the prosecution. Before their trial, they had the opportunity of discussing their line of conduct. They had every reason to expect that the Agreement would be used to prove the "counter-revolutionary character of the Zionist movement," thus involving heavy sentences. Some suggested that, should the question be raised by the prosecution, all should disavow Jabotinsky. According to Mr. Weinstein, it was Mr. Bar Rav Hoi who indignantly rejected this strategy. "He was not proposing," he said, "to volunteer any positive statements; but should the question be raised and should some of his comrades condemn Jabotinsky, he, Bar Rav Hoi, would openly proclaim his solidarity with Jabotinsky." It was finally agreed that the accused themselves were not to touch upon the issue; should the prosecution do so, they were not to disavow Jabotinsky, but to insist that they had no knowledge of the agreement and that no opinion on this question had been expressed by the Convention. "Fortunately," says Mr. Bar Rav Hoi, "this topic was completely omitted during the trial, in August, 1922; many of our comrades, who were ready to back Jabotinsky at any price and not to permit that his name be torn to pieces by the *Yevsektziya*, have thus escaped the lot that was probably in store for them." The Soviet authorities for some reason dropped the subject; possibly they did not consider it of sufficient importance to them. Nor were subsequent arrests and trials of Zionists in the Soviet Union ever connected with the Affair.

The first edition of the *Great Soviet Encyclopaedia* (1932) still described Jabotinsky as "one of the most outstanding enemies of Bolshevism" and specifically mentioned that "during the period of the Civil War [in Russia] he concluded an agreement with the representatives of Petliura concerning the organization of 'Jewish Self-Defense' to help Petliura's troops" (Vol. 24, p. 600). The second edition of the *Encyclopaedia*, which appeared in 1952, does not mention Jabotinsky at all.

At an early stage of the "Petliura Affair," Jabotinsky confidently expected the hue and cry to be short-lived. In a letter from New York, he wrote on December 18, 1921:[21] "I have a definite feeling that very soon people will say:—Jabotinsky wanted to organize Jewish gendarmery, and in this he was perfectly right, and for such a purpose one has to negotiate even with the devil." He was sure that "the noise will continue one more month," and then when he returned from America and visited Berlin or Vienna, "this pack will cheer me as usual."

In this belief Jabotinsky was greatly mistaken. The "Petliura Affair" pursued him for the rest of his life. On almost every occasion, his political adversaries would revive the issue and utilize it as "evidence" of his inveterate "reactionary leanings." When asked what other preventives against pogroms they offered, they had no answer; but they continued to accuse Jabotinsky of "concluding a pact with pogromists." Disgusted but patient, Jabotinsky repeatedly explained to the Jewish public the true circumstances and meaning of his agreement with Slavinsky, seemingly disposing of the accusations in a convincing fashion. But in a year or two, the accusations reappeared; like a shadow, they followed Jabotinsky throughout his life. He fully realized that no reasoning, no arguments of political, moral, or practical nature would ever put an end to this kind of attack; and, obviously overstating his case in the face of perennial malicious criticism, he defiantly declared shortly before his death that he was "even more proud of the Petliura agreement" than he was of the part he played in the creation of the Jewish Legion and in the defense of Jerusalem: "even though ultimately nothing came out of it—when I die you can write as my epitaph 'This was the man who made the pact with Petliura.' "[22]

TWENTY

AT THE CROSSROADS

The Herbert Samuel Issue

Absorbed as he was in his daily grind of fund-raising in the . United States, Jabotinsky was at the same time intently watching the political developments in Palestine and London. What he saw was anything but comforting. Particularly distressing to him was the growing realization of the truly sinister role Sir Herbert Samuel had been playing in the steady deterioration of the Zionist cause.

We have seen that in his Jerusalem speech Jabotinsky heartily welcomed this first Jewish High Commissioner of Palestine. Upon his arrival in London, six weeks later, he told the *Times* correspondent: "We are proud that a Jew has been selected for this high task; his impartiality is our pride."[1] An article "The Political Position" in *The Keren ha'Yesod Book* (1921)— unsigned as were all others, but known to have been written by Jabotinsky —stated (p. 27): "No better choice could have been made even by a Zionist Congress, had it the right, under the Mandate, to nominate the High Commissioner."

This infatuation with Herbert Samuel was one of the major political errors Jabotinsky made. Yielding to universal enthusiasm, he reversed his early intuitive skepticism and gave a practically unlimited endorsement to the High Commissioner. Even the Jaffa pogrom, and the subsequent suspension of Jewish immigration by Samuel, did not shatter this attitude. With his customary loyalty to ideas and men he had once endorsed, he was reluctant to withdraw the trust he had placed in the High Commissioner.

357

However, Herbert Samuel made him do so. After the Jaffa pogrom, he appointed (on May 7 th) a commission of inquiry under the chairmanship of Chief Justice Sir Thomas W. Haycraft. The report of the Commission, submitted on August 10, 1921, was openly hostile to Zionism and Palestine Jewry, and practically blamed the Jews themselves for the Jaffa riots.[2] Jabotinsky read this report in New York. In a letter to the Zionist Executive written on November 24, 1921, he was, of course, very critical of this obviously biased document; but, he pointed out, "what lends it the character of a heavy blow is Sir Herbert Samuel's following letter to Mr. Churchill.[3] He recommends this document with all its innuendos and direct calumnies as a 'very thorough and impartial review'! This praise is naturally reflected in Mr. Churchill's answer.* Both these letters together constitute an official confirmation of the findings of the Commission, and will do us considerable harm."

Stressing that Samuel's letter was dated August 25th and therefore constituted one of his last political acts before the Zionist Congress in Carlsbad, Jabotinsky said:

I regret we did not know this at Carlsbad. Had I known it then, I would have taken upon myself the responsibility of bringing the whole Samuel question to the forefront. But I feel compelled to tell you now that I consider the limits of justifiable patience on our part reached and overreached, and I beg formally to insist on decisive steps being taken with regard to Sir Herbert Samuel. We have no right to abuse the confidence of the Congress by condoning the policies of a man who is openly inciting public opinion in Great Britain and in the Arab world against us, who confirms as "impartial views" slanderous allegations imputing to us "ferocity," in addition to all the rest of his policy which is sufficiently known to every one of you.

Jabotinsky concluded his letter with an insistent plea to dispatch "as quickly as possible" the special delegation which the Carlsbad Congress decided to send to Palestine in order to submit to the High Commissioner a frank statement on the merits and results of his policy, to point out the need for a drastic change, and to report his answer, if any, to the Executive and the Actions Committee (political resolution No. VII).

---

*In his letter to Herbert Samuel of September 21, 1921, Churchill described the Haycraft report as "most ably compiled, lucid and well reasoned."

However, no delegation was sent to Sir Herbert Samuel either in November, 1921, or during the following eleven months.

In the fall of 1922, Jabotinsky, for strictly personal reasons (to see his mother who was ill), paid a short visit to Palestine. He stayed there incognito, in order not to be disturbed by extraneous matters.[4] Nevertheless, he found time for several moves of political significance. On October 17th, he met—not on his own initiative— with Sir Herbert Samuel. During this audience Jabotinsky told the High Commissioner that in his opinion, based on two years' experience in *Keren ha'Yesod* work, it was the policy of the Palestine administration which, by discouraging the enthusiasm of Zionist workers throughout the world, was responsible for the grave financial difficulties from which Zionist constructive work in Palestine was suffering; a perpetuation of this policy could only lead to inevitable bankruptcy. The following night, the Zionist Executive in Palestine invited Jabotinsky to present a report on the political situation; members of the *Vaad Leumi* also participated in this closed meeting. Jabotinsky repeated what he had said to Sir Herbert Samuel and told the gathering that, unless the Executive were to adopt stiffer tactics to combat this situation, a split in Zionist ranks would become inevitable. At this meeting, Jabotinsky reported, "the most bitter complaints against the Administration's attitude were voiced by every one present without exception."[5]

Upon his return to London, Jabotinsky submitted to the Executive a memorandum dated November 5, 1922, in which he insisted that

the wobbling attitude of the present [British] Government is merely the logical consequence of the High Commissioner's policy in Palestine and of our own meekness in dealing with his administration. With the sole exception of the case of Transjordania, every other restriction imposed on the Zionist Movement or every measure detrimental to our interests had its origin in Jerusalem at the Government House, the Colonial Office merely sanctioning Sir H[erbert] S[amuel]'s suggestions. Very often, as for instance after the Jaffa events, prominent officials of the Colonial Office admitted to us that the H[igh] C[ommissioner]'s panicky behaviour was entirely unjustified in their opinion, but so long as we Zionists wanted him to remain High Commissioner they naturally had to accept his views as approved or at least condoned by us.

Neither in 1921 nor in 1922 was the Zionist Executive ready to accept Jabotinsky's contention that Herbert Samuel's policy was undermining the very foundations of the Zionist political position; nor were they prepared to heed Jabotinsky's insistence on actively opposing Samuel's policies. "I am deeply dissatisfied with the state of affairs in Palestine," Jabotinsky wrote to I. Trivus on February 9, 1922: "The worst is that the Executive deems it its duty to profess that it is satisfied. This is stupid. Zionism is entirely based on confidence. If we say that the situation is bad, and we are honest, everybody will at once endeavor to overcome the misfortune. But if we are lying and trying to cover up the Samuel régime. . . ."

The White Paper Controversy

In the meantime, Jabotinsky's long absence from London had considerably weakened his influence in the conduct of Zionist political affairs; it gave a chance to defeatist forces to gain the upper hand, leaving him uninformed and showing utter disregard for his views.

On February 10, 1922, the London *Times* published a resumé of the government draft of an order-in-council providing for a constitution for Palestine, with a partially elective Legislative Council. The very next day Jabotinsky cabled from New York to the London Executive: "Disquieting reports [on] constitution project. Please cable essentials, instruct Secretariat [to] send me all political correspondence from September [1921] and future." He fully realized the danger implicit in any attempt at giving the intensely hostile Arab majority a voice in the administration of the country, and the necessity for actively combating any step in this direction. The prevailing influence in political matters in the London Executive was, however, at the time exercised by Leonard Stein, the Executive's political secretary, who held extremely conciliatory views on policies to be pursued by the Zionist movement toward the Mandatory Power; he also had little consideration for an absent member of the Executive who once dared to criticize him. The answer Jabotinsky received from the Executive, signed by Mr. Stein on February 16th, was to the effect that, though the Executive had been supplied with a copy of the full draft of the projected constitution, there was "none available for transmission to you"; Stein also "regretted that it would be impossible without incurring very heavy expense to cable an intelligible summary of the draft"; he therefore simply mailed to Jabotinsky a clipping from the *Times* saying that "copies of the principal political documents from September onwards were being collected" for Jabotinsky and "will be sent in the next few days."

At this critical juncture, Jabotinsky was thus left practically without substantial documentation. Stein also made it clear that it would be futile on his part to try to say something in this matter: "as we [the Executive] are asked [by the government] to submit our observations without delay, it would, in any case, unfortunately, be impossible to await your comments." A dangerous double precedent had been thereby established: the Zionist Executive had permitted itself to be intimidated into accepting the alleged necessity of assenting "without delay" to any suggestion of the government; and it deemed it proper to do so without giving to an absent member of the Political Department a chance to express his views and to press for their consideration. Four months later, a similar procedure was followed in regard to Churchill's White Paper. As to the contents of the projected "Constitution," Stein wrote that the Executive was

> disposed at present to feel that though the draft requires strengthening from our point of view, there is not very much in it to which we can take strong exception if there is to be a constitution at all. Whatever our own views on the latter point, we should be putting ourselves in the wrong both with the Government and with public opinion if we attempted to obtsruct the development of self-governing institutions and all we can do is to face the situation as it actually is and make the best of it.

The fear of putting themselves "in the wrong" induced the Executive not only to accept the Legislative Council scheme, but even to "express its satisfaction,"[6] thereby establishing a pattern of endorsing every government proposal. This pattern was followed to the bitter end four months later in the case of Churchill's White Paper of July 1, 1922,[7] which was drafted on Herbert Samuel's insistence and was intended to appease the Arabs by a restrictive interpretation of the Balfour Declaration and of Zionist aims. The document asserted that the terms of the Balfour Declaration "do not contemplate that Palestine as a whole should be converted into a Jewish National Home, but that such a Home should be founded in Palestine." Professor Paul L. Hanna rightly describes the gist of this document by saying that "it foreshadowed the creation of Samuel's ideal of a duo-cultural state in the Holy Land."[8]

The draft of the White Paper was presented to the Zionist Executive on June 3, 1922, with a request for assurances that it was acceptable to the Zionist Organization. Jabotinsky was at that time still in the United States, where he spent eight months on behalf of the Keren ha'Yesod.

According to his own account, he returned to London on June 17th, at four or five P.M.:

> A secretary who met me at the station asked me to come immediately to the offices of the Executive. In the office I was shown by Dr. Weizmann the Memorandum dated June 3 which we now call the White Paper; he informed me that the Government was demanding the Executive's consent to this document, and that this consent must be in the hands of the Government the very next morning, June 18. If this were not done, we were being threatened with drastic and very serious changes in the text of the Mandate to the disadvantage of the Zionist Organization. Dr. Weizmann at the same time assured me that the Executive had taken very energetic steps in order to dissuade the Government from this demand, or at least to mitigate certain passages in the document, but that nothing had been of avail, and that the Colonial Office was insisting on its ultimatum: consent the next morning, or changes of the Mandate text. Therefore, the meeting of the Executive, reinforced by invited members of the A.C., must take place that night and arrive at a decision before the following morning.
>
> In the six hours at my disposal between this information and the meeting of the Actions Committee which was called for the same evening, it was naturally impossible for me to do anything positive, or to investigate whether Dr. Weizmann and the Executive had done in absence "everything" (as he maintained) to persuade the [British] Government to change their attitude. But one thing was clear to me: almost any sacrifice was worthwhile—if only the [Jewish] Agency would remain in our hands. True, I did not agree to the form of our answer. . . . I insisted that our acquiescence should be qualified. The formula proposed by me was to the effect that the Executive, while unable to agree with the spirit of the statement, did not wish to increase the complications which H. M. Government had to face and was, therefore, prepared to conform in their activities to the main principles of the document. This formula was rejected and a practically unqualified acquiescence sent instead. . . . I voted against it; and it is not true that I signed the answer, but I did not resign, and thus assumed responsibility.[9]

In his subsequent opposition to Dr. Weizmann's policies, Jabotinsky never reproached him for his acceptance of the White Paper. Dr. Weizmann raised this question on his own initiative at the Fifteenth Zionist Congress in August, 1927. Answering Jabotinsky's criticism of the Executive's defeatist policies, he said:[10] "When Mr. Jabotinsky, like the rest of us, was confronted with the grave trial of having to sign the White Paper, he did not make the speech he has made here. Why did he not try then to face up to the British Prime Minister, or to Samuel or the Colonial

Secretary and make the speech he has made here? He has signed, because he could do nothing else."

Referring to this statement, Jabotinsky stressed that, within the few hours that were at his disposal, he

no longer had time either to take any political steps myself or, as Dr. Weizmann is pleased to express it, make a speech before the British Premier.

To be sure, I still had the rather alluring possibility of withdrawing from any share in the impending decision, to decline all responsibility for it, and to resign from the Executive over this issue. But I felt that this would have meant deserting my colleagues in a desperate emergency. I felt it my moral duty to share with my colleagues even the shame of a defeat, even though I had taken no part in the battle lost during my absence and had had no knowledge of it only a few hours previously. I therefore decided to accept Dr. Weizmann's presentation not merely as subjectively sincere—this goes without saying—but also as an objective fact, and to give him and the other gentlemen in the Executive full credit for really having taken all possible steps in combating the [Government] ultimatum; I thus decided loyally to share in the grave responsibility borne by my colleagues.

Today, having heard the quoted words of Dr. Weizmann, I regret my decision. I now realize that loyalty is a thing with which one should be very sparing. Had matters been reversed—had I lost a battle and another man had come at the last moment, had learned the situation from me, had accepted my presentation in full confidence and without scrutiny—then I would never in my life have reproached him for it; and if a third party were to blame him on that score, I would get up and state that I assumed full responsibility. Dr. Weizmann feels differently—something I note with great regret and leave for public opinion to judge.[11]

It can be easily assumed that Jabotinsky never was happy or proud over this particular chapter of his Zionist career. But he refused from the very beginning to attribute to Churchill's White Paper too great an importance, or to consider it a major blow to Zionist rights and interests. In a letter to the *Jewish Chronicle* (February 2, 1923) he wrote: "The tone and spirit [of this document] are decidedly humiliating—but one should not, in my opinion, attach overdue importance to the tone of official literature. As to the contents—it does not contain one line which, under strict legal analysis, would formally preclude the attainment of the aim of Zionism, which is the gradual formation of a Jewish majority in Palestine; and, as the statement does not preclude this, all the rest, though most unpleasant, is immaterial."

This restrained appraisal of the White Paper's actual political harmfulness, coupled with loyalty for and confidence in Dr. Weizmann, permitted Jabotinsky not only not to resign from the Executive, but for months to come to remain a faithful friend and collaborator of Dr. Weizmann; he was doing his very best to secure League of Nations' ratification of the Mandate which had then been badly jeopardized by opposition on the part of Italy and the Vatican. The Zionist Executive asked him to utilize his old journalistic connections in Italy and to try to improve the "political climate" for Zionism. He accepted the assignment, though he was rather doubtful whether he would be able to achieve tangible results within the short time at his disposal. "I hope," he wrote Dr. Weizmann on July 10, 1922, from Milan, "that the Executive does not entertain any sanguine expectations as to the probable success of my mission . . . but, of course, I am glad to be present and at least trying to do something at this moment." He reported that "the tone of the press was slightly improving." A Jewish Telegraphic Agency dispatch from Rome reported that he also was "holding conversations with representatives of the Vatican and the [Italian] Government."[12]

When, on August 1st, he received in Rome the full text of the ratified Mandate, he wrote Dr. Weizmann a letter full of praise for the latter's personal achievements. "When I call to mind the beginnings, i.e. Manchester and Justice Walk [where they both roomed in 1915], and how all this was being built up bit by bit or sucked out from the finger of one single man, I must tell you—*je me pique de connaître un peu d'histoire générale*—that it is something unexampled as personal performance. . . . You don't need congratulations and compliments. I wish you a good rest."

Parting, of the Ways

Jabotinsky did not resign from the Executive after the acceptance of Churchill's White Paper and continued his Zionist work. But there had been an ever increasing chasm between his appraisal of and reaction to the course of political events and that of his colleagues. This cleavage came to the fore at the Annual Conference at Carlsbad in August, 1922, where sharp divergencies broke out in the midst of the Executive. "The main underlying factor," Jabotinsky later recalled, "was again the same—the deep difference in the appreciation of the political situation, as between some influential members of the Executive and myself. The conflict ended in an empty compromise, leaving the door open for further internecine struggles."[13]

In an intimate conversation with S. Gepstein, whom he met again at Carlsbad after seven years of separation, Jabotinsky reported a long talk he had the same day with Dr. Weizmann: "It was a good, friendly talk. We both argued in a very intelligent, wonderful way. But, you know, I intuitively felt one thing: I cannot go in his ways, and one shouldn't go in these ways, because they are bound to bring us to self-abdication. Weizmann believes that his way is that of a compromising realist, and mine is the way of a stubborn fantast, of a utopian; and I feel that his line is the line of renunciation, of subconscious Marannism, while mine is a difficult, stormy way, which will, however, lead more quickly to a Jewish State."[14]

Probably the most lucid presentation and motivation of his concept of Zionist policy can be found in a memorandum Jabotinsky sent to all members of the Executive on November 5, 1922. At the meeting of the Executive held the previous day, he introduced a resolution demanding that a memorandum be sent to the British government with the request to inform the Zionist Organization "whether the Government intends to adhere to the Mandate"; and if so, that "measures be taken immediately, in order to remove anti-Zionist officials, to ensure the safety of the Jewish population and the unhampered development of Zionist constructive work, and generally to restore Jewish confidence throughout the world."

Jabotinsky put special emphasis on the necessity for "restoring Jewish confidence throughout the world." Knowing that his colleagues had been mainly concerned with the meager results of Zionist fund-raising and the catastrophic state of the Zionist budget, he tried to make them realize both the depth of the financial crisis and its political causes:

The present situation has been described by me in speaking to the High Commissioner on October 16th as "the verge of bankruptcy," and by Mr. Sokolov in speaking to Major Ormsby Gore a few days ago as "not only the verge of a catastrophe, but the catastrophe itself." Unfortunately, both statements are by no means exaggerated.

My experience of two years' work for the K.H. [*Keren ha'Yesod*] fully convinces me that the main reason of our present financial plight is political. K.H. moneys are hardly ever sent in or brought to the collecting office by the contributors themselves on their own initiative: these moneys are being *collected* in every country by a relatively small army of Zionist workers. The success of the collection, therefore, mainly depends on the energy and the *Arbeitsfreude* of these Zionist workers. Theirs is a hard and unpleasant task; they can only carry it out with the full weight of their enthusiasm if they know that the ultimate aim is still the same old Zionism—the creation of a Jewish commonwealth in Palestine. When they see this ultimate aim officially clouded by such statements as Samuel's speech of June 3, 1921, or the White Paper of July, 1922; when they hear and read about the anti-Zionist activities of the Palestine Administration; and when they hear no word of manly protest against all this on the part of the Zionist Executive, but, on the contrary, see that this Executive keeps smiling and bowing as though everything in the government's behaviour were quite satisfactory:—then the confidence and energy of the Zionist worker inevitably weakens, he begins to neglect his work, and K.H. income is not forthcoming. This is exactly our present situation.

There was, in his opinion, no other way out from this predicament than "to have it out" with the Mandatory government and to ascertain its real intentions and policy:

I have given the most careful consideration to the contention that we should not put any such straight questions to this government because there may be a danger of a negative answer. I must reject this contention on both tactical and moral grounds. Personally I believe as firmly as ever that there is a real coincidence of interests between Zionism and the British position in the Eastern Mediterranean; and I firmly believe that any serious revision of the problem by whatever government will only result in their re-confirming this view. Furthermore, I firmly believe that no British government will break the Balfour pledge. . . . I am sure, therefore, that a straight question—which the government, under the Mandate, and in view of Bonar Law's declarations, is under legal obligation to answer—will bring about a favorable reply. But to those who think that the community of interests is questionable and that the pledge may be broken because the tax-payer is tired of paying two million pounds a year*—to those I must say that it would be both dangerous and immoral to prolong the existence of a misunderstanding. If the Mandate has no foundation but bluff, it is no use keeping up the appearances for another couple of months. Our movement can only thrive in an atmosphere of clearness. It was the policy of drift and bluff that has brought us to the present situation. This policy—to avoid a straight talk with the government for fear that they have up their sleeve a ready and unpleasant reply, and at the same time to tell the Jewish public that everything is in perfect order—this policy can no more be countenanced. With great reluctance I must even say that it will no more be possible to carry on this policy unless the Executive is prepared to face an open split in its own ranks.

---

*Jabotinsky refers here to £2,000,000 expenditure for the maintenance of British armed forces in Palestine.

"This memorandum," Jabotinsky later reported, "was discussed by the Executive, but no decision was arrived at, and we went to the Actions Committee [January, 1923] meeting divided as before."[15]

Resignation

This decisive Actions Committee session opened in an atmosphere of pent-up tension. According to *The New Palestine* correspondent, Dr. Weizmann's inaugural address on the political situation "was interrupted by a series of questions by Mr. Jabotinsky who charged Dr. Weizmann with displaying excessive leniency in representing the Zionist cause before the British, and in his negotiations with Arab leaders."[16] Jabotinsky's own analysis of the situation followed the line presented in his memorandum of November 5, 1922, and culminated in three resolutions he submitted to the Actions Committee; their gist was:[17]

1. To inform both the home government and the Palestine administration that the continuance of the present policy in Palestine threatens to ruin the Zionist movement financially, and to bring our enterprise in Palestine to bankruptcy.

2. To declare that the presence of anti-Zionists or anti-Semites in the British personnel of the Palestine administration was contrary to the Mandate; and to instruct the Executive to insist on their withdrawal.

3. To proclaim, in view of the widespread assumption that Zionism had renounced its ideal, that the movement stands on the basis of its historic aim, and that our obligations *vis-à-vis* the Mandatory Power admit of no other interpretation.

The discussion over Jabotinsky's views and the resolutions he introduced was marked by pointed irritation and hostility on the part of most of the speakers. There was not only strong disagreement in opinion, but unconcealed annoyance, resentment, and anger against a stubborn dissenter. There was also a pronounced tendency to dispose of this troublesome member of the Executive.

The Berlin correspondent of the *Jewish Chronicle* reported that there was "a body of opinion both in the Executive and on the Actions Committee, which considered Mr. Jabotinsky's resignation to be desirable, since he was not in agreement with the policy of the Executive."[18] Even more explicit was the well-informed correspondent of *The New Palestine*, who related that, even before the political resolutions were put to vote, "various speakers, emphasizing the necessity of a homogeneous Executive, either gently hinted to Mr. Jabotinsky, or bluntly demanded that he should resign."[19]

The official minutes of the political discussion fully confirm these reports. Published in *Rasswyet* of February 4, 1923, they make depressing reading. Jabotinsky was subjected to a relentless barrage of demands to submit unconditionally to the policies of Dr. Weizmann's Executive or, even better, to quit. Georg Halperin said: "The Executive is our Government, and members of a Government have to abide by the majority. Who is not ready to do so, must leave the Government." Richard Lichtheim, who had joined the Executive together with Jabotinsky and stressed that during the last few years he had "shared Jabotinsky's views on many questions of Zionist political and organizational work," nevertheless found it proper to say: "It is impossible that every member of this responsible body should have the right to say whatever he wants, things which are in full contradiction to the policies of the Executive." Leo Motzkin insisted that a member of the Executive "who disagrees and is in a minority, must resign." S. Kaplansky concurred with this view. I. Grinbaum accused Jabotinsky of "dramatizing things which are not at all dramatic" and of "eternal sharpening of some single question: once it was Hebraization, then Helsingfors, and now it is criticism of England and Samuel." When Jabotinsky asked: "Then what is the way out?" Grinbaum replied: "I will tell you—your resignation from the Executive." Defending his position, Jabotinsky said: "Believe me, the most unpleasant thing in the world is to work in a group where one is unwelcome. It would, therefore, be very convenient for me to step out. But my conscience tells me: 'you have been elected [by the Congress] to defend your convictions. . . .' Shall I walk out?" The minutes register here a characteristic reaction from the audience: "Exclamations: 'Of course!' "

It was in this intensely hostile atmosphere, saturated with the desire somehow to get rid of a non-conformist colleague, that Jabotinsky had to defend his position and to struggle for his right to independent opinion. He tried hard not to be forced either to capitulate or to leave. He reminded his colleagues that the Actions Committee had no right to dismiss a member of the Executive elected by the Congress. "I am defending my viewpoint, and this is my duty. I always understood that a Coalition Government meant that if there are in it different opinions, its line of conduct must be the resultant of these opinions. . . . I will remain in the Executive and will plead my cause and will try to fight for my views. I will endeavor to mitigate the danger of contrasting views, or, admitting that there is a difference between your conscience and mine, I will draw the last consequences. Maybe there is no place in the organization for this kind of people."

The resolutions of the Political Committee "taking note" (and thus approving) of the Executive's statement on the political activities and further plans, were adopted by thirteen votes against two. Jabotinsky requested that the resolutions introduced by him be put to the vote as amendments. By a majority of six against four, the Actions Committee refused this plea.

When all the resolutions had been voted upon, Jabotinsky rose and stated: "I declare that I will henceforth remain in the Executive and will struggle for my views." The same evening, he attended the regular meeting of the Executive and participated in the discussion on budgetary questions.

However, the next morning (January 18th), he sent to the President of the Actions Committee a letter stating that, by the decision it had taken, the Actions Committee had "sanctioned a policy which threatens to bring the Movement to a decay and the Jewish work in Palestine to bankruptcy." Considering "the attitude of the Executive and the A.C. as incompatible with the interests and the principles of Zionism," Jabotinsky informed the president of his decision to resign from the Executive, and, moreover, to consider himself as "no longer bound by the discipline of the Zionist Organization—therefore no longer a member of it."[20]

In his letter "Why I Resigned," published in the *Jewish Chronicle*, Jabotinsky mentions that his letter of resignation was sent "after taking consultation with some of my political friends."[21] It is difficult to accept this reference at its face value. At that time there were as yet no "political friends" of Jabotinsky to speak of, and, so far as this writer was able to ascertain, none of his personal friends then in Berlin had been consulted. Moreover, there hardly was time for doing so. As related above, Jabotinsky participated on the evening of January 17th in the meeting of the Zionist Executive; this meeting was over by eleven P.M. According to S. Gepstein, for the next three hours Jabotinsky walked along the Kurfürstendamm with him and Dr. M. Soloveitchik: the latter— who was in no sense a "political friend"—tried to convince Jabotinsky not to take any precipitate action, and Gepstein listened silently to their discussion. They parted after two A.M.[22] It is most improbable that "some political friends" could have been reached and consulted between two A.M. and the early hours of January 18th when the letter of resignation was dispatched to the Chairman of the Actions

Committee—in time to be read at the morning session of this body. It can be safely assumed that—as had been the case with several other previous and subsequent major decisions— Jabotinsky made this one after having taken counsel with his own mind and conscience.

Aftermath

The reaction of Zionist public opinion to Jabotinsky's resignation was anything but favorable.

The Yiddish press in the United States received it with unconcealed scorn and derision.[23] *The Day* wrote editorially: "Dr. Weizmann has triumphed, and with him has triumphed common sense. Healthy, human understanding is opposed to the hysterical helter-skelter politics of Jabotinsky. . . . It is well that the Zionist Administration has freed itself from his influence." The *Jewish Morning Journal* said: "Jabotinsky in this case has acted like a child who once said something clever and felt ever since that he had become imbued with wisdom and that everything he says from now on belongs in the same category. Concerted political action in Zionist work is dearer to us than all of Jabotinsky's wisdom, and if he cannot adjust himself within the sphere of Zionist discipline, then the organization must be prepared to lose him." Somewhat more restrained in tone and style, but equally prepared, even glad, "to lose him," was the editorial in *The New Palestine*, the official organ of the Zionist Organization of America. Forgetting its own laudatory editorial, published on the preceding June 16th, the paper was "surprised that he should have remained so long within the official fold." The editorial admitted that Jabotinsky "served Zionism well when he fought for the Jewish Legion," but claimed that "he is by temperament and inclination resentful of official authority. . . . What a man may say or do in his individual capacity is wholly different from what is expected of him when he becomes identified with an administration. In order to be himself, Mr. Jabotinsky was bound to shake himself free from official restraint and sally forth as the insurgent, the free Knight breaking the lance with the Administration and taking his chances." The editorial concluded ironically: "We may expect from him an interesting performance, probably more interesting than anything he has contributed toward the strengthening of the Weizmann administration."[24]

Hardly more sympathetic was the reaction of the Zionist press in other countries. The only two Zionist organs which expressed understanding for Jabotinsky's position were the *Jewish Chronicle* in London and *Rasswyet* in Berlin.

The *Jewish Chronicle*, which had already for a long time been very critical of the official Zionist policy, opened its columns to Jabotinsky's letters
explaining and defending his views and action. It also devoted an editorial
to this question, which praised Jabotinsky's "luminous account of the circumstances that led up to his resignation" and said:[25]

What Mr. Jabotinsky seems to have found in the work of the Zionist Organization incompatible with the principles to which he has for many years so valiantly
devoted himself, was the manner in which the [Zionist] organization, in obedience
to the demands of the [British] Government, estimated Zionist doctrine as of no
account, when compared with the prime necessity of securing the smiles and com-
mendation of Government officials. Mr. Jabotinsky is held up in certain quarters,
particularly by pseudo-Zionist, as an extremist and a firebrand, whose absence
from the Executive is a distinct advantage rather than otherwise. . . . But Mr. Jabotinsky's "extremism" and his fire resolve themselves into nothing more terrible than
a desire to abide by principles. That is, we admit, a sufficiently disturbing attitude
to those who are wedded to Peace at any price. The worship of calm resulting from
lifelessness of spirit, and of the death-sleep of opinions that do not coincide with
those of the majority, is an appalling phenomenon among certain sections of our
community. . . . That Mr. Jabotinsky has refused to submit himself to moral eutha-
nasia for fear of being considered unamenable is good hope for the movement.

Leopold J. Greenberg, the editor of the *Jewish Chronicle*, was himself an
ardent Zionist who had for years opposed the policies of Dr. Weizmann and
had left the Zionist Organization. The *Jewish Chronicle* editorial was therefore a
reminder that "Mr. Jabotinsky is not the only one who, refusing to cast Zionism
and all it means to the winds, has recently decided to stand outside the Organization," and unconditionally approved not only Jabotinsky's views, but also of the
last consequences he drew from his disagreement with the official Zionist policy.

The position taken by *Rasswyet* was different. As the organ of the Federation of Russian-Ukrainian Zionists, it was edited by an editorial board of
six, nominated by the Conference of the Federation held in Berlin in September, 1922. The board consisted of S. Gepstein (editor), J. Schechtman
(Secretary), Ch. Grinberg, V. Jacobson, M. Hindes, and M. Aleinikov. The
last-named three had been for years outspoken opponents of Jabotinsky's
views and tactics. The first two were, however, determined supporters of
the position Jabotinsky had taken during the session of the Actions Committee, though they disagreed with his leaving the Zionist Organization

(Ch. Grinberg did not actively participate in *Rasswyet* and did not take a definite stand on this question). Though a minority, they held the key executive
positions in *Rasswyet* and in the past, too, had largely determined the paper's
editorial policy. They therefore took upon themselves the responsibility of
formulating *Rasswyet's* position in the conflict between Jabotinsky and the
majority of the Actions Committee. As a gesture of loyalty toward the other
members of the board, this position was expressed not in an unsigned editorial, but in an article signed by this writer, which appeared on February 4,
1922; there was, however, no footnote stating that the article was being published "on the basis of free discussion."

The position of *Rasswyet* as expressed by this article was: full and unconditional approval of Jabotinsky's appraisal of the political situation in
Palestine, of his criticism of the official Zionist policy, and of his concept
of an activist Zionist policy; since the Actions Committee rejected Jabotinsky's views and proposals and, instead, endorsed Dr. Weizmann's line, it was
but natural and logical that Jabotinsky resigned from the Executive.

He was right in doing so [the article stated]. Up to this point, he would have
found agreement and support among wide Zionist circles. But he went further.
Jabotinsky also left the World Zionist Organization. . . . We do not accept this
move of his. We regret and condemn it. We see in it a threatening symptom. The
[Zionist] Organization is our highest and dearest possession. It bears the mark
of Herzl and Nordau. It has the radiance of the Congresses, the pride of national
traditions, of triumphs and defeats; in the organization lies the assurance for the
future. The World Zionist Organization is the "Jewish State on the march," the
strength of the whole movement.

Other members of the editorial board were highly dissatisfied with the
position expressed in this article. Yet they chose not to fight, and for several
months simply remained aloof. Jabotinsky himself, as he wrote to S. Gepstein
from Paris on February 9, 1923, had mixed feelings. He was, of course, glad
that *Rasswyet* had endorsed his views, but he resented that too much stress
had been put on criticism of his leaving the Zionist Organization: "I read
J. B. Schechtman's article, and here is my honest opinion. I had, naturally, neither expected nor demanded that you approve of my leaving the Organization.
But Schechtman's article conveys the impression as if my *entire* position is
essentially a trifle in comparison with my resigning from the Organization."
He was therefore reluctant to accept Gepstein's and this writer's offer to join

the *Rasswyet* editorial staff. Ultimately, an agreement was reached to the effect that *Rasswyet* was to become the mouthpiece of Zionist policies advocated by Jabotinsky; the question of his relationship with the Zionist Organization was, by mutual tacit consent, left open, and neither Jabotinsky nor the editorial staff ever mentioned it in the paper. On July 1, 1923, about five months after Jabotinsky's resignation, *Rasswyet* announced that Messrs. V. Jabotinsky, J. Brutzkus, I. Klinov, I. Trivus, and M. Schwarzman had joined the editorial board—the last four had fully endorsed Jabotinsky's political position—and, concurrently, that M. Hindes, V. Jacobson, and M. Aleinikov had at different times announced their resignation from the board.[26]

Rasswyet became Jabotinsky's organ. In its pages he published a series of illuminating articles devoted to the clarification of major political problems in Zionism. He started, on July 1st, with an essay "The Perspectives of the Gvirocracy" devoted to a devastating criticism of the plan of "extending" the Jewish Agency through the inclusion of several wealthy and influential individual Jews (*Gvirim*); this topic was followed up the next week by a second article "De Profundis"; Jabotinsky returned to this issue in January, 1924, in two powerful articles "On the Path of Liquidation." A series of articles dealt with "The Three Years of Sir Herbert Samuel," summarizing the sad record of the regime established by this much praised Jewish High Commissioner of Palestine. In three articles on "Pressure," Jabotinsky developed his concept of the methods the Zionist activist policy could use in order to bring about a basic change of the Mandatory regime in Palestine. Another article stressed the decisive importance of a clearly voiced demand for a Jewish majority as the prerequisite for the realization of Zionism (this article was reprinted *in extenso* by the Arab nationalist paper *Falastin*). "An Arab Agency," "The Iron Wall," "The Ethics of the Iron Wall," "A Parliament for Palestine," and "Islam" presented in their totality a clearly defined policy with regard to the Arab population of Palestine; "*Schutzjuden*" motivated the demand for the restoration of the Jewish Legion.[27]

Yet these articles were all that Jabotinsky was then ready to contribute to the Zionist cause. In the light of the statement he had published after his resignation, it somehow appeared as a disappointing anti-climax. Announcing his plans for the future, he said in this statement: "I have resigned from the Executive and I have stepped out from the Zionist Organization because I came to the conclusion that I can no longer remain a mere critic of our present policy, but that I must become a fighter, a rebel. . . . Another reason for my resignation is the fact that I do not wish to embarrass the Zionist Organization through my actions which may become very serious. . . . Being outside of the organization, I will employ every means I find feasible to defeat [the present Zionist] policy. I will listen to no authority, not even to the Zionist Congress. The Zionist Organization will soon be faced with accomplished facts."[28]

In fact, none of the far-reaching consequences announced by Jabotinsky followed. No "actions which may become very serious" and "embarrass the Zionist Organization" were undertaken in the external political arena. He limited himself to publicistic action. His *Rasswyet* articles have undoubtedly largely influenced and revolutionized the thinking of certain circles of Zionist intelligentsia and youth. They did not, however, in any way exceed the limits of "mere criticism" and were completely compatible with membership in the Zionist Organization. Moreover, Jabotinsky steadfastly resisted all attempts by friends and admirers to induce him to go beyond pure journalism. He repeatedly stated that he had had enough of practical politics and was determined to stick to his pen. He saw his mission—if any—in just presenting his views, clarifying the issues, destroying illusions and fetishes, and thus preparing the foundation of a realistic and courageous Zionist conception. This was the limit he was then firmly determined not to cross. "My job," he used to say to this writer, "is to tell the truth as I see it. I don't intend to move a finger in order to 'sell' it to the Jews or to try to implement it in the non-Jewish world. I have been trying, in both fields, too long and too hard. Now I will just write what I have on my mind, and sit quietly in my room. If somebody wants to 'buy' and spread my ideas he is free to do so. But without me. I am no more in this trade. And nothing and nobody in the world will be able to put me back into this damned harness."

He was steadfastly declining stray invitations from various quarters to start organizing those who shared his views. Typical of his state of mind was the friendly but firm answer (March 13, 1923) to a letter he received from I. Beder, Chairman of a youth group *Ezrach ha'Tzair* in Palestine, offering him the cooperation of this organization: "I should be glad if a unit would emerge with which I would be able to cooperate; but I cannot take the initiative, for I have not found people who would *fully* [underscored in the original] share my views—or very few. My conclusion from this state of affairs is that I am an element totally unsuited for the Jewish field. If there are people who feel differently, it is up to them to speak up."

NOTES

ONE

1. Most of the facts pertaining to Jabotinsky's family history and his childhood this writer owes to Mrs. T. E. Jabotinsky-Kopp, with whom he had several interviews at her home in Haifa and who kindly checked this chapter for factual accuracy. A second major source is Jabotinsky's autobiographical *Sipur Yamay* (Story of My Life), which is referred to throughout this book as *Autobiography*. This source is used very often, and in order not to encumber the book with too many footnotes, no page numbers are given for each specific quotation. *Sippur Yamay*, written in 1934 and first published in Hebrew in 1936, had been preceded by a series of autobiographical articles which appeared early in 1933 in the New York Yiddish daily *Jewish Morning Journal* under the heading "Zikhroines fun Mein Ben-Dor" (Memoirs of My Contemporary, later referred to as "Memoirs"). Written in the third person, they are often more candid than the later Hebrew version, and are used concurrently with it, the source in each case being specified. Titles of books and pamphlets published in Hebrew and Russian are given in English translation; when first quoted, the original title is given in parentheses. Titles of articles are given in English translation only.

2. Interview with Eliahu Ravnitzky, Tel Aviv.

3. Letter to Mrs. Jabotinsky-Kopp, December 8, 1926.

4. V. Jabotinsky. "Memoirs of My Contemporary" (Zikhroines fun Mein Ben-Dor), later referred to as "Memoirs." Jewish Morning Journal, February 5, 1933.

5. V. Jabotinsky. *A Pocket Edition of Several Stories Mostly Reactionary* (later referred to as "Pocket Edition . . ."). Paris, 1925, pp. 97-114.

6. V. Jabotinsky. "Memoirs." *Jewish Morning Journal*, January 15, 1933.

7. Jabotinsky's reply to Dr. Isaak Epstein's questionnaire of July 9, 1920. *Jewish Herald. Jabotinsky Memorial Issue,* July 21, 1950.

8. Letter to Mrs. Jabotinsky-Kopp, July 7, 1929.

9. V. Jabotinsky. *The Five* (Piatero). New York, 1947, p. 81.

10. Interview with Eliahu Ravnitzky, Tel Aviv.

11. V. Jabotinsky. *Poetry* (Stikhi). Paris, 1930, p. 85.

12. Itamar Ben Avi. "Jabotinsky the Fearless." *Bnei Zion Voice,* Septembe: 1940.

13. Ernest Jones. *The Life and Work of Sigmund Freud.* Vol. I. 1856-190(The Formative Years and the First Discoveries. New York, 1954, p. 15.

14. Ch. Tchernowitz. "His Origin and Destiny." *Zionews,* September 1, 1942.

15. Letter to Mrs. Jabotinsky-Kopp, December 3, 1923.

16. Interview with Eliahu Ravnitzky, Tel Aviv.

17. V. Jabotinsky. "Memoirs." *Jewish Morning Journal,* January 15, 1933.

18. *Ibid.*

19. *Ibid.,* February 5, 1933.

20. V. Jabotinsky. *The Five,* p. 186.

21. Letter to Isaak Epstein.

22. I. Heifetz. "Altalena." *Rasswyet,* October 19, 1930.

23. Piotr Pilsky. "Jabotinsky." *Novoye Slovo,* September 11, 1921.

TWO

1. Sh. Stupnitzky. "Leaders and Dreamers." *Frimorgen,* February 14, 1926.

2. V. Jabotinsky. "Memoirs." *Jewish Morning Journal,* March 26, 1933.

3. This author is indebted to Count Mario Vannutelli for securing for him Jabotinsky's personal records from the archives of the University of Rome.

4. The most fundamental of Labriola's writings are: *Saggi intero dell concezione materialistica della storia:* I. *In memoria del Manifesto de Communisti.* Roma, 1895; II. *Del Materialismo storico.* Roma, 1896; III *Discorrendo di Socialismo e di filosofia.* Roma, 1898.

5. V. Jabotinsky. "Sketches Without a Title." *Yevreyskaya Mysl,* October 12 1906.

6. Ferri's main works are: *La Sociologica criminate.* Torino, 1884; *Socialism et criminalita.* Torino, 1883; *Socialismo e scienza positiva.* Roma, 1894.

7. V. Jabotinsky. *The Five,* pp. 99, 27.

8. *Encyclopaedia of the Social Sciences.* Vol. XI. New York, 1942, pp. 558-59.

9. V. Jabotinsky. *Feuilletons* (Russ.). Berlin, 1922, p. 185.

10. Interview with S. Gepstein, Tel Aviv.

11. V. Jabotinsky. *The Strangers. Sketches of a "Happy" Ghetto* (Chuzhiye Otcherky "Stchastlivago" Ghetto). Odessa, 1903, p. 18.

12. V. Jabotinsky. *A Pocket Edition* ...,p. 129.

13. Interview with Eri Jabotinsky, Haifa.

14. V. Jabotinsky. *The Five,* p. 96.

15. V. Jabotinsky. *Poetry,* p. 89.

16. V. Jabotinsky. *The Strangers*, pp. 8-9, 18-19, 13.
17. I. Heifetz. "Altalena." *Rasswyet*, October 19, 1930.
18. Piotr Pilsky. "Jabotinsky." *Novoye Slovo*, September 11, 1921.
19. Interview with Mrs. Jabotinsky-Kopp, Haifa.
20. V. Jabotinsky. *A Pocket Edition* ...,pp. 63-64, 56.
21. V. Jabotinsky. "The Lesson of Shevchenko's Jubilee." *Feuilletons*, p. 187.
22. V. Jabotinsky. *A Pocket Edition* ...,pp. 73-74.
23. Postcard from Rome, July 11, 1901.
24. *Ibid.*

THREE

1. I. Heifetz. "Altalena." *Rasswyet*, October 19, 1930.
2. Interview with S. Gepstein, Tel Aviv.
3. V. Jabotinsky. *Poetry*, pp. 103-12.
4. V. Jabotinsky. *The Five*, p. 186.
5. Letter to I. Galperin, June 7, 1935.
6. Letters to S. D. Salzman, March 19 and June 15, 1935.
7. "My Village" in *Causeries*, (Russ.) Paris, 1930, pp. 87-88.
8. "The Literary-Artistic Circle" is vividly described in *The Five*, pp. 17-19.
9. Interview with I. Trivus, Tel Aviv; also: I. Trivus: "The First Steps." *Rasswyet*, October 19, 1930.
10. M.G.A. (one of Jabotinsky's pen names). "Mirabeau." *Rasswyet*, 1931, No. 11.
11. Shlomo Salzman. *From the Past* (Min ha'Ovar). Tel Aviv, 1943, p. 241.
12. *Ibid.*, pp. 241-42.
13. V. Jabotinsky. "Two Tables of the Commandment—One Torah." *Rasswyet*, April 4, 1934.
14. I. Trivus. *The Beginnings of the Haganah* (Rashita Shel Haganah). Tel Aviv, 1952,pp. 10-11.
15. L. Sherman. "The Man of Will and Courage." Reminiscences and Impressions. *Our Voice*, January, 1935.
16. V. Jabotinsky. "In the Days of Mourning." *Feuilletons.* p. 23.

FOUR

1. S. M. Dubnov. *The Book of Life* (Kniga Zhisni). Vol. I. Riga, 1934, p. 407.
2. *Stenographisch.es Protokoll der Verhandlungen des VI. Zionisten-Kongresses in Bael.* Wien, 1903, p. 93.
3. *Ibid.*, p. 100.
4. Chaim Weizmann. *Trial and Error.* An Autobiography. New York, 1949, p. 63.

5. V. Jabotinsky. "Current Problems." *Yevreyskaya Zhisn,* January, 1904.

6. Interview with Eri Jabotinsky, Tel Aviv.

7. *Stenographisches Protokoll der Verhandlungen des VII. Zionisten-Kongresses in Basel.* Berlin, 1905, p. 55.

8. V. Jabotinsky. *Doctor Herzl.* Odessa, 1905, pp. 17, 18, 19.

9. S. Gepstein. *Zeev Jabotinsky. His Life—Struggle—Achievement* (Zeev Jabotinsky. Chayav—Milchamto—Hisigav). Tel Aviv, 1941, p. 30.

10. N. Sorin. "V. Jabotinsky and 'Yevreyskaya Zhisn.' " *Rasswyet,* October 19, 1930.

11. S. Gepstein, *op. cit.,* p. 32.

12. J. Brutzkus. "Jabotinsky in Russian Zionism." *Rasswyet,* October 19, 1930.

13. S. Gepstein, *op. cit.,* p. 44.

14. *Ibid.,* pp. 44-45.

15. N. Sorin, *op. cit.*

16. S. Gepstein, *op. cit.,* p. 46.

17. N. Sorin, *op. cit.;* also: Ossip Dymov. "What I Remember." *Forward,* April 9, 1947.

18. V. Jabotinsky. "Fairy Vagabunda." *Causeries,* p. 50; also: V. Jabotinsky. "Your New Year." *Odesskiya Novosti,* January 3, 1908.

19. Communicated by Mrs. Leah Brown, New York.

20. Interview with Zalman Shazar, Jerusalem.

21. Interview with I. Grinbaum, Tel Aviv.

22. Interview with J. Sprinzak, Tel Aviv.

23. V. Jabotinsky. *Bund and Zionism* (Bund yi Sionism). Odessa, 1906, pp. 44-45.

24. V. Jabotinsky. "Sketches Without a Title." *Yevreyskaya Mysl,* October 12, 1906.

25. V. Jabotinsky. *Bund and Zionism,* p. 4.

26. V. Jabotinsky. *Doctor Herzl,* pp. 16-17.

27. S. Gepstein, *op. cit.,* p. 48.

28. Interview with Dr. M. Soloveitchik, Jerusalem.

29. V. Jabotinsky. "In the Days of Mourning," *loc. cit.*

30. V. Jabotinsky. "Jews in the Russian Literature." *Rasswyet,* March 29, 1908 (first published in the Russian weekly *Svobodniya Mysli).*

31. S. Gepstein, *op. cit.,* p. 35.

32. Sh. Goldenberg. "Encounter with Kuprin." *Jewish Times,* London, October 28, 1938.

33. Reproduced in O. O. Grusenberg's *Sketches and Speeches* (Ocherki yi Ryetchi). New York, 1944, p. 229.

34. M. Ossorgin. "To the Foreigner Jabotinsky." *Rasswyet,* October 19, 1930.

FIVE

1. *Pravo,* 1905, No. 9.
2. Oscar J. Janowsky. *The Jews and Minority Rights.* New York, 1933, p. 94.
3. *Khronika Yevreyskoy Zhisni,* December 25, 1905.
4. *Ibid.,* February 16 and 28, 1906.
5. S. Gepstein, *op. cit.,* p. 50.
6. *Ibid.,* p. 38; also: J. Brutzkus. "V. Jabotinsky in Russian Zionism." *Rasswyet,* October 19, 1930.
7. *Khronika Yevreyskoy Zhisni,* August 10, 1906.
8. *Ibid.,* June 15 and 22, July 6, 13, and 20, 1906.
9. Janowsky, *op. cit,* pp. 107-08.
10. *Yevreyskaya Mysl,* December 7, 1906.
11. *Dos Yiddishe Folk,* No. 27, 1906; *Yevreysky Narod,* December 2, 1906.
12. *Yevreyskaya Mysl,* December 7, 1906.
13. *Rasswyet,* August 19 and 26, 1907.
14. V. Jabotinsky. *The War and the Jews.* New York, 1942, pp. 112-13.
15. V. Jabotinsky. "An Open Letter to M. M. Vinaver." *Ryetch,* January 4, 1907.
16. *Rasswyet,* February 22, 1907.
17. V. Jabotinsky. "My Typewriter Speaks." *Jewish Morning Journal,* December 4, 1932.
18. *Yevreyskaya Mysl,* February 1, 1907.
19. *Ibid.,* January 25, 1907.
20. *Rasswyet,* February 22, 1907.
21. Sh. Schwarz. "Election Campaign in Odessa." *Rasswyet,* October 19, 1907.
22. *Rasswyet,* November 3 and 10, 1907.
23. *Ibid.,* October 27 and November 10, 1907.
24. *Ibid.,* August 3 and 10, 1912.
25. *Ibid.,* October 5, 1912.
26. Quoted in *Rasswyet,* October 5, 1912.
27. Letter from D. Bar Rav Hoi, Haifa, to this writer.

SIX

1. Letter to Mrs. Jabotinsky-Kopp, July 27, 1927.
2. Interview with A. Poliakov, New York.
3. Interview with Mrs. Jabotinsky-Kopp, Haifa.
4. Interview with A. Poliakov.
5. Interview with I. Grinbaum, Tel Aviv.
6. Interview with Mrs. Jabotinsky-Kopp.

7. *Dtto.*

8. Interview with A. Poliakov.

9. Interview with E. Kutzenog, Tel Aviv.

10. S. Gepstein, *op. cit.,* p. 54.

11. V. Jabotinsky. "Your New Year." *Odesskiya Novosti,* January 3, 1908.

SEVEN

1. Letter to M. M. Ussishkin, May 15, 1907.

2. V. Jabotinsky. "The Center of the Party Life." *Rasswyet,* April 13, 1907.

3. V. Jabotinsky. *What to Do* (Chto Dyelat). Yekaterinoslav, 1905, p. 13.

4. The full text of the letter in *Yevreyskaya Mysl,* October 10, 1906.

5. S. Gepstein. "The Alien Land." *Rasswyet,* March 28, 1910.

6. V. Jabotinsky. *Feuilletons,* pp. 106-30.

7. *Ibid.,* pp. 78-82.

8. *Ibid.,* pp. 83-95.

9. *Ibid.,* pp. 39-50.

10. Shlomo Salzman. *From the Past,* p. 279.

11. *Ibid.,* p.280.

12. S. Gepstein. "Feuilletons." *Rasswyet,* January 25, 1913.

13. V. Jabotinsky. "Homo Homini Lupus" and "I Don't Believe." *Feuilletons,* pp. 213-33.

14. Quoted in *Rasswyet,* October 24, 1910.

15. A. Hartglas. "Resistance to Resistance." *Rasswyet,* April 19, 1913.

16. M. Aleinikov. "The First Balance." *Ibid.,* March 15, 1915.

EIGHT

1. *Rasswyet,Ju\y* 3, 1911.

2. *Ibid.,* January 18 and 25; February 1, 15, and 22; March 8 and 22, 1909.

3. Sh. Schwarz. *Jabotinsky—Fighter of the Nation* (Jabotinsky Lochem ha'Umma). Jerusalem, 1942, p. 7.

4. Reprinted in *Rasswyet,* January 16 and 21, 1911.

5. Quoted from a reprint in the *Jewish Standard,* January 2, 1942.

6. Emil Bernhard Cohn. *David Wolffsohn. Herzl's Successor.* New York, 1944, p. 205.

7. A. Hermoni. "Jabotinsky's Struggle with a Revisionist 'Avant la Lettre.' " *Hadoar,* May 4, 1945.

8. Sh. Schwarz, *op. cit.,* p. 155.

9. Quotedinii<maJ)>eí,January 18, 1909.

10. V. Jabotinsky. *A Pocket Edition* ...,p. 127.

11. J. H. Karín. *Erez Israel, Das Jüdische Land.* Köln and Leipzig, 1909, pp. 175, 178, 179.

12. Adolf Böhm. *Die Zionistische Bewegung.* Vol. I. Vienna, 1935, p. 394.

13. J. H. Kann. *Eretz Israel, Le Pays Juif.* Brussels, 1910.

14. Wolffsohn's Letter to Jabotinsky, February 10, 1909.

15. Wolffsohn's Letter to Jacobson, February 17, 1909.

16. Jacobson's letter to Wolffsohn, February 26, 1909.

17. Wolffsohn's letter to Jacobson, April 12, 1910.

18. Wolffsohn's letter to Jacobson, May 19, 1910.

19. *Ibid.*

20. *Ibid.*

21. Jacobson's letter to Wolffsohn, May 23, 1910.

22. *Ibid.*

NINE

1. Interview with Eliahu Ravnitzky, Tel Aviv.

2. V. Jabotinsky. *On Territorialism (Zionism and Palestine).* Odessa, 1905, p.l.

3. L. Sherman. "The Man of Will and Courage." *Our Voice,* January, 1935.

4. S. Gepstein, *op. cit.,* pp. 64-65.

5. Shlomo Salzman. "His First Speeches in Hebrew." *Hamashkif,* July 7, 1943; J. S. "The Mendele Week." *Rasswyet,* January 16, 1911.

6. S. Ben Baruch. "Hebrew Fanaticism." In *Zeev Jabotinsky.* Published by the National Labor Organization, Tel Aviv, August, 1951, p. 33.

7. S. M. Dubnov. *The Book of Life.* Vol. I, pp. 384-85. 8. V. Jabotinsky. *Jewish Education* (Yevreyskoye Vospitaniye). Odessa, 1905, pp. 5, 8, 19.

8. Interview with Mrs. Jabotinsky-Kopp, Haifa.

9. V. Jabotinsky. "My Typewriter Speaks." *Jewish Morning Journal,* December 4, 1932.

10. "Our Languages." *Rasswyet,* March 7, 10, and April 4, 1910.

11. S. Gomelsky. "Jabotinsky on the Bench of the Accused." *Hamashkif,* October 19, 1949.

12. Dr. P-r. "The Speaker and the Hecklers." *Ibid.,* October 23, 1940.

13. *Rasswyet,* April 19, 1913.

14. D. Pasmanik. "The Jewish Creative Power in the Diaspora." *Ibid.,* April 26, May 3, 10, 17, and 24, 1913.

15. *Rasswyet, August 2$,* 1913.

16. *Ibid.,* August 30, 1913.

17. *Ibid.,* August 23, 1913.

18. *Ibid.,* September 6, 1913.

19. *Ibid.,* September 27, 1913.

20. V. Jabotinsky. "Activism." *Di Tribune*, October 10, 1915.

21. "The 'Tarbut' Conference in Danzig." *Rasswyet*, July 15, 1928.

22. *Jewish Standard,Septembei* 13, 1941.

TEN

1. *Stenographisches Protokoll der Verhandlungen des XI. Zionisten-Kongresses in Wien.* Berlin, 1914, pp. 300-09, 365.

2. *Rasswyet*, November 22, 1913.

3. Letter from Nikolayev, March 16/29, 1914.

4. Letter from St. Petersburg, March 20 (April 4), 1914.

5. Letters of April 22 and May 20, 1914.

6. Letter to the University Committee, May 11, 1914.

7. *Ibid.*

8. Jabotinsky's letter to the Hebrew University Committee, February 25, 1913.

9. Mordecai Ben Hillel Hacohen. *The War of Nations* (Milkhemeth Haamim). Book V, p. 109.

10. 10. *The Keren ha'Yesod Book.* London, 1921, p. 137.

ELEVEN

1. Ivan Turgeniev. "Two Quatrains." In *Poems in Prose.* Boston, 1883, pp. 43-50.

2. V. Jabotinsky. "Horoscope." *Feuilletons*, pp. 262-67.

TWELVE

1. Quoted in *Jerusalem* (Brussels), July 12, 1953.

2. V. Jabotinsky. *The Story of the Jewish Legion* (later referred to as "The Story ..."). New York, 1945, p. 30.

3. *Ibid.*

4. *Ibid.*, p. 29.

5. "Jewish War Relief Work." *The American Jewish Year Book, 5678.* Philadelphia, 1917, pp. 219, 223.

6. D. Judelowitz. "With Jabotinsky During the Days of the Creation of the Gdudim." *Hamashkif,* July 30, 1943.

7. V. Jabotinsky. *The Story* ...,p.34.

8. *Ibid.*, p. 41.

9. *Ibid.*, pp. 42-43.

10. Trumpeldor's letter to Jabotinsky, dated Gallipoli, Cape-Helles, December 14, 1915.

11. V. Jabotinsky. *The Story* ...,p.43.

Notes 383

12. Trumpeldor's letter in *Di Tribune*, October 22, 1916.

13. Itzhak Ben Zvi. "About the Jewish Legion." In *Gesammelte Schriften* (Yiddish). Vol. I. New York, 1935, p. 171.

14. V. Jabotinsky. "Letters from a Journey." *Odesskiya Novosti*, June 16, 1916.

15. V. Jabotinsky. *The Story* ...,pp. 43-45.

16. ʃₐmž.,pp.50-51.

17. *Ibid.*, p. 52.

18. *Ibid.*, pp. 31-32.

19. Anna and Maxa Nordau. *Max Nordau. A* Biography. New York, 1943, pp. 225-26.

20. Itzhak Ben Zvi, *op. cit.*, p. 178; also: interview with D. Ben Gurion, Sde Boker.

21. Dr. Joseph Klausner. *Menachem Ussishkin. His Life and Work.* New York, 1942, pp. 104-05.

22. M. Grossman. "The First Encounter." *Unser Welt*, August 3, 1951.

23. V. Jabotinsky. "Instead of a Speech." *Rasswyet*, October 10, 1928.

24. V. Jabotinsky. *The Story* ...,pp. 55-56.

25. Interview with B. Weinstein, Tel Aviv.

26. V. Jabotinsky. "Activism." *Di Tribune*, October 10, 1915.

27. *Di Tribune*, October 10, 1915.

28. "An Opposition Move." *Yevreyskaya Zhisn*, January 24, 1916.

29. Joseph Trumpeldor. *Tagebücher und Briefe.* Berlin, 1925. Letters dated October 27 and 28, November 1 and 10, 1915, pp. 296-98.

30. *Ibid.*, pp. 304-05.

31. V. Jabotinsky. "Activism." *Loc. cit.*

32. Interview with S. Gepstein, Tel Aviv.

33. Chaim Weizmann. *Trial and Error.* An Autobiography. New York, 1949, p. 167.

34. Interview with Mrs. Vera Weizmann, Rehovoth (communicatd by I. Trivus).

35. V. Jabotinsky. *The Story* ...,p.60.

36. *Hadar*, November, 1940.

37. V. Jabotinsky. *The Story* ...,p.70.

38. *Jewish Standard*, August 9, 1940.

THIRTEEN

1. V. Jabotinsky. *The Story* ...,p.75.

2. *Ibid.*, pp. 76-77.

3. V. Jabotinsky. "Joe." *Rasswyet*, June 5, 1932.

4. V. Jabotinsky. "Mÿ Typewriter Speaks." *Jewish Morning Journal*, December 4, 1933.

5. V. Jabotinsky. *The Story* ...,p.78.
6. Interview with Y. M. Machover, London.
7. V. Jabotinsky. *The Story* ...,pp. 85-86.
8. *Ibid.,* pp. 82-84.
9. *Yevreyskaya Nedelya,* June 4 and 11, 1917; *Yevreyskaya Zhisn,* June 18, 1917.
10. V. Jabotinsky. *The Story* ...,p.89.
11. *Yevreyskaya Nedelya,* September 3, 1917.
12. Interview with B. Weinstein, Tel Aviv.
13. J.▪B. Schechtman. "VladimirJabotinsky." *Oif der Wach,* March 24, 1918.
14. J. Fischer. "Who Was Right?" *Yevreyskaya Mysl,* January 17, 1919.
15. Dr. Joseph Klausner, *op. cit.,* p. 111.
16. S. Gepstein, *op. cit.,* p. 82.
17. V. Jabotinsky. *The Story* ...,p.98.
18. Lieut. Col. J. H. Patterson. *With the Judeans in the Palestine Campaign.* New York, 1922, p. 6.
19. *Jewish Chronicle,* August 10, 1917.
20. *fò¿d.,*August17,1917.
21. Chaim Weizmann. *Trial and Error,* p. 167.
22. V. Jabotinsky. *The Story* ...,pp. 102-03.
23. Interview with Mrs. Jabotinsky-Kopp. Haifa.
24. Interview with Eri Jabotinsky, Haifa.
25. V. Jabotinsky. *The Story* ...,pp. 103-04.
26. Lieut. Col. J. H. Patterson. "Jabotinsky as I Knew Him." *Hadar,* November, 1940.
27. V. Jabotinsky. *The Story* ...,p.46.
28. Amery's letter to Jabotinsky, January 23, 1917.
29. V. Jabotinsky. *The Story* ...,p. 182.
30. Quoted in the article by Sh. Schwartz, "The Declaration and Its Factors." *Haolam,* November 17, 1937.
31. D. Ben Gurion. *Chaluzischer Zionismus oder Revisionismus.* Berlin, 1934, pp. 11-18.
32. Barnet Litvinoĭĭ. *Ben Gurion of Israel.* New York, 1954, pp. 63-68.
33. *Ibid.,* p. 75.
34. V. Jabotinsky. *The Story* ...,p. 109.

FOURTEEN

1. V. Jabotinsky. *The Story* ...,pp. 108-09.
2. Lieut. Col. J. H. Patterson. *With the Judeans in the Palestine Campaign,* pp. 43-45.
3. Eliahu Golomb. *Hidden Strength* (Khevion Oz). Vol. I. Tel Aviv, 1953, pp. 149, 357.

4. Mordechai Ben Hillel Hacohen. *The War of Nations.* Book IV, pp. 170-71.

5. *Ibid.,* Book V, pp. 20, 27-28.

6. *Ibid.,* p. 93.

7. Eliahu Golomb, *op. cit.,* pp. 149-50.

8. V. Jabotinsky. *The Story* ...,p.H6.

9. Quoted by Sh. Schwarz, *op. cit.,* p. 19.

10. V. Jabotinsky. *The Story* ...,p.H6.

11. *Ibid.,pp.* 114-15.

12. Eliahu Golomb, *op. cit.,* pp. 159-61.

13. *Ibid.,* p. 357.

14. L. Sherman. "The Man of Will and Courage." *Our Voice,* January, 1935.

15. V. Jabotinsky. *The Story* ...,pp. 159-60.

16. Elias Ginsburg. "Jabotinsky the Soldier." *Jewish Standard,* September 27, 1940.

17. Lieut. Col. J. H. Patterson. "Jabotinsky as I Knew Him." *Hadar,* November, 1940.

18. Lieut. Col. J. H. Patterson. *With the Judeans* ...,pp. 63-64.

19. Letter to Mrs. Jabotinsky, October 25, 1918.

20. Lieut. Col. J. H. Patterson. *With the Judeans* ...,p.99.

21. V. Jabotinsky. *The Story* ...,pp. 136-37.

22. Lieut. Col. J. H. Patterson. "Jabotinsky as I Knew Him." *Loc. cit.*

23. Letter to Mrs. Jabotinsky, October 25, 1918.

24. V. Jabotinsky. *The Story* ...,pp. 138-39.

25. Sh. Ben Baruch. "His Will in 1918." In *Zeev Jabotinsky.* Published by the National Labor Organization. Tel Aviv, August, 1951, p. 35.

26. *Yevreyskaya Mysl,* February 14, 1919.

27. Letter to Mrs. Jabotinsky, August 11, 1918.

28. Interview with Miss Bella Berlin, Tel Aviv.

29. Letter to Mrs. Jabotinsky, October 25, 1918.

30. *Yevreyskaya Mysl,* October 11/24, 1919.

31. *Minutes of the Zionist Commission* (later referred to as "Minutes"), March 25, 1920.

32. *Ibid.,* December 31, 1918.

33. *Ibid.,* January 6, 1919.

34. *Ibid.*

35. V. Jabotinsky. *The Story* ...,p.l66.

36. *Minutes,* February 26 and March 12, 1919.

37. Eliahu Golomb. "Ze'ev Jabotinsky and the Jewish Legion Movement." In *Hidden Strength.* Vol. II, p. 429.

38. V. Jabotinsky. *The Story* ...,pp. 166-67.

39. Letter to Abraham Recanati, July 5, 1919.
40. Lieut. Col. J. H. Patterson. *With the Judeans* ...,pp. 215-16.
41. V. Jabotinsky. *The Story* ...,p. 175.
42. Letter to Abraham Recanati, July 5, 1919.
43. *Minutes,* September 11, 1919.
44. Lieut. Col. J. H. Patterson. *With the Judeans* ...,pp. 243-44.
45. *Ibid.,* pp. 244-48.
46. Lieut. Col. J. H. Patterson. Foreword to the English edition (1945) of *The Story of the Jewish Legion,* pp. 9-10.
47. V. Jabotinsky. *The Story* ...,pp. 178-79.
48. Letter to Mrs. Jabotinsky, October 25, 1918.
49. *Ibid.*

FIFTEEN

1. *David Eder.* Edited by J. B. Hoffman. London, 1945, p. 148.
2. Interview with Miss Bella Berlin, Tel Aviv.
3. *Yevreyskaya Mysl,* February 14, 1919.
4. Sh. Schwarz, *op. cit.,* pp. 55-56.
5. "Demands of Palestine Jews." *The Maccabaean,* Vol. XXXII, 1919, p. 197.
6. Chaim Weizmann. *Trial and Error,* p. 227.
7. *Minutes,* January 6, 1919.
8. *David Eder,* p. 148.
9. Chaim Weizmann. *Trial and Error,* pp. 227-28.
10. *Military Operations: Egypt and Palestine.* Part I. London, 1930, p. 300.
11. A. Remba. "The Founder of the Haganah." *Hamashkif,* July 17, 1947. (This episode was related to Mr. Remba by Raphael and Israel Rosov.)
12. Quoted in Jabotinsky's article "Patience." *Rasswyet,* February, 21, 1932.
13. *Ibid.*
14. *Minutes,* January 20, 1919.
15. *Ibid.,* February24, 1919.
16. *Ibid.,* January6, 1919.
17. Letter of Mr. Robert Szold to this writer, June 15, 1954.
18. *Minutes,* July 11, 1919.
19. *Ibid.,* January6, 1919.
20. *Ibid.,* March 12, 1919.
21. Sh. Schwarz, *op. cit.,* pp. 31-32, 41.
22. Jessie E. Sampter. "Snow-Bound in Jerusalem." *The Menorah Journal,* August, 1920.
23. Ben Yeruham. "The First to Aid His Brethren" (as told by Ziskind

Abramowitz). *Hamashkif,* August 8, 1940.

24. A. Remba. "The Founder of the Haganah." *Ibid.,* July 17, 1947.

25. Mordechai Ben Hillel Hacohen, *op. cit.,* Book V, p. 57.

26. Shlomo Salzman. "The Year 1919 in the Life of Jabotinsky" (later referred to as "The Year 1919"). In *The Leader of a Generation* (Manhigha'Dor). Tel Aviv, 1946, p. 117-29.

27. Quoted by Sh. Schwarz, *op. cit.,* pp. 63-64.

28. *The Maccabaean,* February, 1920.

29. Quoted by Sh. Schwarz, *op. cit.,* pp. 56-58.

30. *Ibid.,* p. 67.

31. Eliahu Golomb, *op. cit.,* Vol. I, p. 357.

32. Sh. Schwarz, *op. cit.,* pp. 48, 77.

33. Interview with Dr. S. Perlman, Tel Aviv.

34. Shlomo Salzman. "The Year 1919 . . ."

35. *Ibid.*

36. Interview with M. Sharett, Jerusalem.

37. Ronald Storrs. *Orientations.* London, 1937, p. 421.

38. Interview with Eri Jabotinsky, Haifa.

39. Lieut. Col. J. H. Patterson. "Jabotinsky as I Knew Him." *Hadar,* November, 1940.

40. V. Jabotinsky. "Between the 6th and llth." *Khasit Haam,* June 8, 1931.

41. *Ibid.*

42. D. Ben Gurion. *Chaluzischer Zionismus oder Revisionismus,* pp. 66-67.

SIXTEEN

1. E. Ben Horin. "The First Pogrom in Palestine. Rutenberg's Evidence." *Rasswyet,* April 21, May 8, 1932.

2. Jeremiah Halperin. "How the Haganah Was Born in Palestine." *Herut,* August 11 and 13, 1954.

3. *Minutes,* June 4 and 9, 1920.

4. Jeremiah Halperin, *op. cit.*

5. *Ibid.;* also: Elias Ginsburg. "Intellectual Charlatinism." *Our Voice,* June, 1935.

6. A. Remba. "Jabotinsky the Defender and Prisoner" (unpublished).

7. Elias Ginsburg. "Jabotinsky in Jail." *Hadar,* November, 1940.

8. Lieut. Col. J. H. Patterson. *With the Judeans* ...,pp.261, 256.

9. V. Jabotinsky. *The Story* ...,p.l72.

10. Jeremiah Halperin, *op. cit.*

11. *Ibid.*

12. Shlomo Salzman. "The Year 1919 ..."

13. Itzhak Ben Zvi. "Der Pogrom fun Pessach 1920." In *Gesammelte Schriften.* Vol. I. New York, 1945, p. 45.

14. *Times* (London), May 14, 1921.

15. A. Remba. "Within the Prison Walls." In *Shilton Betar Editions*. Tel Aviv, 1949, pp. 94-101.

16. Jeremiah Halperin, *op. cit.*

17. Elias Ginsburg. "Jabotinsky in Jail." *Loc. cit.*

18. A. Remba. "Within the Prison Walls." *Loc. cit.*

19. Interview with Mrs. Jabotinsky-Kopp, Haifa.

20. Interview with Dr. S. Perlman, Tel Aviv.

21. Elias Ginsburg, *op. cit.*

22. *Ibid.*

23. A. Remba. "Within the Prison Walls." *Loc. cit.*

24. V. Jabotinsky. "Twenty-four Hours. An Interlude in the Life of the Acre Prisoners." *Jewish Standard*, April 10, 1941.

25. Interview with M. Sharett, Jerusalem.

26. V. Jabotinsky. "Twenty-four Hours . . . ," *loc. cit.*, and *The Story . . .* , p. 175.

SEVENTEEN

1. Sh. Schwarz, *op. cit.*, p. 95.

2. *Parliamentary Debates* (Hansard). House of Commons, Official Report, 29th June, 1920.

3. Elias Ginsburg. "Jabotinsky in Jail." *Hadar*, November, 1940.

4. *Evening Standard*, April 30, 1920.

5. *Parliamentary Debates* (Hansard). House of Commons, Official Report, 29th June, 1920.

6. Elias Ginsburg. "Jabotinsky in Jail." *Loc. cit'.*

7. Interview with Eri Jabotinsky, Haifa.

8. *Dtto.*

9. Interview with Johnny Tamir (Kopp), Haifa.

10. Marvin Lowenthal. *Henrietta Szold, Life and Letters.* New York, 1942, p. 142.

11. Letter to S. D. Salzman, February 26, 1930.

12. Itamar Ben Avi. "Jabotinsky the Fearless." *Bnei Zion Voice*, September, 1940.

13. The Appeal was quoted in *Herut*, July 30, 1954.

14. Text of the petition in the Jabotinsky Institute.

15. *Jewish Chronicle*, June 18, 1920.

16. Lieut. Col. J. H. Patterson. *With the Judeans ...*,p. 263.

17. *Haaretz*, May 28, 1920.

18. *Parliamentary Debates* (Hansard). House of Commons, Official Report, 27th, 28th, 29th April; 3rd, 4th, 11th May.

19. *The Maccabaean*, June, 1920.

20. *Haaretz,* May 28, 1920.

21. *Jewish Chronicle,* June 4, 1920.

22. Sh. Schwarz, *op. cit.,* p. 100.

23. *Minutes,* June 4 and 9, 1920.

24. Elias Ginsburg, *op. cit.*

25. Full text of the letter in: Chief Rabbi Abraham I. Kook, *The Vision of Redemption* (Chason ha'Geulah). Jerusalem, 1941, pp. 273-74.

26. Sh. Schwarz, *op. cit.,* pp. 104-05.

27. Elias Ginsburg, *op. cit.*

28. Quoted by A. Remba in his unpublished study, "Jabotinsky the Defender and Prisoner."

29. "Jabotinsky on His Release." *Jewish Chronicle,* August 13, 1920.

30. Sh. Schwarz, *op. cit.,* p. 107.

31. Telegraphic report of the Zionist Commission to the Zionist Executive in London, July 13, 1920. Also: Sh. Schwarz, *op. cit.,* pp. 108-09.

32. *Jewish C/irom⁻ctø,*September3, 1920.

33. Jabotinsky on His Release." *Ibid.,* August 13, 1920.

34. *Stenographisches Protokoll der Verhandlungen des XII. Zionisten-Kongresses in Karlsbad.* Berlin, 1922, p. 161.

35. *Times* (London), September 2, 1920.

36. Letter to Dr. Weizmann, September 28, 1920.

37. Letter of the Zionist Executive to Jabotinsky, October 1, 1920.

38. Letter to the Zionist Commission, September 30, 1920.

39. *Jewish Chronicle,* March 11, 1921.

EIGHTEEN

1. *Times* (London), September 2, 1920.

2. *Daily Express,* September 2, 1920-

3. I. Naiditch. "The First in the Second Generation." *Rasswyet,* October 19, 1930.

4. *Stenographisches Protokoll der Verhandlungen des XII. Zionisten Kongresses in Karlsbad,* pp. 174-84.

5. "Mr. Jabotinsky and the Movement." *Jewish Chronicle,* November 26, 1920.

6. Interview with M. Grossman, Herzlia.

7. Sir Leon Simon. "The Moderation of Weizmann." *Jewish Chronicle,* October 30, 1953.

8. The full text of the letter was published in *The New Palestine,* May 13, 1921.

9. *Minutes* of the First Meeting of the Zionist Executive, March 2, 1921.

10. *Reports of the Executive of the Zionist Organization to the Twelfth Zionist Congress. II. Organizations Report.* London, 1921, pp. 42-43.

11. Letter to Mrs. Jabotinsky-Kopp, September 22, 1922,

12. *Minutes* of the Zionist Executive, March 3, 1921.

13. *Ibid.,* May 6, 1921.

14. *Minutes* of the Political Committee, May 19, 1921.

15. *Minutes* of the Zionist Executive, March 31, April 1, 1921.

16. Eliahu Golomb, *op. cit.,* pp. 213-15.

17. D. Ben Gurion. *Chaluzischer Zionismus oder Revisionismus,* p. 70.

18. "Das Grosse A.C." *Jüdische Rundschau,* July 19, 1921.

19. D. Ben Gurion, *op. cit.,* p. 73.

20. *Ibid.,* p. 70.

21. "Das Grosse A.C." *Jüdische Rundschau,* July 19, 1921.

22. A. Böhm. *Die ZionL·tische Bewegung.* Vol. II. Jerusalem, 1937, p. 154.

23. *Stenographisches Protokoll der Verhandlungen des XII. Zionisten Kongresses in Karlsbad,* p. 263.

24. "Some Impressions." *Jewish Chronicle,* September 30, 1921.

25. Interview with M. Sharett, Jerusalem.

26. V. Jabotinsky. "The Jewish Legion." *Di Tribune,* June 25, 1921.

27. Eliahu Golomb, *op. cit.,* p. 275.

28. Interview with J. Beder, New York.

29. Interview with M. Sharett, Jerusalem.

30. I. Klinov. "Interview with Jabotinsky." *Rasswyet,* January 28, 1923.

31. *Great Britain. Parliamentary Papers 1921.* Cmd 1499, p. 18; Cmd 1540, p. 35.

32. *Minutes* of the Zionist Executive, May 4, 1921.

33. *Ibid.,* May 6, 1921.

34. Interview with M. Grossman, Herzlia.

35. *Jewish Chronicle,* June 3, 1921.

36. *Stenographisches Protokoll der Verhandlungen des XII. Zionisten-Kongresses in Karlsbad,* pp. 174-84.

37. *Ibid.,* p. 174.

38. *Ibid.,* p. 328.

39. "The Personal Element." *Jewish Chronicle,* September 2,1921.

40. Interview with Georg Halpern, Jerusalem.

41. Communicated by Meyer L. Brown, New York.

42. Communicated by Dr. Mordecai Soltes, New York.

43. *Statement to the Delegates of the XII. Zionist Congress on Behalf of the Former Administration of the Zionist Organization of America,* p. 41.

44. Letter to I. Trivus, February 9, 1922.

45. "Vladimir Jabotinsky" (editorial). *The New Palestine,* June 16, 1922.

46. Letter to I. Trivus, February 9, 1922.

47. *Jewish Review,* April 28, 1922.

48. Interview with Meyer Weisgal, Rehovot.

49. *Jewish Criterion,* November 21, 1921; *Dos Yiddishe Folk,* November 18, 1921; *Jewish Daily News,* November 15, 1921; *Di Zeit,* November 15, 1921.

50. A. Tulin's letter to this writer.

51. *Der Yiddischer Soldat* (New York), July-August, 1922.

52. "Vladimir Jabotinsky" (editorial). *The New Palestine,* June 16, 1922.

53. Interview with Mrs. Jabotinsky-Kopp, Haifa.

54. Letter to Mrs. Jabotinsky-Kopp, September 12, 1923.

55. Letter to Mrs. Jabotinsky-Kopp, July 10, 1927.

56. Letter to Mrs. Jabotinsky-Kopp, September 12, 1927.

57. Letter to Johnny Kopp, September 24, 1922.

58. *Ibid.*

NINETEEN

1. *Stenographisches Protokoll der Verhandlungen des XII. Zionisten-Kongresses in Karlsbad,* p. 184.

2. The photostatic copy of Slavinsky's report to his government, dated September 16, 1921 (No. 825), is in the Jabotinsky Institute in Tel Aviv.

3. Comité des Delegations Juives. *Les Pogromes en Ukraine sous les Gouvernements Ukrainiens, 1917-1920.* Aperçu historique et documentaire. Prepared by J. B. Schechtman in collaboration with E. Tcherikover and M. Tsatskis. Paris, 1927.

4. Nahum Levin. "Jabotinsky and the Petliura Agreement." *The Jewish Standard,* August 16, 1940.

5. Slavinksy's report.

6. Full text of the agreement in *Jüdische Rundschau,* December 23, 1921.

7. Interview with Y. M. Machover, London.

8. Jabotinsky's letter to the Zionist Executive, November 24, 1921.

9. *Zionist Work During 1921-22.* Report of the Executive of the Zionist Organization to the Annual Conference. Carlsbad, August, 1922, p. 40.

10. *Jewish Chronicle,* December 30, 1921.

11. *Jüdische Rundschau,* December 9, 1921; February 21, 1922.

12. Lichtheim's letter to Dr. Weizmann, December 5, 1921.

13. Letter to I. Trivus, February 9, 1922.

14. Nahum Levin, *loc. cit.*

15. *Rasswyet,* September 17, 1922.

16. "How Jabotinsky Resigned. Significance of the Slavinsky Affair." *The New Palestine,* February 9, 1923 (correspondence from Berlin).

17. *Ibid.*

18. I. Klinov. "Interview with V. Jabotinsky." *Rasswyet,* January 28, 1923.

19. Letter to Y. M. Machover, December 18, 1921.

20. Itzhak Rabinovitch. "The Jabotinsky-Slavinsky Agreement Before the Bolshe-viks." *Haolam*, August 5, 1943.

21. Letter to Y. M. Machover, December 18, 1921.

22. Nahum Levin, *loc. cit.*

TWENTY

1. *Times* (London), September 2, 1920.

2. *Parliamentary Papers 1921*, Cmd 1540.

3. Herbert Samuel's letter, dated August 25th, *ibid.*, p. 61.

4. Sh. Schwarz, *op. cit.*, p. 115.

5. V. Jabotinsky. "Why I Resigned." *Jewish Chronicle*, February 2, 1923.

6. *The New Palestine*, February 17, 1922.

7. *Parliamentary Papers 1922*, Cmd 1700.

8. Paul L. Hanna. *British Policy in Palestine.* Washington, D.C., 1942, p. 82.

9. *Stenographisches Protokoll der Verhandlungen des XV. Zionisten-Kongresses*, p. 229.

10. *Ibid.*, pp.211-I2.

11. *Ibid.*, pp.229-30.

12. *The New Palestine*, July 7, 1922.

13. V. Jabotinsky. "Why I Resigned." *Loc. cit.*

14. S. Gepstein, *op. cit*, pp. 97-98.

15. V. Jabotinsky. "Why I Resigned." *Loc. cit.*

16. "Actions Committee Meeting." *The New Palestine*, January 19, 1923.

17. Full text in *Rasswyet*, January 28, 1923.

18. "Meeting of the Actions Committee." *Jewish Chronicle*, January 26, 1923.

19. "How Jabotinsky Resigned." *The New Palestine*, February 9, 1923.

20. V. Jabotinsky. "Why I Resigned." *Loc. cit.*

21. *Jewish Chronicle*, February 2, 1923.

22. Interview with S. Gepstein, Tel Aviv.

23. Quoted in *The New Palestine*, January 26, 1923.

24. "Mr. Jabotinsky Resigns" (editorial). *Ibid.*

25. "Mr. Jabotinsky's Resignation." *Jewish Chronicle*, February 2, 1923.

26. *Rasswyet*, July 7 and August 5, 1923.

27. *Ibid.*, July 8, 1923; January 1, 1924; July 15, 22, and 29, 1923; August 5, 13, and 20, 1923; October 21, 1923.

28. *The New Palestine*, January 26, 1923.

INDEX